DISCRETE SIMULATION
AND RELATED FIELDS

organized by
Research Institute for Measurement and Computing Techniques
Central Research Institute for Physics
Hungarian Academy of Sciences

NORTH-HOLLAND PUBLISHING COMPANY
AMSTERDAM · NEW YORK · OXFORD

DISCRETE SIMULATION AND RELATED FIELDS

Proceedings of the IMACS European Simulation Meeting on Discrete Simulation and Related Fields held in Keszthely, Hungary, 10-12 September, 1980

edited by

A. JÁVOR
Central Research Institute for Physics
of the Hungarian Academy of Sciences
Budapest, Hungary

1982

NORTH-HOLLAND PUBLISHING COMPANY
AMSTERDAM · NEW YORK · OXFORD

ISBN: 0 444 86429 6

Published by:
NORTH-HOLLAND PUBLISHING COMPANY – AMSTERDAM · NEW YORK · OXFORD

Sole distributors for the U.S.A. and Canada:
ELSEVIER SCIENCE PUBLISHING COMPANY, INC.
52 VANDERBILT AVENUE
NEW YORK, N.Y. 10017

Library of Congress Cataloging in Publication Data

IMACS European Simulation Meeting on Discrete
Simulation and Related Fields (1980 :
Keszthely, Hungary)
Discrete simulation and related fields.

. 1. Digital computer simulation--Congresses.
I. Jávor, András. II. International Association
for Mathematics and computers in Simulation.
III. Title.
QA76.9.C65I4 1980 001.4'34 82-7961
ISBN 0-444-86429-6 AACR2

PRINTED IN THE NETHERLANDS

PREFACE

It was an honour to have been asked by European Coordinator of IMACS, Professor Vansteenkiste, to organize and chair the European Simulation Meeting on Discrete Simulation and Related Fields.

Judging from the comments expressed by the participants, Keszthely, at Lake Balaton, Hungary, provided a very pleasant venue for the meeting.

In accordance with the general rules of IMACS European Simulation Meetings, participation was held low. Scientists from eleven European countries, viz. Belgium, Bulgaria, France, FRG, GDR, Greece, Hungary, Poland, The Netherlands, UK, USSR, were present thereby demonstrating that participation was international. A pleasant opportunity was provided for the fruitful exchange of fertilizing thoughts on the subject matter. The addition of "Related Fields" was a consequence of the fact that in modelling real complex systems with a considerable degree of fidelity, in some cases no strict border can be kept and artifical restrictions should be avoided.

Apart from the sessions on Methodology, System Modelling, and Applications a very lively Round Table Discussion took place under the title "Future Tools of Simulation versus the Future of Simulation Tools". This proved to be a highly stimulating part of the Meeting enabling the different thoughts and ideas on future trends including both software and hardware aspects to be aired; the informal give and take was highly interesting.

The discussion was recorded and is presented in this volume. Only a limited amount of editing was done to correct trivial errors and to remove some of redundancies due to the colloquial form. A few omissions were due to the quality of the recording at certain parts. Similarly, the papers of this volume are presented as the authors submitted them apart from the correction of minor typing or translation errors.

The present monograph is based on the Preprints Volume of the papers submitted prior to the Meeting. There are here: extended versions of papers presented at the Meeting; the edited version of the Round Table Discussion; and additional invited papers. This last category deserves further mention. We have the valuable invited papers presented by Professor Ameling and Professor Vansteenkiste that could not be included in the Preprints Volume. We also have papers invited from authors who were not present. Of these, I should like to draw particular attention to the paper of Professor Greenspan whose views and proofs by practical examples on the extended usage of discrete simulation in fields employing classically continuous methods are highly stimulating; and the contribution of Professor Shub representing a valuable survey paper.

The papers in this volume thus tackle discrete simulation and its related fields from various angles: methodology and principles of simulation, simulation system and language design principles, various fields of application, digital logic simulation and testing to be used as CAD tool, and the emerging possibilities provided by the boom of microelectronic technology in the application of new - parallel processing - multiprocessor based computing systems. Accordingly, the book is divided into four parts, viz. "Philosophy, Methodology, General Questions"; "Simulation Systems"; "Applications"; "Round Table Discussion".

The realization of this book owes much to the initiative of Professor Vichnevetsky, president of IMACS. Acknowledgements are due to the Central Research Institute for Physics, Budapest, and to the Hungarian Academy of Sciences for their support in organizing the meeting.

András Jávor

CONTENTS

I. PHILIOSOPHY, METHODOLOGY, GENERAL QUESTIONS

DISCRETE SIMULATION AND RELATED FIELDS
A. Jávor (editor)
North-Holland Publishing Company

TRENDS IN THE ROLE OF MODELLING AND SIMULATION

J.A. Spriet
Belgian Fund for Scientific Research

G.C. Vansteenkiste
University of Ghent and Brussels

Coupure Links 653
9000 Ghent, BELGIUM

The role of the digital machine in man's scientific and engineering endeavour has grown steadily. Formerly many problems could not be solved because the analytical skills were insufficient to properly utilize abstract and formal methods. The computer, however, has opened a new road to solutions. The approach has been called simulation. There has been a steady development of hardware and software tools so that the impact of the computer on the overall problem solving process has increased. This has caused shifts in the relative roles of modelling and simulation and even in their meaning. The paper gives a picture of the issues involved when formal and abstract models are used to solve real world problems. Based on the analysis, the concepts of modelling and simulation are developed and the trends in their roles are identified.

1. INTRODUCTION

In recent years one has witnessed a steady growth in the field of simulation. Especially the digital machine has become pervasive in scientific work as well as in engineering and industrial activities. The computer has changed man's scientific and engineering approach towards reality. A brief historical perspective will illustrate the point. Modelling in the physical sciences, whether it is approached physically by analogy or mathematically, has a long history. Newton was one of the first to construct formal, mathematical representations of a vast class of physical phenomena. During several decades abstract models have extensively been used to build complex physical theories or to develop formal descriptions. Unfortunately, the approach was not always succesful or it yielded results that could not be utilized due to a lack of analytical capability. Indeed one may have a faithful mathematical description for a given process, but in many cases one must have the analytical ability to manipulate the describing equations in order to be able to take profit of them. The advent of the electronic computer in the 1940's has brought a decisive change in the utility of the formalization process mentioned before. Initially it was mainly used for complex calculations that were formerly too tedious to perform. Quite rapidly it was realized that thanks to numerical schemes the machine was able to solve and manipulate equations that were analytically untractable. At first, around 1955, it was the aerospace industry which accepted the computer as a major tool in reaching its goals. Soon, the machine was accepted by other industries and since the early sixties it was also used for military and industrial operations scheduling. At the end of the sixties, it was realized that electronic machines could be assigned more complex tasks. Research in pattern recognition and artificial intelligence provided a basis for new developments. In the last decade, there has been a steady growth of the computer's performance for almost all its applications : one could mention advances in numerical techniques for solving partial differential equations and stiff equations, computed-aided design, computer-aided education, advances in artificial intelligence and robotics, developments in data storage and manipulation, etc... .

It is certainly beyond the authors capabilities to give a detailed picture or analysis of the issues that are involved when digital or discrete computing power is introduced in the many fields where the machine can be of use. In the paper here, we focus on the role the computer can play when a specific problem or a real world process is approached with formal and abstract means, like mathematical models and descriptions. In order to be able to refer to this approach, it is called here the scientific-engineering approach.

The text is organized as follows. Section 2 analyzes the scientific-engineering approach in order to show how and where the digital machine can be of help. An analysis of the process is given before the digital machine was introduced and a second present day overview is given. The reasons for the developments are given. Then the concept of simulation is presented in section 3, followed by the concept of modelling in section 4. Section 5 gives a sharper description of man and machine cooperating to solve a problem. Section 6 finally discusses the trends that has occurred in the role of modelling and simulation. It is the hope that in that manner, the reader will have obtained a better insight into the manner the electronic machine did and will modify human scientific-engineering endeavour.

2. RELATIONSHIPS AND ACTIVITIES IN THE SCIENTIFIC-ENGINEERING APPROACH

2.1. An example for illustration

Before giving a more general discussion on the relationships and activities that characterize the scientific-engineering approach to reality, an example is provided. It may serve as an illustration for the general discussions that will follow.

A bioengineer is working in a fermentation plant where micro-organisms are cultivated to obtain a useful product, for instance an antibiotic. Suppose that there is evidence that the temperature of cultivation is a crucial factor of the overall process. The engineer's objective may be to look for a temperature profile during the actual fermentation process, which optimizes the product yield. Clearly the brute-force approach consisting of trying out all temperature profiles is unfeasible. An approach to the problem may be the following : first a deterministic dynamic state space model is looked after. The model describes growth and product formation and it incorporates the influence of temperature on those variables. Then a suitable cost is defined and a mathematical optimization technique is applied. The scheme makes use of the dynamic model and its result is a temperature profile which optimizes the cost. Having the example in mind it is quite easy to recognize and define the major interactions between man and reality in more general terms. In the next section the case is considered when no explicit reference is made to computers or advanced computational power. The discussion is appropriate in case the model builder has no computer at his disposition ; or in other words the discussion was the only valid one before the advent of the digital machine.

2.2. Interactions between man and reality

Before the widespread use of the digital machines relationships and activities in the scientific-engineering approach were largely determined by the human mind and its formalization and analytical powers. A description of the process can most easily be given with the help of a diagram shown on Figure 1.

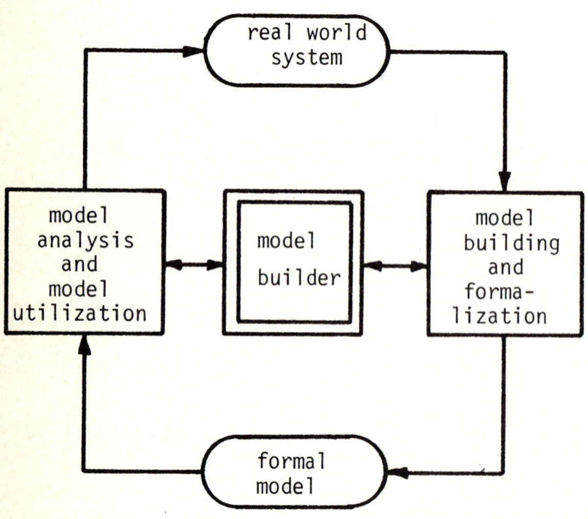

Fig. 1. Interactions between man and reality

At first the scientist or engineer who approaches a real world process or system tries to gain insight or an understanding of the phenomena or the processes under study. One of the very powerful methods consists in trying to obtain an abstract or formal model or representation of the process. The activity is defined here as model building and formalization. In essence the procedure requires abstraction and simplification. A typical example of the abstraction process is the representation of a property of the real world system by a quantitative or numerical quantity. Simplification is necessary to restrict the complexity of the representation. One only chooses those properties within given boundaries of space or time which are believed to be connected with each other but unconnected with other properties or other parts of the world. Basically the model builder proceeds by hypothesis, induction and deduction. However, the procedures for model building are seldom straightforward especially when the model is not overly trivial. The complete body of methods is called modelling methodology.

The formal model, though a simplified representation of reality, always summarizes a vast amount of information, comprising facts, axioms and hypotheses. If its validity is high or in other words if its descriptive quality good, then it can be used to obtain useful knowledge on the system under study. This knowledge is not directly available in the sense that the model has to be analyzed, manipulated or incorporated in other mathematical procedures in order to provide the answers required. The latter step is called model analysis or model utilization. In giving the picture of the approach we have glossed over many difficulties and sensitive points. Those will be discussed next.

2.3. Difficulties inherent in the scientific-engineering approach

The scientific-engineering approach discussed up to here certainly does not guarantee success. All formal descriptions whether they are complex theories of a vast class of phenomena or they are more simple mathematical equations describing a more restricted process are subject to error. Indeed, one single experiment that is in clear contradiction with the derivations of a theory or model topples that theory or model or at least sets their limits. Because theory or model building always encompasses inter- and extrapolation, its validity is a direct function of the precision of the measurements and the number of validity checks performed. Those are facts of life and they are well-known and accepted as the limits and dangers involved when utilizing the scientific-engineering approach.

Unfortunately, the approach may fail for much more down to earth reasons. It may happen that methodology is lacking or that carrying it through by hand is inconceivable, so that the formal model cannot be obtained. It also happens that a model is available but that manipulation is not possible because man's analytical skills are much too limited. As an example, consider the Schrödinger equations ; they are a useful model but in many circumstances, they cannot be solved. Such problems are frustrating and it is here that the advent of the digital machine has opened new vistas and revolutionized the field. Here lies the birth of simulation.

2.4. Interactions between man, machine and reality

As long as calculating devices are used as simple and straightforward computational support, it is not necessary to modify the basic picture on Figure 1. In fact the most dominant and important interactions are present. Clever computation on a digital machine, however, adds a new methodological dimension. It is agreed upon that in certain cases the computer's availability may be the crucial factor in reaching the goal. More recently however, it has been realized that a digital machine endowed with vast amounts of software may be of tremendous help in the whole approach. From this point, it is useful to consider the machine as a crucial part of the scheme and a more complex picture follows - see Figure 2.

The basic scheme can directly be recognized. Besides the computer as an active agent, which cooperates directly with the model builder, there is a new entity termed programs. The programs may take different forms. This will be discussed later on. Very often the main part of the program follows from the formal model or is related to methodology for building or using those models. There are basically two new activities. The first consists in preparing the digital machine for useful work. It is called programming, taken in a broad sense. It may actually comprise writing program code for the computer but it also means preparing the machine through data input, through conversational interaction, through program setup, through library search, etc... . The second activity is for a large part the job of the digital machine and consists in actually doing the computations and calculations. It is important

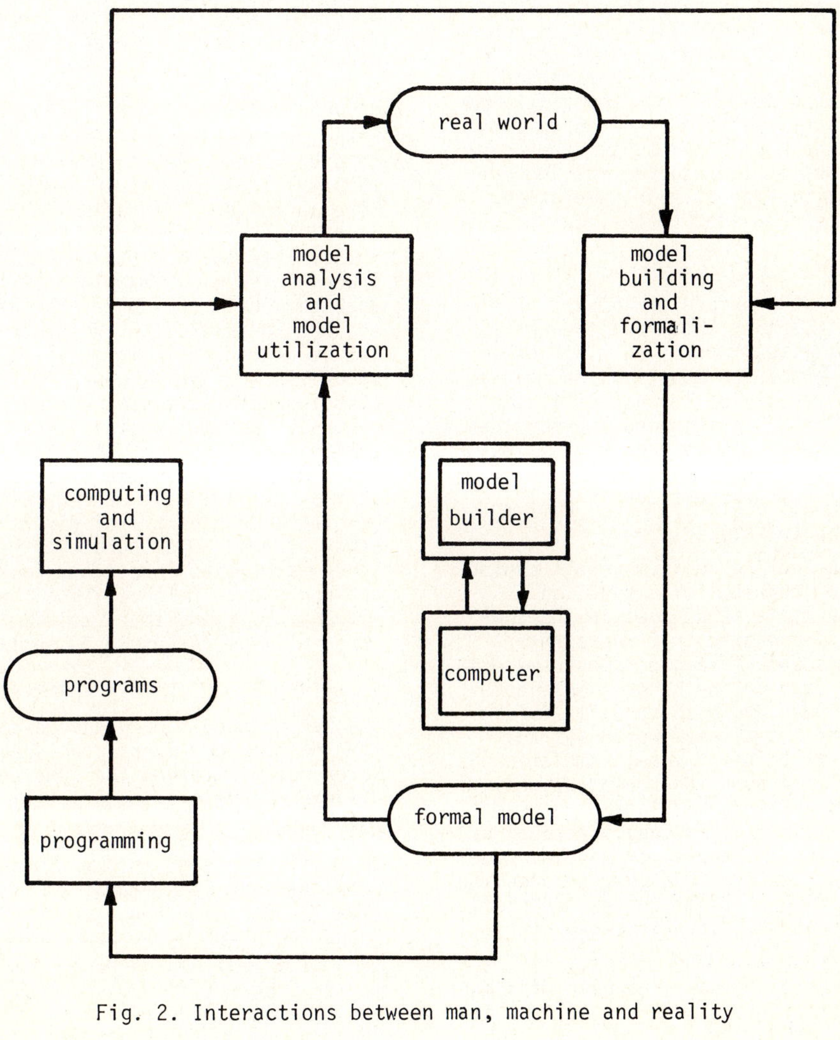

Fig. 2. Interactions between man, machine and reality

to note that the work may be in support of the model building and formalization step as well as in support of the model analysis and model utilization step.

In order to see the relevance of the new activities and interactions, the example presented in section 2.1. can be considered again. Due to the nature of the process under study, it will happen that the impact of the temperature on the growth and product formation equations can only be introduced with the help of experimental outcomes. The model equations will contain parameters and the numerical values of those parameters will have to be inferred from the data points. Though approximate procedures may exist a statistically appropriate approach will require a numerical parameter estimation scheme which is computationally much too demanding in order to be executed by hand. Programming may be required to prepare the parameter estimation session and computation will be needed to obtain the actual values.

Once the model is obtained, Pontryagin's principle can be applied on a suitable cost. Unfortunately the formal model is likely to be nonlinear and there is very little chance that an analytical solution can be found. Here again the computer has to be used and again the programming and computation steps are required to find a solution. The changes in the scheme representing the major steps in the problem solving process indicate the growing role of simulation. This trend will be discussed in the next section.

3. SIMULATION

It is fair to say that before the advent of electronic devices simulation activity, though it existed, was of limited importance. The ability of the computer in solving equations and models has quickly been recognized and out of it the field of simulation has originated. During the years, shifts in meaning have occurred. Therefore the concept is developed in the light of the discussion of the previous paragraph.

3.1. Simulation in the small

The original idea and the 'core-meaning' behind simulation is the 'running' of a model on a machine. Herewith it is meant that on the computer a program is executed that represents a given physical process. As a consequence experimentation can be done on the machine in a hopefully much faster way and much more flexible manner than on the actual real world system. From a mathematical point of view, simulation is equivalent to solving equations computationally. The tremendous impact that simulation has had is a clear indication that in many practical problems the methodological tools for solving models analytically were lacking. This corroborates the statement made before that very often technical issues have hampered the scientific-engineering approach.

It is now possible to evaluate the role of simulation in the context of this paper. It is quite obvious that simulation will be useful in the model analysis and model utilization stage. In order to put the formal model to use, it is very often required to solve the equations under a number of conditions that are specific to the problem at hand. Some further thought however reveals that very often simulation will also be useful in the model building and formalization stage. Indeed, many modeling techniques require the solution of 'candidate' models because a comparison has to be made between measurements and model equations.

Having established those facts, it is now interesting to turn back to the scheme on Figure 2. Clearly simulation belongs to activities summarized under the heading computing and simulation. The program consists in a numerical solution technique for the formal model together with a programmed specification for the equations. The programming task consists in designing those programs or in providing the specifications for a suitable simulation language. It is the thesis of the paper that simulation with the meaning given here is only a part of the computational solutions that are available to the model builder. Therefore, it has been called here simulation in the small.

3.2. Simulation in the large

Based on the scheme in Figure 2, it is possible to give a more general meaning to the concept of simulation. One could define simulation or more adequately simulation in the large as the global set of computational activities that are involved as support during the problem solving process. There are many useful numerical and computational procedures that are not directly related to simulation in the small, but which may be of real help in building a formal model of utilizing such a model. To be mentioned are structure characterization methods, direct or recursive parameter estimation schemes, optimization procedures, dynamic non linear and linear programming techniques, experiment design methods, statistical analysis procedures, etc... in as far as those methods are of direct help for the study at hand. One could even go further and include activities like table look-up, model base search, etc... . Those issues and the trend from simulation in the small to simulation in the large will be discussed in section 6.

4. MATHEMATICAL OR FORMAL MODELLING

The act of modelling and more specifically modelling methodology is basically more oriented towards human intervention. One can distinguish different levels of such intervention.

4.1. Modelling in the small

The basic meaning of mathematical modelling - referred to here by modelling in the small, consists in applying inductive and deductive techniques in order to obtain a formal representation of a real world process. Modelling itself is for a part still considered as an art. There are a large number of factors that come into play.

As mentioned before, the representation process involves almost always 'inter- or extrapolation'. Certainly, a large body of methodology is objective and mathematically sound. Many tools are well-defined and clearly stated. Statistical techniques, parameter estimation procedures, etc... have a firm logical basis. Standard techniques cannot solve all problems. The final product is the result of careful trade-off's between existing facts, decisions on the choice of representative details, careful experimental work and its interpretation. Examples of such issues relate to the choice of formalisms, the evaluation of the validity of a priori facts, the required level of descriptive details, etc.

It is to be noted that modelling and its methodology only refer to one of the branches on Figure 1. In general one will have to draw on analysis and model utilization techniques in order to reach one's goal. Those procedures are by no means always straightforward, but by tradition they have not been included in the concept of modelling.

4.2. Modelling in the large

Modelling in the large has yet been given different meanings. Zeigler for instance, refers to modelling in the large when model integration is performed. Herewith it is meant, that different descriptions of the same real world process are compared, screened for consistency and integrated into a whole. Notice that the activity is a basic step in scientific work, especially in the process of developing a theory and working out general principles. Because modelling in the large, in the sense mentioned, is nothing else but a modelling activity at a higher abstract level, we simple consider it here as modelling.

With modelling in the large we mean here the act of model building and model utilization and its methodology refers to the techniques that can be utilized to execute that act. In that sense, modelling in the large refers to both branches on Figure 1 as well as on Figure 2 and it is a more complete concept when we refer to the scientific-engineering approach in general.

5. INTERACTION BETWEEN MODELLING AND SIMULATION

According to the Figure 2 simulation activities support model building and model utilization. Before discussing the trends in their role, it is useful to have an idea concerning the way the activities are supported. Modelling and simulation are performed by man in cooperation with the computer. A better understanding is obtained if one considers a more complete diagram of the levels involved - Figure 3. Modelling and Simulation activities are in fact highly sophisticated processes that require the availability of a number of hierarchically organized levels.
In case of the model builder, the lowest level refers to the body which supports the human mind. The mind itself allows man to think. In case of the processes involved, logic and mathematics are the basic substrate for more complex processes. At the highest level one finds human modelling methodology, know-how concerning the real world system under study and model building

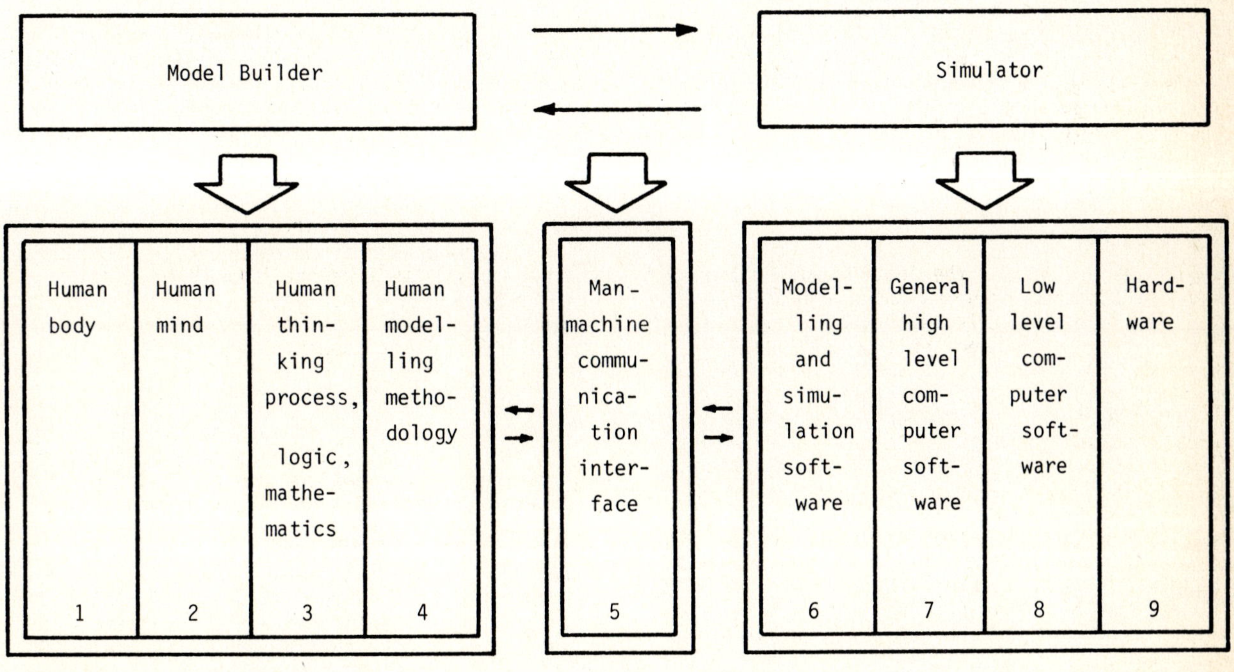

Fig. 3. Build-up of the model builder and the simulator

experience. For simulation activities one first has a hardware level. The hardware has to be provided with low level computer software : machine language and other elementary software tools. Then one has a higher level of general computer software : higher level languages, data storage facilities, etc... . Finally there is the specific advanced modelling and simulation software. As the processes at both sides are rather complicated, smooth cooperation is only possible if there are provisions for suitable man-machine communication.

It is important to note that levels 4, 5 and 6 on Figure 3 have not reached complete maturity. Furthermore though the human side is rather stable, new developments in computer hardware still continue and so the simulator is in continuous development. This fact will been of interest in the next section.

6. TRENDS IN MODELLING AND SIMULATION

Having in mind the build-up of the principal agents during objective problem solving, it is clear that nowadays modelling and simulation have to go hand in hand. It is now more easily to describe the trends that we have witnessed in the few last decades.

Before the fifties modelling and especially modelling in the small was dominating the overall approach, simulation activity was very limited. The advent of the digital machine has dramatically changed the picture. Simulation in the small supported first the model building and model utilization process. The availability of computing power has however also had its impact on modelling methodology. Indeed formerly methodology was developed for its user : the model builder. Man is especially apt in reasoning and in recognizing patterns. His computational powers however are limited. The digital machine however is extremely fast in calculatory operations. Such computational powers can be exploited in methodology. Consequently in the last decades a vast amount of techniques have been developed, which assume implicitly the existence of the machine. At the same time higher levels of computer software were implemented. Modelling in the large and simulation in the large developed concurrently. As mentioned before, nowadays there still are few cases were simulation software is developed to its very limit, while human modelling methodology is utilized at its highest level, partly for cost reasons, partly because the simulator is still in development.

It is difficult to say where the future leads to. There has been arguments that with time, modelling methodology could be incorporated for its major part in 'intelligent', 'self-organizing' machines, so that human intervention could be brought to a bare small level. In such cases, simulation would in a sense supplant modelling. Whether this is possible remains to be proved. In any case rules for 'intelligence' and 'self-organization' would be required which as a human activity would result in a new trend in the meaning of modelling. Much more likely is that developments in modelling and simulation will go hand in hand, maximizing the particular aptitudes of both man and machine.

DISCRETE SIMULATION AND RELATED FIELDS
A. Jávor (editor)
North-Holland Publishing Company

PROPOSALS ON THE STRUCTURE OF SIMULATION SYSTEMS

A. Jávor

Central Research Institute for Physics
of the Hungarian Academy of Sciences
Budapest, Hungary

The problem of building efficient discrete simulation systems is treated in a general way, taking into consideration the amount of work needed for system design and utilization of the system. The application is proposed of a single invariant internal structure with several different user oriented outer layers, i.e. languages. The suggested solutions for the structuring, state representation as well as the executive of the internal structure are presented.

1. INTRODUCTION

The need to investigate and penetrate into the different aspects of the complex world around us has led to the rapidly increasing use of simulation. This has had two consequences:

a/ A great deal of knowledge about simulation tools has been accumulated from practice.

b/ The contradictory demands for efficient "high fidelity" and simultaneously low cost simulation have to be met.

More than a decade earlier, the question "Do we need all these languages?" arose [1], initiating a debate on whether a single general purpose tool or specialized tools are necessary. In recent years an enormous number of simulation tools (languages, packages, systems) have emerged indicating that this problem has still not been settled [2][3].

Simulation now seems to be sufficiently mature for us to attempt a unified approach to the problem because clear theoretical concepts have been distilled from practice on outlining the concepts allowing simulation tools to be used [4][5][6][7][8]. Activities on standardization in the framework of IMACS have also begun. This paper sets out to add some ideas to these efforts based on the more than ten years of research and development in the field of discrete simulation.

2. THE PROBLEM

It seems that a very definite controversy does exist between those having a highly specialized approach and the wide community of people who require their well-defined practical problem to be solved by simulation. The latter group are from different disciplines, they have problems to be solved and they are concerned solely with their own problem. To the simulation expert a well structured highly sophisticated language that enables model building in practically every field looks attractive whereas the latter category requires a highly specialized tool directed to a specific field of interest, enabling model-building to be performed as conveniently as possible in what tends to be a narrow field, with its special terminology and which deals with as few general simulation concepts as possible. The problem is somewhat similar to that of ALGOL 68 in general purpose high level languages. A theoretically well structured very powerful language has been developed but just this high complexity poses a problem for the average user who would be satisfied with a far simpler structure with less possibilities but with a language more closely fitted to his specialized demands.

This aspect is even more important in the field of simulation because modelling is of interest mainly to people who are experts in the subject matter of the field to which the model belongs (i.e. chemistry, biology, microelectronics, economy, agriculture, etc.) and *not* in programming languages, computer science or simulation as a discipline on its own. This is a matter for serious consideration since it is a fact that simulation is already used practically everywhere.

A useful analogy might be that of railways which are used by everyone everywhere but we have to keep in mind that the great impact of railways on transportation results from the fact that it is not only railway personnel that use the trains. It can thus be seen that contradictory requirements for universality and specialization exist.

3. ONE INNER STRUCTURE - SEVERAL LANGUAGES

Let us try to resolve the problem. Laski's concept [9] of the simulation system consisting of a simulation language and an executive can be extended further. Let us divide the simulation system into an inner structure and an outer layer. The invariant inner structure has to be such as to be able to handle effectively model structures in general; it needs also to provide an effective time advancement method that adapts itself well to the different event distributions of different models [10]. The outer layer means that the languages can be fitted to each field of application. This concept may lead to considerable savings in time (i.e. money) spent on simulation.

In the conventional way, the amount of work needed for simulation can be expressed as

$$M = \frac{M_D}{N_M} + M_M \tag{1}$$

M being the amount of work needed to solve a single simulation task

M_D the amount of work needed to develop the simulation tool used

N_M the number of models simulated using the above tool

M_M the amount of work needed to simulate a single model

(the above values are, of course, mean values).

M_M decreases if the simulation tool used is more specialized for the given field, but at the same time N_M decreases if the field of application is more restricted.

By using our proposed construction the overall amount of work can be expressed as

$$M' = \frac{M_{DL}}{N_L} + \frac{M_{DS}}{N_S} + M_M \tag{2}$$

M_{DL} being the work needed to develop the language (and its compiler) used

M_{DS} the work needed to develop the inner structure (executive)

N_L the number of simulations using the same language

N_S the number of simulations using the inner structure,

where

$$M_{DL} + M_{DS} = M_D \tag{3}$$

If we use the level of specialization usual in specialized packages, the values M_M in formulae (1) and (2) are equal, $N_M=N_L$; and because $N_S>>N_L$,

$$M' < M \tag{4}$$

Q.E.D.

This concept does not contradict the need for an advanced general purpose simulation language for two reasons

a/ In cases when the field of application (i.e. N_L) is very limited the development of a specialized language cannot be justified and it is better to let M_M grow thereby making $M_{DL}=0$.

b/ A universal language attached to the inner structure can serve as an intermediate language into which the other languages are mapped (see Figure 1).

4. SOME CONCEPTS FOR THE INNER STRUCTURE

In order to have a universally applicable inner structure it is necessary to design it in such a way that models from a wide range of applications could be mapped conveniently into it. Simultaneously, the inner core has to provide for an effective model representation both statically (i.e. storage space used) and dynamically (i.e. run time required).

In order to achieve this end a number of measures have to be taken in designing the inner structure. In the following we outline some principles whose application would seem to be advantageous.

1. The structure of the model should be built up from - a generally large number of - interconnected "element modules" with inputs, outputs, states and algorithms describing their operation, i.e. next state and output functions analogously to the quintuples of automata [11][12]

$$A = \langle Q,X,Y,\Psi,\Phi \rangle \tag{5}$$

where Q, X and Y represent the internal, input and output alphabet respectively; Ψ is the next state function and Φ the output function performing the mappings:

$$q(t+1) = \Psi[q(t),x(t)] \tag{6}$$

and

$$y(t) = \Phi[q(t),x(t)] \tag{7}$$

where

$$q(t),q(t+1)\in Q;\ x(t)\in X;\ y(t)\in Y.$$

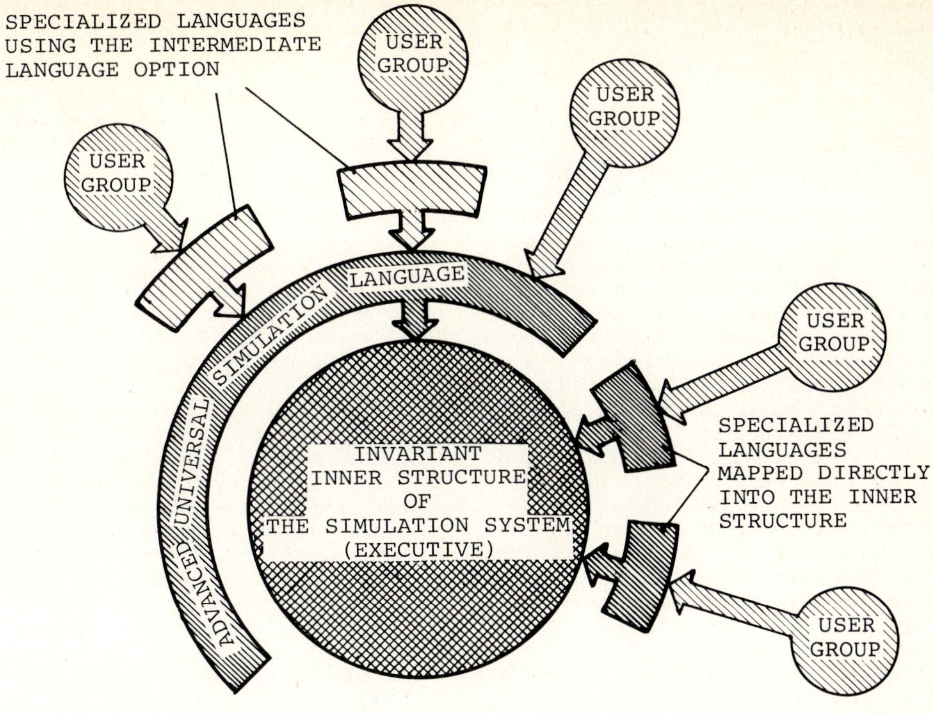

Figure 1 : Proposed simulation system structure

A generalization of the ordinary deterministic automata results in the probabilistic automata. Here an input letter $x \in X$ transfers the automaton from state $q_i \in Q$ into any state $q_j \in Q$ with constant, time independent probabilities $\Pi(x, q_i, q_j)$. As we do aim at the realistic description of systems in simulation, the description very often takes the form of a very important subclass: the automata with delay (i.e. Moore automaton). Here the only difference to the formulae above is that the function Φ takes the form $\lambda(q)$, i.e.

$$y(t) = \lambda[q(t)] \tag{8}$$

and the present value of y does not depend on the present value of x. This can be interpreted as the mapping of reality considering the fact that changes in physical systems never occur instantaneously although in a number of cases this time delay can be ignored.

The operation of the models in simulation however is controlled by mechanisms of time advancement different from those used in the classical description of finite automata, since in the former case some time advancement algorithms are based on unequally quantized time steps, by skipping those time increments where no change in the existing $\langle q_i, y_i \rangle$ takes place.

Thus the following problem may well arise.

At t_1 the letter $x_1 \in X$ schedules the next change to t_2 from $q_i \in Q$ to $q_j \in Q$ and analogously from $y_i \in Y$ to $y_j \in Y$. At time instant t_3 where $t_1 \leq t_3 \leq t_2$ (or in delayed automaton representation $t_1 \leq t_3 < t_2$) another letter $x_2 \in X$ changes the anticipated next states $\langle q_j, y_j \rangle$ to $\langle q_j', y_j' \rangle$ and the anticipated time of the change to t_2'.

More precisely speaking: generally there are scheduled subsets $Q_2 \subset Q$ and $Y_2 \subset Y$ respectively to the set of future time instants T_2, i.e. for which the relation holds

$$(\forall t_{2i} \in T_2) \ (t_{2i} \geq t_1) \tag{9}$$

or

$$(\forall t_{2i} \in T_2) \ (t_{2i} > t_1) \tag{10}$$

for "delayed automata".

The letter x_3 may change the scheduled subsets to $Q_2' \subset Q$ and $Y_2' \subset Y$ and their respective sets of times to T_2' in the case

$$(\exists t_{2i} \in T_2)\ (t_3 \leq t_{2i}) \tag{11}$$

or, for "delayed automata"

$$(\exists t_{2i} \in T_2)\ (t_3 < t_{2i}). \tag{12}$$

This means that in the implementation of the model in simulation the information about the present and scheduled conditions with their uncertainties, has to be stored and the algorithms performing transformations on them have to be chosen in such a way that if the "forecasts" are modified repeatedly the "last should be the best", i.e. the last transformation applied should supply the correct state or output of the system.

This is in fact the same concept as the aggregative system description [13][14].

2. In view of our goal to design a general purpose internal structure we have to consider that models of different types have to be represented from the viewpoint of the occurrence of events. Generally they are categorized as *deterministic* and *stochastic*. This, incidentally, is an abstraction in itself since practically every physical phenomenon is of stochastic nature; it is only the numerical values of the probabilities of the events involved that determine how we regard the system.What is meant here is that if these probabilities are very close to "1" or "0" we can treat the system as deterministic, otherwise as stochastic.

The examination of real systems often shows that the question of how they should be treated depends on the "resolution" or "level" of the examination: with gradually more detailed examination, i.e. increased "resolution", the system can be interpreted alternately as stochastic or deterministic.

When investigating real systems we often encounter a third - intermediate - category called Quasideterministic Systems (QDS) [11].

This, of course, is an abstraction too, by which we shall understand the following

Definition 1. We shall designate a system as "quasideterministic" if it is such that in the majority of cases (or time) its behaviour can be regarded as deterministic and in the minority of cases (or time) as stochastic.

These systems were generally intended to be deterministic by their designers, or hoped to be such by their investigators, at some level at least.

A closer view of such systems shows that - based on their nature - the "uncertainties" or "indeterminacies" can be divided into two distinct groups:

Definition 2. Indeterminacies of first order (IFO).

Uncertainties in the system due to transient periods between deterministic states $q_i, q_j \in Q$.

Definition 3. Indeterminacies of second order (ISO).

Uncertainties, meaning that the system is in a deterministic state (or in a condition to be described by IFO) but the state (or the direction of the transient state described by the IFO) is not known and the state of the system is to be found in a subset of states:

$$Q^* \subset Q.$$

Another term is the *relevancy* of the information yielded by the simulation. Considering the types of indeterminacies and bearing in mind the features of QDS's already mentioned the following can be stated.

(a) The occurrences of IFO's have to be described entirely according to the system modelled since this type of indeterminacy occurs frequently practically in every system and cannot be considered as irregular operation.

Their occurrences have to be tracked however because on the one hand they may cause ISO's, and on the other hand in some particular cases they should not be allowed during operation.

Their inclusion in the model however does not cause too much trouble since they are transient states by nature and their values and existence are clearly defined by the transient times and states in between which the change takes place.

(b) In order to reduce complexity the representation of ISO's can however be restricted both in time and "space". By this we mean that the occurrence of an ISO at a time t should not influence the ISO signalized at t'>t.

This representation can be arranged in a way that if an ISO occurs the next state of the system is chosen arbitrarily as

$$q^*_{io} \in Q^*$$

according to Definition 3.

Using the formalism given in Eqs (5), (6) and (7) the description of a QDS can be performed by replacing the values q, x,y by vectors

$$\bar{q} = \{q_s, q_{IFO}, q_{ISO}\} \quad (13)$$

$$\bar{x} = \{x_s, x_{IFO}, x_{ISO}\} \quad (14)$$

$$\bar{y} = \{y_s, y_{IFO}, y_{ISO}\}. \quad (15)$$

The indexes of the components designate thereby

s value of the parameter (deterministic description),

IFO IFO value of the parameter (i.e. transient value),

ISO ISO state of the parameter (i.e. being actually in some subset of the whole set of possible values).

Equations (2) and (3) may be rewritten in the forms of

$$\bar{q}(t+1) = \Psi[\bar{q}_r(t), \bar{x}_r(t)] \quad (16)$$

and

$$\bar{y}(t) = \Phi[\bar{q}(t), \bar{x}_r(t)] \quad (17)$$

where, in the case of "delayed automata", the term $\bar{x}(t)$ is obviously deleted from (17). The notations $\bar{q}_r(t)$ and $\bar{x}_r(t)$ mean reduced forms of the state and input letters where the last components - for ISO representation - are assumed to equal zero, i.e. are deleted.

In the description according to Eqs (16) and (17) the substitution of symbol $\bar{q}_r$ provides for the restriction of propagation in time, and $\bar{x}_r$ for the restriction in model space. Regarding the latter it should be noted that the whole system may be represented as formed from a network of automata and the output of an elementary automata $\bar{y}_{ei}$ will provide the input $\bar{x}_{ej}$ of others.

This three component vector representation is well descriptive:

- The first component supplies the state assumed;
- The second indicates whether it is in a stable condition or has already begun to change its state and the direction of the changeover;
- The third component indicates major possible discrepancies in the deterministic operation.

Concerning the handling of ISO's it is obvious that some information on the cases in which they are liable to occur has to be determined prior to the dynamic phase, i.e. run of the simulation. This can be arranged in two ways.

(a) The elements of which the whole model consists must themselves have well-known behaviour and the algorithms describing them have to provide for the representation of ISO's that they inherently cause.

(b) The other class of origins giving rise to ISO's is due to the outlay of the topology of the whole system consisting of element modules (i.e. feedback paths). The solution in such cases may be a prior analysis of the system during the model building phase thereby determining those segments of the network the topology of which enables ISO's and during a dynamic simulation run should such a segment be activated a special algorithm attached to the segment is needed to determine whether the next possible state is unique and to provide for the enforcement of one possible state if necessary as well as indicating an ISO.

This method also enables the description of fuzzyness in systems using the extension of the state description into the above mentioned vectors [15].

3. The inner structure has to provide for the handling of models whose state can be described in different ways. In a considerable number of cases the events are characterized by the motion i.e. change of the location, of "entities" in the model rather than the change of some state parameter values. These systems (to be described generally by stochastic processes dealing with queueing, storage problems) are of great significance in the fields of traffic, production control, information traffic systems (e.g. data transmission, computer networks) and in general bulk service problems.

Here the questions are answered by statistical distributions and their characteristic values (mean value, standard deviation, etc.) from which efficiency, waiting time, queue length, etc. values can be obtained. This means that in general we are interested not so much in the individual events but rather in the rate of their occurrence. Nevertheless there are cases when the detection of certain anomalies is of great importance.

Let us consider, for example, that we wish to obtain information about the working conditions of a computer system using a sophisticated operating system (efficiency, throughput, response times, memory utilization, etc.).

It is desirable that the investigation by simulation should be able to bring to the surface the possible faults of the system (such as the system being stuck in a state under certain conditions) that can be caused by the indeterminate operation of the system.

In addition, systematic errors in the results can appear when events occurring at the same instant have to be simulated.

An illustration of indeterminacies in such systems can be seen in Figure 2 where three storage units - connected serially - are shown. The storage cells as well as the entities they contain are also indicated. The operation of the model is assumed to be such that in every discrete simulated interval an entity moves from each storage unit to the next - assuming that there is a vacancy - in the direction of the arrows. As simulation is executed sequentially, if the activation sequence of the element routines is I,II,III there will be no entity transfer from I to II whereas for a calling sequence of II,III,I or II,I,III entity transfer will take place.

This problem may occur - beyond the sequential simulation of parallel events - because of the undeterminacies in real systems due to race conditions of simultaneous events where the choice of the sequence is generally determined by differentially small time differences existing in reality.

It is not always easy to foresee such events in a complex model and even so to build in the special handling of such events requires special considerations and extra programming. Therefore a general solution for the automatic treatment is required.

Systems based on the movements of entities seemingly differ basically from those whose states are represented by parameter "level" values (e.g. digital logic); handling of indeterminacies for these systems was dealt with earlier. With entities, however, the interpretation of statements like "it either exists or not", "it is either here or there", "it is here and there simultaneously" is necessary. Our problem can nevertheless be deduced from the original QDS representation in the following way.

Considering the inputs and outputs of such "entity oriented" elements it can be seen that their operation is entirely different from that of the "level-type" elements. Namely if an output provides an entity for the input for another element that is connected to it, the state of the transfer takes place depending on the condition whether the latter accepts the entity or not. This is entirely different from the case where the appearance ("emission") of a level on an output is unconditionally received by the input of the element connected to it.

A solution of the problem can be based on the *dual nature of the events* [16]. The processes in such systems can be described in two equivalent ways.

- Firstly by the network of elements through the inputs (to be called the

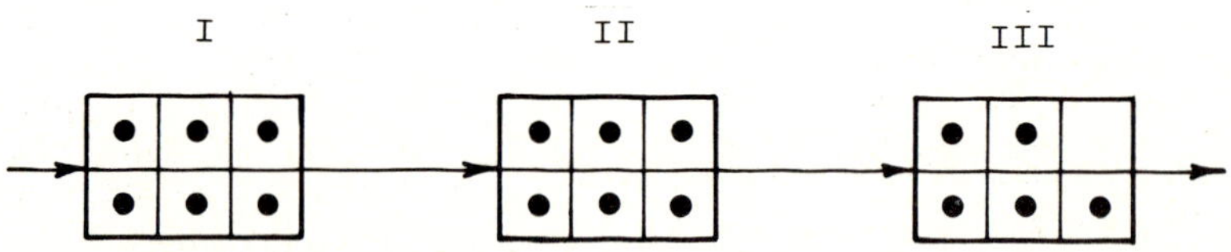

CALLING SEQUENCE	ENTITY MOVEMENT
I, II, III	II → III
I, III, II	II → III
II, I, III	II → III; I → II
II, III, I	II → III; I → II
III, I, II	II → III
III, II, I	II → III; I → II

Figure 2 : Illustration of indeterminacies in "entity oriented" systems

acceptors) of which entities can enter the element depending on the internal state of the element, and through the outputs (to be called *donors*) they can emit entities.

- Secondly by an *equivalent* network of elements where as a function of levels appearing on their inputs and their internal state, their output level and internal state may alter.

To show this, let us introduce the following notetion

I: denotes the input of a "level-type" element

O: denotes the output of a "level-type" element

A: denotes the input of an "entity-type" element

D: denotes the output of an "entity-type" element.

Mention is made of the fact that while the I-s are always passive and the O-s always active, with A and D this is by far not so unambiguous. It is for instance possible that D is the output of an element representing a passive storage of entities from which an active A input of another element "takes the entities out".

Let us denote the active or passive nature of the A and D points by the indexes a or p respectively. The connected pointpairs thus can form either D_aA_p or D_pA_a interfaces.

If we examine the topological routes in the model via which the effects propagate in the case of "level-type" networks we can see that this will be

$$(I\ O)\rightarrow(I\ O)\rightarrow(I\ O)\rightarrow\ldots$$

In the notation the points belonging to the same element are in brackets; the arrows indicate the connections, their direction shows the direction in which the activity propagates.

The route for the propagation of activities in the case of "entity-type" networks can be described by a series like

$$\ldots)\rightarrow(\cdot\cdot_p\cdot\cdot_a)\rightarrow(\cdot\cdot_p\cdot\cdot_a)\rightarrow(\cdot\cdot_p\cdot\cdot_a)\rightarrow\ldots$$

where in place of the dots to which the indexes p and a belong the letters A and D can be inserted either as

$$D_a)\rightarrow(A_pD_a)\rightarrow(A_pD_a)\rightarrow(A_pD_a)\rightarrow\ldots$$

or

$$A_a)\rightarrow(D_pA_a)\rightarrow(D_pA_a)\rightarrow(D_pA_a)\rightarrow\ldots$$

It should be noted that the arrows indicate the direction of propagation of the activity not of the entities!

In the second case, for instance, the movement of the entities takes place just in the opposite direction, i.e. from right to left.

With such entity oriented networks there is also another effect propagating in the opposite direction. Namely when an active point intends to transfer an entity to the passive point connected to it or if it tries to take an entity from the passive point the completion of the transfer depends on the readiness of the passive part (whether it can accept or give an entity) and this - reverse - effect influences the state of the element to which the active point belongs.

If we want to substitute the "entity-type" network with an equivalent "level-type" one based on the existing duality between them, then a single D-A connection has to be replaced with a pair of oppositely directed O-I connections (see Figure 3).

In Figure 3 it can be seen how the formally hidden feedback loops of an "entity-type" network are caused to surface by substituting it by its "level-type" equivalent.

In Figure 3/a the original "entity-type" network is shown, in Figure 3/b its "level-type" dual equivalent.

Redrawing Figure 3/b into a somewhat other form shows clearly that the whole network consists of a system of interconnected loops (see Figure 3/c).

Accordingly the QDS system representation and handling can be used in the following way

(a) The nonzero transfer time of the entities between elements can be described by the indeterminacy of first order.

(b) Indeterminacies caused by race conditions and similar phenomena can be treated using indeterminacies of second order.

(c) As the existence of loop systems is not exceptional in such models, it is advised for practical implementation of the method that their determination be undertaken dynamically meaning that the activation of special loop handling procedures should be restricted to critical segments (i.e. storage elements so close to their full or empty end states that they might immediately reach an over- or "under"-flow).

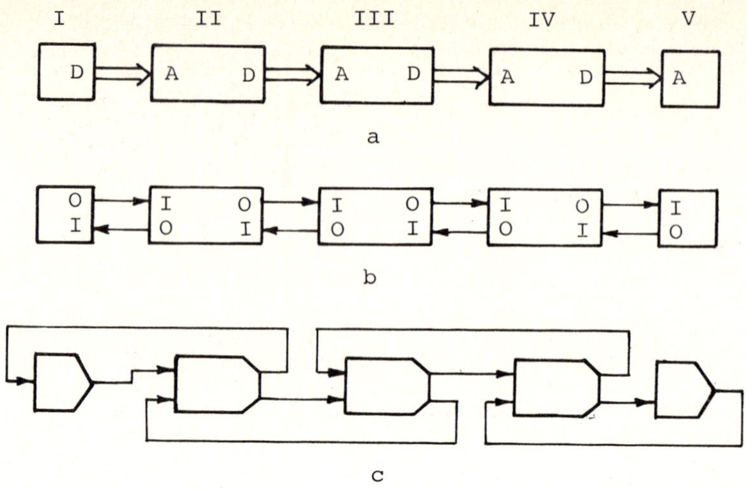

Figure 3 : Substitution of an "entity-type" network by its "level-type" equivalent

4. Lastly a universally effective time advancement algorithm (i.e. executive) has to be used.

This means that on the one hand it should provide robustness under different conditions, i.e. different practical event districtions. On the other hand it should adapt itself automatically to them.

Without going into detail usage of the Delft Algorithm [10] is suggested. This has a hierarchical structure and makes use of the clustered nature of events in a large number of practical systems.

5. CONCLUSIONS

In this work an attempt has been made to summarize the concepts that have proved useful in building simulation systems during our research work in the last decade. Some of the principles have already been verified in practice and others are being implemented [17].

Although our experience has been exclusively in discrete simulation it seems that at least some of these principles may be useful in combined system building as well. It is hoped that these results will serve as a brick to construct the theoretically well established, - and in practice verified, - future building of simulation.

6. REFERENCES

[1] Garwick, J.V., Do We Need All These Languages?, in Buxton, J.N. (ed.), Simulation Programming Languages (North-Holland, Amsterdam, 1968) 143-157.

[2] Kay, I.M., An Over-the-shoulder Look at Discrete Simulation Languages, Spring Joint Computer Conference, (1972) 791-798.

[3] Jávor, A., Benkő, T.né., Diszkrét rendszerek szimulációja (Müszaki Könyvkiadó, Budapest, 1979).

[4] Ören, T.I., Zeigler, B.P., Concepts for Advanced Simulation Methodologies, Simulation 32(3) (1979) 69-82.

[5] Ören, T.I., Concepts for Advanced Computer Assisted Modelling in Methodology in Systems Modelling and Simulation (North-Holland, Amsterdam, 1978) 29-55.

[6] Elzas, M.S., What is Needed for Robust Simulation? in Methodology in Systems Modelling and Simulation (North-Holland, Amsterdam, 1978) 57-91.

[7] Cellier, F.E., Bongulielmi, A.P., The COSY Simulation Language, Simulation of Systems IMACS Congress 1979 Sorrento (North-Holland, Amsterdam, 1979) 271-281.

[8] Jávor, A., Diszkrét rendszerek szimulációjának néhány elméleti kérdése, Számitógépes Rendszerszimuláció Szimpózium, Budapest(1975) 155-165.

[9] Laski, J.G., Two Proposals Towards Discrete Modelling, in Buxton, J.N. (ed.), Simulation Programming Languages (North-Holland, Amsterdam, 1968) 175-197.

[10] Jávor, A., An Adaptive Time Advancement Algorithm for Discrete Simulation, Information Processing Letters 6(3) (1977) 83-86.

[11] Jávor, A., An Approach to the Modelling of Uncertainties in the Simulation of Quasideterministic Discrete Event Systems, Problems of Control and Information Theory 4(3) (1975) 219-229.

[12] Trakhtenbrot, B.A., Barzdin, Ya.M., Finite Automata (North-Holland, Amsterdam - London) (American Elsevier, New York, 1973).

[13] Kalashnikov, V.V., Simulation System Based on Aggregative Mathematical Scheme, Simulation of Systems IMACS Congress, Sorrento (1979).

[14] Buszlenko, N.P., Bonyolult rendszerek szimulációja (Müszaki Könyvkiadó, Budapest, 1972).

[15] Jávor, A., A Representation of Fuzzyness in Discrete Simulation, Problems of Control and Information Theory 7(2) (1978) 111-114.

[16] Jávor, A., Indeterminált helyzetek szimulációja "részecske-orientált" diszkrét rendszereknél, Report of the Central Research Institute for Physics (KFKI-1978-83) (November 1978).

[17] Jávor, A., Révész, Á., Tóbiás, P., Simulation System with a Single Core and Several Outer Layers, in Jávor,A. (ed.), Discrete Simulation and Related Fields (Nort-Holland, Amsterdam, 1978).

DISCRETE SIMULATION AND RELATED FIELDS
A. Jávor (editor)
North-Holland Publishing Company

SIMULATION USING MULTIPROCESSOR SYSTEMS

by o. Prof. Dr.-Ing. Walter Ameling

Lehrstuhl für Allgemeine Elektrotechnik und Datenverarbeitungssysteme
Rheinisch-Westfälische Technische Hochschule
Aachen, FRG

Multiprocessor systems and parallel processing opens entirely new applications to simulation. A large number of proposals and pilot configurations exist using quite different types of architecture and techniques. Unfortunately there is no unifying concept behind these different configurations. This paper surveys different structures of multiprocessor-systems and discusses their utilization for simulation purposes.

INTRODUCTION

Simulation is the technique of constructing and running a model of a system (real or abstract) in order to study the behaviour of that system without disrupting the environment of the real system. By system we mean the connection of parts or events which are given by nature or made by man. The behaviour of many technical and physical systems is determined by physical laws and they depict dependent output variables as functions of independent input variables. An engineering approach is to decompose a system into subsystems and to describe these by mathematical relations. If the mathematical description reflects the behaviour of the system, we have a "mathematical model" of the system and are able to prove the accuracy and effectiveness of the model. In this sense, the term model is used for the image or representation of the original system. The quality of the simulation depends on the quality of the chosen model.

If we are able to simulate all subsystems or parts of the system, then the behaviour of the whole system can be derived from the model. The parallelism of actions in the subsystem can best be suited with parallel oriented devices, machines, components or computing-units.

Since the availability of commercial electronic analog-computers in the early 50's the analog-computer has been proven to be a valuable tool for the simulation of continuous models and processes. Analog simulation is well known for physical models, whose behaviour can be described by differential equations. For solutions of these equations the integral calculation is in a broad field of great importance. The desire, to solve problems by integrating methods has led to the development of integrating instruments and special purpose computers. The analog-computer was the first type of a multiprocessor-system and involves parallel computation.

The general purpose digital computer offers the accuracy of computation, of which the analog-computer is incapable. It is an advantage, too, that a digital machine is not tied to one problem at a time, as the analog-computer tends to be and problem changes are very simple.

In order to control the programmed model and its environment a block oriented simulation language is required. The length of computation time for the general purpose digital computer using numerical methods is undesirable for repetitive solution of the same set of equations.

Performance limitations and time restrictions, Monte Carlo studies, adaptive or learning control simulations etc.

With the Hybrid-computer the class of solvable time-restricted problems has been extended, but the limitations and disadvantages of the analog and digital computing elements remain. Especially in applications in which rapid repetitive solutions are required with a high degree of accuracy the digital incremental computer or digital differential analyzer (DDA) is an appropriate tool.

The progress in technology in the last years has stimulated the discussion about parallel computing structures. Computers as the Star 100 from Control-Data-Corporation, the ASC (Advanced Scientific Computer) from Texas-Instruments and the Cray I, II from Cray Corp. with their vector- and pipelining-capabilities did not give the advantages to simulation, because the application of their approach to simulation-tasks has the difficulties, that the mathematical models for dynamic systems do not lead automatically to vector-processing or pipelining.A considerable work has to be done, to adapt the software packages to get the advantages out of these high sophisticated machines.

Nowadays with microprocessors as computing elements multi-processor systems can be built up, so that real-time requirements can be fulfilled.

ANALOG SIMULATION

Simulation languages have been developed for two distinct fields:

1) Simulation of discrete, serial processes.
2) Simulation of parallel, more or less continuous systems.

In most cases the languages don't care about the possibilities of parallel working processors or units. The advantage is accuracy and the problem is often the time, because of serial execution reasons!

Behind both cases is the distinguishing characteristic of the engineering-analysis approach to break down a system into its functional blocks or components. If we have blocks, than we can work in parallel! These blocks and parts are basically the constructs of block-oriented languages which have been introduced to handle discrete and continuous system simulation.

The continuous and discrete system simulation and data manipulation are used in the following fields:

The study of monetary relationship in economics, the study of information flow in business organization, the solution of partial differential equations in dynamic systems and transportation systems, the study of queuing systems and cell growth and the broad field of pattern recognition and image processing.

Languages for these applications are different from languages used for analog computer simulators, block diagram system simulators. Simulating the analog computer generally results in an operator (or statement) repertoir which reflects the fundamental physical limitations of analog computer elements. For example, in control simulation transfer functions and non-linearities are not conveniently expressable in equation form. In spite of these disadvantages the analog-computer block language has proven itself to be an easily learned programming tool for simulation. It is possible, to handle these blocks or multiprocessor systems in parallel.

Desired blocks are named by appropriate language statements. Generally, these programs provide a large number of different functions, including standard simulation tools, such as integrators (with different integration formulas), relays, many special purpose functions, random number generator, generalized Laplace Transform, variable flow transport delay and facilities for handling distributed systems.

If the user can define and add functions especially suited for his application then the simulation language may be viewed as a tool for general purpose simulation.

HYBRID SIMULATION

Most of the available general purpose digital computers have only a single arithmetic unit. For this reason the computer must perform the required operations sequentially and digital simulation proceeds at a slowed time scale. To overcome the time problem and yet to preserve the advantages of accuracy and information storage, hybrid computers have been developed. A hybrid computer is a combination of both analog and digital computers (Fig. 1). These machines provide the high speed, parallel or simultaneous processing capability of analog computers and the accuracy and information storage capability of digital computers.

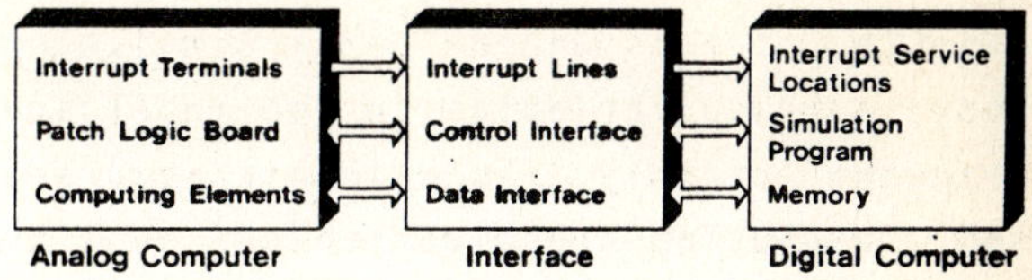

Fig. 1 Hybrid computer system

The programming of a hybrid computer system must consider both the analog and digital points of view /27, 30/. Programming the analog components of the hybrid computer will not be very different from conventional analog computer programming. However, because of the timing restrictions of real-time operations,the programming of a hybrid system will be quite different from conventional digital programming. Even the use of high level languages, which assist the programmer in handling the analog and digital system parts does not solve the programming problems.

The major factors which effect software in a hybrid facility are:

- timing and synchronization,
- the interfaces between the analog and digital computers,
- extensive diagnostics and control interactions.

The ability of a digital computer to handle real time simulations largely depends on its ability to handle priority interrupts and on the software responding to these interrupts.

For iterative and repetitive problems the analog components can be triggered in such a way that the digital parts act immediately upon requests from clocks or analog logic devices through a priority interrupt system and the digital and analog actions run in parallel.

It is quite common in hybrid simulation to use many priority interrupts in both synchronous and asynchronous ways. An example of this would be a simulation where certain variables in the model are changing rapidly. To maintain accuracy and resolution these variables must be calculated and integrated, for instance, more frequently than other more slowly changing and less critical variables. To handle these variables, the problem could be separated into different tasks where each task is processed by a subroutine.

Fig.2 illustrates the relative time that the digital computer spends on each subroutine as a result of an interrupt occuring in lines 1 through 3. Subroutine SUB i services interrupt line i (i = 1,2,3) and has the highest (i = 1), second (i = 2) or lowest (i = 3) priority, respectively. In addition, several asynchronous higher priority routines could be added to handle special system conditions, such as amplifier overload, errors etc.

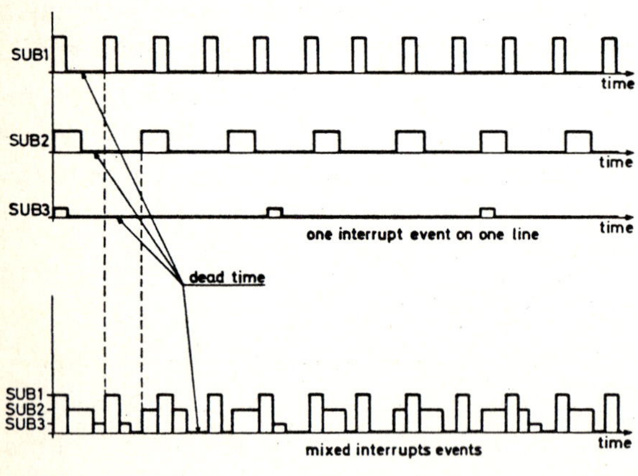

Fig. 2 Interrupt controlled processing of subroutines

In a general purpose real time interrupt environment it is most efficient to make use of re-entrancy. This arises from the fact that, especially for simulation, many portions of a digital program and its subroutines share other routines and normally if one of these routines is interrupted, it cannot share another routine which will reenter that common routine.

Peripheral processors or automatic data channels are very important for a simulation to handle input and output, since I/O operations require a large amount of time. I/O programming can become very complex to the programmer. So he should have access to software tools supporting the powerful hardware I/O features.

Manual intervention in hybrid simulation is a necessity. For this purpose there are hardware sense switches at the console of the digital computer. The programmer may use these to suit his needs.

With an operating system the programmer is able to debug both the analog and digital portions of his program with the digital computer. System software allows him to sit at the typewriter and address and print voltage of amplifiers, potentiometers and any addressable point in the analog computer or interface. He also has the ability to change settings and to change control modes in the analog and digital computer.

DIGITAL DIFFERENTIAL ANALYZER

The structure of conventional Digital Differential Analyzers (DDAs) is the same as of analog computers. The DDA consists of a large number of elements and function generators /4/. A DDA solves differential equations by digital integration.

The advantage is that all quantities are represented digitally, and successive values of a dependent variable are obtained by adding increments to previous values. The independent variable is handled as a succession of small incremental steps, for each of which one step of the integration is performed. This principle is illustrated by Figure 3.

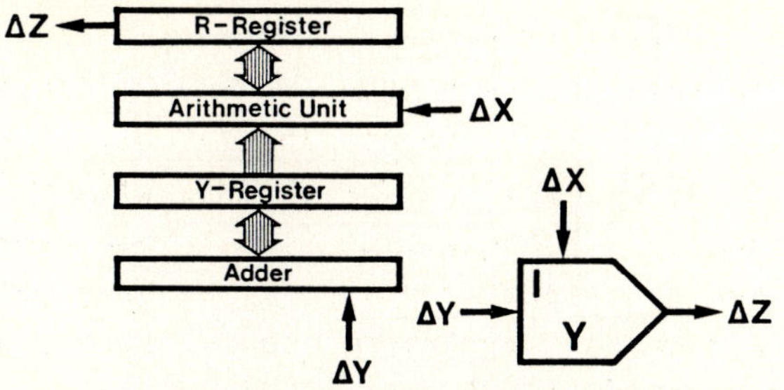

Fig. 3 Blockdiagram and symbol of an integrator

If $Y = f(x)$, and $Z = \int Y\ dx$, then using the simple rectangular integration rule at each step we get $\Delta Z = Y \cdot \Delta X$. Summing over all such steps

$$\Sigma\Delta Z = \Sigma Y \cdot \Delta X$$

gives
$$Z \simeq \int Y \cdot dx \ .$$

As decision element the servo may be used to control running programs or to regard thresholds. If the value of the product $Y \cdot \Delta X$ is greater than zero the servo generates a positive ΔZ-increment, a negative ΔZ-increment is submitted if $Y \cdot X$ becomes negative; ΔZ is zero if the product $Y \cdot \Delta X$ is zero.

A constant multiplier generates the output increment $\Delta Z = K \cdot \Delta X$ with the constant K as initial value.

Sometimes it is necessary to generate functions. The easiest way is the linear interpolation between the ordinates. Basic elements are two integrators, the first is used for defining the interval $[X_k, X_{k+1}]$, the second is used for defining the slope of the straight line connecting the ordinates $f(X_k)$ and $f(X_{k+1})$.

In DDAs truncation errors as well as round-off errors are produced. Generally, the computation of quadrature formulas produce no exact values; there always remains a remainder.

For a quadrature formula a remainder order can be defined for the truncation, which depends on the degree of the polynomial exactly integrable by this quadrature formula. The greater the number of used abscissas the greater is the remainder order. Therefore it seems desirable to choose quadrature formulas of high order for the algorithms of DDAs. But they cause high implementation expenses, so that it is finally indicated to use quadrature formulas of low degree.

A round-off error is inherent with the DDA integrator procedure. And the rounding process is due to the incremental processing, i.e. that only the overflow of the R-register is relevant for the DDA-integration while the remainder in the R-register is not taken into consideration.

Investigations about both errors in DDAs have revealed, that the round-off error dominates. DDAs and their system elements may be organized in different ways. Here, differences are made between the processing structures between the system elements.

Parallel-parallel

In each system element the registers and the processing units are organized parallel. All interconnection paths between system elements are parallel.

Serial-parallel

The system elements consist of shift registers and the computation is done in a serial way. Interconnections between elements are parallel.

Parallel-serial

Parallel execution takes place within the system elements; the transfer of input/output data between the system elements is done serially.

Serial-serial

Every system element and the data transfer between the system elements are organized in a serial way.

The functions such as integration, addition, constant multiplication, and the servo function performed by the above mentioned system elements are different. However, the construction of the system elements show a certain amount of common structure, such that it is obvious to develop a universal system element, which is capable of performing all functions asked for. This complies with the tendency in large scale integration to build general elements (Fig.4), because it will be more economic to waste element functions instead of developing a different element for each function.

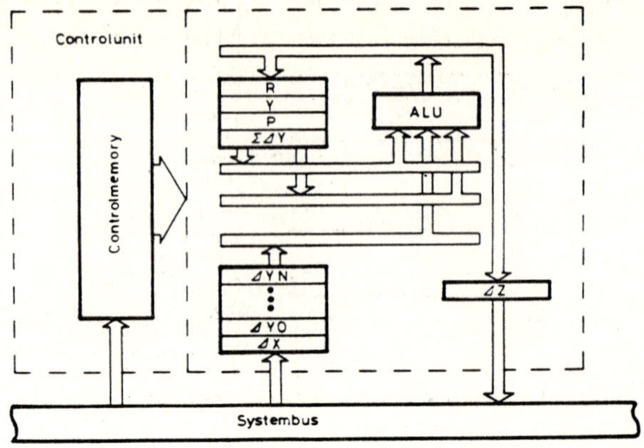

Fig. 4 Universal system element

Important is, that the actual postulated structure of the system element, its function, is defined by a microprogram. The microprograms are stored as information, they define the specific structure of the universal system element.

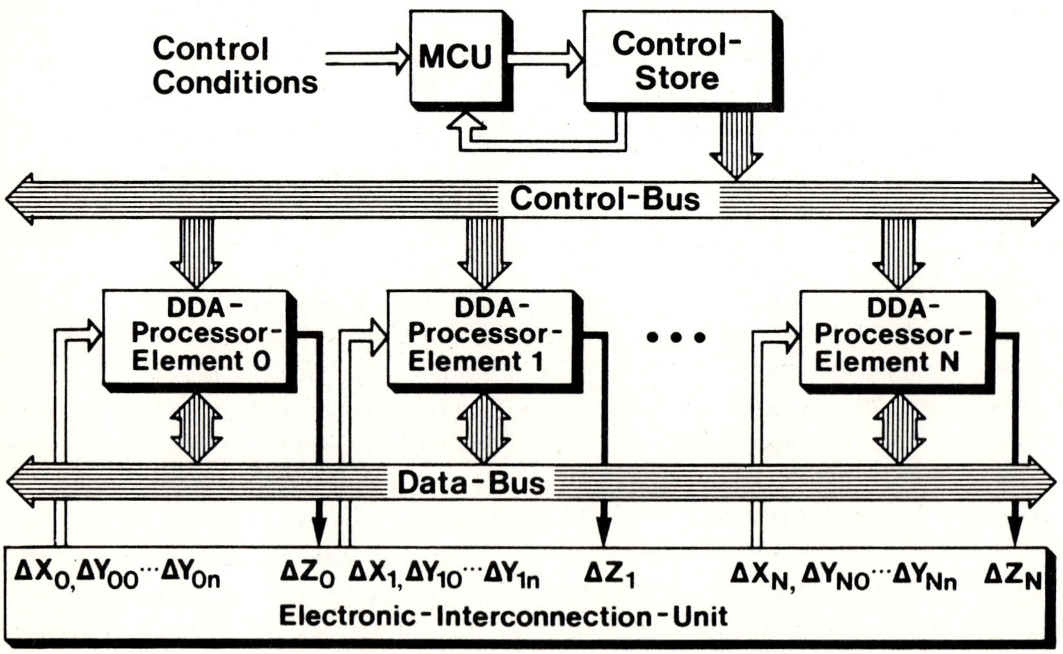

Fig. 5 Parallel DDA with parallel processor elements

Regarding the accuracy one can also make available several quadrature formulas in form of microprograms in the case of integration. When rounding the results is concerned, one may select between microprograms, which support fixed point or floating point arithmetic or whole numbers for fractional number incrementation.

For processing purposes the output information of some system elements has to be transferred to the inputs of the same or other system elements, where the structure of these connections depends on the actual problem that has to be solved.

In most cases, connecting the system elements through coupling information /25/. The configuration (Fig.5) should be controlled automatically by the problem to be solved, the appropriate connecting structure has to be deduced by an automatic analysis of the problem. The problem, for example a differential equation, will be delivered to a separate host computer (Fig. 6). As one result, the compilation phase yields the source and destination addresses of the input and output registers of the system elements to be involved in the solution of the problem. These addresses are transferred to the interconnection unit (Fig.5).

Principally, the DDA can always be applied where the description of the problem is reducible to the solution of equivalent differential equations. Typical examples are investigations concerning aircraft simulators or simulations in connection with missiles. In these cases parameter variations are of great importance for navigation problems, stability investigations and coordinate-transformations.

One can already see by this enumeration, that beside its accuracy the speed of the DDA is decisive for its selection in solving such real-time problems. A very pleasant facility is given by the cooperation of a DDA with a digital computer (Fig. 6), because there is no need for data conversion; both machines are working in the digital mode. Normally, all arithmetic is done with fixed point decimals. To avoid scaling problems, floating point DDAs have been developed /4/. The combination permits each computer to take over that workload it is best suited for. Such a hybrid system may also be used in discrete or combined continuous-discrete simulation.

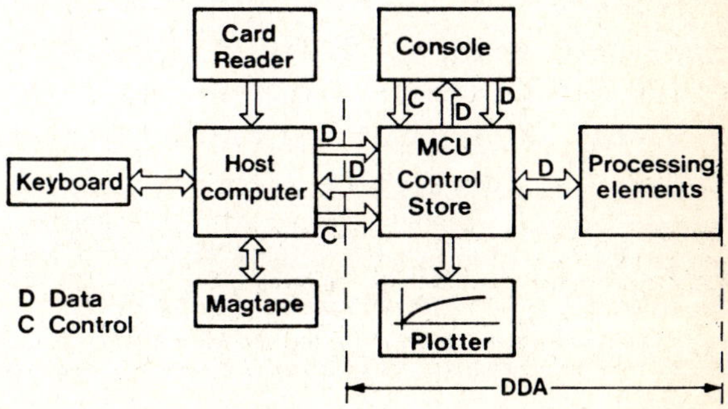

Fig. 6 Hybrid-DDA

PARALLEL-COMPUTERS IN SIMULATION

In the past, analog and hybrid machines and DDAs have been well known as parallel computers for discrete and continuous systems simulation. Current low cost large-scale integrated microprocessors offer the potential of cost-effective multiple microprocessor systems. Compared with conventional digital computers the following advantages can be gained by these systems /16, 17/.

- high throughput
- improved real-time response
- modular extension
- high availability and reliability.

In addition to these features some simulations may be eased and some new problems may be handled by simulation due to the overall digital nature of the information in the simulation system. Some new problems are the following:

- Solution of partial differential equations by finite-difference equations.

  Problems are weather and climate simulation, plasma confinement, fluid dynamics, and problems in geophysics. A considerable increase in speed is possible because of parallelism carried out by a suitable multiprocessor structure. Such a system allows some degree of on-line interactive operation in large problems, as in estimation of parameters and initial conditions which require a large number of runs and interaction with the user.

- Solution of partial differential equations by finite-element techniques.

  Finite-element methods have been valuable in the solution of certain static problems in elasticity, particularly in cases where the boundaries are irregular. The form of a finite-element formulation, so that a multiprocessor structure may be useful in finding solutions.

- Monte Carlo solution of partial differential equations.

  A Monte Carlo method my be useful in problems with difficult boundary conditions.

  With the Monte Carlo approach a solution at a point is determined by averaging the solutions encountered at a boundary after a large number of random walks started at the point and terminating at the first boundary reached.

  Serial digital simulation or the use of a hybrid computer for this approach have not been satisfactory because of the time needed to make some hundreds or more runs. With a parallel computer, runs may be made simultaneously thus providing many times the speed of a single serially working computer.

- Continuous system simulation.

  As explained above, it is quite common to use a serial digital computer for simulation of dynamic systems, sometimes with programming aids such as CSMP. Particularly in the study of electric power systems, ecological and environmental systems, socio-economic systems, and physiological systems, the size of the system makes dynamic simulation both slow and expensive. In addition, a higher speed is necessary if optimization or parameter estimation is required. The speed advantage of a parallel computer would also be useful in problems involving stochastic signals or parameters.

- Discrete system simulation.

  Discrete systems arise in the study of transportation problems, queuing systems, cell growth etc. These problems are better handled by serial computers than by continuous systems. But the increased size of these problems may result in difficulties, concerning speed and size of system components. A parallel computer may be extremely suited for simulation of discrete and continuous-discrete systems.

- Data manipulation

  In some simulations related to radar signal-processing or pattern recognition it is necessary to manipulate the data. Coordinate transformation, Fast Fourier-Transforms etc. are quite common.

A parallel computer may process several tasks simultaneously thus gaining a speed suited for real-time simulation.

Unfortunately, there is till now no unique approach to implement a simulation model for the above problems. The reason is that design techniques, structures, and organizations of multiprocessor systems are not well defined. Research on a large number of problems has to be done before implementation progress can be made. These are in particular process partitioning into parallel tasks, allocating tasks, sequencing and interaction between processors, controlling system resources, the physical and architectural limits of microprocessors /26/.

To provide a system configuration with multiprocessors and distributed processors suitable for specific simulation problems, existing microprocessor architectures, organizations, and strategies must be analyzed to derive those characteristics deemed mandatory for workable multiple microprocessor systems /22, 31/.

Two organizations of multiple processors can be described: the single instruction multiple data (SIMD) and the multiple instruction multiple data (MIND) organization.

In SIMD structures (Fig.7) a single control unit fetches and decodes instructions. The instruction (e.g., jump, conditional branch) is executed in the control unit itself or conveyed to other processing elements. Three subcategories of SIMD exist:

1) Array Processors.

   An instruction manipulates vectors or strings of data simultaneously; the control unit has a limited capability (e.g. ILLIAC IV, WISPAC) /7, 12/.

2) Processing Ensembles.

   The control unit is a complete computer and processing elements communicate by passing messages through it (e.g. PEPE) /14/.

3) Associative Processors.

   Access and operations on data take place by content rather than address (e.g. STARAN) /8/.

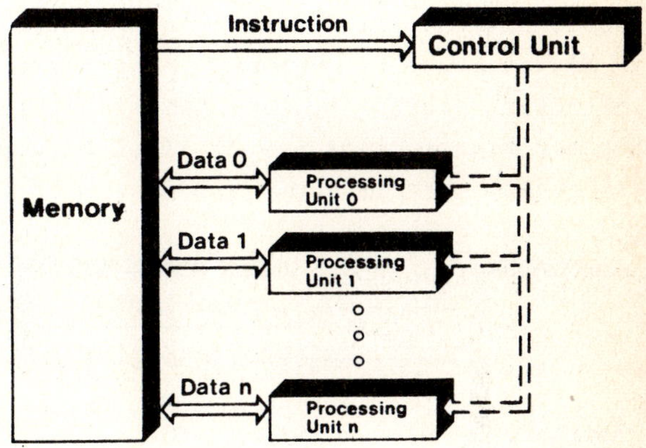

Fig. 7 SIMD-Computer

The array processor is the only one so far, to be cost effective for very specific applications /19/. The advantage of this processor is the great throughput obtained by simultaneous (parallel) operation of processors on different data streams. To obtain parallelism, the array processor system must have the following specific characteristics:

- Computations must be describable by vector instructions, e.g., many identical operations are in action on different data.

- High speed data routing between processors is necessary.
- Operands that are manipulated simultaneously must be fetched simultaneously.

Examples of this type of computation are the solution of partial differential equations, matrix manipulations, grid problems etc. in weather prediction, air traffic control, radar signal processing etc.

As processing elements bipolar bit-slice microprocessors are used in array processors. Bit-slice processor configurations permit application-dependent structures and built-in fault tolerance. Further characteristics are fast technology (e.g. ECL), microprogramming, pipelining through prefetched instructions, carry look ahead logic, external hardware for fast multiply/divide and other arithmetic, microlevel interrupt capability, and pipelining at the macroinstruction level in the control unit.

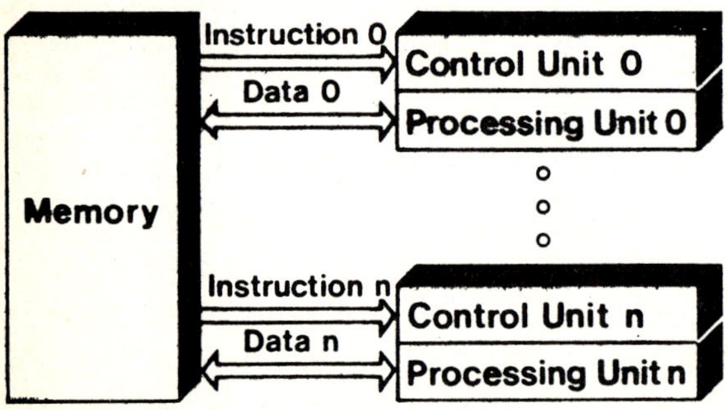

Fig. 8 MIMD-Computer

This organization (Fig. 8) achieves parallelism by performing independent tasks on separate data sets concurrently, and combining results of the execution of the execution of the independent tasks. High efficiency is obtained in this structure by proper synchronization of processors and allocation of tasks. This is quite different from SIMD structures, where synchronization is done automatically by instruction execution and where there is no task allocation problem because all processors perform the same task on different data. Subclasses of MIMD structures are distributed systems and multiprocessor systems.

- Distributed Systems.

  Multiple processors perform dedicated functions as part of a single partitioned system. Processors can be locally distributed (e.g. factory) or geographically distributed (e.g. communication network). Tasks and their actions must be known a priori so that the system function can be subdivided for the separate processing components. This decomposition includes segmentation of software into dedicated program segments and assignment of variables and resources to each processor. These fixed a priori allocation for tasks minimizes program interaction and this in return permits simplified devèlopment and debugging of separated program segments.
  Communication between processors is usually restricted to passing messages through shared resources. This may be a peripheral or a serial communication link (e.g., IEC-Bus).

  Distributed systems have some disadvantages:
  - System load is rarely known explicitly. This can result in inefficient utilization of processors and awkward segmentation of programs.
  - System modification due to changes of controlled variables, tasks or processors may require extensive offline setup preparation.

- Failure of any processing component may seriously degrade system performance so far as the system cannot shift tasks that have been assigned to the defective processing module.

- Multiprocessor Systems.

  A system of this class employs a single integrated operating system to dynamically allocate tasks as they are invoked. The operating system can run on each processing module (floating executive/, or on a master processor which allocates tasks to shared processing modules (resource allocation). The multiprocessor structure is symmetric if all processors are identical and capable of executing any task; the structure is asymmetric if some processing units handle special functions.

  Multiprocessor systems may be further classified according to the degree of interaction between the processing modules. Two of such classifications are:

  - Tightly coupled processors,
  - Loosely coupled processors.

  In the case of tightly coupled processors (i.e. sharing a common memory in the case of a large number of processors on a high speed multiplexed bus), the processors operate under the control of a strict bus assignment scheme, which is implemented in hardware at the busprocessor interface.

The characteristic of this scheme is, that two or more processors may at a certain time execute independent instructions simultaneously. Fig.9 shows the bus utilization of a system with 3 processors. One processor needs the bus only for one cycle. A bus control unit resolves all bus requests for the next cycle and assigns the bus to the requesting processor with the highest priority.

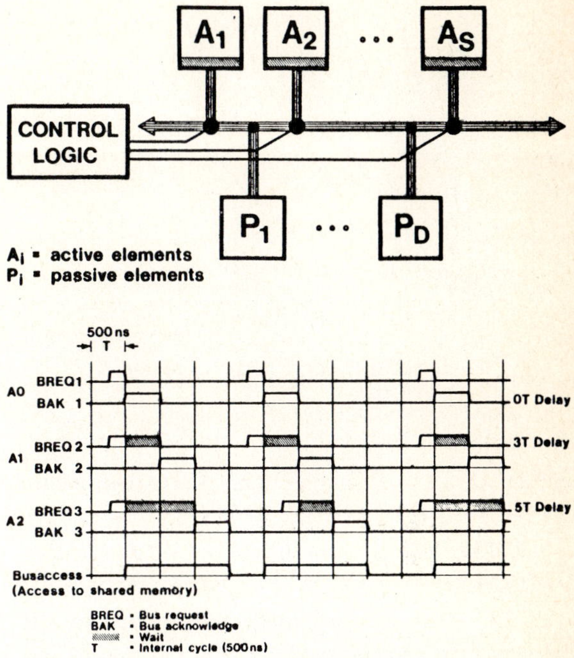

Fig. 9 Time multiplexed bus
a) System
b) Timing diagram

As depicted in the figure, the processor P1 will run with an efficiency of 100 %. The second and all other processors will have an efficiency less than 100 % because their operations (bus accesses) will be delayed if a conflict arises due to bus requests of any processor with higher priority.

Supposed that each of the closely coupled processors needs access to the common memory with a probability of p_i (one access every $\frac{1}{p_i}$ cycles) the probability p_c for a delayed access is shown in Fig.10 /18/.

The probability p_i is instruction dependent and 1/3 is a good mean value for the microprocessors INTEL 8080 and ZILOG Z 80.

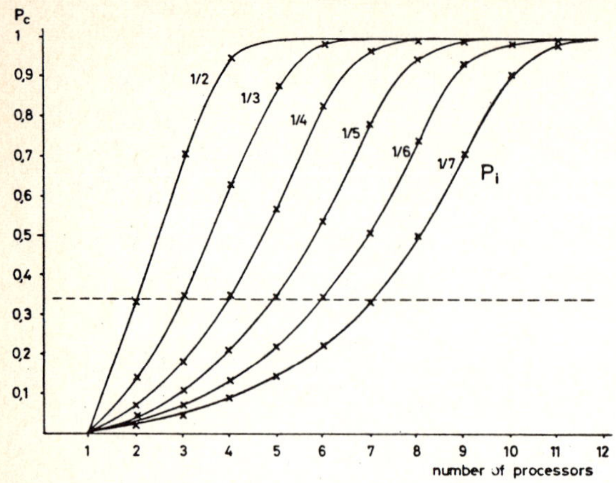

Fig. 10 Probability p_c for a delayed process

As opposed to tightly coupled processors there is no instruction interaction between loosely coupled processors, although they may share a common memory to pass information (Fig. 11). When the system is to consist of numerous modules for general purpose applications, the connections are necessarily of the loose type giving each processor exclusive access to bus and resources for the execution of at least one complete instruction.

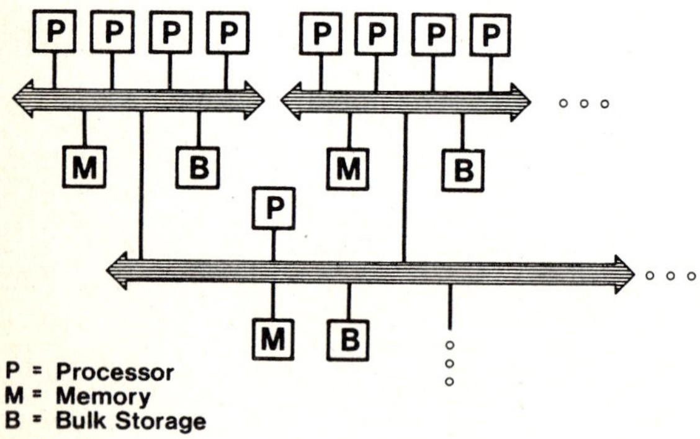

Fig. 11 Hierarchical computer-system

For simulation performance, cost reliability and flexibility of a multiprocessor system are influenced by /3/:

- allocation and synchronization of processors and tasks,
- control of system resources,
- interconnections of functional modules,
- interprocessor communication.

The first two points are in the essence identical to those mentioned for hybrid simulation.

Types of interconnections /2/ between processors, shared memory, and shared I/O are the time-shared commom bus, multiport memory and crossbar switch.

The smaller the ratio of bus cycles required by an individual processor to the total number of possible requests, the higher the system throughput. For this reason, private memory and private I/O are highly advantageous.

Multiported systems, as shown in Fig. 12 employ multiple dedicated buses, and arbitration logic must be available for each multiported part. Major disadvantages of this organization are the high cabling and connector costs.

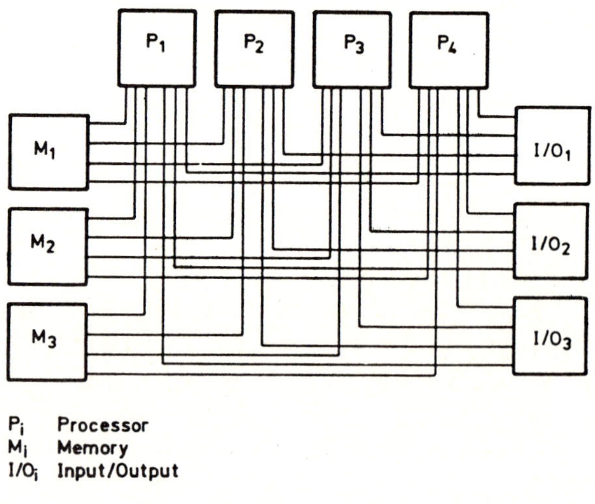

Fig. 12 System with multiport components

The crossbar switch is sometimes referred to as space division multiplexing (Fig.13). With this connection type the same problems arise as in telephone exchange systems. Specific problems are: complex structure, costly to control, physically large, reduced reliability /2, 9/.

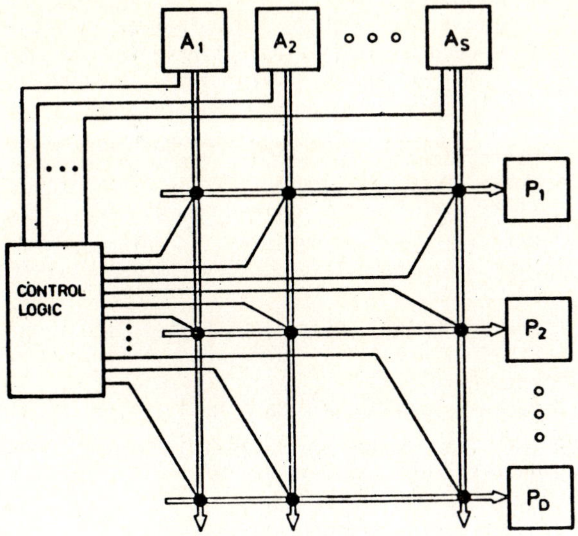

A_i = active element (processor)
P_i = passive element (memory)

Fig. 13 Space multiplex system

In MIMD structures a mailbox memory (common memory) may function as a principal interprocessor communication media. Competition for a mailbox memory must be resolved by arbitration.

A semaphore memory is an unsharable resource and is in this sense a special mailbox memory with arbitration logic.

In reviewing some aspects of parallel systems one must recognize, that technology is considerably ahead of software and architecture. Currently there is no operating system known which controls tasks and processes as easily as block languages handle functional blocks. Probably Petri nets or related nets are a step in the desired direction /6, 13, 15/. Further related approaches are data flow schemes and special hardware /23/. Some implementations have shown, that dedicated parallel systems have been successfully used in computing with real-time constraints. For a large class of simulation problems there will be an appropriate parallel architecture in the near future.

CONCLUSIONS

Several conclusions can be drawn about the usage of the explained systems. The first arises from the amount of time and effort of programming the different systems. An easy-to-program analog computer competes with a digital system. Setup, debug and execution times must be taken into account.

Real-time considerations influence the choice of a system. Often hybrid and/or analog simulation will permit real-time operation. Another consideration is,that special purpose equipment like digital differential analyzers may be included in the simulation and replace any analog working system component. An even more flexible configuration is gained by multiprocessor systems with parallel computing capabilities on several tasks or data strings.

The ultimate purpose of the simulation, the complexity of the problem and many other factors influence the choice of the computing system. One should avoid the temptation to oversimplify the decision on the basis of only a few of these factors, because each system has also some advantages in simulation.

The technological advances in the digital computer field will furtheron have a strong influence on the simulation with multi-processor systems.

REFERENCES

1 Ameling, W.: Aufbau und Wirkungsweise elektronischer Analogrechner, Vieweg & Sohn, Braunschweig, 1963.

2 Ameling, W. u.a.: Interconnection structure for parallel processor systems, Parallel Computers - Parallel Mathematics, IMACS Symposium S. 297 - 300, 1977.

3 Ameling, W. u.a.: Parallel processor solutions for a certain class of optimization strategies, Parallel Computers - Parallel Mathematics, IMACS Symposium S. 243 - 246, 1977.

4 Ameling, W. u.a.: Planung und Entwicklung einer programmierbaren digitalen Integrieranlage. Forschungsbericht des Landes NRW, Nr. 2607, Fachgruppe Physik/Mathematik, Westdeutscher Verlag GMbH, Opladen, 1976.

5 Annino, J.S., E.C. Russel: The ten most frequent causes of simulation analysis failure - and how to avoid them, Simulation, Vol. 32 (6), 137 - 140, 1979.

6 Agerwale, T., M. Flynn: Modeling with Extended Petri Nets, Proceedings at the Conference on Petri Nets and Related Methods, MIT, Mass., 1975.

7 Barnes, J.H. et al.: The ILLIAC IV computer, IEEE Trans. Comp., Vol. C-17 (8), p. 746 - 757, 1968.

8 Batcher, K.E.: STARAN/Radcap hardware architecture, Sagamore computer conference on parallel processing, 1973.

9 Chen, C.J., A.A. Frank: On programmable parallel data routing networks via crossbar switches for multiple element computer architecture, Parallel Processing, Lect. Notes in Comp. Science, Springer, Vol. 24, p. 338 - 369, 1975.

10 Chu, Y.: Digital simulation of continuous systems. Mc Graw-Hill Book Comp. N.J., 1969.

11 Clancy, J.J., M.S. Fineberg: Digital simulation languages, a critique and a guide. Fall joint computer conference, p. 23 - 36, 1965.

12 Cyre, W.R. et al.: WISPAC: A parallel array computer for large-scale system simulation, Simulation, 165 - 172, Nov. 1977.

13 Dijkstra: Solution of a Problem in Concurrent Programming, Communications of the ACM, 569-570 (9), 1965.

14 Evenson, A.J., J.L. Troy: Introduction to the architecture of a 288-element PEPE, Sagamore computer conference on parallel processing, p. 162 - 169, 1973.

15 Francesco, De, N., G. Vaglini: On the Decomposition of Parallel Computations, Parallel Computers - Parallel Mathematics, IMACS Symp., p 221 - 224, 1977.

16 Gracia, O.N., J. Mc Nally: Parallelism in Simulation. Parallel Computers - Parallel Mathematics, IMACS-Symposium, North Holland, p. 133 - 138, 1977

17 Havranek, W.A.: A new digital peripherial computer for simulation problems and its influence on real-time computer techniques. Parallel Computers - Parallel Mathematics. IMACS Samposium, p. 197 - 202, 1977.

18 Hoener, S., W. Roehder: Efficiency of a multimicroprocessor system with the time shared buses, Proc. of Euromicro 1977, J.D. Nicoud, et al. (ed.) North Holland, p. 35 - 42, 1977.

19 Hufnagel, St. P.: Comparison of selected array processor architectures, Comp. Design. 151-158 (3) 1979.

20 IBM, CSMP 1130, Continuous System Modeling, Program, Program No 1130 - CX - 13X, 1966.

21 IBM: CSMP III, Continuous System Modeling Program III, Program No 5734 - XS9, 1971.

22 IEEE Trans. Comp., Vol.C-26 Nr.2 (Special issue on parallel processing), 1977.

23 Jensch,P., W. Ameling: A computer architecture for multiple data flow programs. Parallel Computers - Parallel Mathematics, IMACS Symposium, p. 189 - 192, 1977.

24 Jensch, P., et al.: Arrhythmia Detection with a Multi-Microprocessor System for Distributed and Parallel Processing. Computer in Cardiology, IEEE Comp. Soc., 1979.

25 Kempken, E., W. Ameling: Parallel DDA based on universal microprogrammable computing units. Parallel Computers - Parallel Mathematics, IMACS Symp. 139 - 142, 1977.

26 Rzehak, H.: Parallel Computers for Continuous-System Simulation. Parallel Computers - Parallel Mathematics. IMACS Symposium, 59-70, 1977.

27 Schmidt, W.E.: Important Considerations in Procuring and Implementing a Hybrid Computer, 5th int. analogue computation meetings, p. 273 - 288.

28 Schöne, A.: Simulation technischer Systeme. Carl Hanser Verlag, München - Wien 1974.

29 Shapiro, S.: Analog, Hybrid and Digital Simulation - A Comparative Evaluation, 5th int. analogue computation meetings, p. 301 - 305.

30 Stephenson, R.E.: Computer Simulation for Engineers, Harcourt Brace Jovanovich, Inc., New York, 1971.

31 Zimmermann, N.J., H.J. Sips: Parallel Data Verwerken, Inform. jaarg. 20, Nr. 1, pag. 1 t/m 70, 3 - 22, jan. 1978.

DISCRETE SIMULATION AND RELATED FIELDS
A. Jávor (editor)
North-Holland Publishing Company

ON A CONCEPTOR LEVEL LANGUAGE FOR THEORETICAL SOLUTION OF PROBLEMS

N.N. Diduk, V.N. Koval

Institute of Cybernetics
Academy of Sciences of the Ukrainian SSR
Kiev, USSR

Presented here for discussion is the CONC language intended for use at all basic stages of the preparation of problem solving prior to computer-aided solution. Such stages include: (1) formal problem statement; (2) search for theoretical solution; (3) algorithmization of the solution. The language makes possible the formal representations of a problem solution at any abstraction level available in modern mathematics with further transition to a lower level. The CONC language provides a means for operation on non-constructive objects and ineffective procedures which places it beyond the group of classic algorithmic languages into a broader class of languages specified as conceptor languages. Mathematical means of the language and the role of conceptor languages in solving complex problems is also discussed.

1. THE PURPOSE OF THE CONC LANGUAGE

Several thousands of algorithmic languages are known today. Some of them were developed for theoretical needs (e.g. Turing machines' language, language of normal Markov algorithms or Kaluzhin flow-charts' language). The majority of the languages are aimed at practical solution of problems by a computer. Why should another language be suggested? We have already a great number of these enabling us to select one of them for recording the algorithm of a given problem solution, and it creates the illusion of versatility of these languages in the sense of universal applicability. Indeed, the opinion shared by programmers and programming theoreticians implies that the major difficulty connected with the solution of problems consists rather in formation of adequate systems of realization for already existing languages than in development of new ones, especially after the advent of such powerful languages as ALGOL-68, SIMULA-67, SETL, PL/1, PASCAL.

Such a conclusion would be true in case all the difficulties arising in solving various problems were caused exclusively by inadequate state-of-the-art programming systems. Unfortunately, it is not so. The initial description of any complex problem and its algorithmic solution which can be written in any programming language are separated by a wide gap. The only tool used up till now for bridging this gap is general mathematics. But mathematics itself is very broad, and there is no domain in it capable to play this role independently.

The CONC language proposed in this paper is the very language to bridge this gap between initial problem description and their final algorithmic solutions (it should be emphasized that all achievements in automated programming can become useful only *after* the algorithmic solution of the problem is found).

The bridging of the said gap can be implemented in three stages: (1) transition from the initial problem description to its formal statement; (2) theoretical solution of the problem; (3) transition from the theoretical solution of the problem to its algorithmic solution. It is difficult to define strictly the term "theoretical solution of the problem", but in the present context it has the meaning of solving the problem at a higher abstraction level than required by the user. The theoretical solution of the problem is always somewhat closer to the problem statement than to the required particular solution (from the modern mathematics' viewpoint, the very formal problem statement can be regarded as its theoretical solution).

The language, intended to be a tool for implementing the three above-mentioned stages, should allow the formal representation of a problem solution at any abstraction level available in modern mathematics (starting from its formal statement) with further transition to a lower level. It is evident that no algorithmic language does suit playing this role, owing to the fact that modern mathematics ensures easy operation on non-constructive objects and ineffective procedures while algorithmic languages fail to serve this purpose in principle. The language under consideration, CONC, provides the means for operation on non-constructive objects and ineffective procedures thus placing itself far beyond the class of algorithmic languages into a broader class of languages which we specify as *conceptor* languages. Texts written in conceptor language are not algorithms in the general sense; such texts are called *conceptors*.

2. GRAPH-DIAGRAM REPRESENTATION OF CONC LANGUAGE

The ability of the CONC language to carry out its main purpose, i.e. to serve as a tool for theoretical problem solutions, depends considerably on the degree of visuality of texts written in this language. The requirements for visuality are multilateral and include compactness of texts, possibility to divide them into meaningful portions, level of heuristics, i.e. the ability of texts to convey the logic of the problem solution process as well as the logic structure of the solution obtained. The principal idea of the visuality requirement lies, in our opinion, in the demand that the texts should be two-dimensional rather than one-dimensional: instead of being strings of symbols, they should be presented as pictures or drawings.

1. *Conceptor*

In order to provide high visibility of texts, the CONC language is supplied with a number of specific means, the principal one being a completely formalized graph-diagram language representation. Within this representation, every conceptor has a form of a partly ordered set of flow-charts, normally expressed on separate sheets of paper and called *constructions*. These constructions to a certain degree resemble block-diagrams of algorithms used by programmers. There is, anyway, an essential difference between them. As a rule, a block-diagram of the algorithm is not an exhaustive prescription ensuring the retrieval of the result by any set of input data. Thus, under normal conditions, the block-diagram of an algorithm (or set of such block-diagrams) is not the solution of any problem at any level (conceptor, algorithmic, computer). At the same time, the order set of constructions, specified as conceptor, at its level possesses a constant feature of sufficiency, i.e. it is always an exhaustive solution of a certain problem. The meaning of the latter phrase will be enlightened in the course of narration. Up to this point we can only note that this feature of sufficiency of the construction set cannot be obtained without formalization of graphic means of the language. Below, we shall consider the basic principles of this formalization without going into details.

The construction set is ordered with a tree order. According to this order, the set contains the only basic construction, the root of the tree. All other constructions fixed to strictly defined positions: the nodes of the tree, some of which are final ones. Each construction consists of a set of *constructs* joined by arrows. The language uses the constructs of two types: *blocks* and *operators*. The construction containing at least one block is called a block construction, while with the absence of blocks the construction is called an operator construction. The operator constructions are the only ones that can be the final nodes of a tree structure. A tree structure may be degenerated; in this case it consists of only one construction (operator) which is both the root and the only final node of the tree. The block constructions are always the roots of non-degenerated trees and their non-final nodes.

The semantics of the conceptor tree structure consists of the following. Each block comprised by structure is to be decoded with the help of the original construction. Thus each block construction generates the number of the tree branches equal to the number of its blocks. Decoding process proceeds until all the last decoding constructions become operator ones.

2. *Block*

The need for the decoding of each block of the block construction means that blocks contrary to operators are non-independent constructs. In the conceptor, blocks play the role of complex marks denoting separate portions of the theoretical solution of the problem. The marking function of blocks is realized through numbering them and marking the input and output arrows. The lexicographic method of numbering the blocks is the most suitable one. It means that the block numbers of the construction which are on the higher branches of the tree structure are obtained from the numbers designated to the lower blocks with some additional digits added. This very numbering determines the tree-like order in the set of constructions.

The block has an oval shape attached with and arbitrary number of inputs and outputs (but not less than one of each) that can be marked. The names of numbers or any other symbols can serve as marks. To simplify the situation, we assume that the absence of the mark denotes an empty mark. The syntactical rules of input and output marking are joined into a single requirement: all *outputs* should be marked by different marks (unlike inputs). An example of a block is shown in Figure 1. The symbol (12) denotes its number; two of the three input marks are labeled with an empty mark.

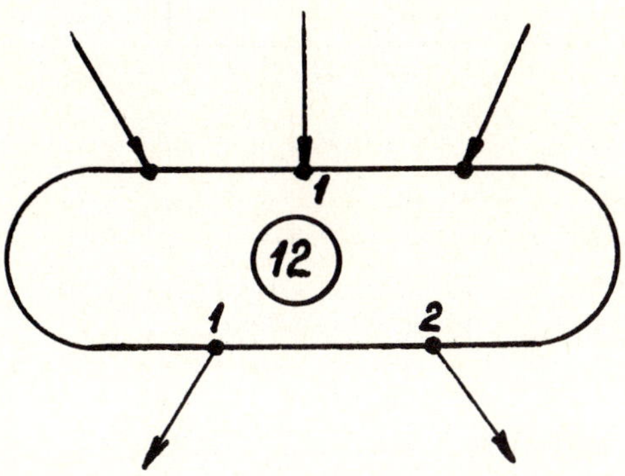

Figure 1 : Example of a block

For each group of the block inputs marked with one mark, the construction decoding this block must have only one input arrow marked with the same mark. Each output of the block must correspond to one or several output arrows of the decoding construction marked with the same mark as the block output.

The semantics of the blocks decoding is reduced to the rules of substitution of them by decoding constructions. For such substitution, it is sufficient to identify all block inputs among each other (and, respectively, all output arrows of the construction) marked with the same mark. This identification results in a mutually single-valued correspondence between the block inputs and outputs on one hand, and between the construction input and output arrows, on the other. The required substitution is performed on the basis of the obtained correspondence.

3. *Operators*

Similarly to blocks, the operators are graphic objects comprising a contour, a body, inputs and outputs. The first difference is that every operator has only one input. Nevertheless, the principal difference lies in the following: the operators are independent constructs of the language, i.e. they contain particular instructions concerning operation on expressions. The totality of all expressions form an independent sublanguage of the CONC language. The next subdivision is dedicated to the description of this sublanguage. Up to this point, we need only the following information. The language of expressions has two levels: the level of *names* and the level of *designates*. Designates fall into two categories: *terms* and *relations*. Terms are the mathematical objects (e.g. numbers, sets, functions, graphs, etc.). Relations are the statements about these jects (e.g. about their equality, equivalence, belonging, type). The language uses *expressions* at the level of names. The expressions specifying the terms are called *forms*. The expressions specifying the relations are called *formulas*.

The CONC language uses four types of operators: (1) subject operators, (2) logic operators, (3) resulting operators and (4) scanning operators.

A *subject* operator is designed for transformation of expressions or computing their designates. The operator has only one output and a rectangular contour. The language uses two varieties of the subject operator: *designation* and *definition*. The operator body of both varieties is $a := A$ and $a \underset{Df}{=} A$. In both cases a is an identifier and A is a certain form. The syntactical difference consists in the fact that in $a := A$, the form A cannot contain free variables, while in $a \underset{Df}{=} A$ it can be arbitrary.

The semantic interpretation of $a := A$ is similar to the one used in algorithmic languages. The difference, however, consists in the fact that at the conceptor level the record $a := A$ is no more an exact synonym of some data record based on a certain adress, since the "recorded" data may be found a nonconstructive object (an infinite set of any type). The meaning of the record $a \underset{Df}{=} A$ is similar to the one already known in mathematics: expression A is assigned to identifier a as a designate, but not the designate of the expression A (as in case $a := A$). The example of the subject operator of assignment is given in Figure 2 (a and b are the identifiers).

A *logic* operator is designed to transform the expressions in order to control the problem solution process. It has also a rectangular contour. The number of

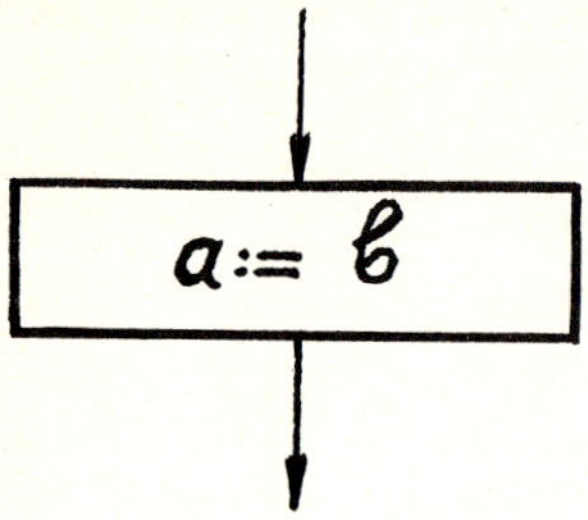

Figure 2 : Example of assignment subject operator

outputs of the logic operator is arbitrary but not less than two. The body of the operator can be any expression containing no free variables. If this expression is a formula, the number of outputs is exactly two. The general view of the logic operator is shown in Figure 3. Here, symbol *A* replaces the expression - the body of the operator. The marks *a*, *b*, *c* are the names of some terms which can become the designates of the expression *A* with different designates of the comprising identifiers.

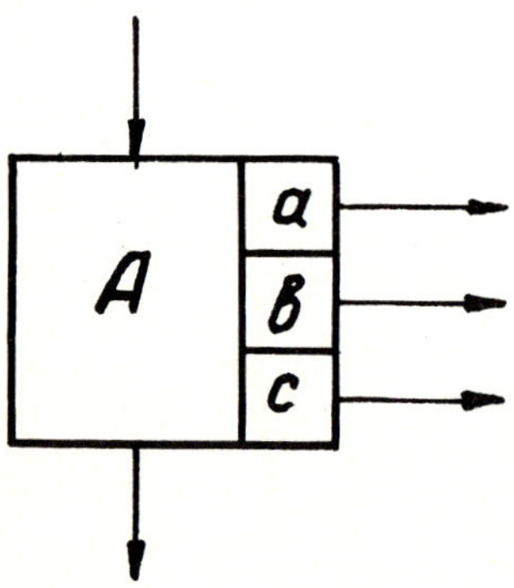

Figure 3 : Logic operator

The semantics of the logic operator consists in the following. After computation of the expression *A* designate, the output of operator is performed by one of the arrows marked by *a*, *b*, *c* provided that the expression *A* designate is equal to the respective designate of one of the names *a*, *b* or *c*. Otherwise, the output is performed along the unmarked arrow. If symbol *A* is a formula, than the logic operator has the form shown in Figure 4, where the mark *T* indicates the output from the operator in case formula *A* is true.

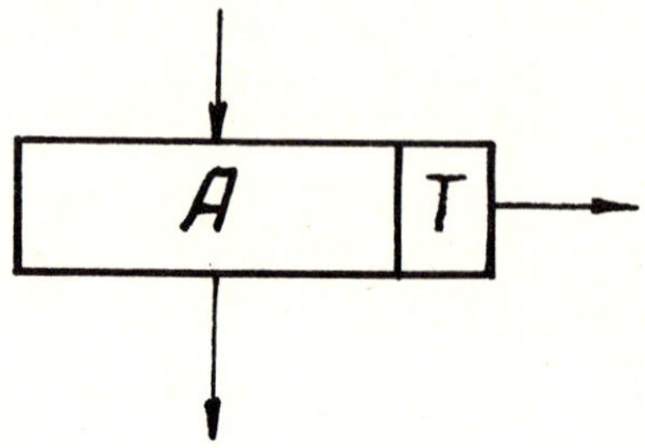

Figure 4 : Logic operator in case symbol *A* is a formula

A *resulting* operator is designed to fix all the data which reflect the results of the theoretical problem solution. Such data may include problem statement, a number of significant intermediate results and, naturally, the answer to the question stated in the problem. The general view of the resulting operator is given in Figure 5. Here, *A* implies an arbitrary expression.

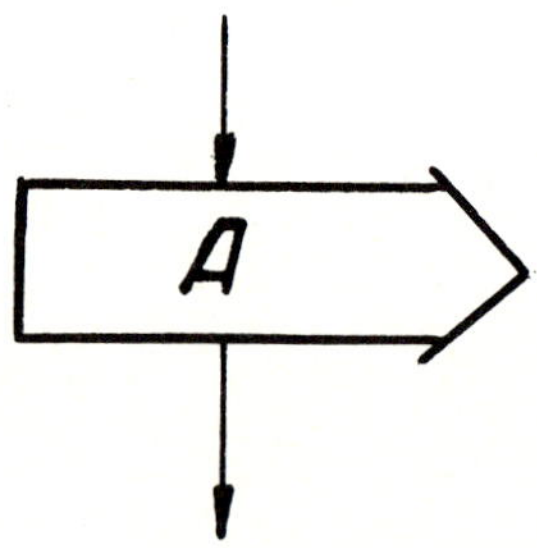

Figure 5 : Resulting operator

The purpose of a *scanning* operator is explained by its name. It facilitates various group transformations of expressions organized through scanning in a certain ordered or non-ordered set. The formal structure of this operator is rather complex and, thus, is not considered here. The character of the CONC language excludes any obstacles for the scanning provided by this operator to be organized within the framework of both finite and non-finite sets.

3. MATHEMATICAL MEANS OF CONC LANGUAGE

The mathematical basis of the CONC language comprises its sublanguage of expressions $\mathcal{X}$, containing the rule of transformation of certain expressions into other and some reduction rules.

1. *The structure of the language of expressions*
Expressions of the language $\mathcal{X}$ are constructed by means of generation rules which are divided into two categories: *transformers* and *reductors*. The transformers are intended for the construction of the expressions with new designates. Reductors, in their turn, are intended for the construction of the compact synonyms for some expressions already contained in the language. The transformers fall into five categories: (1) *functors* which transform forms into forms; (2) *predicators* which transform forms into formulas; (3) *connectors* which transform formulas into formulas; (4) *subnectors* which transform formulas into forms (this part of our classification coincides partially with the classification of functors by Curry [1]) and (5) *specificators*-transformers of special type which hardly fall into the previous four categories. Reductors are divided into two categories (1) *substantive* reductors intended for reduction of forms and (2) *relational* reductors intended for reduction of formulas.

All generation rules of the expression language $\mathcal{X}$ (transformers and reductors) are applicable to the expressions. Therefore, a class of elementary expressions $\mathfrak{a}$, which is the basis of the language $\mathcal{X}$, should be assigned for the construction of the language $\mathcal{X}$ in addition to the generation rules. All elementary expressions included in the basis $\mathfrak{a}$ are forms. These are: (1) simple identifiers, (2) variables, (3) names of numbers and (4) names of number sets. Simple identifiers (as well as complex ones) are names whose designates are not determined by their structure, but rather through forced assignment. Variables, in their turn, are distinguished from identifiers by the lack of any fixed designates. The rules of treatment of the number names in the CONC language are similar to the corresponding rules for modern algorithmic languages. The basis $\mathfrak{a}$ includes the following names of number sets: N for the set of natural numbers, Z for the set of integers, Q for the set of rational numbers and R for the set of real numbers.

2. *Functors, predicators, connectors*
The functors of the expression language $\mathcal{X}$ are used as names of operations on the following types of terms: numbers, sequences of numbers, number functions, sets, families of sets, random variables (all mathematical notions, such as a term, a relation, a set, a family, a function are treated in the CONC language according to Bourbaki [2]). All traditional arithmetic and algebraic operations belong to the group of operations on numbers. Operations of summation, multiplication and passing to the limit are used in sequencing of numbers. For numerical functions, the language has operations of definite and indefinite integration, operations of differentiation and operations on testing the minimum and the maximum of a given function.

Besides, the language $\mathcal{X}$ provides standard operations on pairs of sets: unions, intersections, differences, symmetric differences and Cartesian products. Among the functors of the language, for single sets, we may define the functors *Card* (find the cardinality of the given set), β (take the set of all the subsets of the given set) and, for ordered singular sets *min* and *max* (find the minimum and the maximum elements of the set) and *inf* and *sup* (find the lower and the upper bounds of the set). Traditional functors of union, intersection and family product are also used for operation on families of sets. Here, it should be emphasized that the names of such objects as a numerical function or a set of families are not presented in the basis $\mathfrak{a}$ of the language of expressions. Therefore, prior to application of such functors as integration of the numerical function, union of the family of sets, etc., we must, first, create forms which name the required designates.

In the language $\mathcal{X}$ there is a pair of mutually reverse functors intended for transformation from a given random variable to its distribution law and vice versa. All arithmetic and algebraic operations are also applied to random variables. Besides, there are operations of integration of random variables and calculation of their initial and central moments. The language of expressions $\mathcal{X}$ has two more functors: [____] and <____>, and the application of each one results in a different manner. The functor [____] denotes operation "take a certain (any) element of the set whose name is in the position of the dash". Functor <____> denotes operation "select the number by sampling in accordance with the distribution law for a given random variable". The choise thus obtained should always be independent from all previous choises, no matter how many times the conceptor is addressed to functors [____] and <____>.

Now, let us consider the predicators and connectors of the expression language $\mathcal{X}$. The predicators are traditional. They are listed without any comments: $=$, $\neq$, $\leq$, $<$, $\in$, $\notin$, $\subset$, $\not\subset$. For most connectors, the situation is similar: these include logical connectives. Besides, the general quantifier $\forall$ and the existential quantifier $\exists$ are also used.

3. *Specificators, subnectors*

The language $\mathcal{X}$ uses different specificators (some of them are intended, for instance, to form complex identifiers). However, we are going to dwell upon only two classes of specificators, namely, the *substitution* specificators and the *designate* specificators. Let S - be an expression, x - a variable and T - a form. Using $(T/x)S$ we shall denote the result of the simultaneous substitution of form T into expression S instead of all (free) occurrences of the variable x in S. For each variable x, there exists a substitution specificator $(\_\_/x)\_\_$, where the first dash is replaced by forms and the second dash, by arbitrary expressions. The specificator of the designate has a form of $\_\_\_!$ The dash may be replaced by identifiers of the second rank, i.e. the names whose designates are names as well. If a - identifier of the second rank, the designate of the expression $a!$ equals to the designate of the name which, in its turn, is the designate of identifier a. This can be explained by the following example. Let $a \underset{Df}{=} A$, $b \underset{Df}{=} B$, where A and B are forms. Then, the formula $a = b$ has the meaning of the statement that the expression A may be obtained from the expression B by means of the identical transformations. The formula $a! = b!$ has the meaning of the statement that the designates of the expressions A and B are equal under the given combination of designates of identifiers comprising these expressions.

Now, let us turn to subnectors. The introduction of subnectors into the language $\mathcal{X}$ should be supported by some mathematical theory. The theory is required to distinguish the class of *true* formulas from the rest of the formulas of the language $\mathcal{X}$. In so doing, the notion of the truth may be determined either syntactically, or semantically. For such reference theory for the CONC language, we have selected the axiomatic set theory of Bourbaki [2] (with corresponding purely linguistic corrections associated with peculiarities of the language $\mathcal{X}$). The truth criterion of this theory is but a syntactic one: a formula is considered true in case it is a theorem in the set theory.

Let R - be a formula, x - a variable and T - a form. The form T is called a *solution* of formula R by a variable x in case formula $(T/x)R$ is true (is a theorem). The formula R is called a *functional* one by the variable x if, according to this variable (1) the formula R has a solution, (2) all its solutions have one and the same designate.

Let formula R be functional by the variable x. Then, there is only one term, according to which, each form, being the name of this term, is a solution of formula R by the variable x. This only term is assigned, in the present language, a name $[x:R]$ (it is obvious that the form $[x:R]$ is a solution of the formula R by the letter x). Therefore, for every variable the language has a subnector $[x:\_]$ applicable to various formulas which are functional by x. So, only this type of subnectots is used in the language under consideration. The role they play is a specific one: they are the basic source of names with non-constructive designates.

4. *Reductors*

Application of various reductors in the language $\mathcal{X}$ enables to introduce in the latter the reduced synonyms of complex expressions. This, in its turn, provides high flexibility of the CONC language which is expressed in the ease of creating its modifications sufficiently adapted to various needs. Owing to this, we do not consider possible (or even desirable) to describe all reductors which can be used in the language. It is convenient to take the CONC language for a reductor-open language. Given below are some of the major examples of reductor construction.

Let R be a formula, functional by the variable x and T is a certain form. Then, let

$$[T:R]_x \underset{Df}{=} ([x:R]/x)T \qquad (1)$$

Thus we have obtained a definition of a (two-place) reductor $[\_:\_]_x$, the first place of which is occupied by an (arbitrary) form, the second, by a formula which is functional by the variable x. In principle, the semantics of the reductor $[\_:\_]_x$ can be traced by means of definition (1): the form $[T:R]_x$ is obtained from form T through substitution of the letter x by the form $[x:R]$.

Again, let R be a certain formula, x and y, certain variables, and y does not occur in R. The formula R is called a *collectivising* formula by the variable x when the formula $(\forall x)((x \in y) \Leftrightarrow R)$ is functional by the variable y (here $\Leftrightarrow$ is a connector of logical equivalence). Let formula R be a collectivising one by x. This means that the designates of *all* solutions of formula R by x form a set. Definition

$$\{x:R\} \underset{Df}{=} [y:(\forall x)((x \in y) \Leftrightarrow R)] \qquad (2)$$

means that this set of designates taken *as a whole* becomes a designate of a new name $\{x:R\}$. In particular, for instance, if formula R has no solutions by letter x, it is then collectivising by this letter. The set of its solutions by this letter is empty and is defined by the symbol $\emptyset$. Thus, in order to be collectivising, this formula is not required to have solutions but rather to have "not too many" solutions. As an example of the non-collectivising formula, we can give the formula $x = x$. The reductor $\{x:\_\}$ assigned by Definition (2) is, in fact, very powerful. It enables to introduce into the language short names of numerous types of sets, e.g. names of functions (as any function is a set of pairs of terms).

The reductors introduced by Definition (1) and (2) are substantive. Here is an example of a relational reductor. The only type of subnectors $[x:\_]$ of the language $\mathfrak{X}$ and both types of reductors considered $[\_:\_]$ and $\{x:\_\}$ are based on the property of formulas to be functional over a certain variable. Now, there is a question of how to express this property of formulas in the language $\mathfrak{X}$. If it is possible, then, for each variable x in the language $\mathfrak{X}$ it would be possible to introduce a (single place) reductor $Func_x$ - whose designate would be a statement of the x functionality of the formula occupying the place of the dash. In fact, it can be done in the following way:

$$Func_x R \underset{Df}{=}$$
$$(\exists x)R \wedge (\forall y)(\forall z)(((y/x)R \wedge (z/x)R) \Rightarrow (y=z)) \qquad (3)$$

4. ROLE OF CONCEPTOR LANGUAGES IN PROBLEM SOLUTION

As it has already been noted, the need for conceptor language application arises at all main stages of the problem preparation prior to computer-aided solving: (1) formal problem statement; (2) search for theoretical solution; (3) algorithmization of the solution. Naturally, in many instances these stages were trivial. Yet we are rather interested in somewhat more complex problems, the solution of which is concerned with overcoming the difficulties of notional, heuristic and realizational character at each of the above mentioned stages.

The notional difficulties mainly appear at the stage of the formal problem statement. For successfully overcoming these difficulties, the language used in formalization of the problem to be solved conditions should meet the following requirements: (1) to have sufficient notional means; (2) to have the most abstracted notions of modern mathematics (such as a set, a relation, a function, and order).

Heuristic difficulties arise at the stage of selecting the theoretical solutions of complex problems. Three principal reasons of these difficulties are known. These are: (1) the desired result of the problem solution is a complex object (e.g. a set with a complex structure, a complex function, etc.); (2) a complicated process of transition from the initial data of the problem to be solved to the desired result; (3) a complicated class of sets of those values that can be taken by the initial data of the problem to be solved (this type of complexity characterizes the problem as a mass problem). For all the three types of the problem complexity there are boundaries of the domain beyond which the problem cannot be solved at an algorithmic level. This domain is characterized by the following requirements: (1) the desired result of the problem solution should be a *constructive* object; (2) there should be an *effective* procedure for the transition from the initial data to the desired result; (3) the problem should be *algorithmically solvable* as a mass problem.

The impossibility of the problem solving at an algorithmic level, as a rule, does not indicate its meaninglessness or uselessness. If such a problem is not absurd (i.e. does not contain inherent contradictions), it can be solved in principal at the level of general mathematics or, what is very much the same, at a conceptor level.

Difficulties of realization are associated with the feasibility of the transition from the conceptor level to the algorithmic one (the algorithmic solution implies a potentially feasible algorithm). Here, several situations are possible:

1. An algorithm for the solution of a given problem does exist. In the same way, there exists a transition from a conceptor to the equivalent algorithm. This algorithm can be written in any suitable algorithmic language in terms of the given problem, in particular, in the sublanguage of the CONC language.

2. There is no algorithm for the solution of the given problem due to one of the two reasons: (1) the given problem is algorithmically insolvable; (2) the desired result is not constructive.

In the first case the problem solution as a whole is possible at a conceptor level only. However, as a rule, it is possible to single out some classes of the problem solvability from the algorithmically insolvable problems. Then, the transition from conceptor to algorithm can be defined for each class of solvability. To this end, the conceptor problem solution as a whole plays the role of guidance for writing the concrete algorithms from the mentioned classes.

In the second case, similarly to the first one, the solution of a given problem is possible at the conceptor level only. However in some cases the approximate conceptor solution can exist whose results would be the constructive objects which are sort of approximations of the initial non-constructive object. These approximate solutions are, in fact, the solutions of another problem. Here, the question arises whether the latter could appear another algorithmically insolvable problem. If it happens so, one must act as in the first case, i.e. to try to single out the solvability classes from the problem, etc. Once the new problem is algorithmically solvable and one or several of the said approximations of the non-constructive object have practical sense for the problem user, then the corresponding conceptor solutions may become the guidance for writing the algorithms-approximations.

We have considered the principal types of difficulties a human faces at the initial stages of the solution of any complex problem and illustrated the benefits obtained from the conceptor level of thinking at these stages. Since the language is the principal tool of thinking and the only tool for fixing the results of thinking, the role of conceptor langauges at the initial stages of the problem solution becomes especially clear.

5. REFERENCES

[1] Curry, H.B., Foundations of mathematical logic (Mc-Graw Hill Book Company Inc., 1963).

[2] Bourbaki, N., Elémentes de mathématique, Premiére partie, Livre 1, Théorie des ensembles, Hermann 1956-1960.

DISCRETE SIMULATION AND RELATED FIELDS
A. Jávor (editor)
North-Holland Publishing Company

THE SIMULATION SCENE IN THE UNITED STATES IN 1981

Charles M. Shub

Computer Science
University of Vermont
Burlington, Vermont 05405

Recent developments in the language development and Statistical methodology areas of Discrete Event Simulation in the United States are chronicled. The current major areas of interest are delineated, and references are given.

INTRODUCTION

Recently, there has been much significant research and development effort expended in Discrete Event Simulation in the United States. The effort has been in many areas. This paper will summarize and delineate a portion of this work. The paper will touch upon two major areas of simulation methodology including both the ongoing efforts in Simulation Language development and the issues of statistical methodology as they relate to simulation.

LANGUAGES

There are numerous Simulation Languages and packages in widespread use. Chief among these are ECSL-CAPS developed by Clementson at the University of Birmingham, GASP-SLAM developed by Pritsker and Associates in West Lafayette, Indiana, GPSS as extended from the original Gordon Simulator developed at IBM, SIMPAS, a Pascal like simulation language developed at the University of Wisconsin, SIMSCRIPT, and SIMULA. In addition, there have been two major efforts in integration of Database functions with Discrete Event Simulation, namely the Simulation Data Language of Standridge, and EAS-E of Markowitz. Using the language survey in 1980 of Shub [SHUB80] and the collection of issues presented by Adam and Dogramaci in 1979 [ADAM79] as starting points, this section will discuss the recent developments in Simulation Languages.

SLAM has been enhanced by a graphics output package called SIMCHART which is totally interactive and can produce up to four charts on a single display screen. [DUKE81a] [DUKE81b] SIMCHART can produce graphs, bar charts, pie charts and tabular data. It does this in an interactive fashion.

The major advance in GPSS has been the implementation of a more efficient GPSS. This new version, developed by Henriksen, is called GPSS/H and involves a processor which translates the GPSS block diagram into object code and then the translated code executes. This change has improved the run time efficiency of GPSS by several orders of magnitude. Currently, GPSS/H is available for IBM hardware, but efforts are underway to recode the compiler in the C language so that GPSS/H will be available on all equipment which has a C compiler available. [HENR78]

SIMPAS is a strongly typed portable discrete event simulation language embedded in PASCAL. It extends PASCAL by adding statements for declaring entities, and scheduling events. It also contains the usual gamut of list routines and statistics routines inherent in most simulation languages. SIMPAS functions as a pre-processor for PASCAL, and has as one of its major advantages that it can be used on many mini and micro systems. [BRYA81]

SIMSCRIPT has been extended with a Process and Resource capability. [RUSS76] This addition makes the language more palatable to those who like to view the world of simulation as a world involving cooperating processes interacting with one another rather than viewing the world as one in which events change the state of the system. This also allows the user to activate and control the progress of processes as well as to provide inter process communication facilities.

SIMULA has been extended to DEMOS (Discrete Event Modeling on SIMULA) by Birtwistle. DEMOS is available on IBM, DEC, CDC, and UNIVAC hardware. DEMOS augments SIMULA with a number of CLASS definitions to allow easier implementation of models. DEMOS appears to have built in a number of GPSS like constructs so that one familiar with the GPSS terminology can code in an algorithmic language. [BIRT79]

Standridge has Developed the Simulation Data Language which allows one to use database management capabilities in the context of simulation. SDL has implemented all the usual database management functions in the simulation context. One can define data relations, and then perform the usual database operations. Several applications have been developed in SDL. These applications involve better capabilities to analyze model output, to allow data gathered from the actual system to be used to drive simulations, and for the decomposition of models. [STAN81]

Harry Markowitz, in his keynote address at the 1981 Winter Simulation Conference, [MARK81a] addressed the practical barriers to the use of simulation in the solving of real problems. He suggested that the barriers to the use of simulation have shifted over the years. In the past, the greatest barrier to the use of simulation was that of programming the simulator. However, with the development of the substantial number of sophisticated simulation modelling languages, he no longer sees the programming as a problem. He pointed out that many, if not all of the major simulation languages really had the Entity Attribute Set and Event view of the world and had its constructs and/or internal mechanisms in that view.

Once a multitude of languages became widely available, the barrier to using simulation became that of collecting and using the data of the real system to drive the simulation model and the analysis of the simulation data. To this end, there has been a group at the IBM Watson Research Center developing EAS-E, an entity, attribute, set, and event language to facilitate the integration of database capabilities into simulation languages. [MALH80] The languages features a SIMSCRIPT like notation, with the major difference being that the language refers to actual data rather than sets defined in terms of simulation. The crucial generalization is that the standard simulation set manipulation activities can also be viewed as manipulation activities being applied to real data in a database.

STATISTICAL METHODOLOGY

The major issues in statistical methodology in simulation are the modeling and generation of inputs for simulation studies, response surface analysis, output analysis, and experiment design. There has been much work in these areas recently.

Law and Kelton [LAW81] present a detailed study of the major issues in analysis of simulation output data. They discuss the the requirements for sample size and the techniques for variance reduction. They also delineate the issues for which there are either no generally accepted solutions or only extraordinarily complex procedures, or unreasonably expensive (in terms of computer time) methods.

Much effort is being expended in looking at the initial transient effects on steady state simulations. Fishman has observed [FISH81] that the effect of the initial conditions can be quantified in terms of the autocorrelation in the process, that truncation of the early observations is not always the best solution, and that even though there are procedures in existence, none of the existent procedures are totally satisfactory.

Kelton [KELT80] suggests a method of averaged time series to handle this problem, but observes that this works well only in the case of monotonic transients, and to have the capability of restarting an interrupted simulation run. He also suggests as a future direction looking at finding better methods for dealing with batch means and selecting better starting values. He also advocates looking at the effect of not ignoring the initial transient in several similar alternate systems.

Schruben has also investigated the initial transient with respect to how it effects correlation between different performance measures in multivariate simulations. [SCHR80a] He has also looked at using a method of looking at partial sums of deviations about the sample mean. [SCHR80b] This technique, of course, is based upon weak convergence theory, and is, according to Schruben, the most generally applicable.

Fox [FOX81] has addressed the issue of using collected data rather than fitting that data to "standard" distributions. He delineates the tradeoffs in terms of computer time and ease of statistical testing of simulation results. He also delineates the situations in which one should use the empirical data and when one should use the approximation of the perceived underlying distribution.

Hora has compared three approaches for estimating the inverse of a distribution function. [HORA81] He presents a regression based procedure to supplement the maximum likelihood and empirical approaches. He shows that the new regression method requires a much smaller sample size in terms of asymptotic relative efficiency.

Marcel Neuts [NEUT81a] is using and investigating the generation of phase type random variates. These variates are absorption time distributions for absorbing Markov chains. Computer algorithms for the generation of this particular class of variates have been developed, and appear to be relatively portable. [NEUT81b]

In the area of sensitivity analysis, Cogliano and Schruben are developing a frequency domain approach. [SCHR81] They show that this method allows them to get greater amounts of sensitivity information per simulation run and that they can use the technique to screen several parameters in a single series of simulation runs.

Neil Marks has investigated the effect of the lag parameter "L" on the standard error term in the use of spectral analysis for confidence intervals. [MARK81b] He found that varying the lag parameter could make highly significant differences in the estimates of the variance. While he was not, in the work published, able to establish a pattern regarding the sensitivity of the variance to the lag parameter, he expressed the hope that additional larger studies would show the answer to that question.

Carson and Seila are dealing with simulation output data which show a natural stratification. They investigate the metrics within the different strata and how they relate to the corresponding overall metrics as well as to the strata quantifications. The have shown that their method is applicable to both regenerative systems [SEIL80] and non regenerative systems. [SEIL81]

Efforts are also underway to quantify the efficiency of random variate generation in terms of the number of computational steps and the amount of storage requirements. Bartels [BART81] has established truncation bounds for series expansion, and both Schmeisser [SCHM80] and Devroye [DEVR81] have surveyed several methods addressing, among other things, the relative efficiencies.

Finally, no discussion would be complete without mentioning that Lewis's data enrichment method [LEWI57] has been applied in a new context by Hurwitz and Quirk [HURW76] to develop new easy to apply measures for significance denoted Iota and Nu.

BIBLIOGRAPHY

[ADAM79] Adam, Nabil R., and Dogramaci, A. (Editors), "Current Issues in Computer Simulation", Academic Press, 1979

[BART81] Bartels, R., "Truncation Bounds for Infinite Expansions for the Stable Distributions", Journal of Statistical Computation and Simulation, Volume 12, 1981, pp 293 - 302.

[BIRT79] Birtwistle, G.M., "Discrete Event Modeling on SIMULA", Macmillian, 1979.

[BRYA81] Bryant, Ray M., "Micro-SIMPAS: A Microprocessor Based Simulation Language", Proceedings of 14th Annual Simulation Symposium, Tampa, Fla, March 1981

[DEVR81] Devroye, Luc, "Recent Results in Non-Uniform Random Variate Generation", Proceedings of the 1981 Winter Simulation Conference, Atlanta, Georgia, December, 1981, pp 517 - 521.

[DUKE81a] Duket, S.D., Hixson, A.F., and Rolston, L. "The SIMCHART User's Manual", Pritsker and Associates, West Lafayette, Indiana

[DUKE81b] Duket, S.D., O'Reilly, J.J., and Hannan, R.J. "SLAM II Enhanced Simulation Capabilities", Pritsker and Associates, West Lafayette, Indiana, 1981

[FISH81] Fishman, George S., Oral Communication, December, 1981.

[FOX81] Fox, "Fitting 'Standard' Distributions to Data is Necessarily Good: Dogma or Myth?", Proceedings of the 1981 Winter Simulation Conference, Atlanta, Georgia, December, 1981, pp 305 - 308.

[HENR78] Henriksen, J.O., "GPSS/H User's Manual", Wolverine Software Corp. Box 1251, Falls Church, VA 22041, 1978

[HORA81] Hora, Stephen C., "A Comparison of Three Methods of Modeling Input Distributions", Proceedings of the 1981 Winter Simulation Conference, Atlanta, Georgia, December, 1981, pp 309 - 312.

[HURW76] Hurwitz, J.A., and Quirk, D.A., "Quirks Iota and Hurwitz' Nu, Statistical Measures of I-N-Significance", Simuletter, Volume 8, No. 1, October, 1976.

[KELT80] Kelton, W.D., "The Startup Problem in Discrete Event Simulation", T.R. 80-1, Industrial Engineering, University of Wisconsin, Madison, Wisconsin, 1980.

[LAW81] Law, A.M., and Kelton, W.D., "Simulation Modeling and Analysis", McGraw Hill, 1981.

[LEWI57] Lewis, H.R., "The Data Enrichment Method", Operations Research, Volume 5, 1957, page 551.

[MALH80] Malhotra, A., Markowitz, H.M., and Pazel, D.P.,"EAS-E: An Integrated Approach to Application Development", Report RC-8457 IBM Watson Research Center, Yorktown Heights, N.Y. August, 1980

[MARK81a] Markowitz, Harry M., "Barriers to the Practical Use of Simulation Analysis", Proceedings of the 1981 Winter Simulation Conference, Atlanta, GA, December, 1981

[MARK81b] Marks, Neil B., "Further Investigation into Spectral Analysis for Confidence Intervals in Steady State Simulations", Proceedings of the 1981 Winter Simulation Conference, Atlanta, Georgia, December, 1981, pp 461 - 464.

[NEUT81a] Neuts, Marcel F., "Matrix-Geometric Solutions in Stochastic Models -- An Algorithmic Approach", Johns Hopkins University Press, Baltimore, Maryland, 1981.

[NEUT81b] Neuts, Marcel F., "Documented Computer Programs and Numerical Results", Technical Report, Mathematical Sciences, University of Delaware, Newark, Delaware, 1981.

[RUSS76] Russell, Edward C., "Simulating With Processes and Resources in SIMSCRIPT II.5", Consolidated Analysis Centers, Los Angeles, California, 1976.

[SCHM80] Schmeisser, Bruce W., "Random Variate Generation: A Survey", Proceedings of the 1980 Winter Simulation Conference, Orlando, Florida, December, 1980, Volume 2, Simulation With Discrete Models: A State of the Art View, pp 79 - 104.

[SCHR80a] Schruben, Lee, "Control of Initialization Bias in Multivariate Simulation Response", TR 455, Operations Research and Industrial Engineering, Cornell University, Ithaca, N.Y., 1980.

[SCHR80b] Schruben, Lee, Singh, H., and Tierney, L.J., "A Test of Initialization Bias Hypotheses in Simulation Output", TR 471, Operations Research and Industrial Engineering, Cornell University, Ithaca, N.Y., 1980

[SCHR81] Schruben, Lee W., and Cogliano, Vincent J., "Simulation Sensitivity Analysis: A Frequency Domain Approach", Proceedings of the 1981 Winter Simulation Conference, Atlanta, Georgia, December, 1981, pp 455 - 459.

[SEIL80] Seila, Andrew F., "A Stratified Regenerative Method for Estimating Mean Waiting Times in Queues with Multiple Renewal Input Streams", Technical Report, Department of Quantitative Business Analysis, University of Georgia, Athens, Georgia, 1980.

[SEIL81] Seila, Andrew F. and Carson, John S., "Methods for Stratified Estimation in Nonregenerative Simulations", Proceedings of the 1981 Winter Simulation Conference, Atlanta, Georgia, December, 1981, pp 465 - 467.

[SHUB80] Shub, Charles M., "Discrete Event Simulation Languages", Proceedings of the 1980 Winter Simulation Conference, Orlando, Florida, December, 1980, Volume 2, Simulation With Discrete Models: A State of the Art View, pp 107 - 124

[STAN81] Standridge, Charles R., "The Simulation Data Language: Fundamental Concepts for Its Use in Simulation Studies", Simulation, Vol. 37, No. 3, September, 1981

II. SIMULATION SYSTEMS

DISCRETE SIMULATION AND RELATED FIELDS
A. Jávor (editor)
North-Holland Publishing Company

A FLEXIBLE MULTIPROCESSOR SYSTEM FOR SIMULATION PURPOSES

W. Roehder, W. Ameling, O. Lange

Institut für Allgemeine Elektrotechnik und Datenverarbeitungssysteme
Rheinisch-Westfälische Technische Hochschule Aachen
Schinkelstraße 2, 5100 Aachen

The following paper describes the realization of a multiprocessor system including software for the simulation of differential equations. Some interesting hardware and software aids are presented.
The rapid development of Large-Scale-Integration gives the possibility to integrate a greater number of processors in a multiprocessor system. The use of multiple processors for simulation purposes shall lead to shorter simulation times at a better price/performance ratio.

1. CHARACTERISTICS OF SIMULATION SYSTEMS

A detailed analysis of simulation problems and of linear differential equations of higher order exposed that the performance of a multiprocessor system is mainly influenced by the interconnection structure.

The interconnection structure should have the following characteristics:

a) A projection of the mathematical model on the elements of a multiprocessor structure must be possible without regarding restrictions due to the specific structure.
Therefore a
fast and simple exchange of data between all elements of the simulation system must be possible.

b) Since the producing and consuming of data are done by different processors it should be guaranteed that the data-production is finished before data are used, and that data are not destroyed if they are used by another processor. (Producer-Consumer-Problem).
Therefore
the synchronization of the data flow should be supported by the structure.

c) Besides the simulation in the true sense the system should be usable for the preparation of the problem to be simulated, for the initiation of the system and for further computations of the results.
Therefore
the simulation system should be usable like a general purpose computer.

d) The input of variables for the simulation must be possible before and during the simulation; results which can be computed by any processor have to be interpreted, stored, printed or displayed in a graphical manner.
Therefore
it must be possible to add any peripheral equipment to the simulation system, and a fast and uncomplicated transport of data between the peripher devices and any processing element must be possible.

e) The utilization of a simulation system is limited by the simulation time and system costs. The simulation of small problems is often possible with a small number of computing elements, but the real-time simulation of complex systems often needs a great number of computing elements. If the system is only used to compute one class of problems, the computing power can be raised by the use of special modules (e. g. function generators).

Therefore

> it must be possible to raise the computing power of a simulation system from a minimum system by modular expansion with computing elements, special modules and peripheral devices just as it is needed in a concrete application.

2. THE SYSTEM STRUCTURE

If different processors use the same data-channel in a time sequential manner, the structure is called a time-multiplex-structure. Pure time-multiplex-structures (Fig.1) have the advantage that only one data-channel is needed, but the exchange of different data between different system components at the same time is not possible. A situation where more than one request for transfer exists is called a conflict. Since in conflict situations the data transfers have to be executed sequentially, wait-cycles have to be added which in case of a great conflict probability lead to an enormous reduction in performance [1].

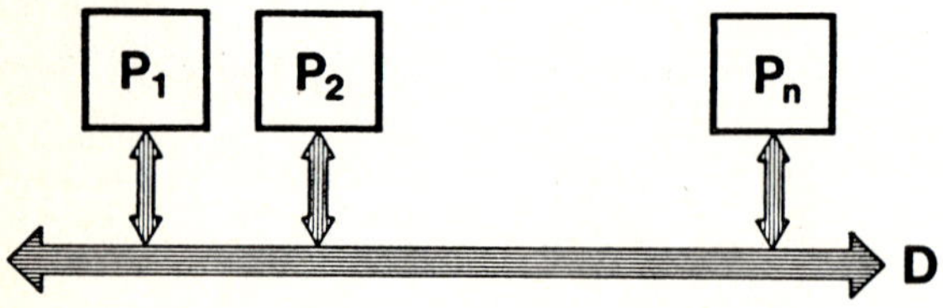

Figure 1: Time-multiplex-structure

The conflict probability depends on the channel capacity and therefore on the transfer speed which is limited by physical problems and costs [2].

On the other hand there are space-multiplex-structures with separate parallel data channels which allow the transfer of different data at the same time. Since usually the immense expense does not allow to connect each element with all other elements directly, one has to find a structure with an optimal cost/performance ratio. Usually this will be a combination of space- and time-multiplex-structures. As amorphous structures are very difficult to control in multiprocessor systems, regular structures like arrays or trees are preferable.

Our investigations revealed that for a practical realization only a closed array structure (Fig.2) or a special tree structure (Fig.3) should be used.

The main advantage of the tree structure is the small number of arcs, the main advantage of the array-structure is that the number of transfers is nearly the same for all data-channels.

As a result of our investigations one should prefer the array-structure if the time between two succeeding data transfers starting from the same node is less than 1000 times the duration for exchanging data between two adjacent nodes. The reason for that is based on the huge number of conflicts in the root region of the special tree-structure.

The multiprocessor-system M^5PS (Modular-Multi-Mode-Multi-Micorprocessor - System) developed at the Institut für Allgemeine Elektrotechnik und Datenverarbeitungssysteme der RWTH Aachen is a general purpose multiprocessor system that is constructed under the previously outlined design principles for simulation systems.

3. THE MULTIPROCESSOR SYSTEM M^5PS

3.1 The Global Structure of the System M^5PS

The Global structure of the M^5PS is designed as a composition of subsystems, which can be arranged as arrays, trees or arbitrary networks (Fig. 2 and Fig. 3) by their up to 8-high-speed data-channels. The transfer rate between two adjacent subsystems will be 16 MBaud.

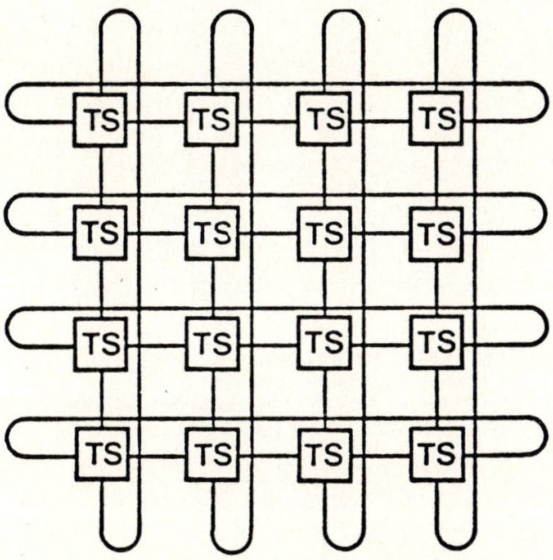

Figure 2: Example of an array-structure with 16 subsystems

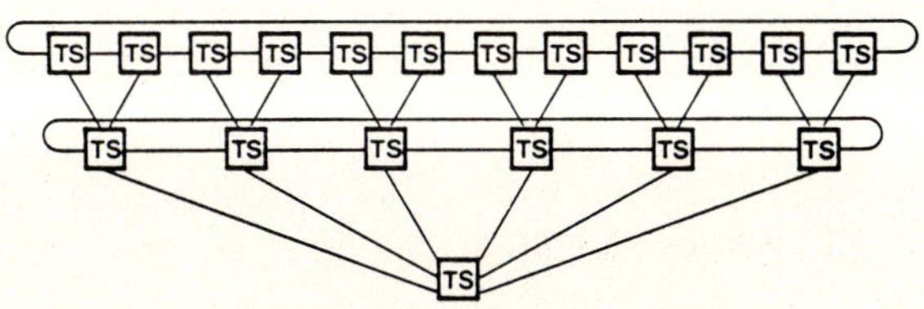

Figure 3: Expanded tree-structure with 19 subsystems

The design of the subsystems opens the possibility to optimize the structure for a given application or for a requested computing power. Since it is possible to build a global system with redundant datapasses and since every subsystem is an autonomous multiprocessor system, fail tolerant structures with a high MTBF can be build.

3.2 Subsystems, Elements of the Global Structure

The subsystems are modular multiprocessor systems built by active modules like processors, DMA-channels and coupling-modules for the interconnection with adjacent subsystems and passive modules like memory boards and non intelligent controllers. For the data transfer between active and shared passive modules a common time multiplexed databus was used. In addition, every processor module has a private bus to which further passive modules and DMA-channels can be connected (Fig. 4). A data transfer on the private bus cannot cause a conflict on the common bus. The use of the common bus is controlled by a bus arbiter which, depending on the actual strategy, gives the bus for a time-slice of 500 ns to one of the processors requesting the bus.

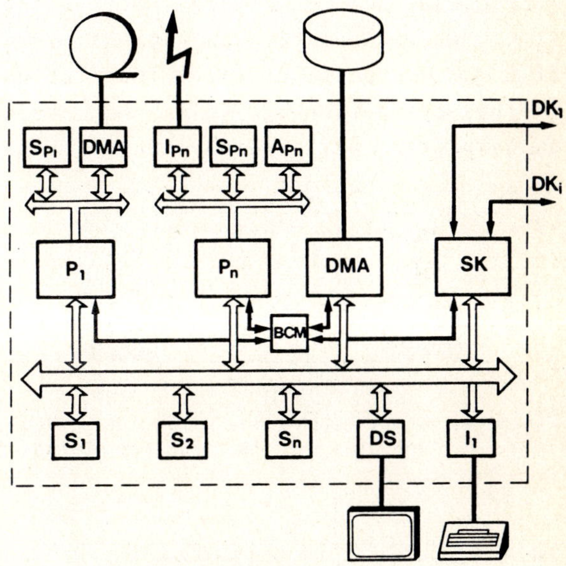

P	Processor-Module
A	Arithmetic-Module
S	Memory-Module
DK	Data-channel
I	Interface-Module
DS	Display Memory
SK	System coupling Module
BCM	Bus control-Module
DMA	Autonomous Data-channel

Figure 4: Example of a subsystem

As all active and passive modules have the same interface to the common bus, a maximum of flexibility is guaranteed. This allows to expand a minimum subsystem by memory, processor modules and peripheral devices in a manner optimal for a given application. The maximum number of active modules depends on the processor speed and the problem-dependent bus utilization factor.

3.2.1 Subsystem Characteristics in MIMD-Mode

The analysis of the bus utilization of microprocessors showed that a machine-cycle can be divided into time slices where memory operations take place and time slices where only internal operations are carried out.

Figure 5 shows time slices during which a processor does not need a bus so that it can be disconnected and the bus cycles of multiple processors can be interleaved. The bus-cycle-time of 500 ns was chosen to guarantee that a memory operation can be finished in one cycle. Other solutions are discussed in [3].

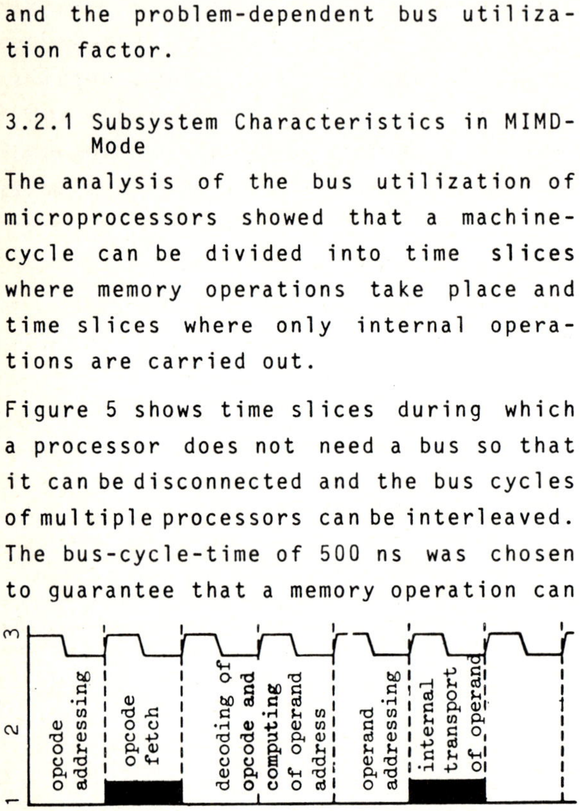

Figure 5: Memory-fetch-cycle during the execution of a register transfer operation

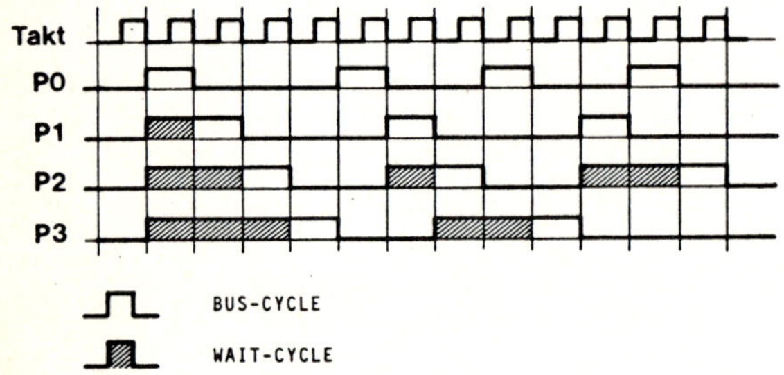

Figure 6: Priority-dependent bus-arbitration to 4 processors

Figure 7 displays the conflict probability and the computing power (effective cpu) for a subsystem in dependence of the number of installed processors built by Z80-microprocessors without private memory and a bus utilization factor of about 25 %.

These theoretical results have been verified by simulation and measurements [1]. They reveal that not more than 4 or 5 processors without private memory should be arranged to a subsystem. Therefore, private memory containing often used programs should be added to reduce the bus load in so far that the bus will only be used for accessing common data.

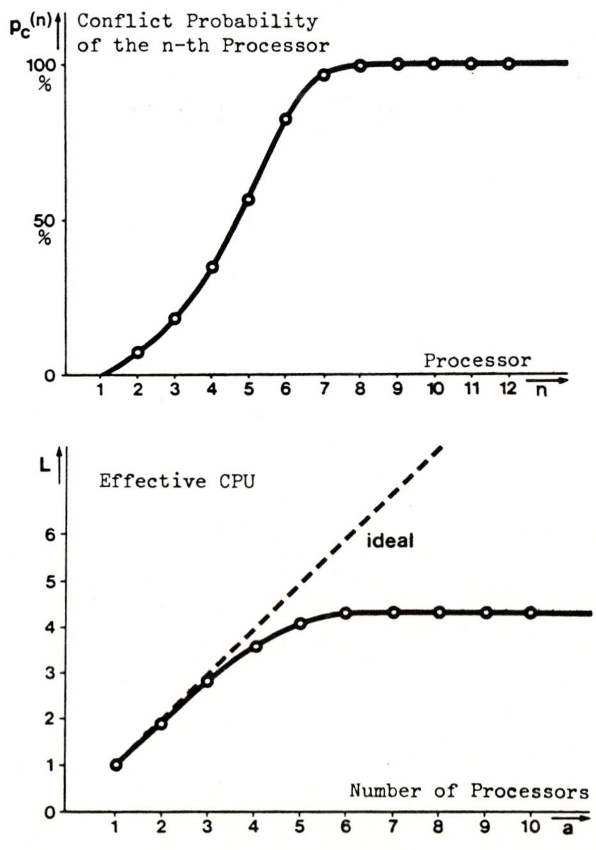

Figure 7: Conflict probability and computing power in a subsystem without use of private memory

3.2.2 Subsystem Characteristics in SIMD-Mode

In SIMD-mode a lot of processors carry out the same operation completely synchronous with different data. This is implemented in the M^5PS-system by the use of the following aids:

a) The bus arbiter will be informed which processors have to work in SIMD-mode; the rest works in MIMD-mode.

b) The fetch of a common opcode or common data is marked by a flag generated by the processor (common-data-bit).

c) The addressing of different data during the execution of the same program is done by transforming the logical address used for memory addressing.

d) The synchronization for the simultaneous execution of a program by all processors is mamaged by the bus-arbiter.

The example in figure 8 shows the simultaneous execution of the instruction: load register from address xy. After the execution the A-register of every processor contains a copy of the logical memory location xy.

a) Operate Fetch Cycle:

The addressing of the next instruction is done internally by every processor in SIMD-mode. Then every processor generates a bus request signal indicating to the bus arbiter that the processor wants to use the common bus. A processor whose "bus-request" and "common data bit" are set is delayed until all processors in SIMD-mode have generated these two signals. If there is no request of higher priority, only the processor in SIMD-mode with the highest priority (master) is allowed to put its address on the bus. The contents of the addressed memory location is read as well by the master as by all other SIMD-processors (slaves). The following internal operation to generate the data address xy is do simultaneously by all SIMD-processors.

b) Fetch of Processor Specific Data:

As the data address was part of the opcode, all processors generate the same logical address xy. To give any processor its specific data, the logical address of each processor is used as an input to a dynamic address-transformation table which can be different for each processor. The contents of the table is used as physical address for memory addressing.

During the next datafetch cycle the "common data bit" is not set. Therefore the bus arbiter delivers the bus to the processors according to their priority as in MIMD-mode, so that every processor gets its specific data. Hereafter, all slaves had been delayed - the internal operations have to be synchronized which is automatically done before the next common fetch cycle (Fig. 8).

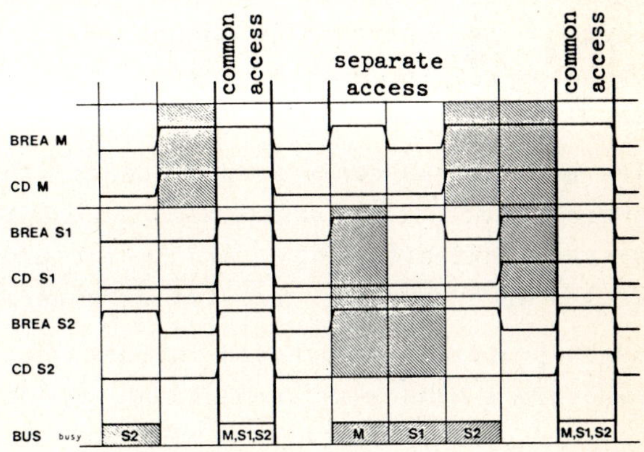

BREQ	bus request
CD	access to common data
M	master
S	slave

Figure 8: Bus arbitration during an instruction execution in SIMD-mode

The SIMD-mode can be used for the synchronization of program execution of multiple processors. It helps avoid time consuming software synchronization for the exchange of data between processors.

Another advantage is the reduction of the busload when all common bus cycles are carried out simultaneously. A fetch cycle in SIMD-mode would need n (n is the number of processors) cycles in MIMD-mode. Therefore if SIMD-mode is used the number of processors in a subsystem can generally be much higher than calculated for a MIMD-system.

3.2.3 Modules; Elements of a Subsystem

During system design much attention has been given to the modularity.

The processor-modules are based on the Z80-microprocessor but other microprocessors can be used without great modifications.

The interface of the processor-module is built by two busses: the common- and the private-bus. Besides the Z80-processor there are 2K RAM and 2K ROM on the processor module. In addition there are drivers used for the separation of common and private bus and the logic to control the data flow.

The private bus can be used to connect the processor module to private memory modules, private controllers or an arithmetic processor to expand the computation power.

Every processor module can further be expanded by a memory-management module, which can be used optionally in MIMD-mode for address transformation, interrupt handling and memory access-control which is necessary in SIMD-mode for the separation of dataspaces.

In SIMD- and MIMD-mode the address transformation gives the possibility to load multiple programs, allocated to the same address in the memory without address-conversion so that they can be executed by different processors. This is necessary for an effective memory management.

The memory management gives further the possibility of virtual addressing as the number of bits of the physical address is only fixed by the word length of the transformation table.

As the physical address of a processor module includes the address of all subsystems, the highest bits of the physical address can be interpreted as the subsystem's address.

The logical address of a processor module is further used for the addressing of a flag-memory. Simultaneously with the physical address the flag memory delivers a dataword whose bits control the access to the physical page. The flags are tested before each memory cycle and if there is an illegal operation the operation is frozen and an interrupt is generated and sent to the processor which controls the system.

This processor can read the state of the frozen processor and the contents of the flag memory. By changing the contents of the flag memory the control processor can force the frozen processor to finish or continue program execution.

4. SOFTWARE OF THE SIMULATION SYSTEM

At the simulation system is based on free programmable processors there is a need for a powerful operating system for resource management of

- processors
- memory, semaphores
- peripheral devices

and scheduling of processes.

Besides the operating system a simulation program was developed which allows the simulation of a system described by the following differential equation:

$$\frac{d^n y}{dx^n} = g(x, y, \frac{dy}{dx}, \ldots, \frac{d^{n-1}y}{dx^{n-1}}).$$

Problem preparation, scheduling and simulation can be done on the M^5PS-system. The results of the simulation can be printed or displayed in a graphical manner.

The program can be divided in 3 parts:

1) Syntactical analysis of the differential equation. According to the theory of formal languages a syntax tree is generated by a syntactical analysis of the arithmetic expression. The nodes of this tree represent the operations; the arcs are the relations between the operations of an arithmetic expression.

2) Generation of a schedule on the tree to distribute the operations among the processors.
   For each processor a list is generated with all operations of an iteration in proper order.

3) Generation of a problem-dependent simulation flow control and fixing of memory space for data exchange.

For the simulation program segments are used which simulate the blocks of a mathematical model (multiplier, adder, function generator).

These program segments are resident in the private memory of each processor. The synchronization is implicitly done during data exchange of three kinds:

a) Data exchange in private memory.

   It can only be used if subsequent operations are executed by the same processor.

b) Data exchange in common memory controlled by semaphores.

   To every dataspace a semaphore for synchronization is added which can be read and manipulated within one memory cycle.

c) Data exchange in SIMD-mode by the use of the common memory.

   This kind of data exchange is used during the integration and forces a hardware synchronization of all processors.

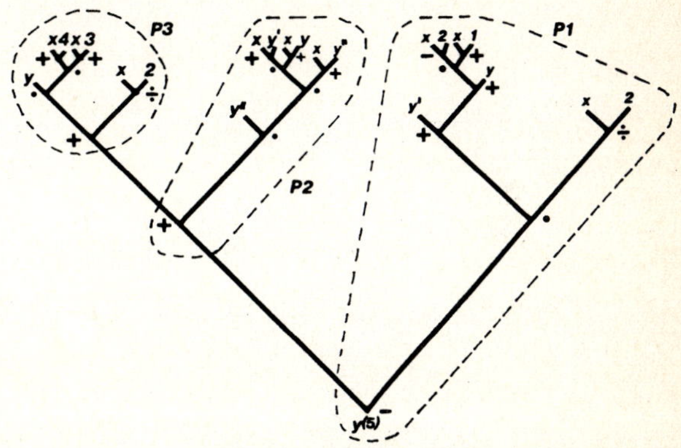

Figure 9: Schedule of the syntax for the differential equation

$$y''''' = \frac{x}{2}\cdot(y+(x+1)\cdot(x-2)+y')-((y''+x)\cdot$$
$$\cdot((y+x)\cdot(y'+x)).y'' +$$
$$+(\frac{x}{2}+y\cdot((x+3)\cdot(x+4))))$$

for three processors.

The control of the simulation is simply done by writing the address for data exchange and the start addresses of the program-segments to be executed into the operation table of each processor.

A speciality of the simulation system is the scheduling algorithm which is based on the algorithm of Hu [4], which guarantees:

a) Minimal simulation time for each number of processors.

b) Minimal number of data exchanges to reduce conflicts.

An example of a schedule for three processors is given in Figure 9.

Figure 10 shows the graphical representation of the simulation results which where computed on the M^5PS by the use of 7 processors in SIMD- and MIMD-mode.

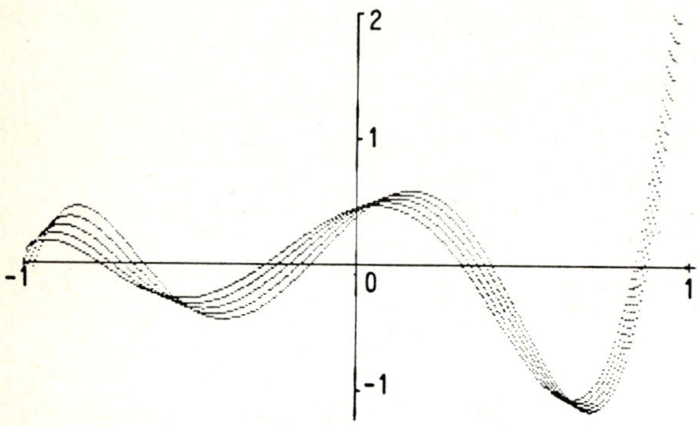

Figure 10: Jacobi-Polynomials

$$y'' = [(1{,}5-\beta)y' + (3{,}5+\beta) x \cdot y' - (37{,}5+5\beta)y] \cdot (1-x^2)$$

5. CONCLUSION

The use of free programmable microprocessors made the simulation system so flexible that it can be used in nearly all applications where today minicomputers or even bigger computers are used, if the problems can be executed in parallel.

But it should be noticed that the flexibility in hardware has shifted many problems into software. For the realization of the operating system problems had to be solved which previously existed only on huge computers.

But the cheap computing power of microprocessors forces us to look for new solution where these elements can be used for the computation of complex problems like simulation.

REFERENCES

1 Hoener, S., Roehder, W.: Efficiency of a Multi-Microprocessor System with Time Shared Busses. Proc. Euromicro Symposium, Amsterdam 1977, 35-42.

2 Hoener, S., Roehder, W., Ameling, W.: Microprocessor Nodes in Computer Networks. Proc. IMMM, Genf, 1977.

3 Ameling, W., Hoener, S., Roehder, W.: Interconnection Structures for Parallel Processor Systems. Proceedings Parallel Computers - Parallel Mathematics, München 1977, 297-302.

4 Hu, T.C.: Parallel Sequencing and Assembly Line Problems Operations Res., Nr.9, 841-848.

5 Hoener, S., Roehder, W.: Modular Multi-Microprocessor Architecture with Virtual Memory. Proceedings Euromicro Symposium, Venedig 1976, 99-108.

6 Hoener, S., Roehder, W.: Microprocessor-Controlled Switching Networks, Proceedings Informatica, Bled, 1976, Bd. 2, 102.

7. Hoener, S., Kempken, E., Lange, O.: Parallel Processing in Specialized Multiprocessor-structures. Informatica in Bled, Okt. 1975.

DISCRETE SIMULATION AND RELATED FIELDS
A. Jávor (editor)
North-Holland Publishing Company

AGGREGATIVE SIMULATION SYSTEM AND DIRECTED SIMULATION EXPERIMENTS

Vladimir V. Kalashnikov

Institute for systems studies, Moscow, USSR

1. INTRODUCTION

While hardware and software for simulation are being developed constantly they are not often suitable for main needs of the modelling and simulation processes. Such problems as validation, estimates of dynamical and structural properties, model transformations, accuracy and so on have not satisfactory decision but only heuristic (if any).

Below some results on methodological, mathematical and software problems will be displayed. These results are based on so-called aggregative approach proposed by N.P.Buslenko [1,2].

2. METHODOLOGY

Because simulation process is some kind of computer experiment it is usually treated as only computer imitation. But it is more natural to include in simulation process the following components: (1) model construction, (2) execution and control of simulation experiments, (3) software tools.

The model construction consists of two main stages: the construction of some formal (analytical or algorithmical) model; the forming of the computer model from formal one. The first stage is the subject for such fundamental disciplines as physics, economics, biology etc. The second stage is the subject for simulation specialists. Further the second stage will be treated as model construction. The main problems here are different kinds of transformations of the models (equivalent or nonequivalent) its enlargings and estimating the corresponding errors [3].

The first component is to be connected with the second one (simulation experiments). Usually these experiments are treated to be similar to the experiments with real systems when such systems are considered to be a "black box" and all conclusions are based on input-output relations. The main problems here are design reduction, factor analysis and so on. Though such approach is rather general its (heuristic) results are not reliable. Many important problems can not be decided in such a way, e.g. convergence rate estimates, continuity and sensitivity analysis. Even for estimations of stationary probability characteristics you need to know the mathematical model [4,5] not only input-output relations.

But computer model is a simplified algorithmical image of a real system. Hence it is possible (in principle) to organize such experiments which take into account the mathematical nature of the model. Such experiments can be called "directed". Main problems in an execution of directed simulation experiments are mathematical analysis of structural and dynamical properties of computer models.

Software problems are well-known: effectiveness, input/output tools, simplicity and so on. But when creating software for simulation one must take into account the following: this software is to provide computer assistance in both model choosing, transformation, simplification, estimating its structural and dynamical properties and execution and control of simulation experiments.

We propose to put some mathematical scheme in the basis of simulation system (see Fig.1).This scheme is to play the following roles: (1) mathematical model of the systems under investigation; (2) base for computer simulation program; (3) subject for mathematical investigations; (4) subject for directed simulation experiments. Therefore we try to decide the above problems on the base of this scheme. N.P.Buslenko proposed an aggregative system to be such a scheme [1,2].

An aggregative system is a complex mathematical object consisting of a finite number of elements $A_1, \ldots, A_N$ and interconnections. Each element can generate some output signals at isolated times. And at these times the above signals are received by other elements. It is easy to see that such a scheme is rather general for discrete simulation. The essence of aggregative approach is that it takes into account the mathematical nature of this scheme. In order to have the possibility to model a wide class of real systems it is necessary to choose rather general dynamic system as an element. One of such systems is so-called piece-wise linear aggregate [1,2,6], its mathematical description being a generalization of queueing models, finite and probabilistic automata, industrial processes, numerical methods for solv-

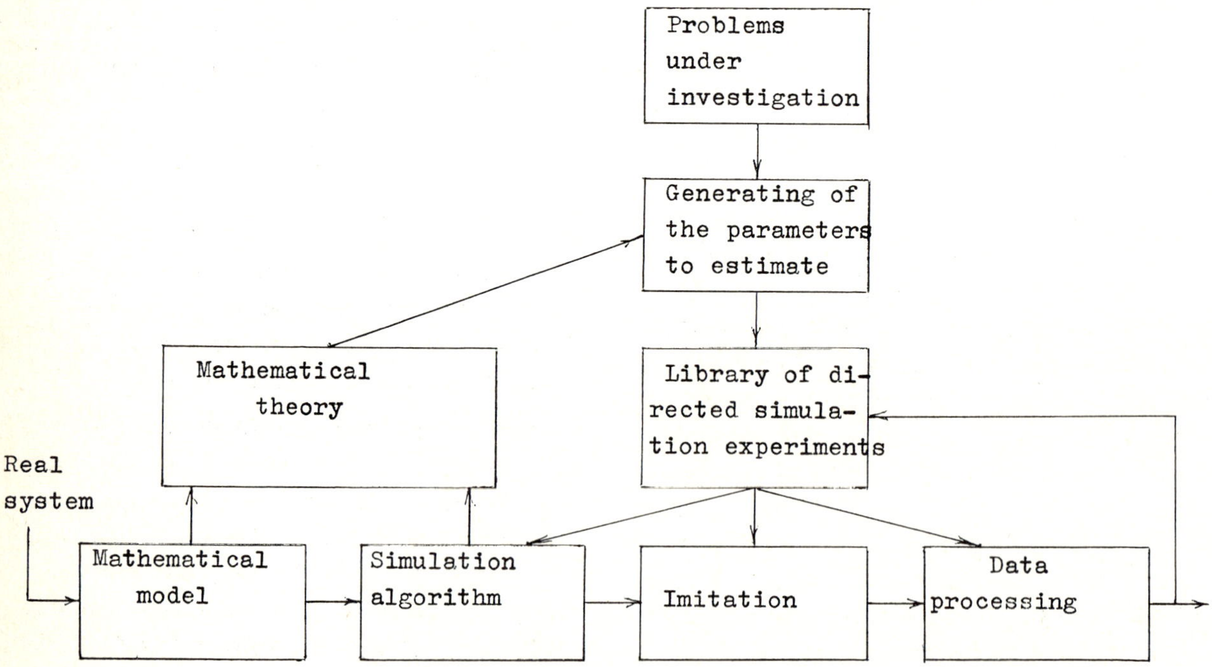

Figure 1

ing differential equations etc. But in spite of such generality it can be analysed by analytical methods [6,7]. Interconnection scheme of aggregative system gives the addresses for output signals generated by the aggregates.

The main advantage of aggregative approach is the following. It gives to programmers, mathematicians and users some common formal scheme as common basis. And in its frame they can consolidate their efforts. As aggregative scheme is rather general it can be used for simulation of wide class of real systems.

3. MATHEMATICS

The aggregative system as a mathematical scheme was intensively studied [6,7]. As the mathematical description of these systems consists of the formalization of the interconnections and that of the elements' dynamic the corresponding theory can be divided in two parts: structural and dynamical ones. The first deals with equivalent and quasiequivalent structural transformations, exposure of "typical" structured configurations (chains, cycles,...) [1,2,6]. This part of the theory can be expoited in the stage of computer model forming. Really, it is convenient for users to compile the model from some elementary blocks. But the corresponding computer model will contain many links and the simulation algorithm will have to process many signals generated by elements. It is evident that such simulation algorithm is not effective. Recently B.V.Nemchinov [8] proposed some algorithms dealing with interconnection scheme and transition functions for each element which permit to joint some elements into subsystems or disjoint them in order to eliminate the above signals and obtain an effective simulation algorithm from a preliminary one (compiling by the user). Nemchinov's procedures run before simulation process on the stage of computer model forming.

Besides the structural theory can be applied to recognize some structural configurations (also before simulation) in order to improve the model.

The second part of the theory deals with dynamical properties of aggregative systems. Namely there are results concerning estimates of continuity [6,7,9], convergence rate [6,7,10], "small" probabilities [11], regularity [7], boundedness [7], recurrence times [7]. These results can be applied for organizing of directed simulation experiments (see below).

We see that in spite of the generality of aggregative system it gives the possibility to develop analytical methods for its investigation. Besides some known methods (e.g. for regenerative processes, queueing systems etc.) can be applied for the analysis of such systems.

AGGREGATIVE SIMULATION SYSTEMS

This simulation system was created in Institute for systems studies [6]. It consists of two parts: internal software (IS) and external one (ES).

The main function of IS is reproducing of the dynamic of an abstract aggregative system. If user has some concrete system he must formalize it as aggregative one and insert its parameters in IS. The simulation program deals with arrays of states of aggregates, their parameters, interconnection scheme. This program reproduces all the fragments of the dynamic of aggregative system. Piece-wise linear processes describing this dynamic imply the simplicity of the above operations. The IS is supplied by some standard transition functions and elements which user can use for the designing of his model in order to simplify user - computer model interface.

The ES serves for designing and running of simulation experiments and works together with the IS. For the lack of mathematical methods for aggregative system analysis it is natural to include in ES heuristic ones. But we restricted ourselves only directed simulation experiments having mathematical foundations because our main aim was testing of our approach.

When working together the ES plays the role of head program and governs the IS. The central place in ES belongs to the library of subroutins. The library can be replenished if necessary. Its subroutines contain the necessary information for directed experiments. Below we shall give corresponding examples. In accordance with the user's order the ES chooses necessary subroutines and marks those signals in aggregative system which must be processed for the execution of the chosen subroutines. Then the investigation of the model by simulation system can be represented as alternating process: running IS up to successive marked signal; processing of this signal by ES.

It is necessary to say that some procedures can be replaced automatically on others if the first are not suitable in the current situation.

5. DIRECTED SIMULATION EXPERIMENTS

Let us list some experiments which are included in ES now. Besides their reviewing will give the reader some impression about corresponding mathematical results.

5.1. Estimates of the accuracy of final characteristics.

Let Z(t) be the state of the aggregative system at time t, $Q_t(\cdot) = Pr(Z(t) \in \cdot)$, $Q = \lim_{t\to\infty} Q_t$. Let us say that $E_Q f = \int f(z) Q(dz)$ is a final characteristic. Usually it is considered that $E_Q f \approx \frac{1}{T}\int_0^T f(Z(t))dt$ where T is "sufficiently large", but the accuracy of this equality is unknown as a rule. If $Z(\cdot)$ is a regenerative process then the accuracy problem can be solved. Appropriate formals can be found in [4,5].

The essense of the corresponding directed experiment is the following. The initial data: time T and the regeneration condition. IS works up to the first regeneration time and transfers the data to ES where they are being processed in accordance with the corresponding formulas. Then IS again generates the trajectory up to the second regeneration time etc. up to T. The output data: the valid confidence interval for the concrete final characteristic. If the aggregative system has not regenerative property or regenerative times are seldom (we can recognize this situation during the simulation) then the above valid procedure can be replaced on approximative one [4].

5.2. Estimates of simulation time

The procedure is dual to the previous one [12]. The initial data: the confidence interval needed for the final characteristic; the regeneration condition. The output data: time T.

5.3. Estimates of convergence rate

Let $\mathcal{V}(Q_t, Q)$ be the total variation distance between Q_t and Q. Let us imagine that we are interested in such "transition" time t^* that $\vartheta(Q_t, Q) < \varepsilon$ for any $t \geq t^*$ where $0 < \varepsilon < 1$ is fixed. It is clear that the estimation of t^* by traditional simulation means is impossible.

But for aggregative systems using their Markov property one can find [6,7,10] that for any $\gamma > 1$

$$\vartheta(Q_t, Q) \leq c t^{1-\gamma} \quad (1)$$

where c is a constant depending on $E\tau_B^{\gamma}$, τ_B is a recurrence time (to some subset B) for $Z(\cdot)$. We can improve this estimate varying γ and B. The initial data for one of the possible directed experiments are: accuracy ε, subset B, constant $\gamma > 1$. During the simulation we estimate $E\tau_B^{\gamma}$.

Then the ES calculates c and $t^* = (c/\varepsilon)^{1/(\gamma-1)}$ (the latter is the output of the procedure). It is necessary to note that during this experiment we need not find out neither Q_t nor Q. Instead we use the estimate (1) (mathematically proved) for designing of the experiment. As a result it will not take much computer time to obtain the necessary estimate.

5.4. Continuity estimates.

As a matter of fact any simulation process is some transformation F of initial data (model parameters) X in output data Y. Usually X consists of different probability distributions or their parameters. Similarly Y are often probability distributions or even sequences of random variables (waiting times, waiting rooms and so on). But there are some problems connected with such transformations.

A) The "input" distrimutions and parameters are known with errors (e.g. because they arised by statistical estimates). Hence instead of mapping $X \to Y$ we deal with $X' \to Y'$.

B) We know X exactly but in order to execute the calculations we need to simplify some relations. And again instead of $X \to Y$ we have to study the model $X' \to Y'$.

It is natural to ask: Are Y and Y' close given that X and X' are close? More precisely, let $\mu(X, X')$ and $\nu(Y, Y')$ are some appropriate distances [13]. Our aim is to estimate $\nu(Y, Y')$ in terms of $\mu(X, X')$. Continuity estimates can be interpreted (depending on μ, ν) as sensitivity estimates, errors implying disturbations of initial data or model simplification; they can be used for proving the effectiveness of dependent trial method. It is possible to point out their interpretations. The continuity estimate can not be obtained by traditional methods though these methods are often used for such purposes (the corresponding results are not correct in general).

In the procedure we choose the whole random process $Z(\cdot)$ describing the dynamic of aggregative system as Y and

$$\nu(Y, Y') = \sup_{t < T} \vartheta(Z(t), Z'(t)), \; T \leq \infty, \quad (2)$$

where ϑ is the total variation distance between distributions of $Z(t)$ and $Z'(t)$. Initial data are: ε - the precision of input parameters X (i.e. we know that $\mu(X, X') < \varepsilon$); time T in formula (2); if $T = \infty$ then one need to know $\gamma > 1$ and subset B in space state (see procedure 4.3). It turns out that in this case one can obtaine some formulas [9] connecting $\nu(Y, Y')$ with $\mu(X, X')$. We don't display these formulas because of the numerous additional notations. It is sufficient to know that they depend on some values obtaining during the simulation process (as in previous procedure). The output of the procedure is the presicion of Y, i.e. such value $\hat{\delta} = \delta(\varepsilon)$ that $\nu(Y, Y') < \delta$ if $\mu(X, X') < \varepsilon$. For obtaining this estimate we need not know neither Y nor Y'.

5.5. Optimization.

This procedure is the only one dealing with the model as "black box". It realizes stochastic gradient method [14].

One can see that each procedure has an analytical part and one of the way to improve the effectiveness of these procedures is to improve some constants and relations consisting of the formulas.

6. PROSPECTS

The above simulation system was applied to different real systems (computers, road traffic, industrial systems, building up the hydro-power stations etc.). The aggregative approach turned out to be flexible and convenient. But when constructing the model we couldn't take rather simple elements as aggregates because of noneffectiveness the resulting simulation program. Namely it implied many extra signals and their proceedings. It is to note that the possibility to take such simple elements as aggregates would follow an essensial simplification (and even an automation) of the model forming.

Hence it would be good to transform the initial noneffective simulation algorithm to an effective one. Besides such transformations are useful for automatic model simplification (e.g.). But the above aggregative simulation system couldn't be transformed because its transition functions were inserted in the simulation program as some subroutines. B.Nemchinov's algorithm [8] gives the possibility to transform simulation algorithms to more effective one before the simulation process. Moreover, writing the procedures of simulation experiments with help of these formulas, we have the possibility to form an effective algorithm of the investigation of the system i.e. realizing both the imitation and analysis of the model. These possibilities together with some improvement of dialog, checking up of the simulation program and others will be realized in the second version of aggregative simulation system which is supposed to be in operating in 1982.

REFERENCES:

1 Buslenko, N.P., Simulation of complex systems (in Russian), (Nauka, Moscow, 1978).

2 Buslenko, N.P., Complex systems and simulation, Kibernetika, N 6 (1976), 50-59.

3 Polljak, Yu.G., General problems of simulation of radiolocation stations, in Simulation in radiolocation (in Russian), (Sov.Radio, Moscow, 1979).

4 Crane, A., Lemoine, S., An introduction to the regenerative method for simulation analysis (Springer-Verlag, Berlin, Heidelberg, New York, 1977).

5 Iglehart, D.L., Shedler, G.S., Regenerative simulation of responce times in networks of queues (Springer-Verlag, Berlin, Heidelberg, New York, 1980).

6 Emeljanov, S.V., Kalashnikov, V.V., Investigation of complex systems by simulation (in Russian), in Itogi nauki i tehniki, Tehnicheskaya Kibernetika, v.14 (All-Union Institute Scientific and Technical Information, Moscow, 1981).

7 Kalashnikov, V.V., Qualitative analysis of the complex systems behaviour by testing functions method (in Russian), (Nauka, Moscow, 1978)

8 Nemchinov, B.V., Structural transformations of aggregative systems and their applications for constructing of simulation algorithms, in Complex systems theory and their simulation (in Russian), (Institute for systems studies, Moscow, 1982)

9 Kalashnikov, V.V., Continuity analysis of aggregative models during simulation (in Russian), Elektronnaya Tehnika, Ser.9, N 4(37) (1980)

10 Kalashnikov, V.V., Organization of complex systems investigations on the basis of aggregative approach to simulation (in Russian), Izv. Akad.Nauk, Tehnicheskaya Kibernetika, N 2 (1982).

11 Kovalenko, I.N., Seldom events analysis for effectiveness and reliability estimates (in Russian), (Sov. Radio, Moscow, 1980).

12 Poljak, D.G., Accuracy estimate for statistical simulation of queueing system (in Russian), Izv.Akad.Nauk, Tehnicheskaya Kibernetika, N 1 (1970).

13 Zolotarev, V.M., Metric distances in spaces of random variables and their distributions, Math. USSR Sbornik, v.30, N 3 (1976).

14 Ermoljev, Yu.M., Methods of stochastic programming (in Russian) (Nauka, Moscow, 1976).

DISCRETE SIMULATION AND RELATED FIELDS
A. Jávor (editor)
North-Holland Publishing Company

SIMULATION SYSTEM WITH A SINGLE CORE AND SEVERAL OUTER LAYERS

A. Jávor, Á. Révész, P. Tóbiás

Central Research Institute for Physics
of the Hungarian Academy of Sciences
Budapest, Hungary

In an attempt to resolve the contradiction between the requirements demanded of simulation systems by highly qualified simulational experts and the average user a principle was suggested to divide the simulation system into a general inner structure and an outer layer of appropriate languages. On the basis of this principle a simulation system was developed which is used for digital circuit design and testing; in this way it becomes possible to handle the modelling and the dynamic observation by the effective and general tools of the inner simulator structure while by means of different outer languages various types of simulation models can be described and investigated conveniently.

1. INTRODUCTION

A simulation system or language can be universally applicable if it provides an adequate framework to model and manipulate large classes of models. At the same time a simulation system provides the best handling of a problem to be modelled if it is strictly problem-oriented, i.e. it adjusts itself to the demands and the descriptive manner of the given problem. In this way the aspects of investigation and information reporting are closely fitted to the behaviour of the real model and the simulation does not need too complex definitions and operations for the model and experiment description.

In recent years plenty of simulation languages have been developed enabling the simulation of different problems with well structured general purpose tools as well as with special ones. Their large number tends to make it difficult to choose the appropriate one for a given problem, while the development and application of several languages increase the costs of simulation. It would be more reasonable from the viewpoint of highly qualified simulation experts if there were only one or a few general simulation systems which could satisfy all the requirements efficiently.

However, this universality to most fields of application, the sometimes complicated simulational tools and the time needed to attain and apply them repel those users who might wish to implement their special problems with as little effort as possible in time as well as payoff. A special purpose simulator would suit them more; a simulator which would not require any knowledge of programming or much abstraction skill but would enable the use of their own special terminology for describing the problem - even to control the simulation runs.

The difference between the attitude of specialized users and programming experts, who need to consider several applications and later developments, causes a great problem with regards to the proper design of simulation systems. The usability for universal and various complex purposes - just as the lowering of costs - makes inevitable the development of general tools, while the ever growing number of average users applying simulation, demands the development of simulation systems which are more user-oriented than at present.

As a means of resolving these contradictory demands, we developed our simulation system [1] as a complex of a universal simulator core together with different language layers according to the principles suggested in [2], where the invariant inner structure ensures the generality and effective handling of models, while the languages offer the users the application oriented convenient description possibilities to various types of simulation models.

Originally our simulation system was intended to aid the development of digital electronics in design verification and to produce correct fault analysing tests. Even now this is the main field of application of our system, and it also includes the simulation of different logic networks, synchronous-asynchronous sequential and combinational ones as well.

The need to develop user-oriented simulation tools is valid to the highest degree in this case of simulation supported design and testing of logic circuits because the usual tools of a hardware designer do not conform to the possibilities of most general simulation languages developed until now.

The choice and/or the forming of the recent layers was greatly influenced by these practical needs; the inner core was developed to be general and effective so that it could be used for other variable fields of application with appropriate general or special layers.

2. SIMULATION WITH INVARIANT CORE

In our system (Figure 1) the invariant core is realized by a discrete simulator. In general it provides an adequate framework to model and manipulate various classes of systems. Flexible model construction can be reached by building up the models modularly from the typical components - element set - of the given application field.

The dynamic investigation takes place according to the interaction of these elements, following the dynamics of the model by the discrete simulation of events. The connection between the applied model representation - event type model - and the modelled reality is assured by the problem oriented description manner of the layers.

The simulator can provide a precise description of model behaviour and high performance design verification by reflecting the realistic time conditions of the models, detecting and reporting on race conditions, undefined situations and other violations of design rules by means of its general and reliable model handling tools, the effective time advancement method and the advanced state representation.

For the efficiency of the program, the original model is represented in the form of a suitable data structure, converted from the model description. The model running is controlled by an executive which also fits the aspects of computer representation.

The internal structure of the model - into which the actual model is mapped - consists of a network of element modules. These individual logic building elements are stored in the extendable universal element library.

These component elements can realize

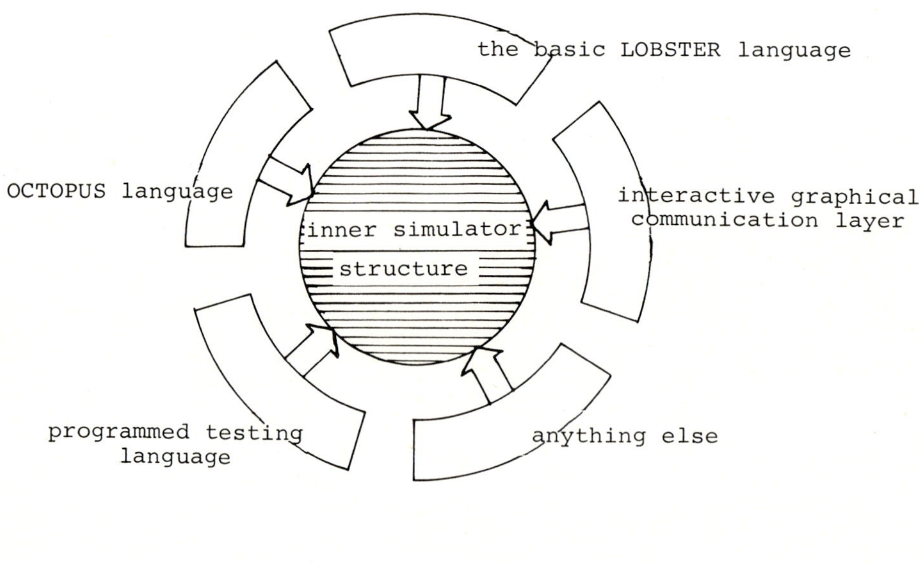

Figure 1 : The complex simulation system

general functions or concrete - less standardized - operations at will, can describe purely a logic operation like a flag, a delay, a queue, a link, a seize function, or a real building block as a certain facility. The degree of abstraction to which the elements are described may increase or decrease the flexibility of the element library to the modelling of different problems.

For strictly special applications, when the simulator is used for a restricted range of problems, more special elements can be stored and referenced in the element library, executing particular or aggregated general logic functions.

The different models are simulated by assembling the appropriate element modules and/or the user defined new blocks according to the given interconnections. The invariant core manages all network components in the same way, disregarding their function or abstraction level. It is their interaction through the I/O ports that makes them in any case a "system", a built model. The building elements are "connected" in a flexible way using pointers, i.e. to change the ways of information propagation only these pointers have to be modified.

Beyond the elements of the "static" model structure, the external input stimuli is also connected and handled as a type of element, serving as an input generator for the static model [3]. The effect of the input stimuli is propagated through the network by the simulator itself, enabling the interaction of the structure elements through the movement of information. The information movement takes place in the form of level changes or entity movement depending on the types of model connections and the input generator.

Other so-called "extra elements", which also interact in the dynamic operation of the whole simulation model, can be built into the model. These extra elements correspond to some temporary component of the model like optional functions, tasks controlling the simulation runs or administration, data collection, monitoring, etc. that may have to be executed during the simulation run.

These components are also handled by the simulator as elements and are described by the attributes and appropriate utility routines similarly to the description structure of the other elements in the element library.

The simulator assembles the necessary functional modules - utility routines - according to the actual requirements of the user's simulation control statements and the operational demands of the chosen element modules and their relations.

The possible set of element modules is constituted according to the relevant application field. In our case the element library of digital electronics can consist of general logical elements (functional groups and single gates like AND, NAND, NOR, INVERTER, flip-flops, counters, registers, memories and other LSI circuit components such as tri-state MOS gates, etc.) and representations of catalogued elements (e.g. TEXAS Instr. Inc. SN series, etc.).

For the implemented objects of the element types all actual parameters must be given; in the case of catalogued elements only the actual I/O list, and the reference name of the element.

As the element modules are handled universally by the simulator referring them through the element library only by their formal parameters and the functional description name, there is a possibility to create any new element to add to the stock of modules, without learning how the simulator works.

The input stimuli elements of circuits have to be given naturally as sequences of state changes of the external input signal levels, or in test patterns. The extra elements connecting special tasks to the model can be given by statements, i.e. keywords and parameters. The user need not consider the input or the extra attributes as elements, it is the language layer that gives the "input" or "extra" information for the core, and the simulator handles them further as elements according to the general conception.

The usual extra elements for digital circuit simulation are the controlling of simulation runs as simulation time, adaptation to event bursts, the actual information printing demands, the requested information store control for the further investigation or for the graphic display results, fictive observational variables for data collection, etc.

The simulator analyses the interconnected network of elements, e.g. it traces the feedback loops in the model, so that it can correctly map the relations of the elements.

The correct tracing of the relations of building elements is of primary importance in the case of digital logic circuits. The detected feedback loops enable one to discover some undefined situations, side effects of the loops and other violations of design rules which can often be caused when designing digital electronics. The analysis of subnetworks consisting of tri-state MOS elements makes possible a special handling for these circuit parts also taking into account the real capacitive relations as a subnetwork of switched capacitors.

While statically the model can be described by the participating elements and their relations, the dynamic operation can be well reflected by the changes of the state descriptive parameters of the modelled system. At any time instant the model is in some particular state, determined by the states and relationship of the elements. The system's state changes when an element's state or its relationship with other elements changes.

The effect of state change between two elements can take place either in the level change of the connecting node, or in the change of the attributes of the moving entities. Both types of events cause a state change in the connected elements themselves.

The applied state representation is of primary importance from the viewpoint of revealing the model's behaviour, the series of state changes and, in particular, the detection of anomalies.

In order to establish an internal structure into which the different model types can be mapped, it is necessary to choose a state representation that covers the requirements of the possible fields. In the practical realization we have dealt only with discrete simulation but the principle can be used for the discrete-continuous case as well.

The theoretical method is based on the separation of uncertainties of different kinds and their separate handling. Beyond the description of deterministic and probabilistic models, for generality a third category, i.e. the *quasideterministic* [4] state representation, is included where, in the majority of cases (or time) the behaviour of the system can be regarded as deterministic and in the minority as indeterminate (probabilistic). This means that a three-component vector representation is used to describe the operation of the real physical systems in a correct way.

This enables the adequate simulation of systems containing feedback loops, race situations and hazardous conditions as well as the simulation of fuzzy systems [5].

In our application field, the model states are described by levels, i.e. state changes usually correspond to logic level changes. (The events, which cause the changes of relations between elements, beyond structural changes, usually also cause level changes at the newly related circuit parts.)

The applied three-component state vector

S: <l;u;v>

where

$l = \{0,1\}$

can describe the stable logical levels, the undefined states deriving from transient periods, and the indeterminate states caused by operational uncertainties like hazard.

The deterministic state component enables the representation of the two logical fixed level values 1 and 0. (At the same time it makes possible the logical true or false value representation of an extra element's state, like "information store at an instant" whether it is needed or not.)

The indeterminate behaviour of an element (probabilistic state) can be represented by the other two vector components.

If the logical level changes at any input node of an element from one stable state to the other during the element's transient delay time the logical value of the output level remains undefined. "Spikes" deriving from oppositely directed simultaneous level changes can also be represented as transients. This indeterminacy of first order reflects the correct real time operation of digital circuits, and can be modelled and reported by the second component of the state vector (Figure 2/a).

The logical levels of any element can become indeterminate for other reasons like hazardous conditions, feedback loops.

A noncorrect operational mode, like illegal control of an element (e.g. an RS flip-flop), can cause its logical states to change to a fixed level, but it cannot be determined whether any of the output levels will change to fixed 0 or 1. The only information is that in real-

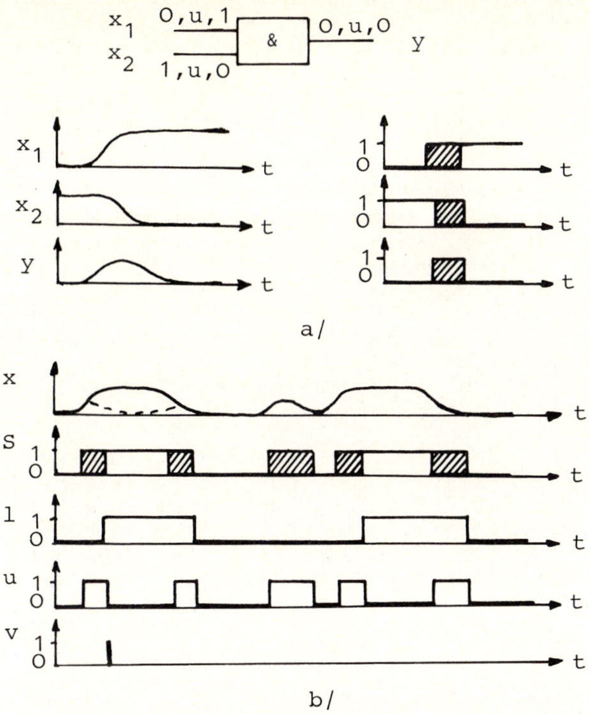

Figure 2 : Uncertainties with QDS representation

ity it results in one of the possible stable states. States are not undefined in the usual sense, but the choice of the stable states is indeterminate.

Similarly, in the case of feedback loops, a loop (or loop system) input level change can cause the loop elements to get into a stable state, but with more possible stable states the real loop state cannot be predicted, the choice will be probabilistic.

The application of the third component of the state vector - called indeterminacy of second order - for the representation and investigation of this hazardous behaviour enables a model description well applicable from the practical aspects of digital logic systems (Figure 2/b).

If an indeterminacy of second order arises, indicating that the system is in a definite but unpredictable logical state, a possible stable state is searched for and the system is forced into it, simultaneously giving signalization of the uncertain operation.

The practical implementation of this solution for those elements in which the second order indeterminacy occurs deriving from their internal features, i.e. a functional hazard, must be provided as a part of the element's functional description. In other case, where it is caused by the feedback loops detectable in the modelled network, the simulation system provides for the investigation and handling of uncertainties by searching for and dynamically handling the loops.

The actual type and number of the values of the state attributes in the three vector component depend on the concrete application demands. They can be changed according to different model types.

If the set of possible values of state parameters is enlarged, the quasideterministic state representation can be used for continuous cases as well.

In a great number of discrete systems the main role is not played by the level type state variables but rather by entities moving through the modules or building blocks of the model "space". This problem of handling uncertainties in this case (rarely mentioned in the simulation of such systems) can also be solved by using the above representation. The race situations, the transient periods and indeterminacies caused by them may block or falsify the simulation (simultaneous requests to access the same facility, storage devices filled and emptied simultaneously, etc.).

It has been shown [6] that a duality between entity and level representation exists where one entity transfer path can be transformed into a pair of bidirectional level paths (see Figure 3) and so the problem of describing such situations when the location of an entity is undefined can be reduced to the - already solved - problem of quasideterministic state representation.

The dynamic changes of the model state are caused by the interaction of the elements taking place in cycles of events. In general, events propagate some kind of information through the elements of the network, in the form of level changes or entities.

In the case of digital electronics this generally corresponds to the propagation of logical state changes of signal levels on the connected elements.

Events can occur at any discrete time instant in zero simulation time. An e-

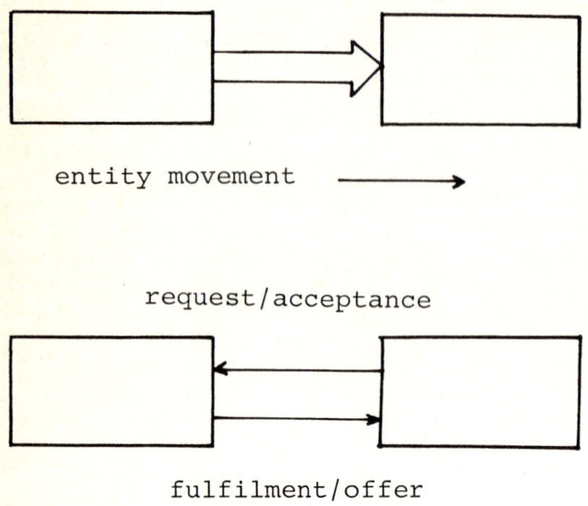

Figure 3 : The duality between entity and level representation

vent is characterized by an event notice containing at least two attributes, the event time when it must have occurred and the event class designator determining the relevant event type and event description.

The types of events and the tasks that have to be executed when the events occur may differ with different applications. When modelling digital electronics the possible event types and the related tasks, defined by the event class descriptions, can be simple events causing a variation in the states (levels) of single individual elements or special events that effect connected subnetworks in the model. These latter type events causing special situations call forth the activation of special tasks, like the dynamic handling of loops, the supervision of the states of the newly related circuit parts, etc. beyond the usual activation of the effected individual elements.

Events are handled by a list-handling method, scheduling them into event lists according to their event notices.

When an event should follow on the output of an element, i.e. a level state change at a prescribed instant, the element's operational algorithm passes a prediction of this event to the executive describing the time instant and the network node the event is predicted for. The executive schedules the activation of this event into the event notice lists by its scheduling mechanism.

The event scheduling mechanism provides for the evaluation and correct administration of event predictions, with due regard to the applied design rules. By scanning the event notice lists it can make a decision for scheduling the event into the list unconditionally, for updating the event list even by the clearing of other already scheduled events, or it can supervise the prediction to neglect the event.

The execution of scheduled events takes place when their predicted conditions are satisfied, e.g. when their predicted time instant comes round. When a scheduled event has occurred, the event is taken off the event list and the tasks provided by the event descriptions are executed.

The propagation of the effect of events between the elements is controlled by the executive according to the given interconnections. It activates the related elements, i.e. those elements where the input nodes have suffered a state change. Disregarding the initial setting of the model where all state values are propagated during the simulation, only the effective events are propagated. Events which have no effect on the connected elements are neglected, i.e. it predicts the actual state to occur. After the executive has activated the related elements, inside these the propagation of the effect is according to their operational algorithms, also resulting in new predicted events.

Up to the time of the last scheduled event, signalizing the end of simulation time, the simulation run takes place in a general recursive way in the following steps: (Figure 4)

- The simulation time steps forward to the next predicted event time.
- The scheduled next events are taken off from the clock, their event notices are cleared, and the events are executed. Special tasks of events for extra situations are also executed.
- The related elements, which are driven by the state changes of the effected nodes as input changes, are activated. The elements using their I/O state descriptors propagate the effect according to their operational algorithms

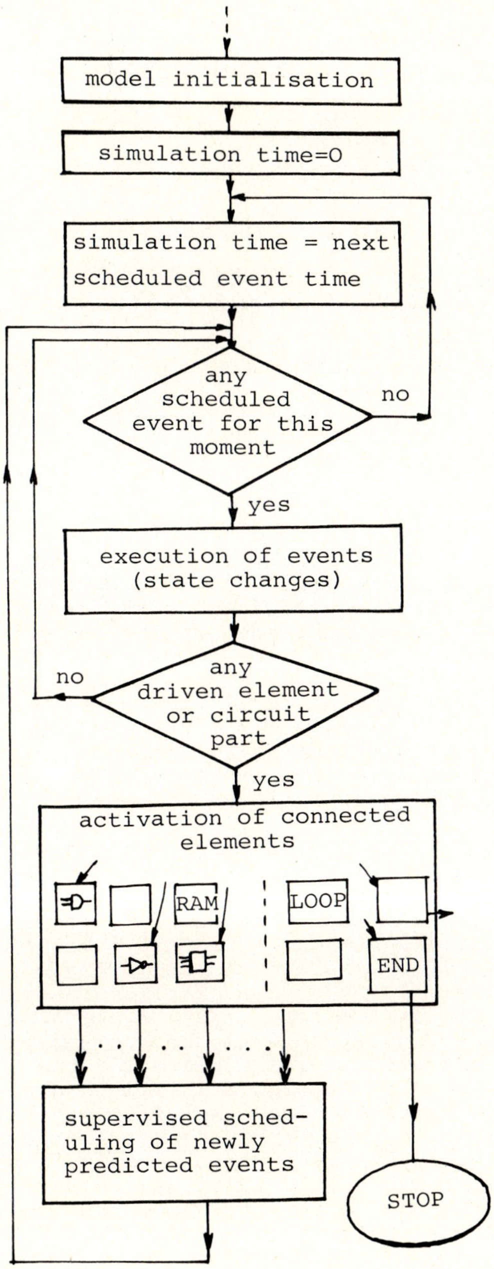

Figure 4 : Event handling

and result in the prediction of new events for their outputs.

- The predicted events are evaluated, the valid predictions are scheduled into the event notice lists.
- Scanning the event notice lists - additionally predicted events - events that can occur unconditionally are scheduled into the clock thereby becoming next events.

For every node of the elements in the network - or attributes of extra elements - the simulator stores the related event notices of the last, already occurred event, the predicted next event and other following events predicted additionally in event notice lists. (The event notices of the last occurred events must be stored because sometimes it is necessary to know the time instant of the last state change of the node, e.g. when investigating a bistable's setup time.)

In principle the core does not restrict the number of events scheduled for a given node. In practice the relevant design rules and the "nature" of the elements of our concrete application field enables us to consider only a certain number of events. There are elements, e.g. a DELAY type one, where the number of scheduled events can be optional, but with most of the "usual" elements it is sufficient to use only two scheduled events, the predicted next event and the secondary predicted one, for physical reasons.

Additional predictions occur when there is already a predicted event for the output of an element, and before it could occur, a new contradictory prediction takes place for a later time. These are the cases when the internal delay of the element is greater than the time elapsing between the changes of the input signal.

The prediction of repeated state changes is conceivable with input changes more quick compared with the element's transient delay time. These are simulated indistinctively, explainable by the physical facts, (Figure 5) which simulation corresponds to the real behaviour of the circuits. Simulation provides a good approach to the real conditions because the speed of the physical signal changes is restricted in nature.

Predictions arriving later but before the activation time of the two scheduled events can cause one or both of the later time events to be cleared and the e-

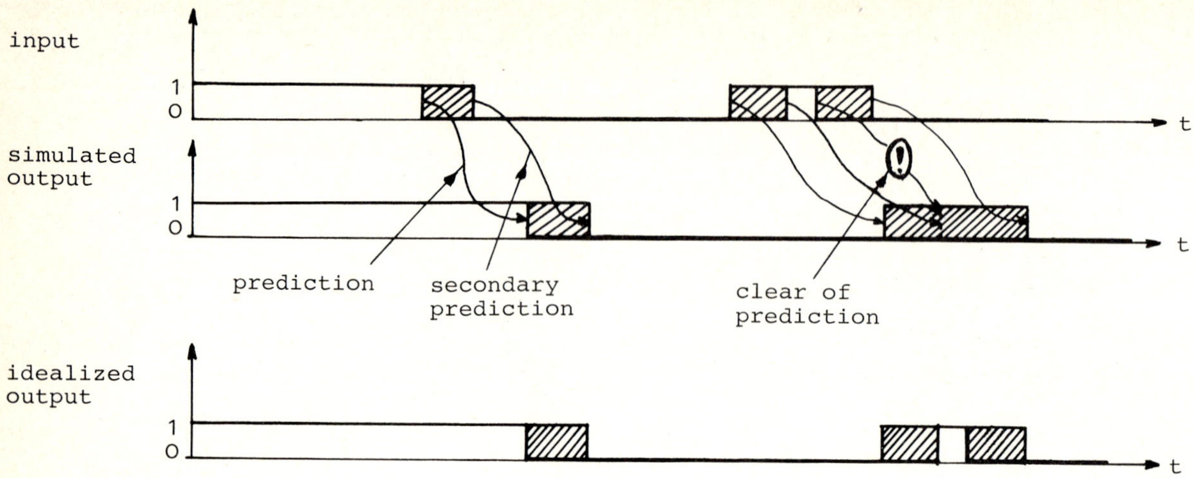

Figure 5 : Indistinct events

vent list to be updated. (Events arising later but predicted before are defined priority according to the design rules: in addition, our application assigns a priority to the maximal representation of uncertain periods.)

Many events can be scheduled to occur simultaneously in model time. Since their execution must be serialized, the scheduling mechanism handles the event predictions caused by simultaneously occurring events on the same element in a special way, eliminating the effect of their handling order.

For the appropriate simulation of the time attribute two main features must be investigated. The applied time representation of the invariant core is the asynchronous simulation, which reflects the realistic time conditions. The state change of the output of an element by the effect of its input change is simulated with delays relevant to the real transient delay times.

By the joint use of asynchronous time and the QDS representation describing uncertainties, it is possible to achieve simulation models according to worst case design rules, where the uncertainties should be simulated with maximal cumulative uncertain periods. It provides more information than from a single hardware model and corresponds to the important marginal investigations of the circuits intended for serial production.

Naturally more optimistic models can be achieved as required with mean- or expected values of delay times even as with delays according to different probability distributions.

The time advancement systems proposed for discrete simulation are many and various, the basic types being the "next event" and the "time mapping" techniques [7] and a number of further developments [8][9][10]. As the choice influences decisively the computer time consumption of the simulation it is very important to use an effective method which adapts itself well to the different types of event distributions. With all this in mind we have chosen the Delft Algorithm [11] which uses a hierarchical structure of circular lists and is highly adaptive to the event distributions, in particular to the bursts of events that in most systems follow certain significant events.

With digital electronics these significant events - or synchronizing events - are usually the state changes of the input signals of the circuit. Until the effect of this input change propagates through the entire model, the events follow each other at very close instants, at almost every time increment. The time periods with bursts of events and the frequency of input element state changes, i.e. the event distribution of the model, can vary within broad ranges depending on the simulated circuit and the given experimental stimuli. This time advancement method can adapt itself to each model structure considering the concrete model propagation time and the input change sequences. Thus an effective and reliable scheduling executive mechanism controls the dynamic simulation.

Having surveyed the general and efficient modelling tools served by the invariant core, such as the flexible model building, the QDS representation, the event handling mechanism and the time advancement method, let us now examine the tasks and the structure of the outer layer languages realizing the problem oriented user interface.

3. OUTER LAYER LANGUAGES

Adequate contact between the inner simulation structures and the real systems to be mapped - the mental model - is established by the outer layers. Actually these layers are languages interacting with the core by means of their language processors. The languages make possible a problem oriented description adapted to the user's requirements, and the processors convert the model and experiment descriptions into relevant data bases according to the aspects of the inner core data structure representation.

Using the same inner structure several simulation packages can be formed by means of the appropriate element sets and relevant language layers fitted to different fields of applications. Any languages needed for general or special purposes, e.g. a standardized simulation language, can be inserted into the structure either by mapping the model descriptions directly to the inner core data bases or by coupling through other already available fitted layers. The only constraint for languages is that the language processors' output is determined to some degree to comply either with the input of another fitted layer or with the existing general data structure at the element references, the applied state representation, etc.

The languages - together with the core - must meet some requirements demanded from simulation systems and languages [12][13], as well as their special field usability. They should be - similarly to the inner structure - portable and machine-independent.

By the detailed semantic and syntactic checking of the descriptions the language processors must force the user to think over and exactly formulate the problems to be solved or tasks to be executed; of course the languages must provide the appropriate tools to make possible the exact formulation of problems. The processors must communicate with the inner structure - or with other layers - in the most appropriate way.

As examples we present some languages which have proved their usefulness in practice, a language which has been planned and finally, disregarding the detailed description, we outline the main features of the language of a possible new application field.

The first three languages together with the inner core supply a simulator system - the LOBSTER - for the simulation of digital logic circuits; the OCTOPUS makes it possible to create a simulation system for information network modelling; the last example suggests a possible simulation system for management decision making.

4. THE BASIC LOBSTER LANGUAGE

The LOBSTER (*L*ogic *O*perational *B*ehaviour *S*imulator for *T*ime and *E*ffort *R*eduction) system provides a convenient tool for the design and testing of digital logic circuits. Using the general inner simulator structure the real time conditions can be reflected and the quasideterministic state representation enables the handling of transient and hazardous states in accordance with the "worst case" principle, as well as the handling of the indeterminacies caused by feedback loops.

The basic LOBSTER language is the modelling language which serves also for model description (giving the elements and their linkage), for describing the experiments and for controlling of the report of the information obtained during the whole simulation.

The language terms are highly adapted to the technical terms of digital circuit designers, they are simple and easy to attain. The description is also promoted by coding sheet forms.

For the building of the model, it provides an easy means to describe and link the model components in modular construction.

The identification of the topology elements and their connection takes place with modular element description. The particular modules of the system refer to the element modules of the library, giving the name or type of the elements and the local data such as the list of their inputs, outputs, and delay or other timing values and all actual values of other necessary formal parameters (e.g. the memory capacity and word length in the case of memory elements). In the case of catalogued elements only the I/O list must be given, but there is a possibility for overwriting some or all of the timing parameters with new tentative values. The user can define new elements according to the formal description of element modules. The interconnection between the elements become definable at the same time by the I/O parameter list of the elements listed, according to the scheme of the circuit.

The description of the network can also be organized in a series of predefined blocks. The aim in constructing blocks is to simplify the specification of the network and the interactions within the entire circuit, especially for repeated circuit parts. Each block describes a part of the system that depends upon a few input variables and results in a few output variables. Blocks should be described only once, giving their inner components' description similarly to the single element definition. They can also include other blocks. The external nodes of the blocks, connecting to other circuit parts, should be collected into a group.

The system as a whole can then be described in terms of the block names and these interconnections between the

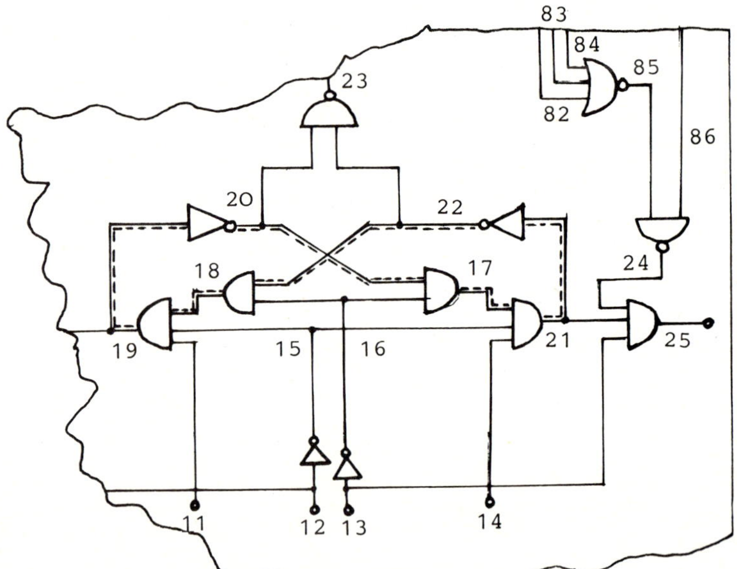

LOOP SYSTEM NUMBER : 3

INPUT NODES :
11 14 15 16

CUT NODES :
21

LOOP NUMBER : 1

OUTPUT NODES :
19 20 21 22

NODES OF LOOP :
18 19 20 17 21 22

Figure 6 : Reporting of feedback loops

blocks and single elements. Correspondingly the system can be represented graphically as a simple block diagram.

At the end of the model building and the connectivity check the simulator offers a detailed topology description, giving information about the detected feedback loops and fan-out of the elements, and it reports the occasional anomalies (Figure 6).

For the description of the experimentation for the dynamic simulation the language offers the possibilities of specifying the whole simulation time, the time increment, the output printing format and density, the initial state of the model, the input stimuli, the fault locations, etc.

The input stimuli may be defined either as time variant sequences of level changes by data items or as fixed values with the SEQUENCE and FIX keywords respectively (Figure 7). Input stimuli can be started from stable or undefined states. With periodically changing inputs only one period of state changes must be described, this sequences will be repeated until the end of simulation.

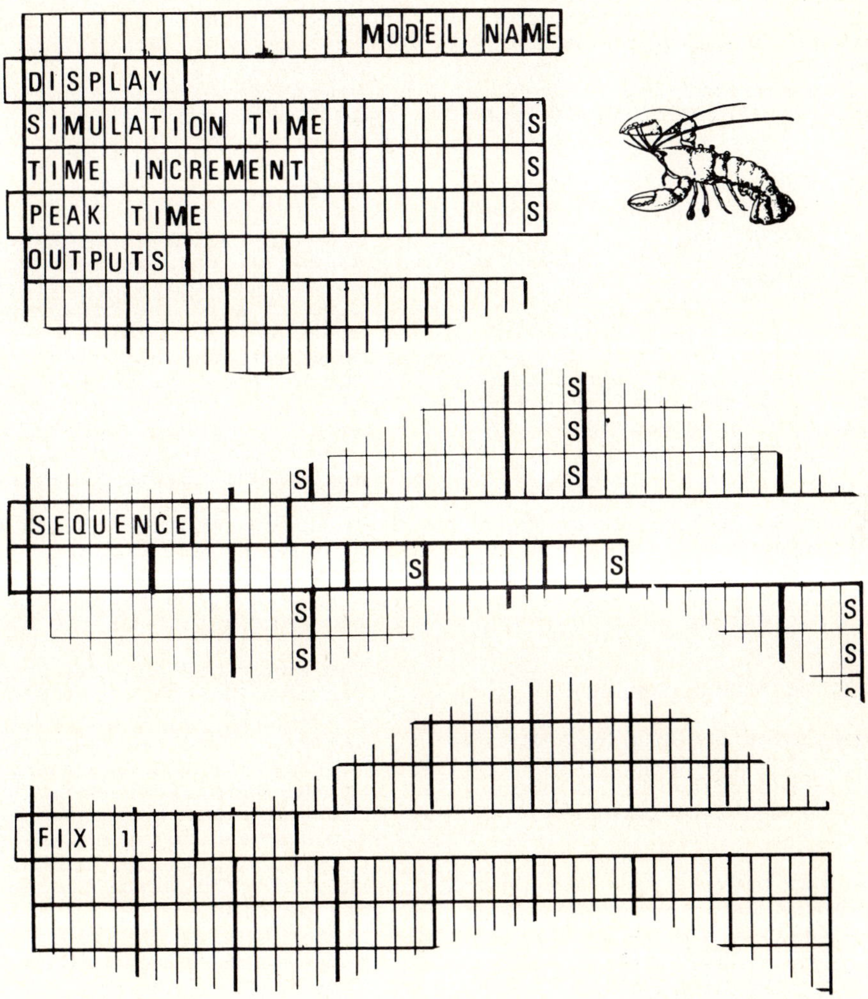

Figure 7 : Input format of the LOBSTER language

The system parameters and input states left uninitialized are detected and reported by the system. The models are initialized automatically based on the input stimuli starting states, the initial values of other element state variables and on the output functions. Initial unstable states are also propagated. After setting the model into its initial states, information is provided about the state variables that remained in an unstable state.

Optional initial states of the model can be reached by presetting the initial state of any internal node of the circuit to a given fixed level (PRESET 0 and PRESET 1 statements). The effect of these state settings is also propagated through the entire network.

Fault detection can be requested by listing the fault locations to be settled to some fixed state - to be stuck at 0, stuck at 1 or stuck at an undefined state.

The utility options - called during the dynamic operation as display or store of results in a special way - can be requested to join in the investigation by means of special keywords.

At the end of the simulation, information is served about the events that occurred during the simulation run together with the signalization of uncertainties like hazards, also providing their sources.

The format of the output provided on lineprinter can be defined so as to choose the testpoints of the model to be reported on as well as to give the density of the printout (intervals of printing or printout at every change in state).

5. PROGRAMMED TESTING LANGUAGE

The experimentation for the dynamic simulation can be described in a higher level language according to the operational flow-chart of the modelled circuit.

The language can provide help mainly at the evaluation of fault detecting test sequences of digital logic circuits but obviously it can be used for simple design and/or testing purposes as well. The option serves as a preprocessor for stimulus sequences definition enabling the algorithmic manipulation of experimentation specifications of the model.

By means of the language several parameters like input sequences, testing conditions and conditional branches can be defined for the time of the simulation runs, specifying the input stimuli module structures, the so called segments. For the closed loop feedback controlled simulation realized with the LOBSTER system [2], the option serves as an efficient means of describing conditional testing, where the conditions under which decisions have to be made on the following steps of simulation must be handled in input stimuli, and complicated or recursive test sequences must be applied to observe the dynamic behaviour of the simulated model.

The language processor (interpreter) connects the experimentation to the inner structure, more precisely to its adaptive generator element, through an appropriately structured modular data base. The input stimuli and the conditions are mapped into the data interface as linkable segments [2] of test sequences. Test sequences can follow the train of thought of the circuit analysts.

Concerning the user-system communication aspect of the language we can also take advantage of its high level possibilities as well as the special purpose user-oriented commands given in the terminology of the hardware designers. The language offers tools for the specification of appropriate model and test variables, propagation delays, definition of test time unit, etc. By the language statements the user can describe time and/or function dependent test sequences, conditional branching between sequences, event controlling in input stimuli and state changes as well as the initialization settings of the model and the termination of the simulation runs.

The structure and the components of the language are shown in Figure 8. Several possibilities of realizing complex test segment libraries are provided with appropriately fitted experiments by means of the compiling techniques [2]. The data base parts, i.e. the sequence of the corresponding experiments, can be chosen adaptively during a simulation run using the name of the experiment entry points.

6. INTERACTIVE GRAPHICAL COMMUNICATION LAYER

This layer is an interactive graphical observation facility by which an efficient analysis and tracing of the simulation results can be performed. It gives the user the feeling of observing

```
<experiment>::=<declaration><entry segment>{&lt;segment>}
<declaration>::=<model name><variable declaration><timing declaration>
<model name>::=<identifier>
<identifier>::=<letter>{<letter|digit>}
<variable declaration>::=<variable type><variable name><variable parameters>
<variable type>::= HWS; scalar model variable| HWV; vector model variable|
                   SWS; scalar test variable|  SWV; vector test variable
<variable name>::=<identifier>
<variable parameters>::=<empty>|(<vector size>)=<model vector component>{,<model
                        vector component>}|=<model signal>|(<vector size>)
<vector size>::=<unsigned integer>
<timing declaration>::=<program clock declaration><delay declaration>
<program clock declaration>::= CLOCK <period length>
<period length>::=<unsigned integer><unit>
<unit>::= ps|ns|ms|us|s
<delay declaration>::= GEN <variable name>{,<variable name>|<vector variable name>
                       (index)}<delay time>
<delay time>::=<rise time><fall time>
<entry segment>::= MASTER &lt;segment name> new line
                  <initialisation of the model> new line
                  <test segment> new line
                   END
&lt;segment name>::=<identifier>
<initialisation of the model>::= INIT<LOW|HIGH|UND>{<variable name>{(index)},}
&lt;segment>::=<SUBROUTINE|BLOCK>&lt;segment name> new line
            <test segment> new line
             END
<test segment>::={<event execution>}{<condition testing>}
<event execution>::={label}{time}<variable setting>|{label}<branch>
<variable setting>::= DATA<vector variable><value|vector variable>|<SET RESET>
                      <scalar variable|vector variable(index)>
<branch>::= GOTO<label|block segment name>|RETURN ; only in subroutine
<time>::=<n * clock period ± m * unit>
<condition testing>::={label}{time} TEST<scalar variable|vector variable(index)>
                      <branch to label1;if high><label2;if low><label3;if undefined>
                      |{label}{time} COMP<vector variable><vector variable|value>
                      <branch to label1;if equal><label2;if not equal>
<label>::=<unsigned integer>
```

Figure 8 : The structure of the programmed testing language

and testing the realized model during operation. A further very obvious advantage is the possibility to easily trace the separate parts of a digital network tested with long variable sequences as opposed to using a detailed list of simulation results.

Results reporting takes place by interactive display techniques. The way of displaying the results is similar to that of the well proved testing method of the hardware designers, providing more information with easier handling. From their viewpoints this tool can substitute the physical hardware model, driving it with sequences of programmable signal generators and the events can be observed on a multitrace oscilloscope (Figure 9).

The event tracing postprocessor of the facility is connected to the effective simulation through the output file of the inner simulator containing data about all simulation events that occurred during the observation like state changes, special situations and so on. The minimal knowledge to get the option running is the DISPLAY keyword which is given to the dynamic simulation to obtain the wanted output file. By the high level commands of the language the user can control the graphical display of sequences of state changes at any point of the simulated models at any selected time interval of the simulation time and, further, can ask several different items of information on event occurrences, groups of events or any other information relating to the simulation run.

The different states are denoted according to the state representation of the inner structure (see Figure 10). The stable states, fix 1 and fix 0, are represented by the high and low level line intervals; the undefined states are denoted by empty intervals. For the displayed test-points all special events caused by hazardous conditions occurring during the selected time interval are specially noted.

Figure 9 : The interactive graphical subsystem

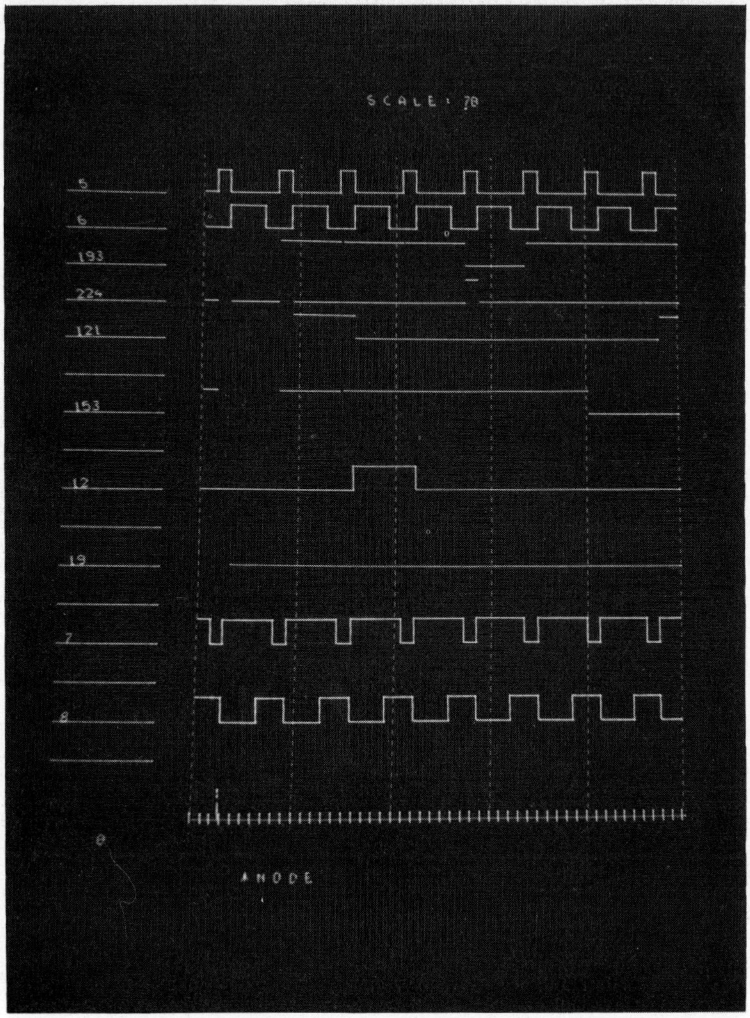

Figure 10 : The picture parameters

The parameters given by the user to create the desired picture - the beginning and the scale of the time interval, the requested nodes' identifiers, the commands - are also displayed on the screen. The way of giving the commands makes use of the advantages of interactivity as well as the available graphic input tools.

As an example let us consider the analysis of the behaviour of a pseudorandom generator realized by an MOS shift register. The simulated circuit can be seen in Figure 11.

The shift register consists of two phase dynamic MASTER-SLAVE flip-flops, each of them is built up from MOSTORE and MOSLAVE element module pairs. The shift register propagates the input level on its stages and with a modulo 2 feedback of the 5th and 9th stages it forms a pseudorandom generator. Shifting takes place according to the clock signals which are delayed with respect to each other to conform to the two phase timing. The feedback is realized through an

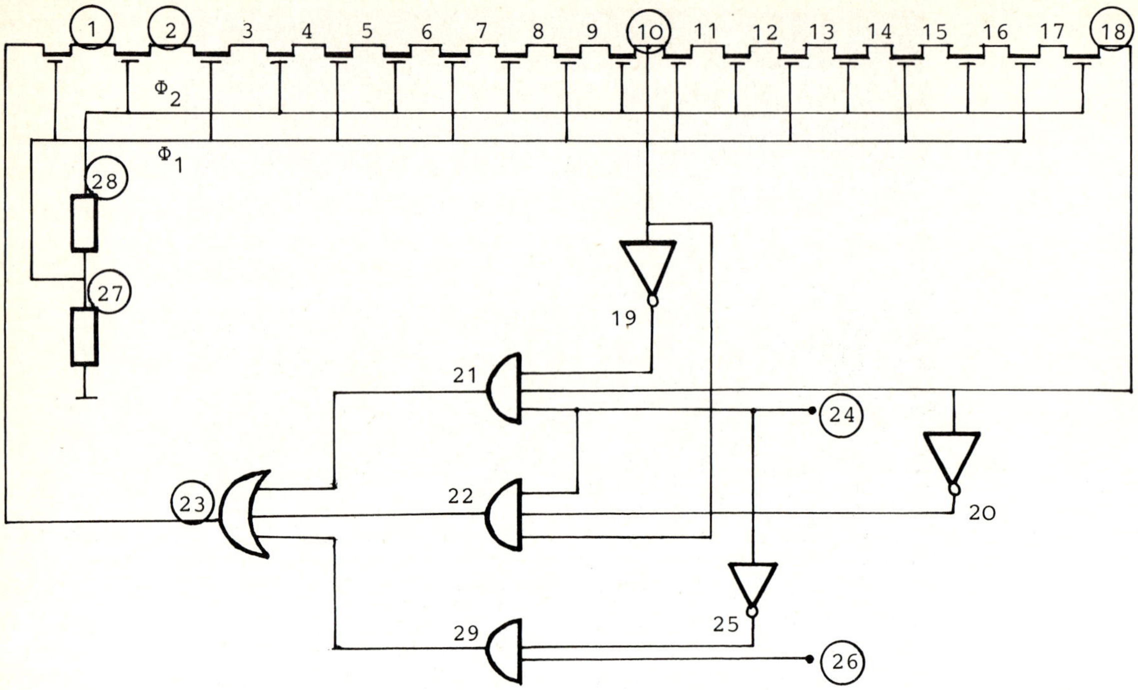

Figure 11 : MOS SHIFT

EXCLUSIVE OR gate that in its closed state enables the feedback of the register's output, i.e. the pseudorandom generation, while switching into its open state it cuts the feedback and enables an external input signal to rewrite the states of the register components.

The aim of the simulation experiment was to investigate the effect of the external input for the initialization of the shift register, and the effect of the clock rate on the operation of the circuit. The simulation results presented in Figure 12 are obtained under normal operating conditions. It can be seen that by the external input signal the shift register can be initialized correctly, the signal propagation through the master-slave stages can be well observed.

The level changes of 26→23 reach the first stage at once (points 1 and 2), the fifth stage (point 10) at about 2600 nsec, the last stage (18) at about 5000 nsec. Until the input sequence reaches the certain stages of the shift register the MOSLAVE elements signalize hazards since "floating", i.e. undefined, states are on their inputs when the clock pulse arrives.

It can also be seen that if the clock rate is too quick hazards arise (vertical dotted lines) at the M-S stages because of the incorrect control of slaves, i.e. their clock pulse comes when the input level was undefined. If the clock rate is too slow the circuit also operates in a faulty way, the output states of the M-S flip-flops become undefined because the storage time of the levels passed before the next clock pulse.

Interactive observation took place in

Figure 12 : MOS SHIFT investigation

the following steps:

- As we initially wanted to see the overall effect of the input changes and the clock rate, we requested a rather long time interval to be displayed, from the beginning of the simulation time in a dense time scale (DISPLAY FROM 0 BY SCALE 200 nsec).
- The operation of the circuit can be illustrated and observed by the series of state changes of the next nodes (signalized by circles on the circuit scheme):
  Statement:

  NODE x TO LINE y

  Φ_1, Φ_2 clock signals (27, 28) to the first two lines

  the points that are fed back (5th and 9th stages): 10 and 18 to lines 3 and 4

  the input point of the shift register (23) to line 5

  the operation mode select (24) to line 6

  the external input (26) to line 7

  the propagation of the states can be observed on the M-S stages, i.e. on the output of the first stage M-S on the master (1) and on the slave (2) to lines 11 and 12 respectively.
- When the state changes of nodes of the shift register are displayed, a simultaneous hazard signalization arises. More information is provided about hazards by the effect of "LIST HAZARDS UNTIL 5000 nsec AT All", when the occurred hazards are displayed together with their sources until the 5000 nsec of the simulation time.
- The propagation of the level changes through the circuit can be followed on the picture. Time parameters such as the interval of transients or the time elapsing between the level changes of nodes can be measured by the INTERVAL

statement, pointing with the light pen or positioning the ball to the relevant signal points. The simulation time instant of a certain state change or the occurrence of hazards can also be requested by the TIME command.

7. THE OCTOPUS LANGUAGE

The draft of a system for simulating computer networks based on the common inner structure mentioned above is now being developed (OCTOPUS - *O*riginal *C*omputer *T*opology *O*riented *P*rognostic *U*niversal *S*imulator). The system should enable the information traffic level modelling of multiprocessor systems with all the relevant modules of this kind (i.e. buffer and operational memories I/O equipment, etc.) in order to find optimal configurations for given purposes. Such problems are widespread in the area of computer networks [14].

The main application field will be the modelling of multimicroprocessor systems with unusual (i.e. experimental) configurations in order to promote the investigation of new architectures [15]. In the development we made use of the experience of our earlier system designed for similar purposes [16].

The events of simulation are mainly described by the movement of information blocks (messages) or, in other words, by the movement of entities from one facility to the other. Nevertheless there are a number of "level type" events, e.g. interrupt request. For the proper description of the system both types have to be handled. Most of the simulation packages of this type provide statistical data on the efficiency of the model operation (utilization of memory areas, throughput efficiency, response times, etc.). These gross data do not reveal the destiny of single entities, i.e. the microstructure of events. Although in a number of cases this is really irrelevant, sometimes they might be of great importance in revealing the anomalies of the operation of the modelled system, such as the attempt to simultaneously access facilities which may result in an "after you, after you" type of blocking of the system [17], simultaneous filling and emptying of buffers in data transmission, etc.

The description of such models can be solved by using the formerly described state representation and mapping the model described by the language in the common structure. The main features of the draft of the language are the following:

1/ Building blocks (elements) of the models
A number of them are predefined and stored in the library with their formal parameters, e.g. processor, random access memory, buffer, input device, output device, I/O device, stack, bus and environment type elements. In addition to these, user defined modules can be stored in the library.

2/ Model description
The interconnection of the elements should be given, the two types of connections (i.e. level or entity exchange) have to be noted.

3/ Boundary conditions of the simulation run are partly given by the ENVIRONMENT type of elements; furthermore, the initialization conditions of the model have to be determined, the simulation time and conditional transfers in the simulation should also be described.

4/ Monitoring, data collection and output statements are also to be given. These have to include statistical routines to obtain mean value, standard deviation, confidence interval calculation and histogram collection. In addition to these functions the monitoring and signalization of "anomalies" or unwanted (race, hazard, overflow, etc.) conditions have also to be solved.

8. SIMULATION OF MANAGEMENT DECISION MAKING

Management decisions for various activities often have to be made under severe time constraints and on the basis of mixed information about the prevailing conditions. Decision makers wish to inquire in advance about the probable consequences of their decisions. The representation of trends, growth rates and other overall statistic provides results at a low level of detail. With logical decisions, which are dependent on the exact state of the system or in the case of stochastic systems with interacting internal and environmental events, the investigation of individual states by discrete event simulation models is of more interest (e.g. resource allocations and job scheduling problems at areas as project management, inventory control, multilevel manufacturing etc.).

By the event oriented modelling of these systems and their environmental effects the management policies can be tested by demonstrating the system's response to various conditions and decisions. A discrete event simulation based upon the invariant core - outer layers simulation structure seems practicable for aiding management decision making.

Once the general tools of the core, like the model building, the time advancement method, the state representation and event handling have been developed forming the main frame of the simulation system, only the strictly problem oriented components need to be described and the appropriate language or languages should be developed to form the desired simulation systems.

For the relevant simulation of the field problems, the system programmer should:

- Constitute the appropriate element library, giving the elements' formal attributes and operational function in an optional way, the only restriction is that it must fit to the element references of the inner system;
- define and construct the entity attributes' format, the number and type of the possible "states" in accordance with the QDS representation and the input generator's output;
- define the special scheduling rules if there are any, and the number and type of lists for the event scheduling mechanism;
- specify the event descriptions and event notices;
- construct the relevant and required language layers;
- write the necessary utility routines in a similar way to the element routines.

The system programmer has a great freedom in the forming of the above mentioned features, realizing several types of simulation systems, without changing the invariant core operation.

For the describing of the permanent components of the management systems several types of implementation may be realized. By storing general logical elements in the library like facilities, buffers, storages, seize and release blocks, delays, generators, etc. universal management simulation can be achieved. By storing more special elements "typists", "bookkeepers", "technicians", "machines" - or enabling the task of abstraction for the language interpreter - special fields and viewpoints of managing can be well simulated, like factory management, job shopping, marketing, financial transactions, etc.

The individual elements can be aggregated into larger elements so the general manager of a factory may be satisfied with the description, while the production control manager will want to consider the shops of the departments as individual elements.

The dynamic behaviour has to be described by information traffic level modelling, as the events of simulation are mainly described by the movement of entities. These entities can be of different types, like information message blocks, materials, orders, jobs, machine component parts, vehicles, funds, etc. The interpretation of the real features of each entity type, as well as their relation to other entities, should be given by the input elements and could be handled by the relevant element modules.

In the case of general simulation the definition of the entity attributes, i.e. the explanation of their features, must be given by the user, whereas for special element libraries the entity types and attributes can be defined in advance. Of course there may be also "level type" events in the modelled systems, like busy/free states, interrupts to give priority to some jobs etc.

The event class description routines according to the predicted event notices must be given to execute the changes of the entity attributes in a fixed automatic way, disregarding the real content of the single attributes but only the type of their changes.

The handling of anomalies - by the element modules or by the simulation system - must be defined in a well documented way according to the QDS conception. These undefined situations, e.g. decision feedback loops on the basis of the prevailing information, ordered-, produced- and sold-products, races between entities (e.g. orders or jobs), can cause hazardous conditions, and may block the management system. For the correct evaluation of the decision effects a possible overstep must be chosen and signalized, or an interactive decision must be asked from the manager.

Considering the world view of the system analyst several types of model descriptions are possible and desired. In the case of material oriented scenario approach the spatial and temporal movement of entities through the network is of interest the permanent elements serve only for passing them, and can be represented merely as flags or counters [18]. The entities, e.g. jobs, have several attributes that the events can cause to change and the users are mainly interested in the information about the entity attributes' changes in time and space. (E.g. a job is waiting for two hours after scheduling but before having been typed, etc.)

In the case of machine oriented world view the individual life cycles of permanent elements are of more importance, the temporary entities are used only for synchronizing the activation of these elements. In this case they are the entities that may be considered as counters rather than the permanent building blocks, which play down their real operation defined by their algorithms. In this world view the required information should be provided about the state changes and attributes of the permanent elements.

It can be shown, that in the inner structure the mechanism of the model building and executing is the same for both cases. The operation of the system at a lower level, i.e. at the handling of events and the activation of elements and entity attribute changes, takes place in the same way. The only difference when using the best fit to a scenario may be in the operational functions and the content of the attributes of the building elements and entities as well as the needed utility functions for data collection.

As with the related element library, the model description and the element references, the experiments just as the information gathering aspects must be defined through the outer layers these being the language layers that must reflect the chosen scenario approach, and should mirror the execution of the model according to the block scheme or flow chart of the management system.

Constructing more layers to the same core, reflecting the basic operation of the systems, several simulation tools can be provided, fitted to different world views and differently abstract description possibilities and investigations.

The necessary and suggested features of the outer languages may be drafted as the following: (special requirements should not be satisfied by all or one general language, but with more differently fitting ones)

1/ The building blocks - temporary elements - of the model should be predefined and stored in the element library with formal parameters. User defined modules are also allowed.

2/ The interconnection between the elements, i.e. the model network emphasizing the connection types, should be unambiguously defined. The description of the system should be organized in a series of blocks to simplify the specification of interactions within the system.

3/ The building blocks of the models as well as the experimentation and information reporting should reflect the chosen scenario approach, and the abstraction level of the model, i.e. the model should include those aspects of the system that are relevant to the study objectives.

4/ The experimentation should be determined by environment elements. The input stimuli generation could be given in test patterns or in algorithms, enabling conditionally programmed testing of the model. Initial settings upon the previous model state and the exogenous events could be prescribed.

5/ Interactive model design and testing is highly suggested. The interaction of the human decision maker and the modelled process have to be ensured at least by conditional transfers.

6/ The necessary data collection with several types of statistics or individual values of parameters as well as other user defined utility functions should also be given for the simulation. The density and the type of the report of the obtained information should be given by the user by report statements.

7/ The use of graphical representation of simple block diagrams for model description is recommended. The report generation should also include graphics capabilities.

8/ The languages should provide a user interface that is easy to learn and mirrors the logical thinking of the managers, usually unfamiliar with programming, to enable the fast and reliable model construction. They must guide the analysts during the model design, validation and experimentation.

9. CONCLUSION

Results obtained in the field of digital logic circuit simulation seem to verify that such simulation system structures containing a general inner core and appropriate outer layers are worth developing and, together with a standardized general simulation language, can meet the requirements demanded by a wide range of simulation users.

ACKNOWLEDGEMENT

The authors are indebted to Miss Á. Vigh for her valuable contribution to this project.

10. REFERENCES

[1] Jávor, A., Benkő, M. Mrs., A User-Oriented System for the Simulation of Digital Logic, CAD Seminar, Budapest (3-5. November 1976) 178-191.

[2] Jávor, A., Proposals on the Structure of Simulation Systems, in Jávor, A. (ed.), Discrete Simulation and Related Fields (North-Holland, Amsterdam, 1982).

[3] Jávor, A., Révész, Á., Tóbiás, P., A Closed-Loop Feedback Controlled Simulation System, in Jávor, A. (ed.), Discrete Simulation and Related Fields (North-Holland, Amsterdam, 1982).

[4] Jávor, A., An Approach to the Modelling of Uncertainties in the Simulation of Quasideterministic Discrete Event Systems, Problems of Control and Information Theory 4(3) (1975) 219-229.

[5] Jávor, A., A Representation of Fuzzyness in Discrete Simulation, Problems of Control and Information Theory 7(2) (1978) 111-114.

[6] Jávor, A., Indeterminált helyzetek szimulációja "részecske-orientált" rendszereknél, KFKI Report, KFKI-1978-83 (November 1978).

[7] Feuvrier, Ch.V., La Simulation de Systémes, Dunod, Paris (1971).

[8] Franta, W.R., Maly, K., An Event Scanning Algorithm of Nearly Constant Complexity, in Dekker, L. (ed.), Simulation of Systems (North-Holland, Amsterdam, 1976) 439-444.

[9] Vaucher, J.G., Duval, P., A Comparison of Simulation Event List Algorithms, Comm. ACM 8(4) (April 1975) 223-230.

[10] Ulrich, E.G., Exclusive Simulation of Activity in Digital Networks, Comm. ACM 12(2) (1969) 102-110.

[11] Jávor, A., An Adaptive Time Advancement Algorithm for Discrete Simulation, Information Processing Letters 6(3) (1977) 83-86.

[12] Ören, T.I., A Personal View on the Future of Simulation Languages Proc. 1978 UKSC Conference on Computer Simulation, Chester (April 1978) 294-306.

[13] Elzas, M.S., Whither Simulation?, Proc. 1978 UKSC Conference on Computer Simulation, Chester (April 1978) 494-501.

[14] Dartois, J.P., On a Traffic Simulation Problem of the Switching Network for a Common Control Exchange, Comm. et Electronique (30) (July 1970) 36-45.

[15] Dekker, L., Kerckhoffs, E.J.H., Systems Modelling and Parallel Simulation, Part I: Present and Future Parallel Prodessing, Delft University of Technology, Dept. of Mathematics (April 1978).

[16] Jávor, A., Csákány, A., Some Achievements in the Investigation of Data Transmission Networks Using a Flexible Simulation System, XVIII. Rassegna Internazionale Electronica e Nucleare Congresso Scientifico Internazionale per l'Elettronica D-5, Roma (Marzo 1971) 331-337.

[17] Dijkstra, E.W., Hierarchical Ordering of Sequential Processes, Acta Informatica 1 (Spinger Verlag, 1971) 115-138.

[18] Kreutzer, W., Comparison and Evaluation of Discrete Event Simulation Programming Languages for Management Decision Making, in Dekker, L. (ed.), Simulation of Systems (North-Holland, Amsterdam, 1976) 429-438.

DISCRETE SIMULATION AND RELATED FIELDS
A. Jávor (editor)
North-Holland Publishing Company

A CLOSED-LOOP FEEDBACK CONTROLLED SIMULATION SYSTEM

A. Jávor, Á. Révész, P. Tóbiás

Central Research Institute for Physics
of the Hungarian Academy of Sciences
Budapest, Hungary

A system enabling the input variables of the model to be controlled dynamically by the results of the simulation during run time is presented. The solution to transform a conventional "straight forward" simulation system into such by adding a single - special - element to its element library as well as the outlines of the language used are shown on a practical example of realization; the LOBSTER system designed for the simulation of digital logic.

1. INTRODUCTION

There are certain points in the simulation process where a decision has to be made on the basis of which the process may alter or become recursive, meaning that some part of it has to be repeated possibly with a modified model structure or test conditions.

This branching point is usually controlled by the simulation experimenter, i.e. by the human part of the man-machine system. The closing of these decision-feedback loops within the simulation system increases the intelligence of the system by automating the experiment.

The goal of this work has been to achive this end by using essentially a system structure that has proved to be useful generally, and the necessary extension should be embedded without modifying the original framework [1].

The principle has been applied in solving a practical problem, viz. the evaluation of fault-detecting test sequences of digital logic circuits by means of simulation.

2. GENERAL PRINCIPLE OF THE SOLUTION

The general principle of the solution is illustrated in Figure 1. The structure of the simulation system used consisted of a set of subsystem modules with the algorithms, state, input, and output variables (describing them), and the framework through which the interconnected element modules - forming a network in accordance with the model structure [1][2] - activate each other analogously to interconnected automata (see Figure 1/a).

There are many advantages of this simulation principle even though it may cause difficulties in providing a comprehensive test sequence as input. The input sequence has to be given in advance and this sequence will provide external events for the experiment.

In this arrangement the simulator consists of a model frame providing the skeleton of the model to be simulated into which the component modules of the model are inserted.

The other important arrangement is that the input stimuli driving the model through the experiment should be treated during the simulation run as one module element (see Figure 1/b). This sort of element is, of course, a special sequence generator which, after generating an input event, automatically sets the timing of the next one. Thereby, the activated generator routines have the following task

```
<generator>::=<generate input event; set
               time for next event in
               system clock structure>
```

This generator type element is also to be found in the widely known GPSS system [3].

The inputs do not have to be treated in a special way but, instead, uniformly as an element module which means that the basis is also provided for the implementation of a more sophisticated input description.

The last step now is to "close the loop", i.e. to automate the experiment by selecting the appropriate input sequences according to the results of the simulation during the simulation process. This element chooses from the sequences given in advance. The advantage over the conventional method is that it does not differ essentially in its structure so we can easily insert it into the structure of the simulator. This "result driven adaptive generator element" gives the possibility to use a higher level input stimuli description.

As the input during simulation run is already represented by an element that is activated by itself through the frame, no problem is caused if it is extended by driving the input(s) from the outputs of other modules and/or the results of the simulation.

In other words a conditional transfer of input stimuli can be realized (see Figure 1/c).

Figure 1/d shows the development of elements from the general element through the generator element to the result driven adaptive generator element.

The results or outputs can - of course - be state variables, statistical parameters such as mean values, standard deviations, etc. where, from the system building point of view, the primary output variables should also be considered as state variables of the "statistical evaluation modules" which can be handled in the same way as the rest.

Let us now consider an example of such a system developed for a well defined practical purpose.

3. PRACTICAL IMPLEMENTATION

The fundamental system used was the LOBSTER digital logic simulation system [4]. The LOBSTER (*L*ogic *O*perational *B*ehaviour *S*imulator for *T*ime and *E*ffort *R*eduction) is a table driven, asynchronous, discrete simulator which has the possibility of describing timing conditions with transportation delays and ambiguity. This three-valued logic simulator is able to simulate tri-state circuits with realistic simulation of time delays. It provides tools for designing and testing digital logic circuits that

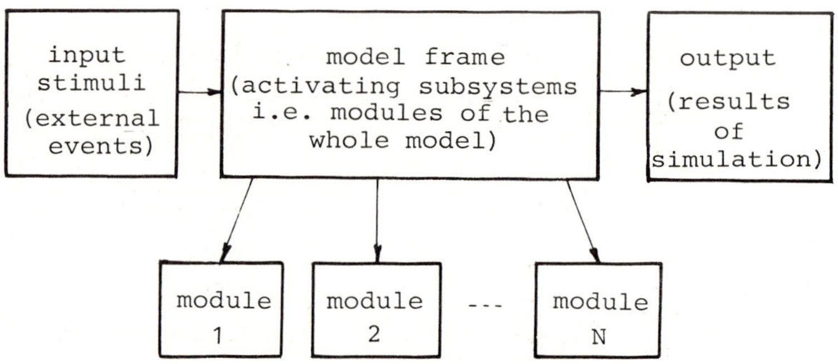

a/

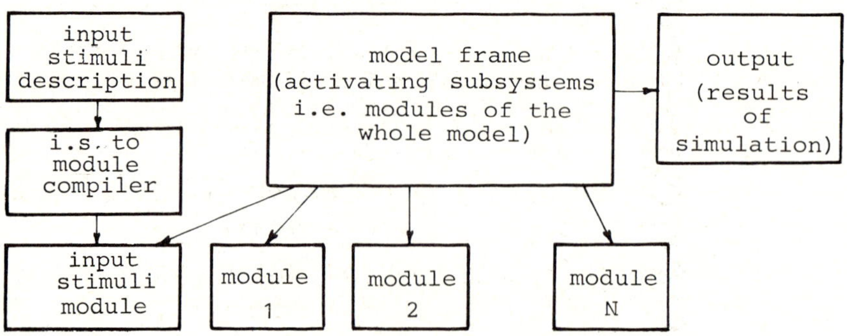

b/

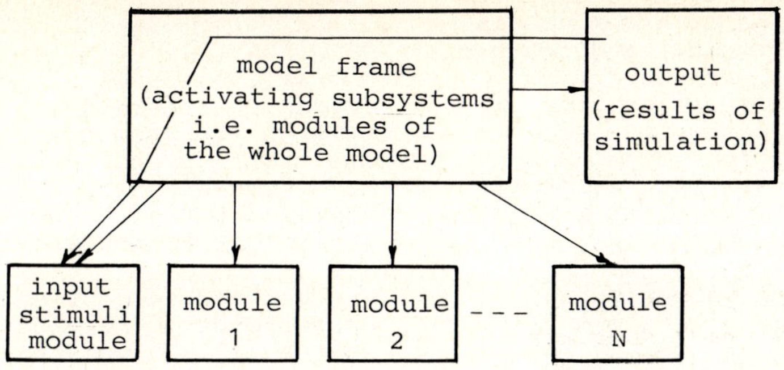

c/

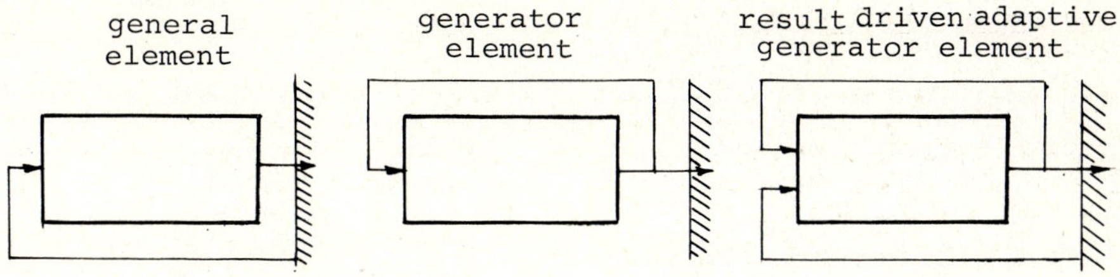

d/

Figure 1 : Development of the proposed simulation system structure

are similar to the means of hardware designers.

The simulation system consists of a set of element modules and the framework executive through which the interconnected elements can activate each other. It also provides languages for the model description and experimentation.

The simulation takes place in two phases. The first phase is the static analysis. The designer of the circuit describes the circuit topology in a user oriented language. This language provides the possibility of defining blocks in the model for the repetitive insertion into the circuit topology. The user can define a circuit block and he only has to call this block description in the circuit description. This possibility saves time and effort in the circuit description. The first phase of the simulation gives the interconnection table of the circuit and searches the loops in the circuit. This is necessary for the dynamic simulation of the asynchronous sequential circuits and enables hazardous situations to be indicated. Having completed the static analysis, the first phase stores the model structure in the background memory thereby enabling multiple independent experimentation. This segregation of the model building and the description and execution of the simulation experiment has proved to be highly advantageous.

The second phase is the dynamic simulation. It operates within the framework of the system containing the description of the model topology, the executive (timing tool), and other factors necessary to activate the modules.

The element set of the LOBSTER system contains the conventional gates (AND, OR, NAND, NOR, INVERTER), many members of the Texas Instr. Inc. SN series, memories (ROM, RAM) and some special elements for LSI and tri-state circuits.

The element set of the simulator can easily be expanded. Because of the modularity, it is only necessary to write a new module to obtain a new element. Every element corresponds to a module. It means that a subroutine or procedure in some high-level programming language has to be written. If the designer of the circuit has some experience in programming he can write it himself but, of course, it is simpler to use the elements of the element set of the LOBSTER system.

AND	Logical "and" function
NAND	Logical "not and" function
OR	Logical "or" function
NOR	Logical "not or" function
INVERTER	Logical "not" function
DELAY	Universal element for time delay
D-E-FLIP	Edge triggered, D-type flip-flop
J-M-FLIP	Master-slave, JK flip-flop
MOSGATE	Special element for modelling MOS LSI transfer gate or connected gate groups
MOSTORE	A variant of the MOSGATE element for storage stage modelling
MOSLAVE	A variant of the MOSGATE element for modelling of the slave stage of a master-slave
RS-FLIP	Static RS flip-flop
JNE-FLIP	Negative edge triggered JK flip-flop

Table I : In addition to elements of the Texas Instr. Inc. SN series the LOBSTER has these general elements

The system is modular so we need use only those modules (elements) which are necessary for the given application. This modularity makes possible the expansion and changing of the program, therefore a model of entirely different nature can be built up on the existing inner structure.

The activation of elements - firstly the input sequence modules - takes place through the executive, on the basis of the signal propagation and/or the scheduled events. After the elements have accomplished their function, control reverts back to the executive.

The general element shown in Figure 1/d corresponds to most circuit elements (gates, flip-flops, etc.). Their operation is very simple. We have to evaluate the effect of the signal arriving at its input (input change) and on the basis of this we predict the output change in such a way that we schedule the event notice of the output point. These simple elements form the major part of a circuit.

The so-called generator elements driving the input points of the circuit have special features. For these input points, the model frame activates these modules (elements) if the time equals a formerly predicted value; a change takes place at its output and it schedules its next event time.

Once the execution of the sequence is started the generator element reschedules itself until the end of the sequence.

In order to make possible the conditional transfer in input stimuli a new element type, the so-called *adaptive generator element* was introduced. The adaptive generator element, beyond the execution of sequences, tests certain conditions, i.e. the state variables and, depending on the result, chooses the appropriate input sequence (see Figure 2).

Input sequences consist of events and condition-testing. "Events" mean that there are some changes in the circuit, e.g. changes from logical low level to logical high level. Every event and con-

<SEQUENCE(t)>::=<EVENT SEQUENCE(t)><CONDITION SEQUENCE(t)>

<EVENT SEQUENCE(t)>::=<EVENT(t)>|<EVENT SEQUENCE(t)><EVENT(t)>

<CONDITION SEQUENCE(t)>::=<CONDITION(t)>|<CONDITION SEQUENCE(t)><CONDITION(t)>

Figure 2 : The definition of an input sequence

dition testing is time dependent, as indicated in the definition. The condition may refer to a test of the state of a given node or other element [2]. As a result of condition testing, the adaptive generator element chooses a sequence from the user written data-base.

There is a considerable difference between the generator and adaptive generator element. The first one requires only one sequence whereas the second requires us to define many sequences among which we place condition testing. Once a sequence is executed, condition testing follows (obviously checking the effect of the sequence). Depending on the result of this test we choose one or another input sequence to be executed and after the execution of this a new condition test may take place and so on until the end of the simulation.

How are these three cases similar? In the simplest, the first case, there was an input change and as a result of this we scheduled an output change. In the generator element there is a feedback, once the operation has started; it is given an input signal to start the evaluation of the sequence and during the operation it schedules itself indicating it wishes to change again. In the present case - the adaptive generator - it also has to start a sequence, but it leads to a condition test whose result specifies the next sequence and so on. It is, of course, assumed that the necessary sequences are given in advance.

In this way we have been able to achieve highly complex input sequences consisting of several sub-sequences which are activated conditionally (depending on the results of simulation) and that can be generated by extending the element library of the simulation system with a - very special - generator element that is treated by the model frame system in the same way as all the others.

4. DEFINING THE EXPERIMENT BY A DESCRIPTIVE LANGUAGE

The experiment undertaken on the simulated model must characterize the set of circumstances under which the model is to be observed. In connection with providing the experimentation two important aspects must be taken into consideration.

The description of the experiment should appear to the simulator as an appropriate data base containing the sequences of input stimuli, and the efficiency of simulation - especially in the case of the above mentioned closed loop feedback method - depends strongly on the structure of this data base while, considering the experimenter, it should take the form of an easy-to-manage description, which meets his sometimes special requirements.

With regard both to the possibility of realizing such a well-structured data base and to the user-system communication aspect of experimentation we can state that the experimental framework can be defined in the most flexible way by means of a suitable descriptive language [2]. In our problem the language suits its purpose well if on the one hand it conforms to general languages to some extent having, for example, a high level structure, advanced specification options, managing and compiling techniques for creating the corresponding structured data base as well as for describing some pecularity of the framework, but on the other hand it provides special purpose, user oriented simple tools - commands - which are adapted to a hardware designer's well proved testing methods.

Bearing this in mind the experimental data base is to be produced by the compiler in intermediate code, and the following requirements should be met. In order to make it possible to automate the simulation experiment, i.e. to control the branching points of dynamic observation by the simulator itself, the experiment should contain sequences of events and tests as well as the conditions of the simulational results under which the transfer in input stimuli can be realized. The sequences of input stimuli should be structured to appropriate segments which correspond to special tests or test sections. These must be easy-to-reach either if there is a conditional transfer to them, or by realizing different test sequence chainings. The segments must be addressable and reentrant, the conditions must contain the addresses of the appropriate segments or sequences to which control is to be transferred so that the simulator - in our case the adaptive generator element - can choose and adapt itself automatically to the next appropriate input stimuli from the sequences of events and tests upon conditions and test results, making it possible to assemble in time the necessary sequences from segments during the simulation run. The individual segments must be defined in relative time, getting their real-time values only when they are activated.

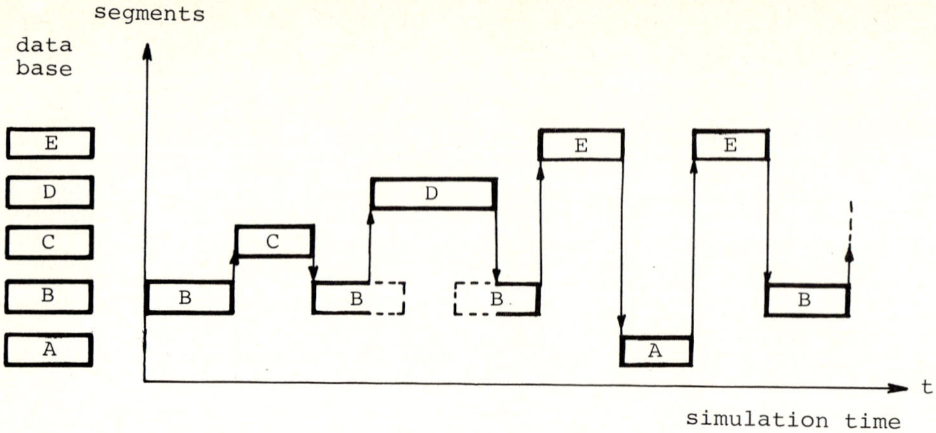

Figure 3 : Conditional linking of input segments

<segment>::=<events><conditions together with branching points>

The method of chaining these segments or sequences by the simulator during one simulation run can be seen in Figure 3.

Where A,B,C,D,E are segments of input stimuli sequences grouped to form special test steps.

We have enumerated some options offered by this language as convenient tools for describing these segments, the sequences of events and tests, and conditions.

The experimenter can

- specify optional and observational variables by means of identifiers (hardware signs and arrays or test flags),
- declare timing delays and give the initialization settings of the model,
- specify input sequences, scheduled state changes and prescribe scheduled tests using special control commands,
- control conditional transfer upon testing variables inside the segments or transfer to other segments,
- define segments of control command and/or conditional branches with relative timing,
- link segments to each other conditionally or unconditionally,
- terminate the experimentation.

In each experiment there must be a special main segment, i.e. the entry point of the experiment, which is applied as the first segment of the simulation run; this must contain the initialization settings of the model. (Initialization concerns only the input variables of the model; output and state variables of the model are initialized automatically by the simulator based on the output functions and the initial values of state variables. Variables which are left undefined are detected.)

The modular structure of the experimental data base and its handling by the simulator make it possible to give the highest variability of testing with relatively few segments which can be linked together to meet the required experiment. If the experimental framework proves to be insufficient in its testing capability it can be enlarged to permit the establishment of an extendable test segment library (Figure 4).

It is possible to give more separate experiments in one framework, e.g. with more main segments assigning a name to each of them.

As the specification and executive segments are separates there may be great variability in the way the segments are linked for different experiments, according to the changing conditions and simulational branches either in its "switching parts" or in "data setting parts".

As an example, let us see a simple se-

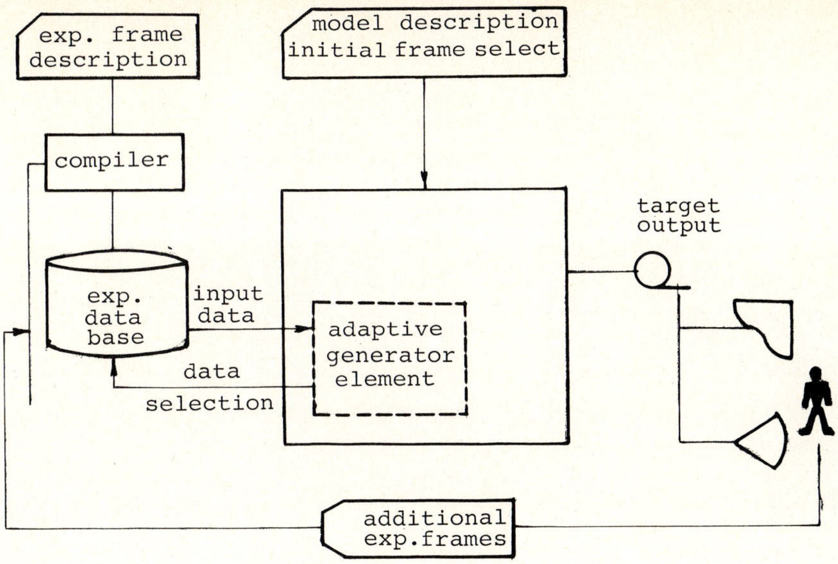

Figure 4 : Simulation system

quence of input stimuli written in the descriptive language for the LOBSTER system. The example is shown in Figure 5. The descriptive language consists of segments like procedures or subroutines in programming languages. A segment corresponds to a special test or test sequence of the input stimuli. A main segment, called master, is shown in the example.

The first part of it is the declarations. Since this can be run after the first phase of the LOBSTER system it has to be said what identifier corresponds to what node in the circuit. This is done by the HWS (Hardware Sign) statement: "A" will be the notation of node 7 and OU3 will be node 12. The SWS (Software Sign) and SWV (Software Vector) declare software variables that can be used as the usual variables and vectors in the common programming languages-

Among declarations there is a CLOCK statement defining a new "time unit" advisably conforming to the clock period of the circuit under test. This is advantageous for the convenient description of the test sequences.

A SET command is the first executable statement. The format of the statement can be seen in Figure 5. It consists of four main parts. First is the label field - this is 10 in the SET statement; secondly there is the time field which is a compound one. After this comes the statement code and some parameter or operand. The time field is not self-evident. It consists of two numbers and an arithmetic operator. The first number gives the number of clock periods until the execution of this statement. The second number is a value in nanoseconds, which gives a shift relative to the time corresponding to the first number. The arithmetic operator gives the direction of shifting. In the first statement, 5+12 means 5 clock periods plus 12 nanoseconds assuming that 1 clock period equals 100 ns. The statement SET sets node A to logical high level.

Similarly, the next statement RESET causes the KK(3) array element to become zero, or if it were a hardware node, logical low level.

The TEST statement is an examination if OU3 is logical high, or if it is in a low or undefined state. The three positive numbers at the end of the line are labels where the execution continues depending on the state of the OU3.

The next new statement is CALL. CALL means a special segment call meaning that after the execution of this segment the simulator will continue the execu-

```
                TESTSEQ
                SWS        ERROR
                SWV        KK(4)
                HWS        A=7
                           OU3=12
                CLOCK      100 NS
                MASTER     EXPERT
10    5+12      SET        A
                RESET      KK(3)
      6         TEST       OU3        12     13     12
12              RESET      A
                CALL       TEST20
                GOTO       15
13              SET        KK(3)
                CALL       TEST10
15    10-30     COMP       KK       1011     16     13
16    10        TEST       OU3        18     20     19
18              RESET      ERROR
                GOTO       20
19              SET        ERROR
20              STOP
                END
```

Figure 5 : Input stimuli sequence description

tion at the next statement. TEST20 is the name of the "subroutine". This is very similar to this master segment but it contains a RETURN statement where the execution returns to the calling segment. The GOTO statement is self-evident.

SET KK(3) means that the KK(3) software element is assigned the value 1. This means that this software variable (or array element) is a one bit binary flag.

The next new statement, COMP (Compare), checks whether this KK vector equals a given binary number. The two positive numbers - labels - at the end of the statement indicate where the simulator has to continue the execution for equal or different values, respectively. The time field of this statement indicates that the statement has to be executed 30 ns before the end of the 10th clock cycle.

The last statements STOP and END mean the logical and physical end of the segment, respectively.

By means of the language one can simply define an overall experimentation framework for the simulated model leaving the evaluation of results and the selection and conditional running of the appropriate segments for the simulator.

5. CONCLUSIONS

A simulation system (language + executive inner structure) has been developed that enables the model input sequences to be controlled by the results of the simulation, i.e. state of the model. The sequences of events and tests, are dynamically assembled from segments during the simulation run. This method is able to provide considerable help to the experimenter using the simulation tool.

6. REFERENCES

[1] Jávor, A., Proposals on the Structure of Simulation Systems, in Jávor, A. (ed.), Discrete Simulation and Related Fields (North-Holland, Amsterdam, 1982).

[2] Jávor, A., Révész, Á., Tóbiás, P., Simulation System with a Single Core and Several Outer Layers, in Jávor, A. (ed.), Discrete Simulation and Related Fields (North-Holland, Amsterdam, 1982).

[3] Gordon, G., System Simulation, (Prentice Hall Inc., Englewood Cliffs, New Jersey, 1969).

[4] LOBSTER User's Manual, (Central Research Institute for Physics, Budapest)

DISCRETE SIMULATION AND RELATED FIELDS
A. Jávor (editor)
North-Holland Publishing Company

FEATURES AND SYSTEM ARCHITECTURE OF THE MODEL BASE SYSTEM MBS

Dr. W. Klösgen, Dr. W. Schwarz

Institut für Planungs- und Entscheidungssysteme (IPES)
der Ges. für Mathematik und Datenverarbeitung (GMD)
D-5205 St. Augustin, Federal Republic of Germany

Construction and operation of planning models are still complicated and expensive in spite of some software packages existing in special areas like econometrics. In the Institute for Planning- and Decision-Systems (IPES) of the GMD the Model Base System MBS was developed for software support of socio-economic modelling. MBS today is used in some Federal Ministries of the FRG. This general purpose software-system offers a comfortable and comprehensive DP-environment for the imbedding of 'model-operators'. MBS covers general modelling functions like user-dialogue, data-management or like presentation, comparison and analysis of simulation results. The following sections describe application fields, features and architecture of the system.

1. APPLICATION FIELDS

MBS adresses to users from government and research, who want to analyse socio-economic real systems by modelling and simulation techniques. Typical application-examples of MBS include:

- demography
- social security
- labor market
- economic structure
- energy
- ecology
- technology assessment.

The following examples describe some tasks in modelling practice and research which can be supported by the system:

- construction of models
- linkage of models
- operation of models
- collection of models
- comparison of models
- research of the implementation process
- training
- methodical research.

MBS was developed for a type of models dominating in socio economic modelling with the following formal structure:

- the development of a real system in time is represented,
- the given time period is divided into a sequence of discrete, generally equal intervals,
- the still unknown (endogenous) variables are computed successively for each time step according to a specification (operator), which is not necessarily step-independent and
- the specification is of the form: $Y(t) = O(Y(t-1),.., Y(t-n),X(t),..,X(t-m),t)$; $Y(t-j)$ and $X(t-j)$ are the vectors of endogenous and exogenous variables for the step lagging j periods behind t.

This computation by an operator representing the core of the model characterises for example econometric-, System Dynamics- or cohort-models. Operator-represented models apply to whatever aggregation level and include also micro-analytic models analysing a total of individuals. Static models are treated in MBS as special (degenerate) dynamic operator-represented models.

Corresponding to this model-type is the data type known as time series. In MBS the numeric values associated to a sequence of equidistant time intervals can be disaggregated to a multi-dimensional matrix. A time-series holds the following attributes:

- name
- time range (first and last date)
- periodicity
- number of dimensions and maximum number of elements for each dimension
- missing data code
- level of aggregation
- presentation characteristics
- comment

2. FEATURES OF MBS

MBS supports the construction and linkage of models, the preparation, monitoring and analysing of simulation experiments as well as the management of the contents of a model-base. The features of MBS were structured in accordance with the working-phases within model construction and operation:

MBS		
modelling-functions	service-functions	central functions
preparation of (external) models	editing of models	guide to MBS-functions
preparation of (external) data	data-input/update	model base documentation
linkage	forms for user dialogue	help
simulation	reports	
analysis	graphics	

2.1 CONSTRUCTION OF SOCIO-ECONOMIC MODELS IN MBS

The following aspects characterize model construction in MBS:

- basic languages for the specification of the structural core of a model (operator) are FORTRAN as well as an own 'modelling language'. The latter is also used for model-linkage.
- the access to modelling techniques like System Dynamics or econometrics is offered. For instance the integration of models specified in DYNAMO or in an econometric system (MEBA(1), IAS(2)) is possible.
- model linkage enlarges the possibilities of special modelling techniques and permits the application of modular concepts.

2.1.1 Basic modelling languages in MBS

FORTRAN:

The 'programming language' by which a model-developer can specify the mathematical-logical structure of a model is one of the central points of a modelling-system.

Although some special modelling languages and model construction systems were developed, in modelling application area FORTRAN is the most frequent used language. Besides the generally wide dissemination of FORTRAN another reason are the constraints of specific simulation languages developed for limited applications, so that the language range of a general programming language often is needed.

However FORTRAN is applied by the MBS - user only for the specification of the structural core of models, that is the transformation of the input- into the output variables for one time step. This 'model-operator' is embedded into a MBS-environment covering those parts of a model not belonging to the structural core like user-dialogue, data management, runtime package, report generation or analyses of results.

To accomplish this embedding, the user has to define the data-interface for a 'model-operator'. This data interface includes the variables, by which the operator accepts and supplies data. The definition of the data interface has to be done in a structured commentary part preceding the operator code. The user has to specify for each interface variable especially its name, internal name in FORTRAN-code, type (Input/output), dimensions and lag. The following example describes data interface for a simple population (cohort) model-operator:

Description of the data interface of a FORTRAN-operator:

```
C OPERATOR: POPUL
CC Population operator calculating the
   population by 100 age and 2 sex
   groups for each year out of an ini-
   tial population
C PERIODICITY: 1
C INPUT: MORT (2,100)=M
CC Mortality rates depending on sex and
   age C SP(2)=SP
CC Sexualproportion
C FERT(50)=F
CC Fertility rates depending on age
C OUTPUT: POP(2,100)=POPNEW,POPOLD(T-1)
CC Population depending on sex and age
   for the current and last year (end
   of the year)
```

The specification of the structural core of the model reduces in this case to three equations representing the calculation of the population of the current year and the calculation of the births:

```
    DO 100 SEX=1,2
    DO 100 AGE=2,100
100 POPNEW(SEX,AGE)=POPOLD(SEX,AGE-1)
    *(1-M(SEX,AGE-1))
    BIRTHS=0
    DO 200 AGE=15,50
200 BIRTHS=BIRTHS+POPNEW(2,AGE)*F(AGE)
    DO 300 SEX=1,2
300 POPNEW(SEX,1)=BIRTHS*SP(SEX)
    RETURN
    END
```

For the linkage of model parts data-transformations are necessary as a rule. The MBS - linkage - language offers the corresponding tools for this purpose but allows also to specify simple models. This language can be characterized as a dynamic simulation language. The user has to specify the relations between the variables (in case with lags) for one time step only. The variables can also be multi-dimensional matrices. Nevertheless a general programming language (FORTRAN) is necessary, if special linguistic constructions are needed.

2.1.2 Integration of external models

MBS offers also an access to models developed in the econometric systems MEBA or IAS or in the simulation language DYNAMO. Model construction is done in the original systems. The accomplished models are integrated into MBS by special integration - procedures which adapt them to the MBS-concept of a simulation-operator with data interface. After this integration process (going on in background) these models can be used in MBS like models developed within MBS.

2.1.3 Development of econometric models

The development of an econometric model usually is done in econometric systems like MEBA or IAS (specification of equations, analysis of model-structure, estimation). On transfer of such a model to MBS the source code is stored in the central MBS-model-file and compiled to an (MBS-own) intermediate code. Further the data (for instance estimation coefficients) are stored in the MBS-database. On simulation of an econometric operator in MBS an econometric subprocessor schedules the solution of the equation system (Gauß-Seidel iteration method). This simulation is done very time-efficient because the intermediate code is transfered into a machine code during the initial phase of the simulation. Further special routines for the decomposition of the equation system into blocks and the 'optimal' arrangement of the equations within blocks bring about a very fast simulation of econometric models within MBS.

Within MBS only least-squares estimation methods are available to the user for econometric model development. If special estimation methods are needed this task has to be done in an external econometric system like MEBA or IAS.

2.1.4 Model linkage

The concept of an operator permits the mutual linkage of several operator represented models to a total model, being also represented by an operator. The linkage is defined by data exchanges between 'partial operators'. An exogenous variable of an operator O1 can be associated with an endogenous variable of an operator O2. Algebraic-logical operations are possible. However an interdependent linkage is not admitted on the operator level. But this does not exclude the specification of a single partial operator as an interdependent equation system. On the other side lagged mutual influences and feedbacks between operators can be specified.

In the following example a very simple linkage of the population model with a labor-market model is shown:

```
POPLAB=POPUL,LABOR
LABOR.POPALL=POPUL.POP
```

In the first equation the constituents (partial operators) of the linked model POPLAB are enumerated (POPUL and LABOR). The second equation is an example for the data-linkage between these two partial operators. The output-variable POP of the operator POPUL is associated to the input-variable POPALL of the operator LABOR.

These features of MBS allow in addition to conventional techniques the development of very complex models. A wide research and experimental area is touched exploring problems in connection with linkage of models of different methodologies.

2.2 OPERATION OF SOCIO-ECONOMIC MODELS IN MBS

Simulation and analyses of results are the dominating activities during model-operation. Moreover MBS offers some features for model-management and -information. MBS provides handling functions in a generally applicable and standardized form for all model-types and models. In addition to the considerable reduction of the programming effort for the model, this contributes to a standardized use of models.

2.2.1 Simulation

During simulation the MBS user is experimenting with models, introduced as 'elementary' or 'linkage operator' into the system. To this purpose he composes a special simulation run (the experimental frame) and controls its execution.

Data-assignment is the main task for composing the experimental frame. This is done in forms, which are presented to the user at the terminal. Forms for an individual model (linked model or partial model) can be defined by the user or can be offered self-acting by the system in accordance with the commentary description of variables stored in data bases connected to MBS. Arithmetic expressions are also admitted.

Default-assignments can be scheduled at form-definition time. The values of selected data-assignments can be shown at the terminal and can be altered. Moreover interpolation and extrapolation facilities are available.

Additional tasks are related to the definition of the report modalities. Among other things the output medium or the time-intervals for the output of results can be specified.

After defining the simulation experiment the user can start, interrupt, put forward and backward the simulation. On interrupting, the experimental conditions can be modified, whatever model variables (results) can be plotted, listed (terminal or printer), stored in data bases or analyzed by statistical methods (available in the MBS-method base) or by ad-hoc calculations specified in the MBS linkage language.

2.2.2 Analysis of results

Methods of mathematics and statistics are offered to analyse variables (which can be also simulation-results) stored in data-bases. If the analysis-subsystem is called during the simulationphase all the variables of the actual run are still available. In the current version of this subsystem elementary methods of descriptive statistics, of extrapolation and analysis of time-series and of validation are offered. This method-base can be extended by the user. Tools are available to integrate existing libraries.

A special dialogue interface is offered by the MBS-system for using these methods. Also the combination of methods and the linkage with presentation-moduls (reports or graphics) is possible.

2.2.3 Service-Functions

Service-functions exist for the management of the objects of the model base, for presentation of results and for user-information. Documentation of models is possible on different levels from a survey of existing models to the full details of a single input variable. Tools are offered for editing source codes of models, updating data, inserting model-operators and defining model specific forms for user dialogue. For the presentation of results a report- and a grafic-generator can be used. The layout of reports or graphics can be constructed, surveyed and modified in dialogue. Presentation operators specified in this way can be combined with methods and models. A help- and information system supports the user in system-handling.

3. SYSTEM ARCHITECTURE

Also on the level of the internal system-concept the special alignment to operator-represented models is dominating. This applies first of all to the simulation processor (with the functions of scheduling the simulation run, access and management of the codes to be executed of the partial operators, access to external data and management of all the data resulting during simulation) and the compiler of the linkage language.

Special interfaces of MBS are fit for models developed in external systems or for data from external data bases. Portability is supported by central interfaces to terminals and system-files.

3.1 MODEL-OPERATOR

A (model-)operator in MBS is represented by its source code, its internal code and an operator-header. On integrating an operator into the system, the internal code and operator-header are produced automatically from the source code.

The header contains informations about the input- and the output-variables, needed by the simulation processor, for model linkage and for documentation. These informations include the dimensions and the lag-structure of an interface-variable. Moreover there is fixed the original system of the operator (needed for selecting the run time environment, which handles the internal code). Restrictions for usage of the operator (for instance limits for simulation-time) are also included.

3.2 CENTRAL SIMULATION PROCESSOR

There are two phases for the activities of the simulation processor: the initial phase and the phase of scheduling the simulation run. In the initial phase the code for model linkage and the internal codes of all linked (partial)-operators are loaded, a data-area for the interface-variables is established, and the exogenous variables are loaded. For loading of the internal code the linkage-loader of the operating system is used for instance in case of operators specified in FORTRAN, otherwise the internal code (to be interpreted) is read into a core area dynamically requested.

On simulation-scheduling the processor has to activate the linked total operator at each time step and to associate those parts of the data-area which correspond to the actual time step under consideration of lags. If the core area is not large enough for the data area (large models or periods of simulation time) parts of the data area have to be stored temporary and loaded again on demand (for instance if simulation time is put backwards, or for postsimulation activities like presentation, analysis, storing of results).

3.3 INTERFACES TO EXTERNAL SOFTWARE-SYSTEMS

MBS has the intention to integrate models developed in external construction systems. For that purpose there exists an interface by which a system administrator can add (for each additional external system) components for integrating models (source and internal code, operator-header), for providing the special run time environment (loading the internal code and the adapted run time package) and for data transfer between special run time package and central data area.

Furthermore interfaces to method libraries and to data base systems are available.

3.4 DATA-MANAGEMENT

MBS supports the access to all external data being structured as time-series (scalar or matrix-values) by a general data base interface. For each specific data base organisation a special interface has to be implemented, which is called by the general interface of MBS. The special interface must offer the following two entries:

- transfer (read/write) of the descriptive part
- transfer of the values for a specified time period (in case of matrices regarding the usual arrangement of elements in FORTRAN).

In the general interface all the other functions are realised like:

- consistency checks and error messages
- extracting of parts of matrices
- establishing of internal control blocks.

The actual version of MBS offers special interfaces to an own data base system, to a data organisation realised in the index sequential access technique of the operating system and to the data organisation of an econometric system.

4. AVAILABILITY, EXTENSIONS AND EXPERIENCES

MBS is running on SIEMENS-computers under the operating system BS 2000. The system can be used on the GMD-computers by teleprocessing. Also external installations are possible. There was paid attention at system development to a potential transfer of MBS to IBM-computers. Because of central routines for the access to terminals, to system files, to dynamic loading components and because of the use of FORTRAN as main-development language an IBM-version can be implemented with comparatively low effort and is available in the near future.

4.1 EXTENSIONS

The maintenance of MBS and the assistance of its external users is done in the GMD-project SOFMOD. SOFMOD is executed within the GMD-program "planning models", which is scheduled for the period 1980 - 1984. This program has the overall aim to increase the qualified application of planning models for public administration. The software- and data-aspects of the program are treated in SOFMOD. In this project an integrated software-pool is implemented, gathering the tools needed for socio-economic modelling such as a model operation system (MBS), special econometric software, a method base of mathematical and statistical methods, or some data analyses packages (survey data). The subsystems of this pool are implementable at distinct places and can be connected with each other and to socio-economic data services in a computer network system. In this way an increased communication and cooperation of the institutions dealing with socio-economic planning (data-distributors, model-developers, model-users) shall be aspired.

4.2 EXPERIENCES

The experiences with the use of MBS result from several applications both in the administration and in some research institutions. Three mainpoints of activities are noticable:

- Ad hoc data analysis,
- Software production system for the development and maintenance of complex disaggregated models,
- Methodical research.

4.2.1 Ad hoc data analysis

This elementary application-area is dominating when decision-preparations are supported by quantitative planning methods. The following tasks determine the pattern of these applications:

- Data assembly,
- Data transformation,
- Application of mathematical and statistical methods,
- Presentation of results.

The GMD has installed a computer network-system to the computer of the Federal Statistical Office, to offer a fast and direct access to socio-economic data bases. The users of the GMD-computers (most governmental offices and ministries have terminal-access to the GMD-computers) facultatively can switch on the Statistical Information System (STATIS) of the Federal Statistical Office from their terminal. Moreover they can transfer directly selected data to the GMD computer and insert these data into the data bases of the modelling software inventory. Often ad hoc situations are predominant where data needs and analysis methods cannot be predefined or anticipated, and where answers are required in short time.

The following features of MBS support these situations:

- Fast and direct access to external socio-economic data bases,
- Ad hoc calculations on data by a time series- and matrix-oriented language,
- Flexible selecting and combining of methods out of a method base of mathematial/statistical methods,
- Easy possibilities of modification of methods.
- Ad hoc result-presentation facilities (reports, graphics).

Most of these tasks can be specified in the MBS-command- and time series-manipulation language in a way that many problems can be supported in dialogue.

4.2.2 Software production system

The second application area relates to complex disaggregated models which have to be developed, maintained and updated over a long period of time by various user groups.

These models mostly are written in FORTRAN; because of disaggregated data (voluminous matrices) the use of econometric systems for instance is not possible. The models can be divided into several partial models, which can be used separately, but which can also be combined in a flexible manner to different model versions.

They use extensive input-data (time dependent matrices), which have to be easily modified for alternative calculations. Examples are models in the area of social security or micro-analytic models in the area of tax or transfer laws. The modularity of the model-implementation is especially neccessary in order that varying users are able to adapt the model to changes in the specifications of laws.

The required modularity is realized in MBS by the linkage-concept. The model is separated into parts which can be combined by the MBS-linkage language in a flexible way to various model-versions.

Especially important for the test of new model versions is the possibility to run the partial models individually. MBS generates automatically a user interface to a partial-model.

The advantages (compared with a conventional implementation of complex models) turned out in a reduction of programming effort both for development and for modification of models. Furthermore also the computer time needed to run a simulation was reduced. The latter surprising result is attributed to the evident structuring of models: The user who implements models in MBS doesn't need to bother about general tasks like data management, simulation scheduling or user dialogue. This brings about another advantage, because the interfaces to the operating system and to hardware components (especially terminals) are centrally concentrated in MBS.

4.2.3 Methodical Research

Another application area relates to methodical and research oriented tasks. Examples are formal analyses of the structure of models (for instance dependencies between variables), the combination of models with optimizing algorithms, or the evaluation and comparison of methods available in subroutine-packages (for instance methods for time series analyses). These tasks can be easily realized in MBS because of its interface to external systems (transfer of models and methods) and because of the possibility to link models with special analyses-packages.

The experiences with the use of MBS show, that a broad application area in the sector of socio-economic modelling and data-analysing can be supported by MBS both in modelling-practice and research.

LITERATURE:

(1) Bundesminister für Wirtschaft (ed.): Ökonometrische Methodenbank, BMWi-Studien-Reihe 22, Bonn 1978

(2) Lösch, M., MEBA-Benutzerhandbuch, MEBA-Bericht 35, Institut für Angewandte Wirtschaftsforschung (IAW), Tübingen (FRG), 1980

(3) Plasser, K., IAS-Benutzerhandbuch, IAS-Level 2.7, Institute for Advanced Studies, Wien 1976

For further information about MBS:

(4) GMD: List of papers and publications of the MBS-project. (Especially an user-manual for MBS is available).

For further information about method- and model base systems:

(5) Böhling, K.H., Spies, P.P. (ed.), GI-9. Jahrestagung - Fachgespräch 'Methoden- und Modellbanksysteme' (Springer Verlag, Informatik Fachbericht Bd. 19, Berlin, Heidelberg, New York 1979)

DISCRETE SIMULATION AND RELATED FIELDS
A. Jávor (editor)
North-Holland Publishing Company

COMPLEX SYSTEMS MODELLING AND ANALYSIS: A METHODOLOGY AND A SOFTWARE SYSTEM

Z. Strezova

Scientific Center
for Management Information Systems
Sofia, Bulgaria

The design of complex, large scale systems requires the use of new tools for systems investigation. This paper presents a methodology for system modelling, simulation and analysis based on the concept of generating and successive evaluation of alternatives. A modular software system (FIMOS) developed for support to the design of management systems with decentralized structure is described and its application is discussed.

1. INTRODUCTION

In the design of complex, large scale systems two important questions arise. The first is that of choice of a method for modelling and analysis of the complex system. The second question concerns the procedures of validation of the modelling process. When the system engineering approach to problems concerning large scale systems treating is applied, three fundamental stages may be distinguished: (a) problem formulation; (b) problem analysis; (c) interpretation of the analysis results. These general stages have been defined in the works of R. Ackoff and interpreted by a number of authors in the system area (see, e.g., Van Gigch (1974), Sage and Thissen (1980)). Considered in some detail the first stage comprises, along with the problem formulation, also defining and structuring of objectives and formulation of alternative solutions. The second stage provides assessment (forecasting) of the impact of alternatives and the refinement of the alternatives. The third stage comprises evaluation, comparison and selection of alternatives and planning for implementation. Thus, the wide-spread approach to complex problem investigation, the system engineering approach, leads to, generally speaking, generating and evaluation of alternatives (policies formulation, decisions making, structures design, etc.).

In large scale systems design the solving of the problems mentioned above is difficult as a rule for lack of comprehensive and acceptable methods and tools for handling such kind of systems. In this paper is outlined a methodology for modelling and analysis of a class of complex systems based on the concept of generating and successive evaluation of alternatives. Taking into account some features of the complex systems under consideration this methodology leads to selection of a set of feasible system structures. A modular software system (FIMOS) developed for modelling and analysis of management systems with decentralized structure is described and its application is discussed.

2. SOME FEATURES OF COMPLEX SYSTEMS DESIGN

A large number of complex systems existing in the real world as power systems, economic and management systems, air and urban traffic control systems, computer communication networks, etc. can be qualified as decentralized large scale systems. They are characterized by decentralized information, decentralized decision making, distributed computations. Usually the research in such systems and their design are concerned with a number of difficulties.

From a point of view of the control theory the problem of a system optimal functioning, and that of a large scale system, too, is a result of a solution of the system structure design problem. The latter can be treated by methods and techniques for handling large scale systems as the methods of large scale linear and nonlinear programming, the techniques of decomposition and aggregation, the methods of the hierarchical and multilevel systems theory, and other tools of the modern control theory. But almost all of them represent centralized design methodologies. The decentralized large scale systems are considered usually as "soft" systems, with ill-defined structure and functioning. To handle such systems one needs tools since the known ones are not applicable. For the present a theory of large scale systems with decentralized structure is lacking but a policy concerning these systems has been outlined by a number of authors and this is the policy of approximations: approximate methods for system structure synthesis instead of exact methods, approximate criteria, an architecture of interacted models instead of explicit models of alternative structures, etc. An approximate approach to decentralized large scale systems design requires the use of a method for system modelling and analysis leading to selection of a set of feasible, suboptimal alternatives (system structures).

3. VALIDATION OF A COMPLEX SYSTEM MODELLING

The term validation appears to refer to activities designed to determine how a model performs. In particular, validity refers to the degree of "fit" between the model and the reality. Some activities as evaluation, verification, model analysis, assessment, certification, are closely related to the validation. Following Ansoff and Hayes (1973) the process of problem-solving (a system design in our case) requires two, non-independent, transformations to be made: T_1, the transformation of the real world problem into an abstract model M_1 (or a set of models), and T_2, the transformation (or a set of transformations) which will be used to perform any analysis on the model. T_2 might be a computer simulation or another technique used for model analysis. Besides the validation of T_1 also this one of T_2 must be investigated.

In well-structured problems the process of validation is relatively easier; there are procedures which assure that not only valid but optimal use is being made of the model M_1. In ill-structured problems as the problems of decentralized large scale systems design, the difficulties associated with the model validation are significantly greater. In such cases the application of known validation procedures leads to unsatisfying results. A combined use of statistical techniques, simulations and heuristic aiming at evaluation of alternatives, comparisons, further assessment and selection of feasible alternatives seems to be a promising approach to model validation in the case of complex systems design. Such a manner is very close to the approximate approach to decentralized large scale systems design stressed in the previous section.

4. A METHODOLOGY FOR MODELLING AND ANALYSIS OF COMPLEX SYSTEMS

Having in mind the considerations mentioned above, in Figure 1 are shown the stages of the general algorithm which can be performed in support of the design of a complex system. These stages comprise the activities of modelling and analysis of system structures.

The first stage (stage A) represents the process of choice of transformations T_1 effected on the real system structure and functioning to produce an abstract model M_1 and the construction of the very model. These activities depend on the particular case having to be treated. Two important points might be stressed here. Firstly, there is not an appropriate procedure ensuring that T_1 is valid, i.e. that M_1 is the best representation of the real world. The adequacy of M_1 depends strongly on the skill and the knowledge of the modeller. Secondly, and non-independently of the first point: as far as the real problem in question, a complex system design, is usually an ill-structured problem which arises in an ill-defined environment, a set of models M_1 must be designed (instead of one model) with various sets of input variables and system parameters. This means several T_1 to be chosen.

In a result of the first stage of the general algorithm for system modelling and analysis *a set of possible system structures* {PSS} are modelled, i.e. a set of alternatives that will be next evaluated, is generated.

The second stage represents a process of evaluation of the consequences of each alternative and a selection of a smaller set of system structures.

The evaluation of variants of systems and the comparison of alternatives have been studied by a number of authors with emphasis on the development of statistical techniques and procedures for analysis of simulations outputs (Naylor (1969, 1971), Kleijnen (1974), Law (1980)). The evaluation of alternatives is related to measuring the outputs of each alternative. But the identification of outputs of interest is one of the most difficult and critical aspects of the system investigation process, particularly when dealing with the outputs of "soft" systems. Another problem is the basis on which alternatives can be compared. An integrating step in the process of alternatives evaluation is to find *a decision model* that embodies a procedure helping the analyst to make

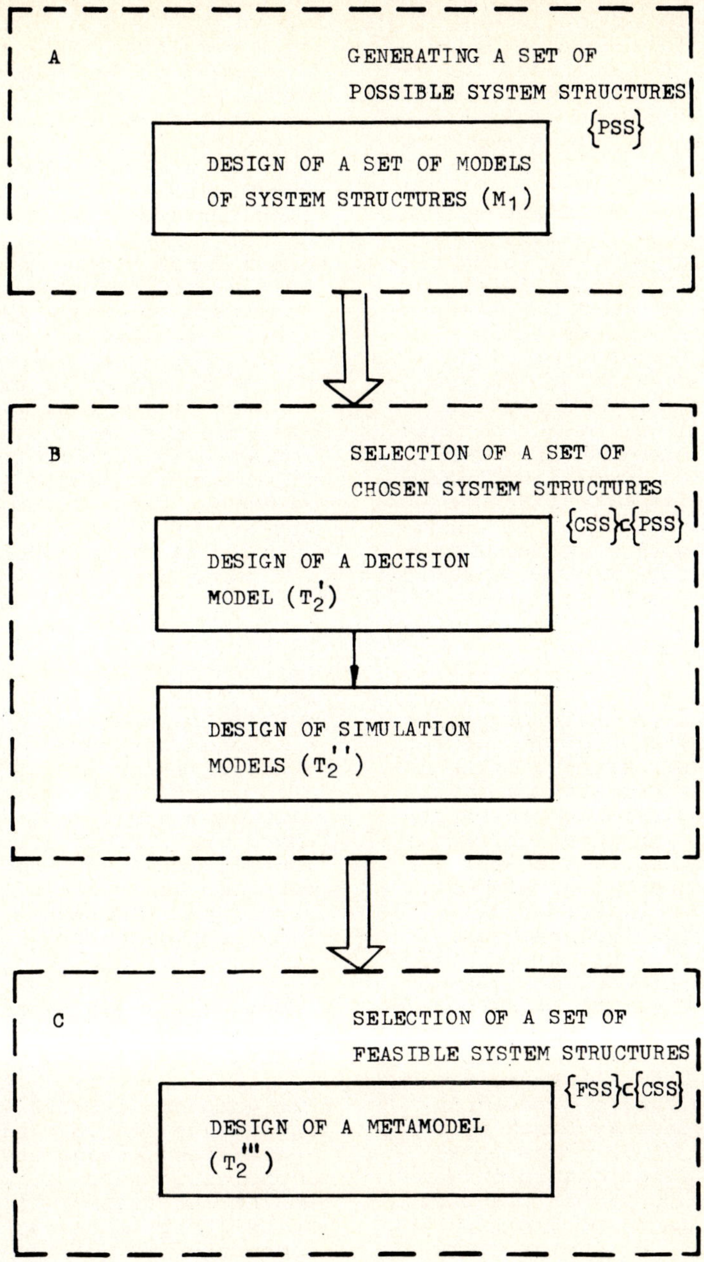

Figure 1 : Stages of the Process of System Modelling and Analysis

choices among possible alternatives. The decision model describes the inputs of the modelled situations which will be next simulated, and the measures for evaluating them. The design of a decision model is the first step of the transformation T_2 to perform an analysis of the possible alternatives.

The second substage of the stage B (Figure 1) is the design of a simulation model (transformation T_2'') by which all of the alternatives described in the terms of the decision model will be simulated. Since simulation can be an expensive technique, a design of simulation experiments that consists in specifying the conditions under which the simulation model will be executed, must be performed. Using the measures supposed in the decision model (input-output relations, permissible values of outputs, etc.) an analysis of all simulated alternatines will be made. Thus, the second step of the transformation T_2 is performed. As a result, *a set of chosen system structures* {CSS}, {CSS} $\subset$ {PSS}, will be selected.

The following stage (stage C) of the system modelling and analysis represents further assessment and selection of the chosen alternative structures. These activities require a sensitivity analysis of the simulation outputs and interpretation of the simulation results. Widely discussed in the relevant literature, these problems have been treated mostly in the terms of the statistical decisions theory. Numerous techniques and procedures have been proposed and some good practical results have been obtained. When a large amount of output data must be investigated an appropriate model for analysis of the simulated alternatives must be used. A promising tool seems to be so-called *metamodel*, discussed in this sense by Blanning (1975) and Kleijnen (1977). The metamodel "models" the relationship between the inputs and outputs of the simulation model. Its purpose is to perform a sensitivity analysis after a prior evaluation of simulated alternatives has been already made, i.e. the metamodel performs further, more precise assessment of the chosen alternatives. As inputs a metamodel uses some of the input and output variables described by the decision model and used through the simulations. An important task in constructing a metamodel is the choice of these variables and the selection of combinations of variables and simulation runs. As a metamodel a linear regression model could be used (proposed by Kleijnen (1977)) and it seems this is a good option.

In a result of the sensitivity analysis performed by the metamodel on the set of simulated alternatives, a final set of feasible alternatives, *a set of feasible system structures* {FSS}, {FSS} $\subset$ {CSS} will be selected. Each one of these structures is a "candidate" to be designed since all of them satisfy a number of formal criterea chosen a priori. But a final choice of a system structure belongs to the decision-maker and is subjected to a range of additional nonformal criterea.

Thus, the modelling and analysis of a complex system aiming at a choice of a feasible system structure can be performed according to the general algorithm outlined briefly above. This algorithm has been applied to the design of a class of decentralized large scale systems as shown below.

5. FIMOS: A MODULAR SOFTWARE SYSTEM FOR MODELLING AND ANALYSIS

In this section is described the FIve MOdular System (FIMOS) which has been developed as a tool assisting the design of large management systems with decentralized structure (DMS). More considerations about the structure and the functioning of this class of complex systems could be found in (Strezova (1979, 1981)). The algorithm on which FIMOS is constructed is shown in Figure 2. The algorithm is based on the general methodology described in the previous section. In the figure are shown in some detail the successive activities required by the algorithm and the intermediate and final results (in double-line blocks).

The purpose of FIMOS is modelling and successive analysis of structures of decentralized management systems aiming at a choice of feasible DMS structures. A DMS includes a set of decision-making units (this is the so-called decision structure (DS) of the management system) and a set of computer resources (the computer structure (CS) of the management system). As is shown in Figure 2 through the first stage of the modelling and analysis process a set of possible DMS structures can be modelled. This is performed applying successively discriminant analysis and optimal allocation modelling. To the purpose, the first module of FIMOS, Decision Structures Modelling, includes a discriminant analysis program package; the second module, Optimal Allocation Modelling, includes an integer linear programming package.

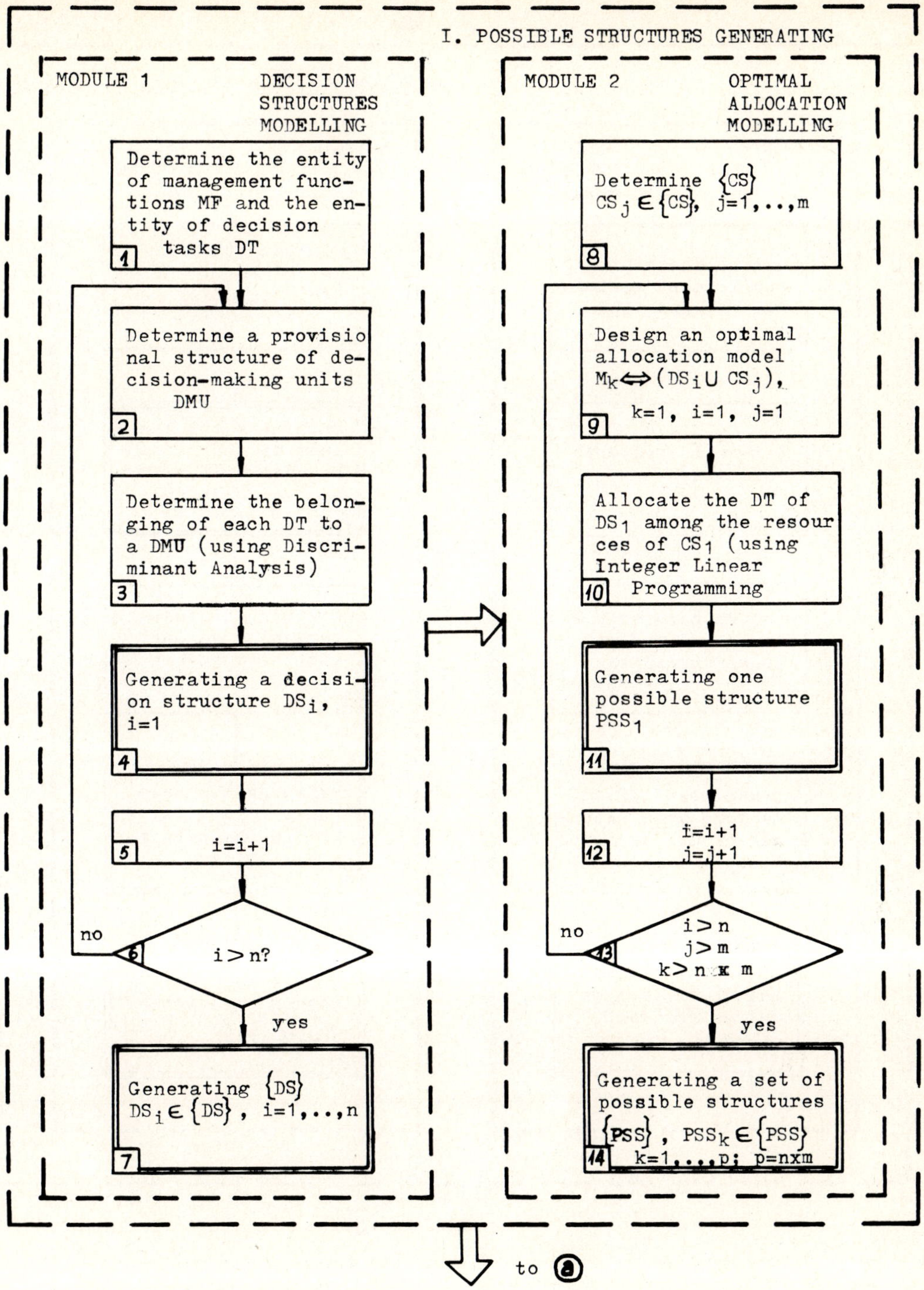

Figure 2 : Algorithm of FIMOS Functioning

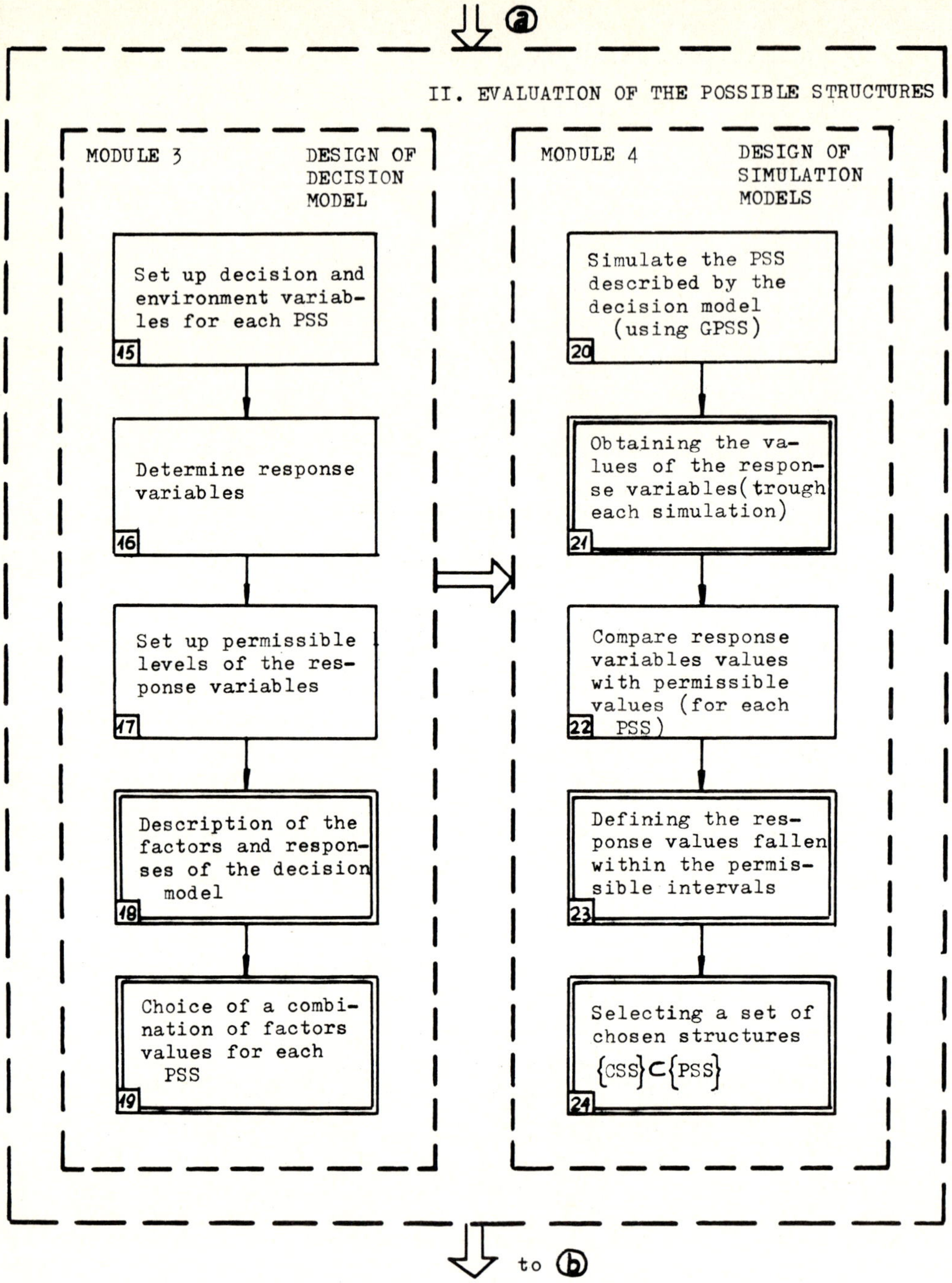

Figure 2 : Algorithm of FIMOS Functioning (cont.)

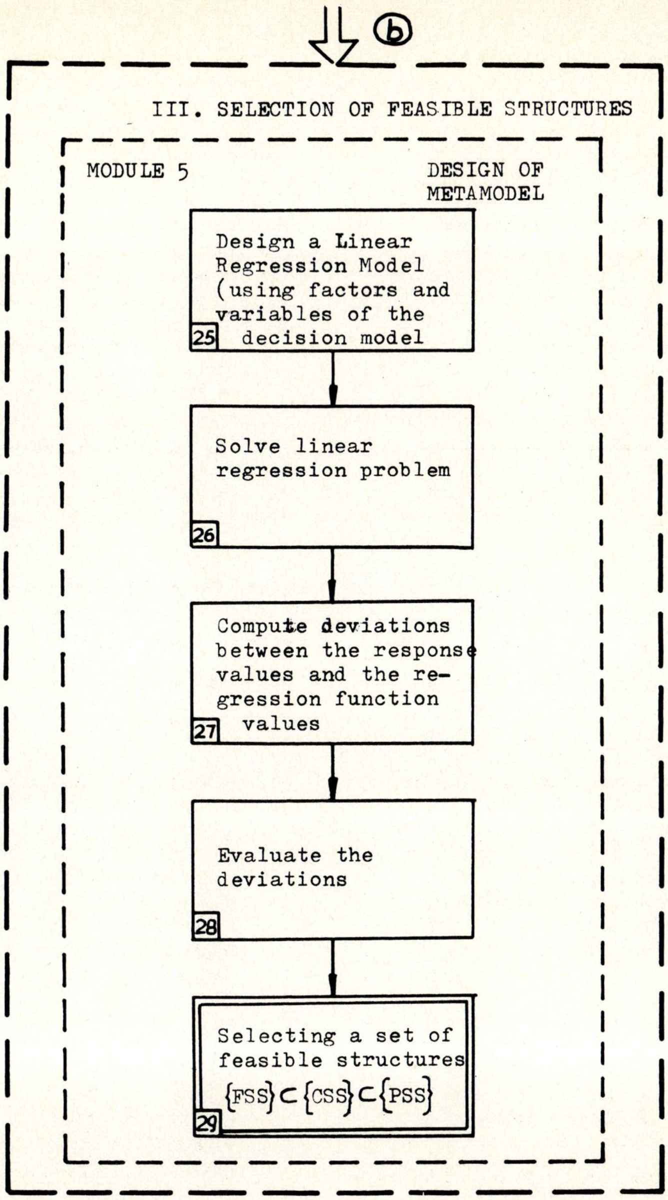

Figure 2 : Algorithm of FIMOS Functioning (cont.)

The second stage of the modelling and analysis process, Evaluation of Possible Structures, is performed by the third and fourth modules of FIMOS. The steps performed by the third module, Design of Decision Model, are described in the terms of Naylor's methodology. The fourth module of FIMOS, Design of Simulation Models, is intended for simulation of the modelled DMS structures functioning and for analysis of the simulation results under the conditions of the decision model. The fourth module includes a GPSS package as a tool for simulation, and also procedures for postsimulation analysis.

The third stage of the system modelling and analysis, Selection of Feasible Structures, is performed by the fifth module of FIMOS, Design of Metamodel. This module includes linear regression program package and procedures for analysis of the metamodel results.

FIMOS is developed on the basis of standard program packages and includes a number of particular programs and a range of non-automated procedures. In some sense FIMOS can be considered as a man-computer system supporting the design of decentralized management systems. The full implementation of FIMOS to a real DMS design is under way. All of the modules of the system have been used successfully in solving a number of real-world problems concerning DMS structures and functioning (Strezova (1977, 1979), Strezova and al. (1978)).

6. CONCLUSION

Usually the main difficulties in complex system modelling and simulation are concerned with: (a) the design of valid models (and estimation of model validity); (b) the choice of procedures for sensitivity analysis and for simulation results analysis, and (c) the development of procedures for comparison and selection of alternatives. In spite of the large number of techniques and tools that have been developed in the 70's the difficulties remain. One reason is that such tools are usually designed for particular cases and their implementation to the overall process of system modelling and analysis is unsatisfying. The methodology described in this paper proposes some advantages. Firstly, the successive ecaluation of alternatives ensures a better choice of the final set of feasible alternatives, without using a complex selection procedure. Secondly, an original modelling of a set of structures and a further simulation of the functioning of these structures makes the model validation easier than in a case of only one modelling cycle. The simulation process here is actually experimentation with models. Thirdly, the decision model facilitates to a great extent the design of simulation experiments including the choice of combinations of factors to be investigated, the number of simulation runs, etc.

In its present version FIMOS includes, along with an efficient library of computer programs, a number of non-automated procedures. When applied to the design of a decentralized management system this version is appropriate enough. An implementation to a larger class of problems requires development of additional tools as, e.g., procedures for automated generation of sensitivity model, procedures for generation of metamodel, etc. Some trends in the design of advanced tools for support to the modelling and simulation process have been already outlined (see, e.g. Zeigler (1980)). Clearly the problems of complex systems modelling and analysis will continue to be a challenge for research in this decade.

7. REFERENCES

[1] Ansoff, H.I. and Hayes, R.L., Role of models in corporate decision making, in: Ross, M. (ed.). Operational Research'72 (North-Holland, Amsterdam, 1973).

[2] Blanning, R.W., The construction and implementation of metamodels, Simulation, June, 1975, 177-184.

[3] Kleijnen, J.P.C., Statistical Techniques in Simulation (M. Dekker, N. Y., 1974/75).

[4] Kleijnen, J.P.C., Design and analysis of simulation: practical statistical techniques, Simulation, March, 1977, 81-90.

[5] Law, A.M., A tutorial on statistical analysis of simulation output data, in: Ören, T.I., Shub, C.M. and Roth, P.F. (eds.), 1980 Winter Simulation Conference, Orlando, Florida.

[6] Naylor, T.H. (ed.), The Design of Computer Simulation Experiments (Duke Univ. Press, 1969).

[7] Naylor, T.H., Computer Simulation Experiments with Models of Economic Systems (Wiley, 1971).

[8] Sage, A.P. and Thissen, W.A.H., Methodologies for systems simulation,

in: Ören, T.I., Shub, C.M. and Roth, P.F. (eds.), Simulation with Discrete Models: A State-of-the-Art View (University of Ottawa, Ottawa, 1980).

[9] Strezova, Z., A man-computer analysis of a class of discrete systems, IFAC Workshop on Computer Application in Discrete Manufacturing, Prague, Sept., 1977.

[10] Strezova, Z. and al., Modelling of chemical branch management system, 1st International School-Conference on Control of Large Chemical Systems, Varna, Oct., 1978.

[11] Strezova, Z., Control problems in management systems, in: Proceedings of the VIIth IFAC Congress, vol.2 (Pergamon Press, 1979).

[12] Strezova, Z., A method and model for analysis of the system "management tasks - computer resources" in an industrial branch, in: Yearbook of the Scientific Center for ESSI, 2, 1979 (in Bulg.).

[13] Strezova, Z., An approximate approach to the design of decentralized management systems structures, in: Preprints of the VIIIth IFAC Congress, vol.XXI, Kyoto, 1981.

[14] Van Gigch, J.P., Applied General Systems Theory (Harper and Row, Publ., N.Y., 1974).

[15] Zeigler, B.P., Concept and software for advanced simulation methodologies, in: Ören, T.I., Shub, C.M. and Roth, P.F. (eds.), Simulation with Discrete Models: A State-of-the-Art View (University of Ottawa, Ottawa, 1980).

DISCRETE SIMULATION AND RELATED FIELDS
A. Jávor (editor)
North-Holland Publishing Company

S I M K O M
A SYSTEM OF SIMULATION SYSTEMS ALSO FOR COMBINED MODELS

Gunter Schwarze
Humboldt-Universität zu Berlin
Sektion Mathematik
Berlin, German Democratic Republic

A short survey of the modeling and simulation software developed and used in recent years in the GDR is given, together with a short global view of combined simulation systems using FORTRAN or SIMULA 67. Conditions for the project SIMKOM ar given as are details of a system of simulation systems including the attributes of the first experimental versions SIMKOM-F/80 and SIMKOM-S/80 being a further development of base simulation software like GASP IV, CADSIM, COMBINEDSIMULATION; GPSS, GPSS-PRAGUE, SIMDIS; CSMP, SPAS, BORIS, DIGSIM, DS 4000.

1. INTRODUCTION

Discrete and related fields invite reports on new results and conceptions referring to the development and use of software assisting modeling, simulation and experimentation. At present there exist new developments of discrete modeling and simulation systems in the GDR. At this point it may be appropriate to mention:

PS SIMDIS	ESER	/1/
SDS	BESM 6	/2/
DDSS	KRS 4200, PRS 4000	/3/
TOMAS	KRS	/4/
SIMULA 67	BESM 6	/5/
SIMDIT	BESM 6	/6/

But also new recommendations for special fields of application-oriented discrete modeling and simulation systems have been presented by Frank /7/ and a comparison of software belonging to the GPSS-family has been conducted by Lorenz /8/. All these results belong to classically discrete models. Furthermore related fields may be interpreted also in the sense of an extension of the model class. In this sense the so-called combined models are an extension of this discrete models, see Gerhardt /9/. Some years ago we started the development of combined simulation and modeling systems with the aim of simulating several types of combined mathematical models. See also Schwarze /10/. According to the interest of the users in detailed analysing we took FORTRAN on the one hand and on the other hand SIMULA. So we just produce the versions

SIMKOM-F/80 using ESER - OS-FORTRAN-compiler

SIMKOM-S/80 using BESM 6 - SIMULA 67-compiler

with a model philosophy being not at all indentical. This paper gives a description of the SIMKOM-development.

2. EXPERIENCE BY USE OF COMPUTERS AS A SIMULATOR FOR DISCRETE OR CONTINUOUS MODELS

Combined mathematical models tolerate discrete or continuous models or a connection of both. That is why we used our experience with continuous or discrete digital simulation systems and analog computers for the development of SIMKOM. To this domain belongs also the digital simulation of analog computer programs. A survey of this development in the GDR is given in /11/. We analysed the use of computers including simulation software needed for research work on the one hand and in high school education on the other hand. The results and conclusions were presented and discussed at several international and national symposia (see /12-26/). Hence follow some assertions referring to model description, model modification and experimentation with the model, production of model output and computations with produced model data during as well as after running the model. At this place we give a listing of continuous digital simulation systems used before and during the SIMKOM development:

BORIS-series	FORTRAN	ESER BESM 6	/27,28/
DIGSIM	FORTRAN	ESER	/27,29/
SPAS	PL/1	ESER	/27,30/
DS 4000	FORTRAN	R 4000	/27,31/

Moreover we studied or used further continuous systems like CSMP /32/, MIMIC /33/, PROHYS /34/. The mentioned analog computers were UNIMAR, ENDIM /35/, MEDA-series /36/. Now we use the hybrid analog computer ADT 3000 /37/. It is also our aim to use SIMKOM in order to simulate typical programs belonging to this computer-series. Listed discrete simulation systems have been mentioned in the introduction and we add only GPSS /38/, GPSS-PRAGUE /39/ and GPSS-FORTRAN /40/. Together with these tasks and the corresponding study of literature, the different use made of the terms modeling, simulation and simulator during the last few years has been analysed. Considering these results, a more exact definition of the term simulation and terms closely connected with it has been formulated. Furthermore the individual stages of abstraction on the way from the original to the establishment of a computing model in simulation are closely considered and the implementation of simulation experiments is considered too. In addition to it Gerhardt developed kombi-nets. These are essential extensions of petri-nets using a new time base and describing dynamical combined models. These basic ideas have been described in the papers /41,42,43,44/. They exert an influence on the model class and model description within the SIMKOM-project.

3. COMBINEDSIMULATION SYSTEMS

Ören /45/ and Kindler /46/ described or listed several important developments of combined simulation systems. But most of them have not been implemented for several computers or used for many simulation projects. Up till today FORTRAN and SIMULA 67 have been the most-used basic languages for the development of simulation languages in this case. The result of the inquiries we made shows the FORTRAN based GASP IV version /47/ as a widely implemented and used combined system. Tarlos presented his FORTRAN based combined simulation system FOCUS /48/. We studied before and during our further development both systems. Cellier developed GASP V and COSY /49/ simultaneous up to SIMKOM-F. Several SIMULA-classes (subclasses of the class SIMULATION) representing combined simulation systems have been developed since 1975:

1975	CADSIM	England	/50/
1977	CADSIM-JOHNSEN	Norway	/51/
1977	CADSIM-J class GPSS	Norway	/51/

1978 COMBINEDSIMULATION Denmark /52/
1980 BOSCOS Czechoslovakai /53/

For the first time Johnsen demonstrated the development and use of a system of discrete and combined simulation systems. Members of this system are the external classes
SIMULATION class GPSS
SIMULATION class CADSIM-J
CADSIM-J class GPSS
SIMULATION class SIMON-75.

We studied before and during our further development the CADSIM-series and COMBINEDSIMULATION. These results influenced also the SIMKOM-project.

4. THE SIMKOM-PROJECT

The utilization of the results put together and pointed out by publications in the sections above led to the following conditions for a further development of combined modeling and simulation systems or a collection of software concerning combined models too.
We have to take into account several types of submodels, including several kinds of model description like

- continuous submodels
  - partial differential equations
  - ordinary differential equations
  - equations without derivatives
  - difference equations
  - block-oriented description
  - time-delay
- discrete submodels
  - event-oriented description
  - process-oriented description
  - components for queueing models
  - block-oriented description
- combined submodels composed of
  - continuous components
  - discrete components
  - hybrid components (with discrete and continuous changes of states)

It is desirable

- to compute submodels in a quasiparallel way,
- to generate and terminate submodels during a run,
- to exchange algorithms also during a run,
- to separate collection, evaluation and reporting of model data (like the actions of data processing plants in industrial processes),
- to unify the different types of reports used up till today in discrete or continuous simulation systems (post run and post case reports),
- to assist the experiments with models; for instance
  options for
  - optimization
  - stability analysis
  - sensitivity analysis
- to assist the validation of models,
- to produce useroriented software in an effective way and simulation programs with practicable runtime.

These are general conditions for our SIMKOM-project. Furthermore the SIMKOM software has to be a basis for the production of special simulation software. This is the background as to why we take only the compiler of the basic language used for the development of SIMKOM. The use of a precompiler may be reserved - if indispensable or desired - for the production of special simulation software (next step).
Now we are working on two versions, SIMKOM-F/80 with FORTRAN parallel to SIMKOM-S/80 with SIMULA 67. During the development there are several exchange effects. Quasiparallel model computation and the generation and termination of submodels during a run was easily realized in SIMKOM-S/80. But now we have developed this for continuous submodels in SIMKOM-F/80 too. We tested the SIMKOM software using standard examples

described in /47,50,52/ but also models running on the hybrid analog computer ADT 3000 /55/.

5. ATTRIBUTES OF SIMKOM-F/80

Continuous submodels:
equation-oriented description,
explicit ordinary differential equations without derivatives, difference equations, times-delay.
Discrete submodels:
event-oriented description,
queueing models may be assisted by special components.
Seperate collection, evaluation and reporting of model data and unified reports helpful to the user.
Offers of several integration methods and methods for step size control and the users own algorithm may be introduced. Exchange of methods or submodels also during a run.
Automatic specification of the simulation control depending on the type of the model.
Now we take first steps for the use of general hybrid analog computer programs and special partial differential equations.

6. ATTRIBUTES OF SIMKOM-S/80

The following text is in accordance with the description in /56/.
SIMKOM-S/80 is a hierarchical system of SIMULA classes which are based on the standard class SIMULATION.

SIMULATION --→ BLOSIM --→ BHYBRID
SIMULATION --→ EQUSIM --→ EHYBRID

The subclasses BLOSIM and EQUSIM do already permit the description of discrete, continuous and hybrid processes and their interactions. Objects of a subclass of PROCESS whose local variables are only changed in a time-discrete manner and whose actions also change variables in this form are called 'discrete processes' in SIMKOM-S/80. Contrarily objects of a subclass of PROCESS are marked as 'continuous processes' if their actions only alter variables in a time-continuous manner (described by ordinary differential equations). If the local variables of objects of PROCESS subclasses are changed in a discrete and continuous manner (simultaneously or in sequence) by overlaying of at least one discrete and one continuous process, these objects are called 'hybrid processes'.

In BLOSIM the description of continuous altering of variables is possible in a blockoriented and in EQUSIM in an equationoriented form.

To support the modeling of discrete and hybrid processes BHYBRID and EHYBRID offer further possibilities which are influenced by GPSS components like transaction, queue, facility, capacity. SIMKOM-S/80 permits the extension of these components to such possessing continuous variables, too.

The fundamental features of SIMKOM-S/80 are based on

- separation of the simulation system, integration methods, plotprograms and experiment control programs into single parts, which are implemented as external classes.
- data collection in external files
- possibilities of exchange of submodels and numerical methods in runtime
- structured development of submodels (complex blocks), which may be stored as external classes in user libraries.

SIMKOM-S/80 offers the following numerical integration methods:
- Euler (1th order)

- Runge-Kutta-Merson (4th order)
- Grag-Burlirsch-Stoer (automatical order control)
- Gear (1st order with a modified Newton iteration method for solving stiff differential equations)

All methods possess their own control strategy in altering the integration stepsize. Each continuous process may be connected with an integration method by the user in runtime. That is why it is possible to solve any differential equation systems in the form of initial value problems with various numerical methods simultaneously (i.e. quasiparallel by various continuous processes). Furthermore the continuous processes may exchange the differential equations which have to be solved. A coupling of differential equation systems, too, is possible in any continuous process. Special features are offered by the class BLOSIM:

- The continuous processes operate over blocks, which are inserted in special local lists in runtime.
- There are elementary blocks (summator, integrator, delays, etc.) and complex blocks (nonlinear differential equation systems)
- Complex and elementary blocks may be connected over input and output variables (references).
- By each altering of the block structure of a continuous process, this process will sort its blocks into a computable order before it continues the work. (algebraical loops will be taken into account)
- The transmission of blocks from a continuous process to another is supported by the class 'blockset' with their attribut procedures GOIN(') and GOOUT.
- All blocks possess a variable number of input and output blocks.
- There are time delay blocks where the death time period may be a function of time.

SIMKOM-S/80 has the following standard output possibilities:

- trace for the continuous processes with remarks for the manipulation of block structures, for the occurence of state events, for the synchronisation of continuous and discrete processes.
- plots in the form of tables, graphs and phases
- GPSS-like standard output of stochastical parameters of queues, facilities, capacities etc.

7.CONCLUDING REMARKS

One of the most important tasks is the development of combined models for real problems which have to be solved by simulation. This is a general one, not only for SIMKOM. The further SIMKOM development may not only be fixed by referring to the conditions and experiences described in this paper. Essential impulses may be emitted by solving real problems. From this point of view it may be necessary to extend SIMKOM to implicite differential equations. The SIMKOM development is today the common work of J. Fischer; H.-D. Gerhardt; G. Schwarze and M. Voß.

8. REFERENCES

/1/ PS SIMDIS, Anleitung für den Programmierer. VEB Robotron ZFT Dresden 1977

/2/ BUCHAM, J.; CARL, D.: GPSS für die BESM 6. rechentechnik/datenverarbeitung, Beiheft 3/1978 pp. 16-19

/3/ DIENHOLD, V. u.a.: Ein dialogfähiges Simulationssystem für diskontinuierliche Prozesse. Wiss. Beiträge der IH Dresden, H. 4/78 pp. 2-25

/4/ DIENHOLD, V.; FRANK, M.: Ein fachgebietsbezogenes Simulationssystem für diskrete technologische Prozesse. Anwendungsaspekte der Systemanalyse, Akademie-Verlag Berlin 1980 pp. 141-157

/5/ HARTWIG, M.; STROBEL, R.: Vorläufige Benutzerbeschreibung für den SIMULA-Compiler der BESM 6. Akad. d. Wiss. d. DDR, ZIMM Berlin 1980

/6/ GERHARDT, H.-D.: SIMDIT - ein diskretes Simulationssystem auf der Basis von SIMULA. 9. Jahrestagung Grundlagen der Modellierung und Simulation, Rostock 1980, Kurzreferate pp. 48/1-48/4

/7/ FRANK, M.: Ein automatentheoretisches Modellkonzept für ein fachgebietsbezogenes Simulationssystem zur Untersuchung diskreter fertigungstechnischer Prozesse. Diss.B, TH Ilmenau 1979

/8/ LORENZ, P.: Vergleich und Bewertung von Simulationssprachen. Diss. B, TH Magdeburg 1980

/9/ GERHARDT, H.-D.: Kombinierte Simulationsmodelle und kombinierte Simulationssysteme. IH Köthen 1978, 3. Wiss. Tagung Mathematik/Rechentechnik, Bericht pp. 57-69

/10/ SCHWARZE, G.: Kombinierte Simulationssysteme. msr 22(1979) H. 2 pp. 97-101

/11/ SCHWARZE, G.: Towards Software for Modeling and Simulation. International Symposium on System Analysis and Simulation, Berlin 1980, Proceedings pp. 113-123

/12/ N.N.: Digitale Simulation mittels Rechenanlagen des ESER. 2. Kolloquium über Simulation, Berlin 1978. ZfR-78.08, pp. 4-32

/13/ GÖRSCH, B.; SUSCHKE, E.: Erfahrungen mit Programmen zur Berechnung erzwungener Schwingungen in elektronischen Schaltungen. Nachrichtentechnik. Elektronik 28(1978) H. 1 pp. 17-18

/14/ SCHWARZE, G.; SUSCHKE, E.: Simulation kontinuierlicher Systeme auf Rechnern. Internat. Sem. Rechentechnik als Mittel und Gegenstand der Aus- und Weiterbildung, TU Dresden 1978, Berichtsband Teil 2 pp.183-206

/15/ SCHWARZE, G.: Test- und Einsatzerfahrungen mit kontinuierlichen Simulationssystemen für Lehre und Forschung. IH Köthen 1978, 3. Wiss. Tagung Mathematik/Rechentechnik, Bericht pp. 242-251

/16/ SCHWARZE, G.: Sachgebietsbezogene Simulationssysteme. Mitteil. d. Math. Ges. d. DDR, Heft 2/3 1979 pp. 189-201

/17/ SCHWARZE, G.: Kontinuierliche digitale Simulationssysteme als Arbeitsmittel des Ingenieurs. Plenarvortrag Festkolloquium IH Köthen, Mathematik/Rechentechnik 1979 (see Mitteilungen der Math. Gesellschaft der DDR, Heft 1/1980, pp. 51-68

/18/ GERHARDT, H.-D.: SIMULA 67 als Basis für den Aufbau von kombinierten Simulationssystemen. Weiterbildungszentrum MKR/Informationsverarbeitung TU Dresden 1979 Heft 40/79 pp. 55-61

/19/ SCHWARZE, G.: Simulationssysteme und Programmiersprachen. see /18/, pp. 139-143

/20/ FISCHER, J.: SIMULA 67 - eine Basissprache der Simulation kombinierter Systeme. TU Dresden 1979. Internat. Seminar Aktuelle Probleme der Rechentechnik, Wiss.Z.Techn. Univ. Dresden 29(1980)H.2, pp.349-350

/21/ SCHWARZE, G.; Wagner, B.: Simulationssysteme in der Aus- und Weiterbildung, rechentechnik/datenverarbeitung Beiheft 4/1979 pp. 14-18

/22/ SCHWARZE, G.: Simulation kontinuierlicher Systeme - Gemeinsame Grundausbildung für Analog- und Digitalrechner. 16. Seminar MEDA, Prag 1979, Seminarbericht Teil 2, Beitrag Nr. 70

/23/ FISCHER, J. u.a.: Zur digitalen Simulation kombinierter mathematischer Modelle. 24. Internat. Wiss. Koll. TH Ilmenau 1979, Reihe Simulation auf Rechnern, pp. 107-110

/24/ GERHARDT, H.-D.: Entwicklungstrends auf dem Gebiet der Simulation. ZfR-Informationen, AdW DDR, Berlin 1979, ZfR-79.16 (14 pages)

/25/ FISCHER, J. u.a.: Digitale Simulation kombinierter Systeme. Anwendungsaspekte der Systemanalyse. Akademie-Verlag Berlin 1980 pp. 109-125

/26/ FISCHER, J. u.a.: SIMKOM-F and EXCADSIM. mrs 23, 1980 H. 8, pp. 443-448

/27/ SCHWARZE, G.: Simulation - kontinuierliche Systeme. VEB Verlag Technik Berlin 1976, R. Automatisierungstechnik Bd. 177

/28/ HEINRICH, G.; KRUG, W.: Modellierung luft- und kältetechnischer Prozesse. Kap. 6. VEB Verlag Technik, Berlin, 1978

/29/ ARNDT, S. u.a.: Anwenderinformation zu DIGSIM 3. VEB KIB Chemie Leipzig, Abt. Anlagenmodellierung, 1980

/30/ NEDO, D.; REIMANN, W.: Programmdokumentation SPAS, Anwenderbeschreibung. IfR Berlin 1977

/31/ SCHÖNEFELD,R.: DS 4000 ein interaktives digitales Simulationssystem für zeitkontinuierliche Systeme. Wiss.Z. TH Ilmenau 22(176) Heft 5 pp. 75-92

/32/ SPECKHART,F.H.; GREEN, W.L.: A guide to using CSMP. Prentice-Hall, Inc., Englewood Cliffs, New Jersey 1976

/33/ SHAH, M.J.: Engineering simulation using small scientific computers. Prentice-Hall, Inc. 1976

/34/ JANOSY, J.S.; SZENTGALI, A.: PROHYS - A program for hybrid Simulation using Digital Computers. Hungarian Academy of Sciences, Central research institute for physics. KFKI-76-37

/35/ SYDOW, A.: Elektronische Analogrechner. VEB Verlag Technik Berlin, R. Automatisierungstechnik Bd. 6, 1. Aufl.

/36/ BIENER, K.; SUSCHKE, E.: Praxis des analogen Rechnens. VEB Verlag Technik Berlin, R. Automatisierungstechnik Bd. 91

/37/ SCHÖNEFELD,R.: Hybrid-Simulation. Akademie-Verlag Berlin, 1979

/38/ MAISEL, H.; GNUGNOLI, G.: Simulation of Discrete Stochastic Systems. Science Research Associates, Inc. Chicago 1972

/39/ KINDLER, E. u.a.: GPSS-PRAGUE - Listing 1979

/40/ SCHMIDT, B.: GPSS-FORTRAN Version II. Springer-Verlag Heidelberg 1978

/41/ SCHWARZE, G.: Allgemeine digitale Simulationssysteme - Sequentielle und pseudoparallele Berechnungen. AdW DDR, ZfR Informationen ZfR-80.08 (186 pages)

/42/ GERHARDT, H.-D.; SCHWARZE, G.: SIMULATION - Begriffe und Benennungen; Original-Modell-Computer. Wiss.Z.d. Humboldt-Universität zu Berlin, Math.-Nat.R. XXVIII(1979)4 pp. 549-565

/43/ GERHARDT, H.-D.: Kombi-Netze und mathematische Modellbildung. mrs 24(1981)11, pp. 606-610

/44/ GERHARDT, H.-D.: Allgemeine Grundlagen der Systemsimulation auf der Basis kombinierter Modelle. Diss. B, Humboldt-Universität zu Berlin 1981

/45/ ÖREN, T.I.: Software for Simulation of Combined Continuous and Discrete Systems: a State-of-the-Art Review. Simulation 28 (2) 1977, pp. 33-45; and Software Additions 29 (4) 1977, pp.125-126

/46/ KINDLER, E.: Simulacni programovaci jazyky (Simulation-Program-Languages) SNTL Praha 1980

/47/ PRITSKER, A.A.B.: The GASP-IV Simulation Language. New York, Wiley Inter-science 1974

/48/ TARLOS, B.: FOCUS - eine neue Simulationssprache. msr 23(1980)6, pp. 333-337

/49/ CELLIER, F.E.: Combined continuous/discrete system simulation by the use of digital computers: Techniques and tools. Dissertation Zürich 1979

/50/ SIM, R.J.W.: CADSIM Users Guide and Reference Manual. Department of Computing and Control, Imperial College London 1975, Publication 75/23

/51/ JOHNSEN, K.: Simulation Classes. Simula Newsletter. Vol. 5, May 1977, pp. 4-6

/52/ HELSGAUN, K.: COMBINEDSIMULATION - Speech given at the sixth SIMULA user's Conference, Lisboa 1978. Roskilde University Center. Roskilde 1978, Report No.2 and COMBINEDSIMULATION-listing 1979

/53/ KINDLER, E.: BOSCOS - a combined simulation system using SIMULA 67. Personal communication Berlin-Prague 1980/81

/54/ FISCHER, J.; SCHWARZE, G.: SIMKOM-S/80 - A simulation system for combined models. SIMULA NEWSLETTER 1981 (in print)

/55/ SCHWARZE, G.: SIMKOM and Analog Computer Programmes. 18. Seminar MEDA, Prague 1981, Report pp. 260-265

DISCRETE SIMULATION AND RELATED FIELDS
A. Jávor (editor)
North-Holland Publishing Company

A PROCESS-ORIENTED MODELLING CONCEPT FOR SPECIAL SIMULATION SYSTEMS

Martin Frank

Ingenieurhochschule Dresden, DDR

In general, Simulation will be understood as an important problem-solving-method. The practical realization of this approach requires full integration of simulation in the problem-solving process so that the problem-author can use simulation without computer specialists. A new type of simulation software is necessary for them. It will be designated as Special Purpose Simulation System (SPSS) and discussed in this paper.

1. THE FEATURES OF SPSS

SPSS is characterized by the following components:

- a set of model elements, which are formal descriptions of typical substructures of the processes in the defined userfield,
- routines, which model functional structures of the whole system (signal transmission, event realization),
- algorithms for preparation, execution and utilization of model experiments.

SPSS help the user by

- identification and formalization of the process elements in a man-computer interaction based on menu-technique,
- connection of the formal descriptions of the process elements to a whole model,
- fixation of the system parameters and initial values,
- data input,
- model variation (parameter variation, structure variation),
- data output and utilization.

The SPSS-language for interactions between user and computer is oriented on the terminology of the user field.

Simulation systems of this type differ from general simulation systems (GSS) such as GPSS in many aspects. A fundamental difference exists between offers for model description. In GSS this offer is a close set of relatively elementary model elements, which as a whole are suitable for modelling discrete processes of a very large class. But this flexibility is compared to special systems, connected with high expenses for acquisition of the system and model or program notation, respectivily.

Opposite to them the set of model elements is open ended in SPSS and moreover, one model element must allow to reflect very different complex substructures of the processes to be modelled in the user field.
There is a second fundamental difference related to the conversational mode, especially to the dialogue language.

Unlike the orientation of the SPSS-language on model description and model variation in technical terms from the application field, the GSS-language is more oriented on programming aspects.

SPSS are less flexible compared with GSS but due to its modularity much more flexible than one-purpose simulation models. Figure 1 shows the position of SPSS in the field of simulation software. This representation shall demonstrate that the flexibility of the stated types decreases but the simplicity of manipulation increases downward. It shall further imply the possibility of building a type based on one of the other types placed above (see fig. 1).

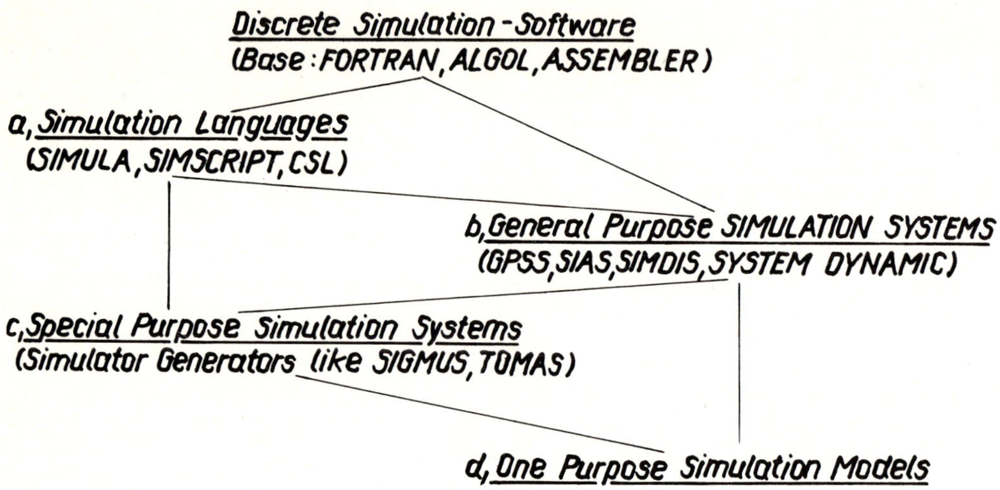

Fig. 1. Simulation software

The demand for the extensibility of the stock of model elements on the one hand and for the possibility of reflecting typical process elements with a very different complexibility in one model element on the other hand, require a uniform transparent mathematical concept for model modules.
Comparative investigations related to usual algorithmical modelling methods showed that an automat-theoretically model concept is in accordance with the demands mentioned above.

2. THE GENERAL FORMALIZATION SCHEME

The uniform mathematical structure of all modules, which are included in the model elements library is defined by

$$\underline{A} = (X, Z, Y, \underline{T}, P_f, P_g, \underline{z}_o) \qquad (1)$$

$\underline{A}$ is being denoted as a general, stochastic, initialized asynchronous automaton. It means:

X - a finite, not empty set of input signals $\underline{X}$, where each $\underline{X} \in X$ is a vector with constant dimension, for whose components $x \in \underline{X}$ an alphabet exists.

Z - a finite, not empty set of states $\underline{Z}$. Each z as component of $\underline{Z} \in Z$ is also characterized by an alphabet. In $\underline{Z}$ three subvectors will be distinguished: $\underline{z}_1$, $\underline{z}_2$, $\underline{z}_3$.

- $\underline{z}_1$ is called parameter vector,
- $\underline{z}_2$ is called vector of master attributes,
- $\underline{z}_3$ is named vector of auxiliary attributes.

The dimension of $\underline{z}_1$ and $\underline{z}_2$ is constant, for dimension $/\underline{z}_3/$ of $\underline{z}_3$ is valid

$$/\underline{z}_3/ = f(\underline{z}_1)$$

Y - a finite, not empty set of output signals, also with an alphabet for each y as component of $\underline{Y} \in Y$.

T - a set of time points t, where the relation $\leq$ is valid. ($T \subset R$, T is a subset of the set of all real digits)

P_f- a table of conditional transient functionals. They present the algorithm which models the function of the reflected process element in the following variant form of the usual notation of transient functionals of abstract automata:

$$\forall \underline{X} \in X: \underline{Z}(t+\varepsilon)_{\varepsilon \to 0} = P_f(\underline{Z}(t), \underline{X}(t)) \quad (2)$$

That means: the transfer in a new state takes place momentarily as soon as an input signal exists.

P_g- a table of functionals of results. They describe generation of output signals at time points, in which an input signal exists and a transfer in a new state, takes place. The function of results also differs from conventional notation

$$\forall \underline{X} \subseteq X: Y''(t+\varepsilon')_{\varepsilon' \to 0} = P_g(\underline{Z}(t+\varepsilon)_{\varepsilon \to 0}, X(t)) \quad (3)$$

That means: It is to guarantee, that the generation of output signals will also be realized without time delay but after transfer in the new state.

$$(Y'' \subseteq Y)$$

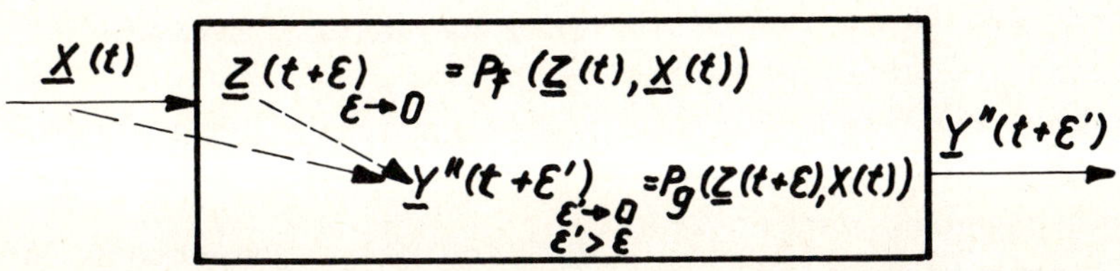

Fig. 2 General stochastic asynchronous automaton

$\underline{z}_o$- determined or stochastic initial state (state is stochastic, for example after the acceleration phase for overcoming the non-stationary phase)

In the combined sets $X' = \bigcup X$ or $Y' = \bigcup Y$ of the input or output signals of all automata $\underline{A}$ of a simulation system eight types of signals will be distinguished

1- event signals: They serve for internal notification of future signals and for actuation of actual signals
2- mark signals: They lead to the change of attributes of a special automat type called Operands (this type reflects temporary process elements)

3- block signals: They stop the transfer of "operands" or dissolve blockade
4- transfer signals: They show the delivery or acceptance of "operands"
5- disturbance signals: They stop the signal interpretation completely or partially
6- separate signals: They realize some auxiliary functions
7- output signals: They activate the result transfer into a result file
0- start-stop signals: They cause start, stop or put-away simulation in accordance with the programme of experiments

The last two signal types realize relations to the complex of experiment algorithms as the second important part of a SPSS, which is not discussed thoroughly in this paper.

The development of this modelling concept has been stimulated by Buslenko's aggregative system. The general stochastic asynchronous automaton may be designated as a special aggregate in the sense of Buslenko. But there is an essential difference in the configuration of the whole signal transfer. The selected form is similar but not identical the known event planning method. It offers some advantages concerning the computation time required.

3. COUPLING OF AUTOMATA

The SPSS possess an extensibility set $\mathfrak{A}$ of different abstract automata of the general form, mentioned in 2. Each element $\underline{A}$ of $\mathfrak{A}$ that is an automaton type is capable of modelling one element of the process to be simulated. For modelling a concrete simulating object to be simulated out of $\mathfrak{A}$ a new set $\mathfrak{M}$ must be build, in which only those $\underline{A}$ are represented, which are needed for O, and each $\underline{A}$ as often as necessary. On this set $\mathfrak{M}$ couple relations $\rightarrow$ have to be defined, so that the system $\mathfrak{M}' = (\mathfrak{M}, \rightarrow)$ can be used as simulation model for O.

Realization of couplings, cooperation of the automata in $\mathfrak{M}$ is effected by transfer of signals.

To guarantee a dynamic coupling of the model elements, which is entirely analogous to the progress in the real system a suitable organisation of signal transfer is necessary.

Thereby signals of future events (signal type 1) and momentary events (signal type 2 ... 6) must be distinguished. The first type of signals will be registered in a special automaton, designated as calendar, ordered at time and transferred to the sender if simulation time equals event time. Signals of momentary events will be stored in another special automaton, designated as signal range, because signal interpretation is only possible in a sequential manner.

4. STANDARD AUTOMATA FOR PRODUCTION OPERATIONS

Particularly, researches for the design of SPSS were carried out in the field of technology preparation for discrete production processes. For the same field, a first SPSS was designed, called TOMAS (Technology-oriented modelling and simulation). Initially the following model element classes and types were defined:

1. A type of automaton, designated as "operand", with which it is possible to model work objects (workpieces). (In the computer, these are temporary data structures, in contrast to the following automata,

which are permanent data structures.)

2. A class of automaton, whose elements were designated as "generator" and realize a relatively autonomous generation of external signals. There are two automaton types:
   - "operand-generator" (GENO), one model element of this type models the generation of "operands" (workpieces, jobs)
   - "disturbance-generator" (GENS) for modelling process interruptions.
3. An automata class with elements, which are designated as "operator" and whose signal interpretation can be connected with the delay of "operands".
   They can be divided into two subclasses: The first class leads to active delays of "operands" and allows modelling of technology operations and can be combined with passive delays.
   Automata types of this subclass are
   - "service-operator" (BEMM) for representing service stations, where M workers operate M machines.
   - "service-operator (BEMN) for representing of service stations where M workers operate N machines, where M   N.

   The second class can only be combined with passive delay and allows organisational operations to be represented at the operand flow.
   Types of automata are
   - "branch-operator" (VERZ) for branching operand flows
   - "union-operator" (VERE) for uniting operand flows
   - "store-operator" (SPEI) for storage of operands
   - "takeout-operator" (ENT) for taking operands out of stores
   - "connect-operator" (ZUOR) for connection of one or some operands with one operand (assembling)
   - "disposal-operator" (DISP) for preparing operands for connection
   - "gather-operator" (PACK) for gathering a fixed number of operands as one job
   - "copy-operator" (KOPI) for splitting up jobs

A further class of automata, designated as control automata with elements above named as calendar and signal range. They are not dependent upon the field for which SPSS was designed. Principally the classes 2 and 3 are extensible. Through addition of new or extension of offered automata adaptation to special user conditions is possible. Thereby the fixed classification and structure of input signals and output signals must be considered. The extension of a module is not difficult because the automaton algorithms have a clear structure. Its general form is shown in figure 3, where the digits 0,1,2,3,... represent a signal type.

The extension of modules or insertion of a new module into the menu should be a task for a specialized programmer. The problem solver must only describe the desired module function in technological terms. It is expected that the extension and insertion will become an exceptional case.

Each type of "generators" and "operators" represent a nonfinite set. One element of a type (designated as object) will be fixed through the user by giving values for parameters connected with the automaton type.

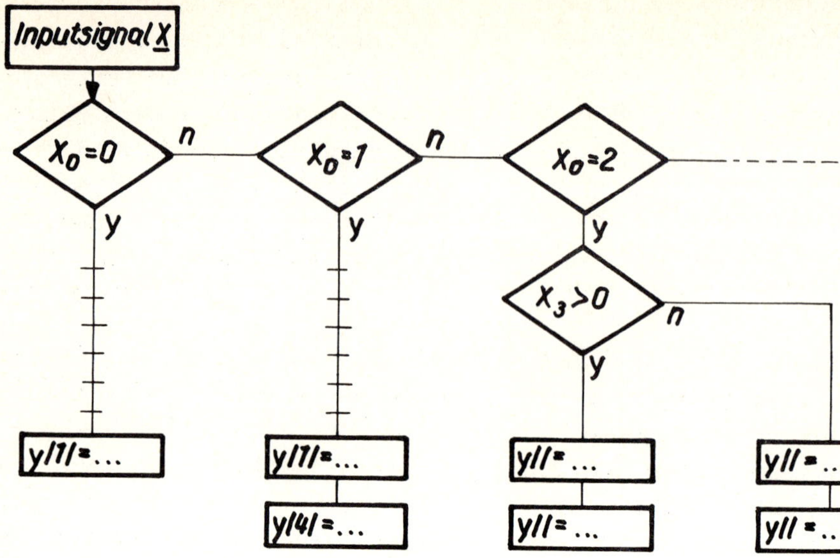

Fig. 3. Structure of automaton algorithm (P_f, P_g)

Function and indication vector of the standard automata can not be described in detail in this paper. Only the parameter vector of the service-operator BEMM may be ennumerated. It contains the following components:

p/1/ - number or name of the connected process element

p/2/ - capacity of the local queue for operands

p/3/ - quantity of machines or working places / areas

p/4/ - number or name of the previous process element (according to the flow of operands)

p/5/ - number or name of the following process element (according to the same)

p/6/ - number or name of a function, which models the time delay for preparing and for finishing the technological operation

p/7/ - number or name of a function, which models the time delay for the realization of operations

The functions must be defined with the help of the computer or provided with parameters when using an offered standard function. The attribute vector of BEMM includes such state variables, which are commonly used for the estimation of technological units.

5. MODELLING AND SIMULATION BASED ON SPSS

The standard automata which are mentioned in section 4 and possible further user special automata allow a static model of the process to be built.in the following manner suggested by figure 4: Generally the user - he should be a production engineer - designs a possible variant of the technological process to be simulated. It may be represented by a graph where the nodes represent service stations, storages and other technologically-conditioned stations but the edges represent flows of discrete workpieces or groups of such.

Using a display he now gets into touch with the simulation system TOMAS. He reviews the offered modules available for modelling his process. Advancing from node to node of the process graph he chooses an appropiate module (for every node) and names it in accordance with the connected process element. After having chosen the system in the same way demands parameter inputs from the user for every named module. In such a dialogue with TOMAS the user designs a simulation model. In a similar manner he states conditions for the first try and later based on the results of previous tries for further tries.

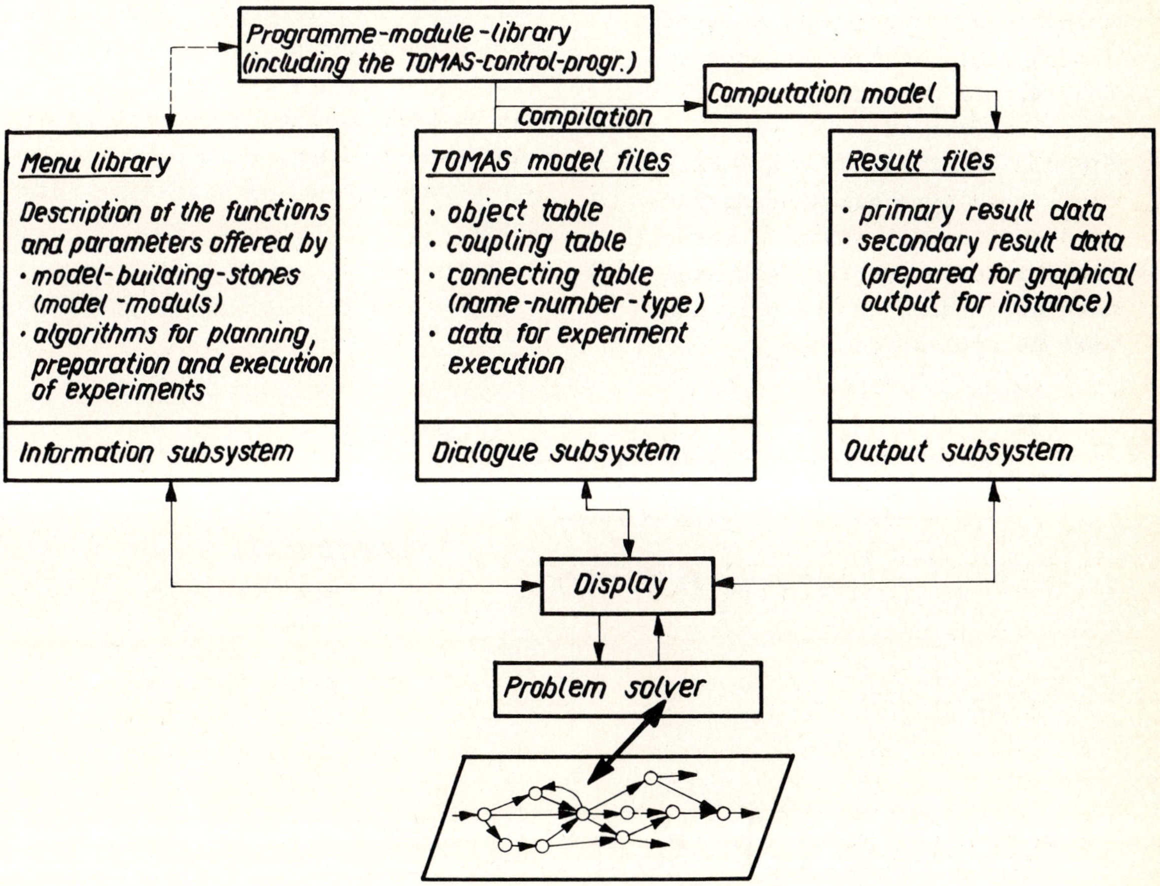

Fig. 4. Simulation based on TOMAS

To consider its dynamics organisation of signal transfer is needed as shown above.

The cooperation of all elements of a simulation model will be realized in following form:

1. Start (and stop) of the computer simulation for a model based on SPSS will be effected by all "generators" of the model.
2. Activation of an automaton by an input signal results in output signals, which will be dealt in the following form:

2.1. Signals of future events at the output of "generators" and active delaying operators will be specified in the calendar as soon as they occur. No signals result directly from it.

2.2. Signals of all other types will be registered into signal range. Sequence of registration is without importance, only block signals make an exception. The rule LIFO must be applied to them.

3. If all output signals resulting from interpretation of an input signal are taken up in to the signal range, the identification of the first signal of range, its transfer to the receiving automaton and its interpretation in this automaton will be executed. (The transferred signal will be extinguished.)
4. Continuation at 2 or - if all signals in range are extinguished - activation of calendar.

Fig. 7 illustrates this couple mechanism. It is related to the submodel in Fig. 6, which presents a formal description of two non-disturbed steps of a production process. These production steps are shown in Fig. 5. The symbols in Fig. 6 are related to the standard model elements, which were discussed in section 4 of this paper.

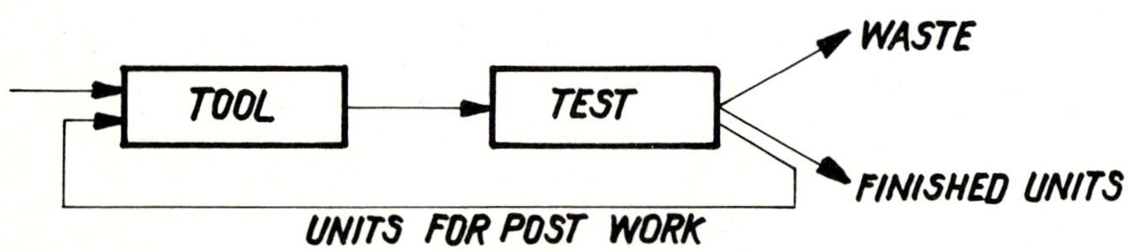

Fig. 5. Process sketch

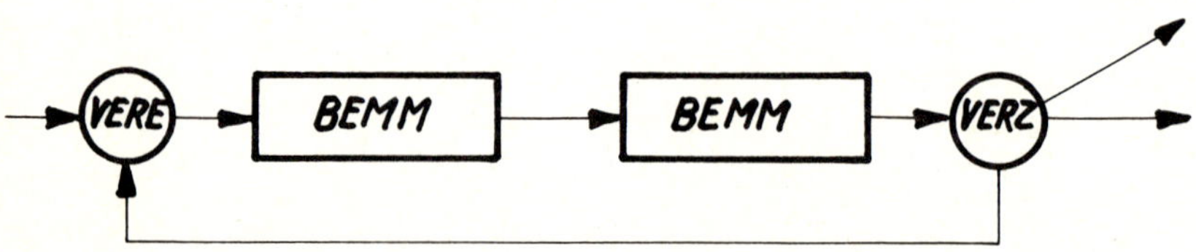

Fig. 6. Model sketch

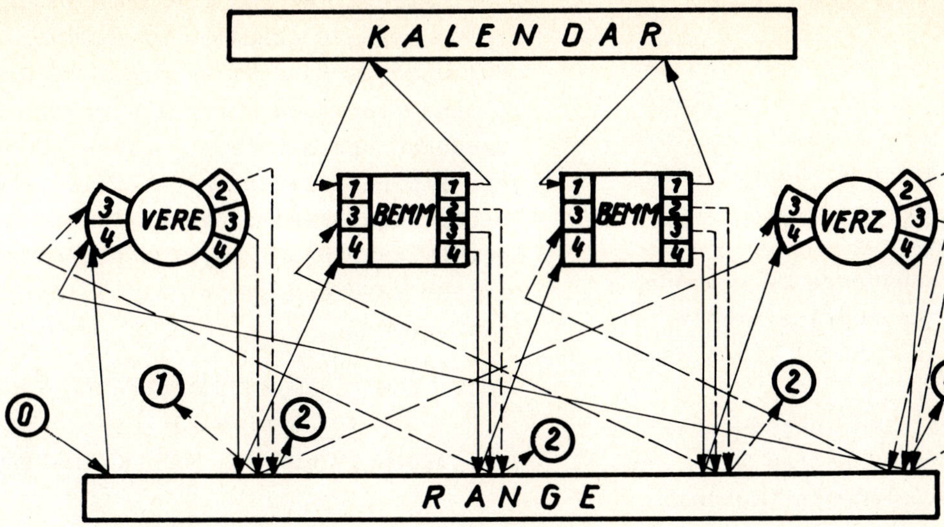

Fig. 7. Occuring signals

Explanation:

0 - from a predecessor (outside of submodel)

1 - to a further predecessor (outside of submodel)

2 - to operand generator (outside of submodel)

3 - to a successor (outside of submodel)

It must be stated that the couple mechanism as shown in Fig. 7, does not become evident for the user. His task at modelling is illustrated in Fig. 6 and also includes the parameter notation for selected model elements in interaction with the computer, whereby for each model element predecessors and/or successors - only related to the flow of operands (workpieces) - must be given.

Example for modelling a workpiece production in jobs by work-shop-principle is shown roughly in Fig. 8.

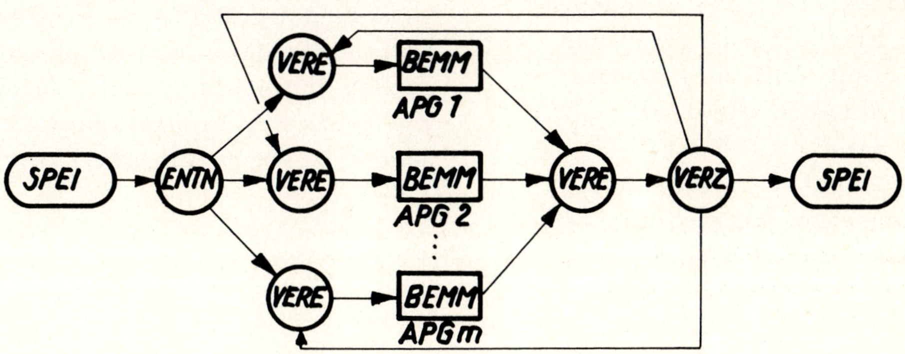

Fig. 8. Workpiece production

6. CONCLUSIONS

The designed model concept allows all above named demands for special simulation systems to be considered. In addition, the concept has the following advantages over general simulation systems:

- avoidance of redundance by reasonable adaptation of the model elements to conditions of user field, thus saving locations.
- saving computer time, because the time variable is connected with the permanent model elements (automat objects) and in general in practical simulation models the number of permanent elements is considerably smaller than temporary elements, so that time for handling the calendar will be less. It is also defined in this concept, that for one automat only one event is specialized in the calendar. Other possible events of the same automaton will be handled in local waitlists. That also reduces time for computing.

Another important question is related to the kind of implementation. Implementation of SPSS will be realized most reasonably by means of simulation languages, such as SIMULA or SIMSCRIPT. Because compilers for these languages for computers of the ESER family and KRS-series are not available in the GDR, implementation of TOMAS is performed in two ways:

1. Based on DDSS, that is a SIMSCRIPT oriented language for minicomputers (KRS and SKR) extended to interactive model building and model variation.
2. Based on FORTRAN for ESER computers.

Parallel to the Fortran-based implementations there are preliminary investigations for the application of SIMULA using a compiler of BESM 6. Obviously, SIMULA is the most effective language for such special systems. Its class concept allows a rational programming realization of the discussed modular modelling concept. The insertion of TOMAS into SIMULA's class concept is shown on principle in the list below:

```
SIMULATION CLASS AUTOMATON(AMAX);
           INTEGER AMAX;
     BEGIN INTEGER I; REF(AUTOMAT)ARRAY
                          ANR 1:AMAX ;
           REF(AUTOMAT)AUTO;
           REF(SIGNAL)SNR; REF(EVENT-
                          SIGNAL)ESNR;
           REF(OPERAND)ONR;
           PROCESS CLASS AUTOMAT .....;
              AUTOMAT CLASS GENO .....;
              AUTOMAT CLASS GENS .....;
              AUTOMAT CLASS BEMM .....;
                   :::::::::::::::::
              AUTOMAT CLASS KOPI .....;
           PROCESS CLASS EVENTSIGNAL..;
           LINK CLASS SIGNAL .........;
           LINK CLASS OPERAND ........;
           REF(HEAD)SIGNALSET,OPERANDLIST;
           SIGNALSET:-NEW HEAD;
           OPERANDLIST:-NEW HEAD;
     END   AUTOMATON;
```

In addition, SIMULA is a reasonable base for complex libraries of algorithms for special user fields; and the tools for simulation will be a subset of those libraries in future

References

1. Buslenko, N.P.; Modellierung komplizierter Systeme. Verlag Die Wirtschaft Berlin 1972

2. Buslenko, N.P.; Kalashnikov, V.V.; Kovalenko, I.N.: Lectures on complex system theory. Sov. Radio Moscow 1973 (in Russian)

3. Frank, M.: Ein automatentheoretisches Modellkonzept für ein fachgebietsbezogenes Simulationssystem zur Untersuchung diskreter technologischer Prozesse. Dissertation B, Technische Hochschule Ilmenau 1979

4. Goscinski, M.: Simulation of complex discrete productional processes. Archives of automation and telemechanic Vol. XIX, No. 4, pp. 497-514, Warshow 1974 (in Polish)

DISCRETE SIMULATION AND RELATED FIELDS
A. Jávor (editor)
North-Holland Publishing Company

A DISCRETE SIMULATION SYSTEM BASED ON ARTIFICIAL INTELLIGENCE METHODS

Iván Futó, János Szeredi

Institute for Coordination of Computer Techniques

Budapest, Hungary

A discrete event simulation system based on the AI language PROLOG is presented. The system called T-PROLOG extends the traditional possibilities of simulation languages toward automatic problem solving by using backtrack in time and automatic model modification depending on logical deductions.
As T-PROLOG is an interactive tool, the user has the possibility to interrupt the simulation run to modify the model or to force it to return to a previous state for trying nes possible alternatives. It admits the construction of goal-oriented or goal-seeking models with variable structure. Models are defined in a resticted version of the first order predicate calculus using Horn clauses.

1. INTRODUCTION

Solving problems using computerised models of real systems is one of the purpose of AI and simulation researches. The developed programming tools, AI [1], [4], [9], [14], [18], [19], and simulation [2], [3], [10], [20], [21], languages differ in many features. We found uselful to construct a modelling system which takes the time handling concept from the simulation languages and non-algorithmic programming concept, pattern matching and backtracking from the AI languages.

Our system is implemented in CDL [11] and in MPROLOG, a logic based AI language with simple syntax, Horn clause and great expressing power due to its logical basis 4

Some features with an application the simulation system called T-PROLOG is presented in the following paragraphes.

The system allows the construction of goal seeking or goal generating and self-organizing models with variable structure [17]

2. INTRODUCTION TO ARTIFICIAL INTELLIGENCE BASED COMPUTER SIMULATION

2.1 Simulation using digital computers

Under simulation in this paper we mean discrete event simulation, when the changes occur in discrete time moments.

Simulation is a problem solving procedure. We prepare a computerised model, a program of a real life system which reflects the interesting characteristics, to examine the behaviour of the original system. i.e. with running the program.

The purpose of the simulation can be: i) Examination of the reaction of the observed system when its structure or parameters are changed. ii) To examine the final state the system reaches from a given initial one and how its structure or parameters have to be changed to obtain a predefined final state. We will call this kind of simulation goal oriented.

The scheme which corresponds to the goal-oriented simulation is the following

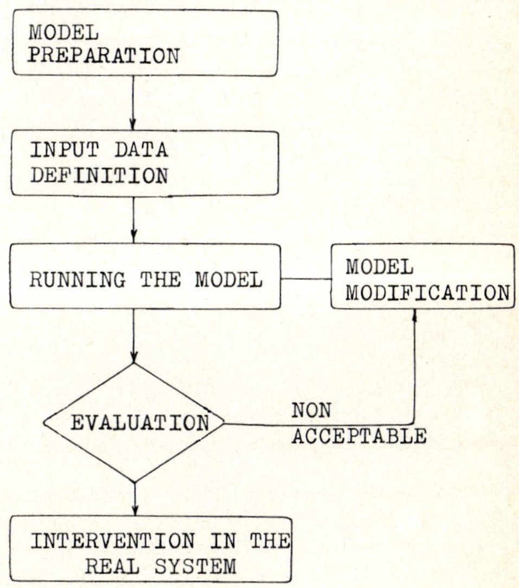

Figure 1: The simulation process

2.2 AI based computer simulation

We call the simulation procedure AI based simulation if the behaviour of the model is tested on different points during the running of the program by control conditions or the structure of the original model is changed automatically according to different predefined rules depending on the actual state of the system. Then the original scheme of the simulation procedure can be modified in the following way.

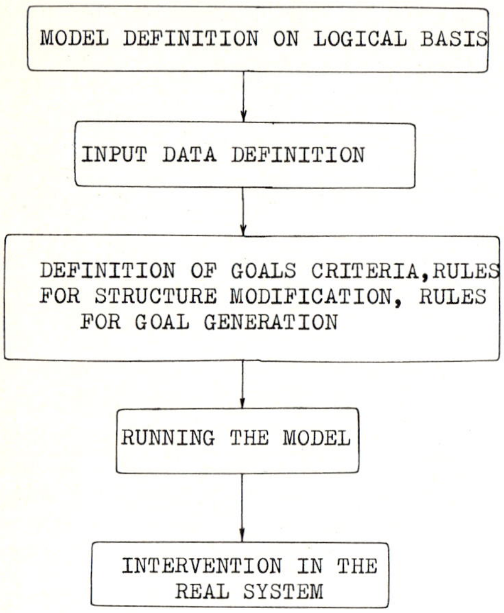

Figure 2: AI based simulation

2.3 Criteria for logic based discrete simulation languages

The following are the basic criteria of a logic based discrete simulation system: i) Models are defined using logical formulas. ii) Changes in the examined system can be described by explicit time dependent predicates. iii) Parallel processes may communicate with each other.

From the system simulation's point of view, the role of time is essential, as real systems work in time. The conditions for synchronising their processes are time dependent.

We want to satisfy the above conditions by the following methods: i) Using a logic-based very high level language which is suitable for the simultaneous description of the processes and goals of the systems, interactive, easy to modify and modular. ii) During the simulation run the program system assigns to each process a theoremprover whose task is to prove the goal of the process by means of the logical statements defining that process. iii) To solve the conflicts shich are arising from the possibility of data base modifications or resource allocations, sophisticated rules of preferences can be given. iv) Backtraking is provided to some previous state from which an alternate path can be schoosen to try to go forward again toward the goal. This is important in dead-lock situations from which goals can not be reached. v) The set of formulas, defining the simulation model can be altered dynamically during program running. This means the original structure of the simulation model can be modified automatically using predefined state dependent rules. vi) During program execution new processes with new goals can be created and old ones can be deleted from the simulation model. In the case of deletion the successful proof of the corresponding goal is not considered.

For traditional simulation problems the system works as a process oriented simulation language [15].

3. THE LOGICAL BASIS OF T-PROLOG

T-PROLOG is [6], [7], derived from PROLOG (Programming language based on LOGic) [1], [5], [18], and discrete simulation languages [2], [10], [20], [21]. An introduction to PROLOG (MPROLOG) [4] concept and logical problem-solving is presented below. [12], [16].

3.1 The Clause From of Logical Formulas

A language, such as the first order predicate calculus, is defined by its syntax. Its elementary components are predicate symbols, function symbols, constant symbols and variable symbols. Predicate symbols are used to represent relations in the domain of discourse. For Eg. if the domain of discourse is authors and their works the statement that Shakespeare wrote Hamlet can be formulated using the two argument predicate Wrote to form the atomic formula Wrote (Shakespeare, Hamlet). Here Shakespeare and Hamlet are constant related by the realation Wrote. In general atomic formulas are composed from a predicate symbol and terms as arguments. Terms are constants, variables and functions which may have as arguments other terms. Divorced (father(Jack), mother(Jack)) can be an example for atomic formulat containing functions. To every atomic formula we assign the value T or F (True or False) if we define an interpretation for that formula. Wrote (Shakespeare, Hamlet) and

Wrote(Diderot,Macbeth) are respectively true and false if the interpretation is the usual.

To express more complex situations connectives can be used in the predicate calculus language. These are $\wedge$(and), $\vee$(or), $\Rightarrow$ (implies) and $\neg$(negation). Syntactically correct formulas formed using connectives are called well-formed formulas (wff). Now we can write the following wff, Loves (Ann,Paul) $\wedge$ Loves (Paul,Ann) to express the fact that Paul and And mutually love each other, and Loves (Ann,Paul) $\wedge$ Loves(Paul,Ann) $\Rightarrow$ Marry (Ann,Paul) to state that if they love each other they will marry.
Sometime an atomic formula like P(x), has value T with a given interpretation for P no matter what assignment is given to the variable x. Or such an atomic formula may have value T for at least one value of x. To express these informations quantifiers $\forall$(universal), and $\exists$(existential) are used. For E.g.: $\forall x$(Human(x) $\Rightarrow$ Mortal(x)) (every human is mortal) or $\exists x$Wrote(x,Hamlet) (There is somebody who wrote Hamlet) are quantified wff-s. Generally composed formulas of the predicate calculus are more complex but every time it is possible to transform them into the so called prenex form. A wff in prenex form consists of a string of universal quantifiers called prefix, and a quantifier free formula called matrix. During transformation we eliminate implications (using the equivalence $X_1 \Rightarrow X_2 \equiv \neg X_1 \vee X_2$), reduce the scope of negation symbols (using De Morgan's laws) to at most one atomic formula, and eliminate existential quantifiers by "skolemization". Any matrix than can be written as the conjuction of a finite set of literals. (A literal is an atomic formula or a negated atomic forma). Such a matrix is said to be in conjuctive normal form. If now we eliminate the prefix (we can drop it since all variables in the wff are universally quantified and the order of universal quantification is unimportant), assuring by convention that all variables in the matrix are universally quantified, and then eliminate $\wedge$ symbols too by replacing $(X_1 \wedge X_2)$ with the set of wff-s $\{X_1,X_2\}$ we obtain a finite set of wff each of which is a disjunction of literals. Any wff consisting solely of disjunction of literals is called a clause.
To illustrate the above procedure consider the following example:

a) $\forall x(\text{Human}(x) \Rightarrow \text{Mortal}(x)) \wedge \forall y(\text{Man}(y) \vee \text{Woman}(y) \Rightarrow \text{Human}(y))$

b) $\forall x(\neg\text{Human}(x) \vee \text{Mortal}(x)) \wedge \forall y(\neg(\text{Man}(y) \vee \text{Woman}(y)) \vee \text{Human}(y))$

c) $\forall x(\neg\text{Human}(x) \vee \text{Mortal}(x)) \wedge \forall y((\neg\text{Man}(y) \wedge \neg\text{Woman}(y)) \vee \text{Human}(y))$

d) $\forall x\ \forall y((\neg\text{Human}(x) \vee \text{Mortal}(x)) \wedge (\neg\text{Man}(y) \vee \text{Human}(y)) \wedge (\neg\text{Woman}(y) \vee \text{Human}(y))$

e) $\{(\neg\text{Human}(x) \vee \text{Mortal}(x)), (\neg\text{Man}(y) \vee \text{Human}(y)), (\neg\text{Woman}(y) \vee \text{Human}(y))\}$

Figure 3: Transformation to clause form

3.2 Resolution refutation systems

Deduction of a formula F from a set of formulas S means the demonstration of the fact, that F is a logical consequence of S, that is every interpretation which satisfies S also satisfies F. (An interpretation satisfies a formula if it is true with this interpretation). These interpretations cannot satisfy the formula $\neg$F (the negated version of F), so they cannot satisfy the set S $\cup$ $\neg$F. This means, that if F is a logical conqequence of S, then the set S $\cup$ $\neg$F is unsatisfiable. The inverse is also true, if the set S $\cup$ $\neg$F is unsatisfiable (no interpretation can satisfy it), then the formula F is a logical consequence of S. Using this fact to deduce F from S we try to demonstrate that there is no such an interpretation that satisfies S'= S $\cup$ $\neg$ F. We will represent by $\square$ the empty clause, which is always unsatisfiable.
It is possible to give a deduction rule that is easy to implement, called resolution. On Figure 4 resolution step corresponds to the application of the rule of inference "modus ponens"; if $X_1 \Rightarrow X_2$ and X_1 is true then we can infer to X_2.

To use resolution we transform the set of formulas $S = \{X_1 \Rightarrow X_2 , X_1\}$ to its clause form $S_c = \{(\neg X_1 \vee X_2), X_1\}$ and then we apply resolution. We search for complementary literals in clauses and deduce a new clause as logical consequence from two parent clauses by eliminating these literals from the original clauses and grouping remaining literals in a new clause [16].

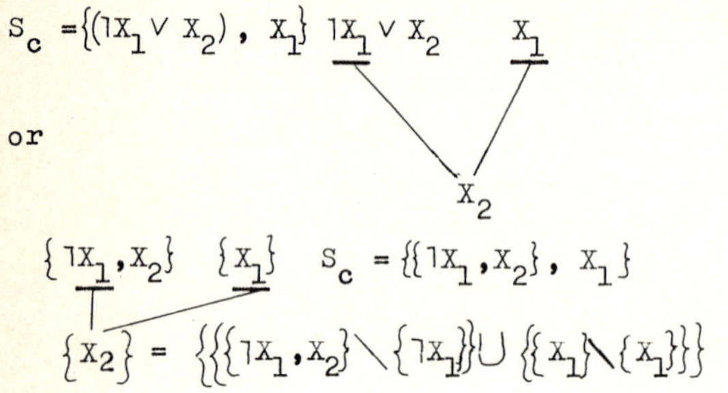

Figure 4: Resolution applied to ground clauses

More precisely: [16] resolution process, where it is applicable, is applied to a pair of parent clauses to produce a derived clause. In order to apply resolution to clauses containing variables, we need to be able to find a substitution (a possible replacement of variables by terms) that can be applied to the parent clauses so they contain complementary literals. Let the perspective parent clauses be given by $\{L_i\}$ and $\{M_i\}$. Suppose that $\{l_i\}$ is a subset of $\{L_i\}$ and $\{\neg m_i\}$ is a subset of $\{M_i\}$ such that a most general unifier s (a substitution) exists for the union of the sets $\{l_i\}$ and $\{m_i\}$. We say that that the two clause $\{L_i\}$ and $\{M_i\}$ resolve and that the new clause $\{\{\{L_i\} \setminus \{l_i\}\}\, s \cup \{\{M_i\} \setminus \{\neg m_i\}\}^s\}$ is a resolvent of the two clauses.

It can be shown that resolution is a sound rule of inference, that is the resolvent of a pair of clauses also logically follows from that pair of clauses. When resolution is used in refutation systems (see later) it is also complete. Every clause that logically follows from a set of clauses can be deduced from that set of clauses using resolution refutation.
In problem-solving using logic and resolution we have a set S_c of clauses from which we wish to prove some goal clause C. Resolution based systems are designed to produce proofs by contradiction or <u>refutation</u>. In a resolution refutation we first negate the goal clause and then add the negation to the set S_c. Then we use resolution in attempt to derive the contradiction represented by the empty clause □. As resolution is a truth preserving inference rule if we deduce the empty clause from $S' = S_c \cup \neg C$ that means, S' is unsatisfiable, so $\neg C$ is not a logical consequence of S_c, and C (the original goal to be proved) logically follows from S_c. To see how resolution works consider the following example.
In our domain of discourse the following is true. If it is raining and there is a good film, then everybody goes to the movie to see that film. It is now raining and Cabaret is a good film. Does Jack go to the movie to do there something?
The corresponding logical formulas are:
(To be more understable variables will be represented identifiers preceded by a _ sign and the use of _ is permitted inside of identifiers composed from more than one word. This notation is a part of the T-PROLOG syntax too. (Figure 5).

As the contradiction was deduced, the negated version of the goal question is not true, so the original version that is "Jack goes to the movie to see Cabaret" is true.

3.3 The AI language PROLOG

The PROLOG language may be introduced in the simplest way using the procedural interpretation of Horn clauses.

Those clauses $\{B_1, \ldots B_m, \neg A_1, \ldots, \neg A_n\}$, where $m \leq 1$ are called <u>Horn clauses</u>.

The various Horn clauses are named as follows:

1) m=0 n=0 , □,
   the empty clause ;
2) m=1 n=0 B,
   the <u>assertion or unit clause</u>;
3) m=0 n≠0 , $\{\neg A_1, \ldots, \neg A_n\}$,
   the <u>goal</u> or <u>goal-sequence</u> ;
4) m=1 n≠0 , $\{B, \neg A_1, \ldots, \neg A_n\}$,
   the <u>rule of inference</u>.

Do not forget, thet notation $\{B, \neg A_1, \ldots, \neg A_n\}$ is equipodent to $B \Leftarrow A_1 \wedge \ldots \wedge A_n$.

A clause representing a goal sequence ,

$$\{\neg A_1, \ldots, \neg A_n\},$$

can be interpreted as a sequence of procedure calls. That is, each literal

(1) ∀_x ∀_film (It_is_raining ∧ Good_film(_film) ⇒ Goes_to_movie (_x,to_see(_film)))

(2) It_is_raining (3) Good_film(Cabaret)

The corresponding clauses:

(1') {¬It_is_raining, ¬Good_film(_film), Goes_to_movie(_x,to_see(_film))}

(2') {It_is_raining}

(3') {Good_film(Cabaret)}

The negated version of the question:

(4') {¬Goes_to_movie (Jack,_doing_something)}

The resolution process:

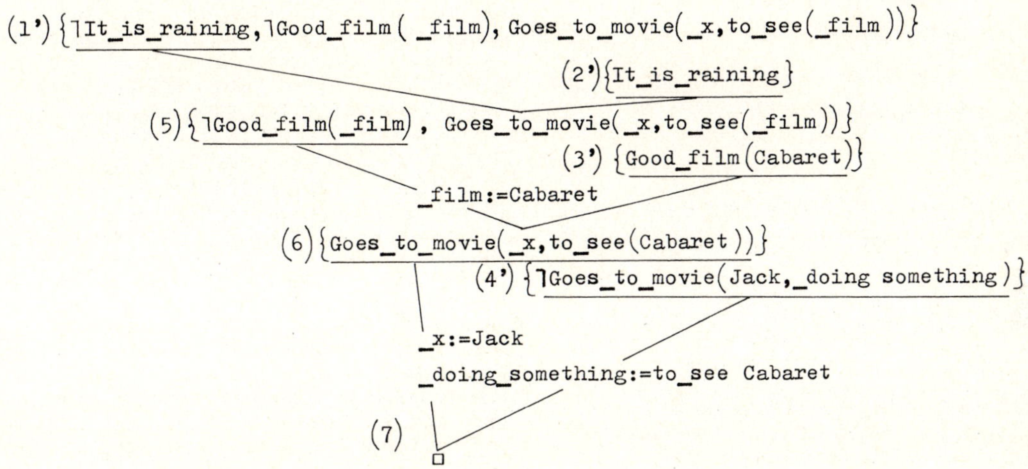

Figure 5: The resolution process

$\neg A_i$, i=1,...,n is interpreted as a procedure call.
A Horn clause,

$\{B, \neg A_1, \ldots, \neg A_n\}$

may be viewed as a <u>procedure declaration</u>, where B is the <u>head</u> of the procedure and the procedure calls A_i , form the <u>body</u> of the procedure. Assertion of form B , may be looked upon as procedures with empty bodies, while the empty clause, □, is the STOP instruction. The arguments of the literals correspond to the parameters of procedures (procedure calls).

In the language, <u>procedures are declared with Horn clauses</u>, whose calls are controlled using, pattern matching, by a <u>theorem-prover</u> with <u>top-down</u>, <u>depth-first</u> trategy. The pattern matcher executes the unification algorithm [16] . Using the procedural view of clauses, it is possible to step outside of the frame of the first order predicate calculus to introduce other procedures.

There are two types of procedures in PROLOG: i) Procedures defined by the user in the PROLOG language. ii) Procedures provided by the interpreter; that is, built-in procedures.
A user defined procedure means that it is the responsibility of the user to provide for each procedure call a literal of the form ¬A, a procedure definition with an applicable head, A . If this is not the case, backtraking results according to the strategy of the theorem-prover contained in PROLOG.

Built-in procedures may be called in the same way as user defined procedures, however, the user does not have to provide their corresponding definition as these are contained in the interpreter.

Such built-in procedures are used to perform arithmetic functions addition, multiplication, etc. , comparisons, input-output, and file handling operations. An important role is played by the program modification procedures which can be used by a running program during the theorem-proving process

to change the set of clauses which comprise the program.
To show how PROLOG works we give as an example an extended version of the previous problem, using the current syntax of PROLOG (T-PROLOG). To $\{B, \neg A_1, \ldots, \neg A_n\}$, $\{\neg A_1, \ldots, \neg A_n\}$, $\{B\}$ corresponds respectively

B: $A_1, \ldots, A_n$, $:A_1, \ldots, A_n$, and B.

```
(1) Goes_to_movie(_somebody,to_see(_film)):
                        Good_film(_film),
                        There_is_ticket_to(_film),
                        It_is_raining.
(2) Good_film(Rocky).
(3) Good_film(Cabaret).
(4) There_is_ticket_to(Cabaret).
(5) It_is_raining.
    End.
(6) :Goes_to_movie(Jack,_doing_something),
    Outterm(_doing_something).
```

Figure 6: A PROLOG program

Outterm(term) is a built-in predicate that serves to output its argument, in this case what Jack will do. The execution of the above PROLOG program is shown on Figure 7.

4. THE T-PROLOG LOGIC BASED SIMULATION SYSTEM

The basic notion of the T-PROLOG system are: i) The notion of process.[15] There can be several processes in the system running conceptually in parallel. Processes can be created at initial phase of the simulation as well as during run time. A goal to be achieved correspond to each of them. ii) The notion of resource. Resources are model elements that can be used only by one process at a time. The use of a resource can take time and may be returned or deleted after use. Resources also may be created at program initialisation or dynamically during program execution. iii) The notion of internal time. A duration time can be assigned to certain program parts independently of their real execution time. An internal clock is maintained by the system which is used for scheduling the processes.(Next event simulation.) iv) Messages and conditions. Processes can wait for fullfilment of conditions or for messages. Conditions can be formulated using the full power of PROLOG. v) Backtrack. The whole system including the scheduler can backtrack into a previous state and try an alternative path of control. Backtrack is caused either by failure in the execution of a process, by deadlock or when the prescribed termination time of a process is exceeded.
The system is written in MPROLOG [4]. and CDL2 [11].

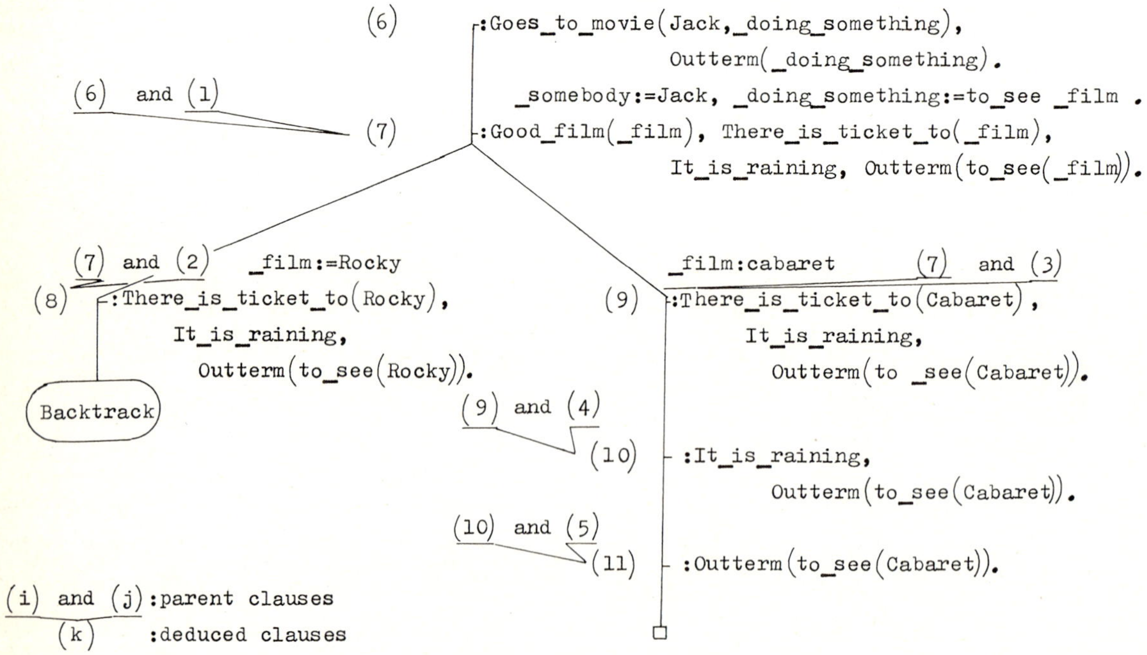

Figure 7: Execution of a PROLOG program

4.1.1 Time handling and synchronising built-in predicates

In the next example we show the different possibilities of communication between the processes and the control of time. The program solves the following problem. Jim and Dick want to rob the PROLOG Savings Bank. Jim climbs in the bank - it takes him 5 minutes -, Dick waits outside. There are different safes in the bank, they need different tools for opening these safes. Jim chooses a safe, and if they have the appropriate tool they rob the bank. The roberry has to finish in 25 minutes. The data are the following: There are there safes in the bank: Wertheim, Milner and Chatwood. Jim and Dick have tools only for the latter two. Opening the Milner takes 40 minutes, while the opening the safe Chatwood takes only 10 minutes. The question is which safe is to be chosen for the succesful robbery?

The program for this problem is show on Figure 8.
(1), (2), (8)-(11) are rules of inference, (3) -(7) are asertions, (12) is a goalsequence, (3) -(5) form the partition "Choses" (6), (7) form the partition "Has".

The program execution is shown in Figure 10. The sequences of execution of the different processes are labeled and they are resumed, Figure 11.

```
(1) Jim_gets_money(_bank,_safe):
        Jim_clims_into(_bank),
        Shooses(_safe),
        Wait_for(Tools),
        Open(_safe,Tools),
        Outputs(_safe,_bank).
(2) Dick_gets_money(_bank,_safe):
        Wait(Identifier(_safe)),
        Has(Tools,_safe),
        Send(Tools).
(3) Chooses(Wertheim).
(4) Chooses(Milner).
(5) Chooses(Chatwood).
(6) Has(Tools,Milner).
(7) Has(Tools,Chatwood).
        End.

(8) Jim_clims_into(_bank): Hold(5).
(9) Opens(Milner,Tools): Hold (40).
(10) Opens(Chatwood,Tools): Hold (10).
(11) Outputs(_safe,_bank):
        Systemtime(_t),
        Outstring("THE BANDITES GOT"),
        Outstring("THE MONEY FROM THE").
        Output(_safe),
        Outstring("SAFE, "),
        Outstring("FROM THE"),
        Output(_bank),
        Outstring(" BANK "),
        Outstring(" AT TIME "),
        Output(_t).

(12)
:New(Dick_gets_money(Prolog_savings),_safe ,Dick,25), New(Jim_gets_money(Prolog_savings),_safe ,
                                                                                    Jim,25).
```

Figure 8: A T-PROLOG program

The function of the different built-in predicates is the following (the syntactical restrictions have to be always fulfilled at the moment of the procedure call, that is when the predicate is executed).
i) Wait (G). Syntactical restrictions: "G" atom. This predicate serves for the suspending of processes depending on different conditions, "G" is the condition of the suspension. The execution of the process is suspended until "G" becomes provable. If it was originally true the execution of the process continues. ii) Wait_for(A), Send(A). Santactical restrictions: "A" term. Predicates serving for the communication through messages, sending and waiting for messages. iii) New (GL), New(GL,X), New(GL,X,ST), New (GL,X,ST,ET) . Syntactical restrictions: "GL" an atom (goal) ,"X" is a term "ST" and "ET" are integers. These predicates serve the creation of processes. "GL" is the goal of the process, "X" is its identifier, "ST" is the starting time and "ET" is the prescribed time for the achievement of the goal. The default values are: "ST"=system time, "Et"=100000, "X"=an identifier differing from any other identifier in the program iv) Hold(T) . Syntactical restrictions: T integer. It serves the unconditional suspension of processes for "T" time units. (For detailed explication of built in procedure see Appendix). The execution of the program is the following. on the left hand side of ":" n the waiting list we give the process identifier, on the right hand side we give the reactivation (activation) time of the process.

At the initialisation phase: i) System time: 0. ii) Waiting list: Dick:0. iii) Blocked list: empty. iv) Message list: empty. v) Active process: Jim.

Executing the goal-sequence of process Jim, the procedure Jim_climbs_into _bank is immediately called, and needs time to run (5 time units) . So Jim is suspended: i)

System time: 0. ii) Waiting list: Jim: 5. iii) Blocked list: empty. iv) Message list: empty. v) Active process: Dick.

The execution of process Dick is suspended because of theproduce call Wait (Identifier(_safe)). The process is appended to the Blocked list. As there is no process which can run at the current system time (0), the internal clock is moved to 5: i) System time: 5. ii) Waiting list: empty. iii) Blocked list: Dick. iv) Message list: empty. v) Active process: Jim.

The execution of process Jim continues with the procedure call Chooses(_safe) and the variable "_safe" gets the value "Wertheim" (state A). The next procedure call is Wait_for(Tools) and Jim is appended to the Message list. But now Dick can continue its running because its waiting condition Identifier (Wertheim) is already fulfilled (state B): i) System time: 5. ii) Waiting list: empty. iii) Blocked list: empty. iv) Message list: Jim. v) Active process: Dick.

The next procedure call of Dick is Has (Tools,Wertheim) . It fails, and so the backtrack begins. The backtraking continues to a previous state when another alternative can be chosen. This is state A. The variable "_safe" then gets the value "Milner" and the program execution continues to state B. The procedure call Has (Tools,Milner) now succeeds and the next call is Send (Tools).

A message is sent to an other process, and Dick finishes his execution (the goalsequence of the process is empty). Now Jim can continue the running as he got the wanted message: i) System time: 5. ii) Waiting list: empty. iii) Blocked list: empty. iv) Message list: empty. v) Active process: Jim.

The processing of Jim continues with the procedure call Opens(Milner,Tools) state C.

As the opening of safe Milner takes 40 time units, the reactivation time of Jim would be 5 + 40 = 45 > 25 (25 is the prescribed time to solve the task) so the backtrack begins again. The choice of a new alternative is possible at state A only. The variable "_safe" now gets the value "Chatwood".

The program reaches, as it was described before, the state C. The opening of the safe Chatwood takes only 10 time units. Jim is suspended and can be reactivated at 15. As there are not other processes, the systemtime is increased to 15: i) System time: 15. ii) Waiting list: empty. iii) Blocked list: empty. iv) Message list: empty. v) Active process: Jim.

Jim calls the printout procedure and its goalsequence becomes empty too. All lists are empty, the execution of the program is terminated sucessfully. The output produced by the program is: the badites got the money from the safe Chatwood, from the PROLOG-savings bank at time 15.

4.1.2 Resources and resource allocation

Processes during problem-solving may need resources. Resources can only be used by one process a time. T-PROLOG ensures -if it is necessary- that all possible distribution of resources are tried among processes waiting for them. Different built-in algorithms help the distribution. Resources may be created at program initialisation or dynamically during program execution. The used buil-in predicates: Resource (R,N) and Addresource (R,N) , where R is a term which identifies the resource and N is the number of resources to be created.

To seize a resource the following built-in predicates can be used: i) Seize (R) and ii) Seize (R,T) . To release a resource the built-in predicate Release (R) is used.

In the above predicates R is a list of term identifying the resources to be sized simultaneously, T is an integer giving the duration of resource control by the given process. (See also Appendix.)

To help the scheduling of processes at resources during backtrack, the notion of homogenous process class and homogenous resource class are introduced.

Processes waiting for the same resource and having the same parameters (unifiable goalsequence, and same termination time) form a homogenous process class. After backtrack to go forward only processes belonging to different process class are permuted to get the control of the resources trying all possible distribution of resources among processes if needed.

Resources having the same parameters form a homogenous resource class. During the backtrack processes belonging to different homogenous process classes and having received resources of same homogenous resource class are not permuted.

To illustrate resource distribution let us consider the following example. There are two homogenous resources and five processes grouped in two homogenous process class, see Figure 9.

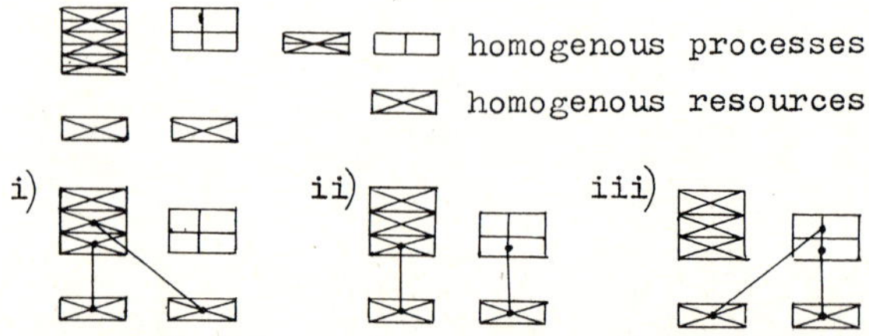

Figure 9: Automatic resource distribution

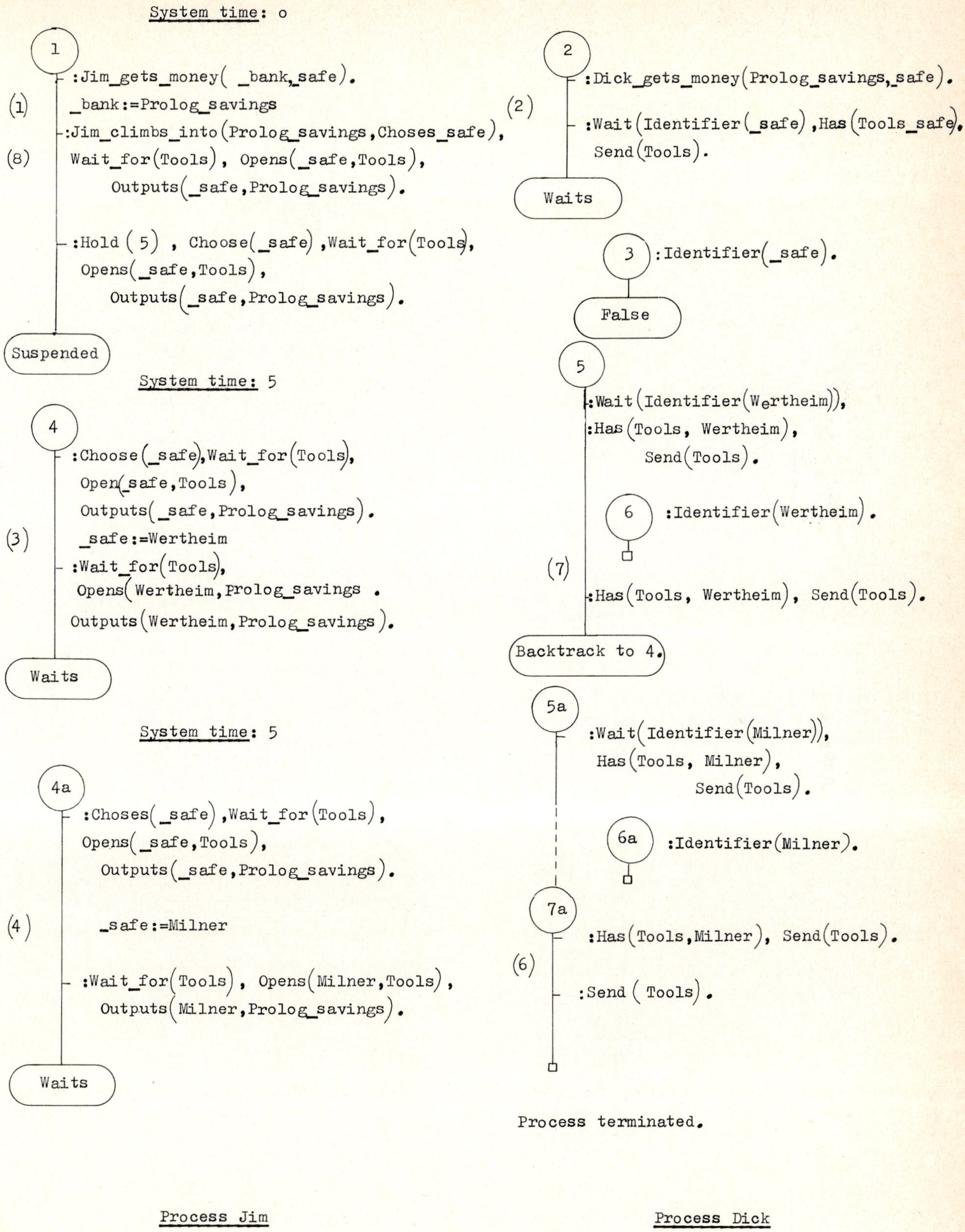

Figure 1o: Execution of a T-PROLOG program

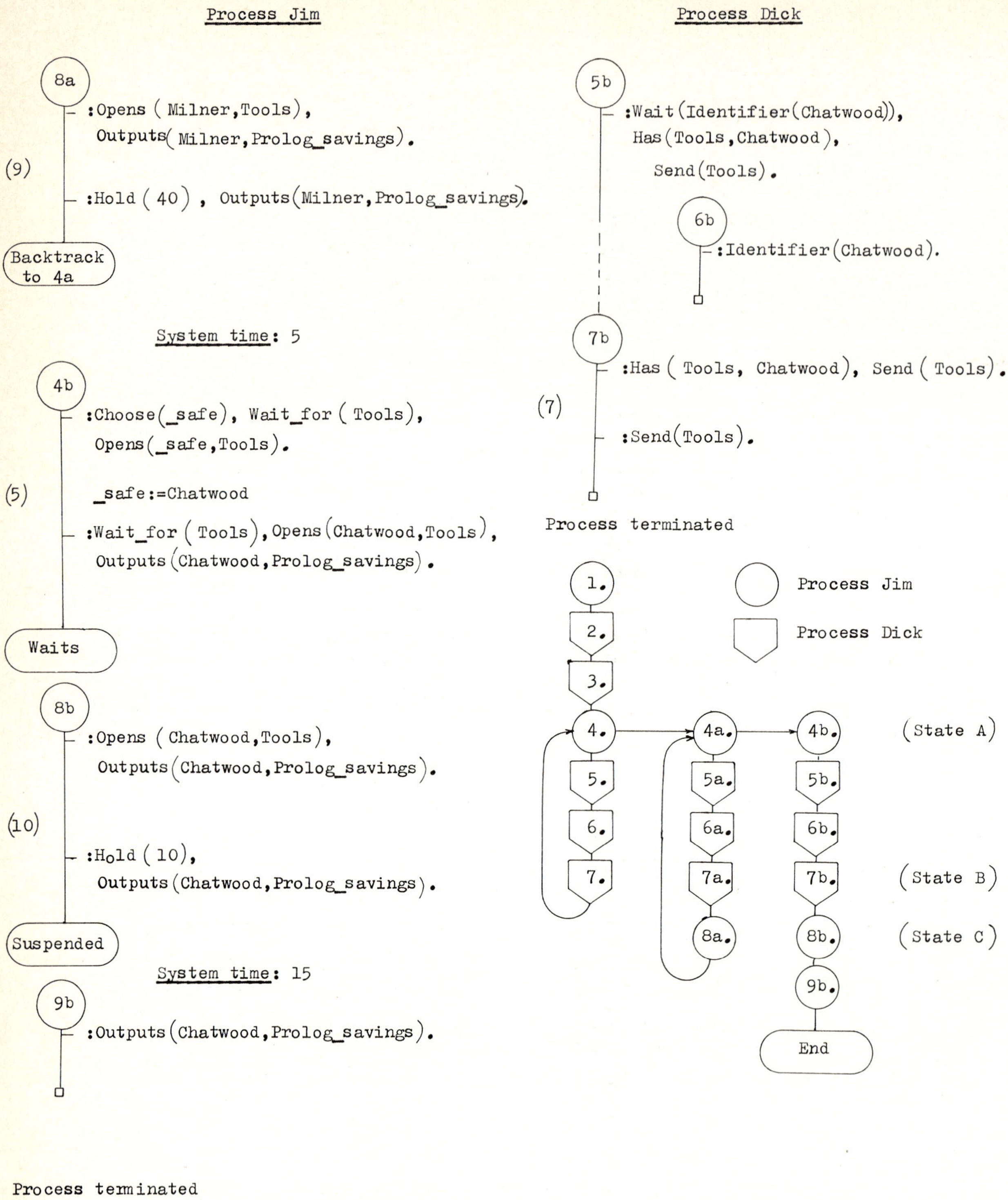

Figure 11: Execution of a T-PROLOG program

First the two processes of the first homogenous process class receive the control of resources (Figure 9. i)). If this distribution was not successful, then during backtrack one process from the first process group and one from the second gets the resources (Figure 9. ii)). If this distribution was not successful too then two processes of the second homogenous process class get the resource (Figure 9. iii)). The system automatically tried all meaningful distribution of resources and if a new backtrack occurs at this state, then backtrack continues without trying other possible distribution by permutation of homogenous processes. For E.g. two other processes of the first homogenous process class . The exact definition of the resource distribution algorithm is given in the Appendix.

To illustrate the operation of the standard resource allocation mechanism we show the solution of a job-shop problem. Traditional simulation run and a simulation using the new possibilities of T-PROLOG is presented bellow.

There are three types of resource "A", "B", "C" and there are two copies of "A", two copies of "B" and only one copy of "C". Jobs to be processed (the processes) arrive at 0. The prescribed sequence of the use of differents resources is shown on Figure 13. The corresponding T-PROLOG program is on Figure 12.

```
  (1) Resource(A,2).
  (2) Resource(B,2).
  (3) Resource(C,1).
  (4) Processing(Nil).
  (5) Processing_resource(_time._remaining):
              Seize(_resource),
              Hold(_time),
              Rélease(_resource),
              Processing(_remaining).
 End.
 (6A)
:New(Processing(A:3.B:4.C:2.Nil),P11,0),
 New(Processing(A:3.B:4.C:2.Nil),P12.,0),
 New(Processing(A:1.B:6.C:2.Nil),P21,0).
 (6B )
:New(Processing(A:3.B:4.C:2.Nil),P11,0,14),
 New(Processing A:3.B:4.C:2.Nil),P12,0,14),
 New(Processing A:1.B:6.C:2.Nil),P21,0,14).
```

Figure 12: A program for resource allocation

The main difference between the two solutions is (Figure 13), that at time 0 there were three waiting processes for the two resources of type "A". First processes P11 and P12 received the resources, and so the jobs can be processed in 15 time units. This is the solution given by traditional simulation. To use AI possibilities of T-PROLOG we give a termination time 14 for the problem. At the beginning T-PROLOG works as a traditional simulation system, but at time 13 when it wants to schedule P12 it remarks that there is no time enough to finish processing for 14 and <u>backtrack</u> begins. When backtrack arrives to time moment 3 processes P11 and P12 are not permuted on the two resources of type "B", because P11 and P12 are homogenous processes, and the resources are homogenous too. So backtrack continues to the beginning where all processes wait for resources of type "A". As P12 and P21 are not homogenous processes, they are permuted and now P21 receives a resource of type "A" before P12. This order gives a solution for the problem.

4.1.3 Dynamic program/model modification

As it was mentioned previously a T-PROLOG program (simulation model) consists of a set of logical statements, Horn clauses .

During run-time it is possible to <u>add</u> or <u>delete</u> logical statements to/from the original set of clauses. This means that the original program/model can be dynamically altered depending on the current state of the simulation by using sophisticated rules (E.g. if backtracks occurs). This feature of the system permits the contruction of allopoietic or autopoietic system models [17].

Together with the possibility of dynamic creation and destruction of processes with goals to be achieved, dynamic program/model modification possibilities suggest the construction of hierarhical, self-organizing, teleozetic system models with variable structure [17].

To insert or delete statements the built-in predicates Add(Cl,N) and Del(Id,M) are used, where Cl is the list of atoms forming the clause to be inserted into the N-th position of the corresponding partition and Id is the name of the partition from which the M-th clause is to be deleted. If backtrack occurs then previousely introduced statements (formulas) are deleted and deleted statements are introduced into the system's database.

To illustrate the use of the above built-in predicates for contructing a simple model of variable structure consider the following example.

There is a little port originally with three

Product	Sequence	Processing time			Arrives at
		A	B	C	
P11	A-B-C	3	4	2	0
P12	A-B-C	3	4	2	0
P21	A-B-C	1	6	2	0

Result of traditional simulation

Result of AI based simulation

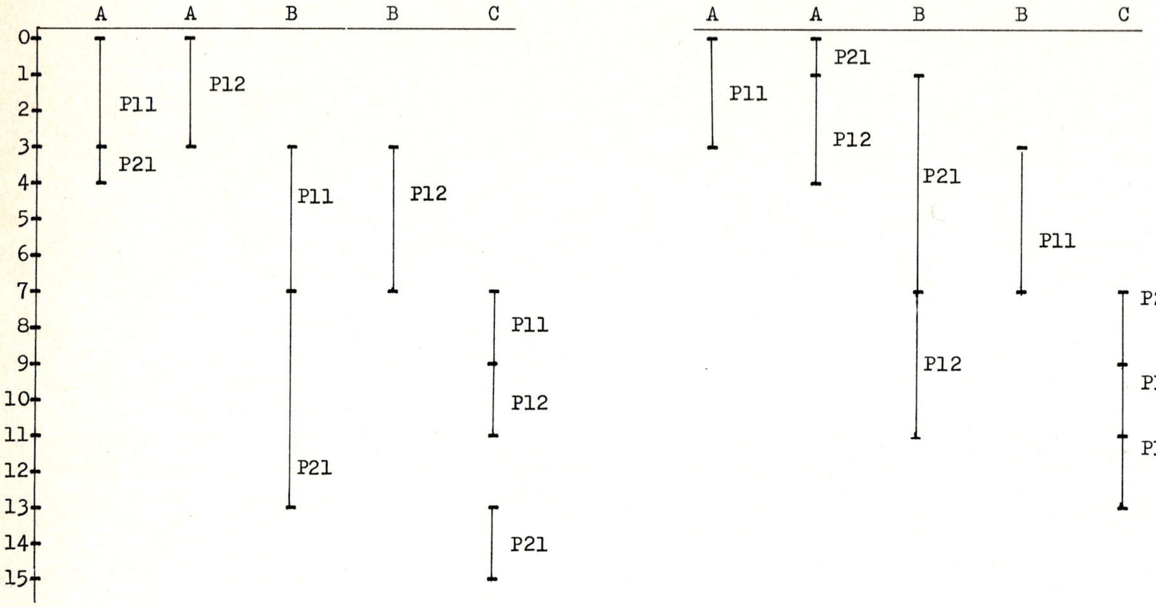

Figure 13: Job-shop scheduling

cranes of type A. Ships arrive to the port with the following rate (Figure 14).

Day	Number of ships
1	3
2	2
3	2

Figure 14: Arrival rate of ships

The unloading of a Ship using crane A takes 3 days. Every Ship arriving at the port must be unloaded without waiting for a crane. If the problem cannot be solved with original number of cranes of type A, then a crane of type A can be changed to a crane of type B. A crane of type B can unload a ship in one day. The question is with how many cranes of type A and B the problem can be solved. The corresponding T-PROLOG program is the following, Figure 15:

```
(1)  Generate_ships:
         New(Arrive_at_port,Ship1,1),
         New(Arrive_at_port,Ship2,1),
         New(Arrive_at_port,Ship3,1),
         New(Arrive_at_port,Ship4,2),
         New(Arrive_at_port,Ship5,2),
         New(Arrive_at_port,Ship6,3),
         New(Arrive_at_port,Ship7,3).
(2)  Arrive_at_port:
         Hold(0),
         Choose(_crane,_t),
         Seize(_crane,_t),
         Release(_crane).
(3) Model_definition(_number_of_a_number_of_b):
       Introduce(Crane ( A),_number_of_a),
       Introduce(Crane ( B),_number_of_b),
(4) Model_definition(_number_of_a,number_of_b):
       Minus(_number_of_a,1,_new_number_of_b ,
       Plus(_number_of_b,1_nes_number_of_b ),
       Model_definition(_new number of_a ,
                       _new_number_of_b).
(5) Introduce(_crane,0).
(6) Introduce(Crane (A),_number_of_a):
       Addresource(Crane (A),_number_of_a),
       Add(Choose(Crane A ,3).
           Available(Crane ( A)).Nil.1) .
(7) Introduce(Crane ( B),_number_of_b):
       Addresource(Crane (B),_number_of_b),
       Add(Choose(Crane(B) ,1).
           Available(Crane(B)).Nil, 2).
    End.
(8) :New(Generate_ships) ,
     New(Model_definition 3,0) .
```

Figure 15: Automatic program modification

The most important program steps are the follosing:

i) Ships are generated by (8) → (1). (Sequence of procedure calls).
The first model is generated by (8) → (3) → (6) → (5), the statement

```
     Choose ( Crane(A), 3):
         Available Crane A  .
```

is inserted into the set of clauses forming the program as the first element of the partition "Choose". This means that a ship can choose the crane A if there was a crane A available and the unloading takes three time units. Available (R) is a built-in predicate to check if a resource R is available. If it is not the case, backtrack occurs. As in this model there are three cranes of type A the problem can not be solved, because at time 2 ship4 and ship5 find no available cranes.

ii) After backtrack a new model is generated using procedures (4)→(3)→(6)→(7). In this model there are two crane of type A and one of type B, the statements

```
Chose(Crane(B),1):
    Available(Crane (B)).

Chose(Crane(A),3):
    Available(Crane (A)).
```

are introduced as first and second elements of partition Choose. (During backtrack the previously introduced statements are forgotten!)

iii) This model fails too, and a third model is created similarly to the previous step with one crane of type A and two of type B. With this model the problem can be solved and the corresponding scheduling is shown on Figure 16.

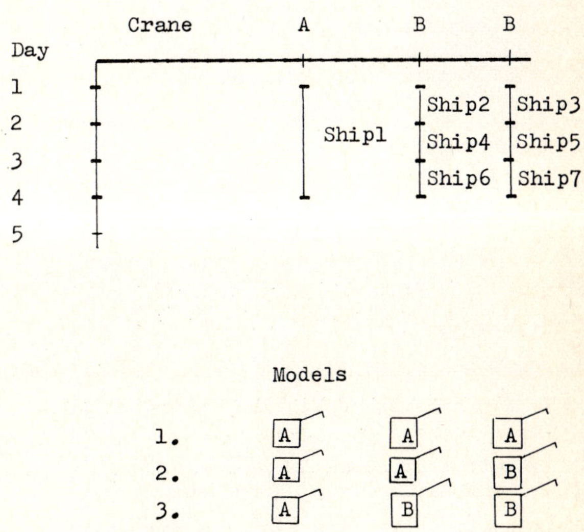

Figure 16: Generation cranes for ships

5 CONCLUSION

We think that T-PROLOG is a step toward decreasing the gap between specialist, modeler and the programer. Using mathematical logic as a programming language and a theorem-prover the programer has to concentrate on the proper definition ot the problem, rather then the exact solution by giving an appropriate algorithm. Logic may be an interface language between specialists of different domains and so it facilitites the contruction of complicated models. As a program consists of a set of logical formulas, not exactly specified sub-models can be tested because the exact structure of data are not needed at every level of testing. In traditional languages before running programs all data structure has to be defined. T-PROLOG is an interactive system, the user has the possibility to interrupt the simulation process and to modify the model by inserting or deleting logical formulas, clauses. It is our plan to extend the current possibilities of the language to forced backtrack to a user defined pevious state and then continue simulation in a defined direction. This extension will be done in the next months. For traditional simulation problems T-PROLOG works as a process oriented [15] discrete simulation language and the actual version is 16 times slower that SIMULA. The speed of T-PROLOG will be improved by using a new MPROLOG compiler. As a planned application field long range regional planning can be mentioned. The system currently works on SIEMENS, IBM and VAX machines.

6. ACKOWLEDGEMENT

We want to thank to our colleagues Péter Köves and Péter Szeredi their help in using the MPROLOG system and to Dr. András Jávor for his advices concerning the paper.

7. APPENDIX

The T-PROLOG scheduler

First we introduce some basic notation and abbreviations:

AP : active process;
ET_P : termination time of process P;
WL : waiting list its elements are pairs of form (P:T), where P is a process identifier , T is the reactivation time of the process P.
WL is ordered by T in monoton increasing way.
BL : blocked list (list of process suspended by a "Wait" call).
LM : list of messages (messages sent by "Send (M)").
ML : messages list (list of processes waiting for messages).
SL : suspend list (list of processes suspended by a "Suspend" call).
RL : resource list, its elements are pairs of the form (R:N), where R is the resource name, and N is the number of available resources R.
SG^R_{Tj} : seize group members are processes suspended by "Seize (R,T), and forming the j-th homogenous group of resource R.
ST : system time
ETL : end time list, its elements are pairs of the form (P:ET),where P is a process identifier, and ET is its termination time.

If L is a list, and X is an element of this list, then L+X is the list obtained appending X to the end of L. $X \in L$ means that X is an element of L. In the case of WL, RL, ETL, $X \in L$ means that there is such an Y that $(X:Y) \in L$.
If $(R:N) \in RL$ then $N(R) = N$.

If L is a list of resources then

$$N(L) = \min_{R \in L} N(R) \quad (N(Nil) = \infty)$$

$|L|$ denotes the length of the list L.

The scheduling algorithm is the following:

1) Initialisation

The general form of a T-PROLOG goalsequence is:

:New(GL1,P1,S1,E1),... ,New(GLn,Pn,Sn,En).
Default values: Pi = new identifier, Si=o, Ei=100000

WL1: = (P1:S1). ... .(Pn:Sn). Nil

EL : = WL1 ordered by Si in monoton increasing way.

BL : = Nil, ML :=Nil, LM:=Nil, RL:=Nil, ST :=0

ETL :=(P1:E1). ... .(Pn:En). Nil

Continuation at 4).

2) Execution of the active process

AP is executed as in PROLOG, until execution is terminated sucessfully or a control built-in procedure (built-in predicate) is called. If execution of AP is finished then continuation at 3), if a control procedure is called then continuation at 4).

3) Continuation if AP's execution terminated

$AP:ET_{AP}$ is deleted from ETL. If ETL=Nil then the T-PROLOG program is terminated sucessfully. If ETL $\neq$ Nil then continuation at 5).

4) Process suspension by control predicates i) Wait G :Let's consider G as a PROLOG goal. If its execution success then continuation at 2) AP remains unchanged. If G fails, then BL: = BL + AP, the "wait" condition of AP is G. Continuation at 5). ii) Wait_for (M): if M ∈ LM then continuation at 2). Otherwise ML: = ML+AP, the message AP waits for is M. Continuation at 5). iii) Send(M): LM :=LM+M, continuation at 2). iv) Hold(T): If $ET_{AP} > ST+T$ then backtrack. Otherwise (AP: ST+T) is inserted into WL after (P:PT) ∈ WL and before (Q:QT) ∈ WL for which PT ⩽ ST+T ⩽ QT. Continuation at 5). v.) New(GL,P,S,E): if S > ST or E < S then backtrack. Otherwise (P:S) is inserted into WL similarly as it was desribed in case of Hold (T). ETL : = ETL +(P:E). The goalsequence of P is GL, continuation at 2). vi) Suspended: SL := SL+AP, continuation at 5). vii) Seize(R,T): (Seize(R) ≡ Seize(R,0)) R is a resource or a list of resources. If R isn't a list then it is replaced by the list of one element R.Nil. If ∃E ∈ R, E ∉ RL then it causes a runtime error. Otherwise if ∃j,P $(P \in SG^R_{Tj})$ that the goalsequences of P and AP are unifiable, then $SG^R_{Tj} := SG^R_{Tj}$ + AP. If there isn't such a seize group, then a new one is created and SG^R_{Tk} :=Ap.Nil . Continuation at 5). vii) Release (R): if R is not a list it is replaced by R.Nil. If ∃E∈R (E ∉ RL) then runtime error. Otherwise for all Ri ∈ R the (Ri:Ni) element of RL is replaced by (Ri:NI+1), continuation at 2). viii) Addresource(R,N): if R:M ∈ RL then R:M is replaced by (R: M+N). Otherwise RL := RL+(R:N) , continuation at 2). ix) Delete_process(P): all process identifiers that are unifiable with P are deleted from the lists, WL, Bl, ML, SL SG^R_{Tj}, ETL (AP is not deleted from ETL!), continuation at 2). x) Replace_process (P,K): the first process whose identifier is unifiable with P is deleted from one of the lists WL,BL, ML, SL or SG^R_{Tj} . If there isn't such a process then backtrack. If K is a number and ST⩽K then (P:K) is inserted into WL with preservation the monotonity of WL. ST > K causes backtrack. If K is not a number then SL := SL+P. Continuation at 2).

5) Choise of the new active process

i) WL ≠ Nil, and the first element of WL is P:ST. Then AP :=P, and P:ST is deleted from WL. Continuation at 2). ii) BL ≠ Nil and P ∈ BL that the "wait" condition of P succeeds. If P is the first of these processes then AP := P and P is deleted from BL. Continuation at 2). iii) ML ≠ Nil and P∈ML and for "message" M of P, M ∈ LM. Then AP is the first of such processes, P is deleted from ML. Continuation at 2). iv) $\exists SG^R_{Tj}$ that N(R)>o, then resource distribution 6). v) The user defined Active_suspended (PL) procedure is called. If it doesn't fail and APL = PL SL ≠ Nil then SL : = SL\APL, and P ∈ APL (P:ST) is inserted into WL. Continuation at 5). vi) WL ≠ Nil, its first element is (P:T), t > ST . If T is less or equal to all elements of ETL then AP := P, (P:T) is deleted from SL, ST :=T, LM := Nil. Continuation at 2). vii) If none of i-vi is satisfied then <u>backtrack.</u>

6) Resource distribution

i) R_1, R_2 , ... , R_r are all the resources for which $N(R_i) > o$ and $SG^{Ri.Xi}_{oj}$ that $N(Xi) > o$, (It there is no such resources then r=o). R_{r+1} is the first resource such that $N(R_{r+1}) > o$ and $SG^{Rr+1.Xr+1}_{Tj}$ that $T > o$ and $N(X_{r+1}) > o$. (If there is any.)

ii) q:=1. iii) $SG^{Rq.Xgj}_{Tj}$, j=1, ... , s are all the seize groups that $N(X_{qj}) > o$. If $g \leqslant r$ then T=o, if q=r+1 then T = o.

$a_j := \min(N(X_{qj}), |SG^{Rq.Xgj}_{Tj}|)$,
$M = \min(N(Rq), \Sigma^s_j = a_j$. M instances of resource Rq will be distributed. In list RL (Rq:N (Rq)) is replaced by (Rq:N(Rq)- M). iv) $V := \{\langle v_1, \ldots, v_s \rangle\}$:

$o \leqslant v_j \leqslant a_j, v_j$ is integer $\sum^s_{j=1} v_j = M$.

In the lexicographic ordering of V the order of elements of V : $w_1, w_2, \ldots, w_z$.

$wk = \langle v^k_1, \ldots, v^k_s \rangle$ k=1,2, ... ,z

v) k:=1. vi) From seize groups $SG^{Rq.Xqj}_{Tj}$ the first v^k_j elements are choosen (j = 1,2, ... ,s). These processes are deleted from seize groups, and they are inserted into WL with reactivation time ST. vii) End of algorithm. If later in case of backtrack this points is reached again then continue at viii). viii) k:k+1. If k⩽z then continuation at vi). If k=z+1 then continuation at ix). ix) q:=q+1. If q⩽r+1 then continuation at iii, otherwise the backtrack continues.

8 REFERENCES

[1] Battani, G. and Meloni, H., Interpreteur du Language de Programation PROLOG (Université d'Aix Marseille 1973).

[2] Birtwistle, G.M. and Dahl, O-j. and Myhrhaug, B. and Nygaard, K., Simula Begin (Studentlitteratur, Lund, Sweden, 1973).

[3] Birtwistle, G.M. Discrete event Modelling on Simula (The Macmillan Press Ltd. London 1979).

[4] Bendl,J. and Köves,P. and Szeredi,P., The MPROLOG system. (Preprints of Logic Workshop, Debrecen, Hungary, 1980).

[5] Futó, I. and Darvas, F. and Szeredi,P., Using PROLOG to implement QA and DBM system, in Gallaire,H. and Minker, J. eds Logic and Data Bases(Plenum Press, New York, 1978).

[6] Futó, I. and Szeredi, J., T-PROLOG User Manual, Institute for Coordination of Computer Techniques, Budapest, Hungary (1981).

[7] Futó, I. and Szeredi,J. and Szenes,K., A Modelling Tool Based on Mathematical Logic -T-PROLOG. Acta Cybernetica Tom 5, Fasc. 3 (1981) 68-74.

[8] Hevitt C., PLANNER: A Language for Manipulating Models and Proving Theorem in a Robot, in Walker, D.E. and Norton, L.M. eds,(IJCAI 1969).

[9] Hevitt, C., Viewing Control Structures as Patterns for Passing Messages, Artifical Intelligence Vol. 8. No. 3. (1977) 323-364.

[10] Kiviat, P.j., Simulation Using Simcript II (Rand Corporation 1968).

[11] Koster, C., A Compiler Compiler, Report MR 127, Matematisch Centrum Amsterdam (1971).

[12] Kowalski, R., Logic for Problem Solving (North-Holland, Amsterdam, 1980).

[13] Mc. Dermott, D. and Sussman, G.J., The CONIVER Reference Manual. MIT AI Laboratory Memo No. 259, Cambridge (1972).

[14] Mc. Cabe., Programmer's Guide to IC-PROLOG. Imperial College London (1978).

[15] Nance, R.E. and Tech.V., The Time and State Relationship in Simulation Modelling, Communication of the ACM Vol.24 (1981) 173-180.

[16] Nilson,N.J., Principles of Artifical Intelligence (Toga Publishtng Co. Palo Alto, California 1980).

[17] Oren, T.I. Concepts for Advanced Computer Assisted Modelling and Simulation in Ziegler, B.P. eds (North-Holland, Amsterdam 1979).

[18] Pereira, F. and Pereira, L. and Warren,D., User's Guide to DECsystem-10 PROLOG, Dept. of AI University of Edinburgh (1978).

[19] Rulifson, J.F. and Derksen, J.A. and Waldinger, R.J., QA4 A Procedural Calculus for Reasoning. AI Center Technical Note SRI Project 8721 (1972).

[20] Schmidt, B., GPSS-FORTRAN (Lecture notes in Computer Science, Springer Verlag, Berlin 1980).

[21] GPSS/360 User's Manual. IBM 420-03261

III. APPLICATIONS

DISCRETE SIMULATION AND RELATED FIELDS
A. Jávor (editor)
North-Holland Publishing Company

COMPUTER MODELING OF DOUBLE-LAYER CIRCULARIZATION AND GASTRULATION

Donald Greenspan

Department of Mathematics
The University of Texas at Arlington
Arlington, Texas

In this paper, certain types of biological cell rearrangements are modeled from a computer point of view. All forces are of a local nature and are patterned on classical atomic and molecular interactions. It is first shown how to induce a double-layered flat tissue to fold into a double-layered circular tissue. Then, it is shown how to induce a section of the circular tissue to pull inward, or gastrulate.

1. INTRODUCTION

In this paper we will develop a new computer oriented approach to the modeling of certain motions of biological cells. Precisely, we will explore circularization, which is the folding of cells into a circular tissue, and gastrulation, which is the pulling inward of part of a circular tissue. Note, immediately, that even though the discussions and examples are given in two dimensions, the vector formulation and the methodology apply equally well in three dimensions.

In recent years the modeling of circularization and gastrulation have received wide attention, but from an abstract, mathematical point of view only (see, e. g., [1] and the references contained therein). Our approach will be from a physical point of view in that we will develop dynamical relationships which are founded on classical molecular mechanics [2]. These relationships will yield gross configurational motions from entirely local interactions, which is completely consistent in spirit with other approaches.

2. CLASSICAL MOLECULAR MECHANICS

For purposes of intuition, it will be important to review, first, how molecules interact.

Within a larger body, molecules interact only locally, that is, only with their nearest neighbors. This interaction is of the following general nature [3]. If two molecules are pushed together they repel each other, if pulled apart they attract each other, and mutual repulsion is of a greater order of magnitude than is mutual attraction. Mathematically, this behavior is often formulated as follows [4]. The magnitude F of the force $\vec{F}$ between two molecules which are locally r units apart is of the form

$$F = -\frac{G}{r^p} + \frac{H}{r^q}, \tag{2.1}$$

where, typically,

$$G > 0,\ H > 0,\ q > p \geq 7. \tag{2.2}$$

The major porblem in any simulation of a physical body is that there are too many component molecules to incorporate into the model. The classical mathematical approach is to replace the large, but finite, number of molecules by an infinite set of points. In so doing, the rich physics of molecular interaction is lost because every point always has an infinite number of neighbors which are arbitrarily close. A viable computer alternative is to replace the large number of molecules by a much smaller number of particles and then readjust the parameters in (2.1) to compensate [5], [6]. It is this latter approach which we will follow.

3. THE COMPUTER ALGORITHM

The general idea outlined in Section 2 will be

implemented in the following, constructive fashion.

Consider N particles P_i, $i = 1,2,\ldots,N$, each of unit mass. For $\Delta t > 0$, let $t_k = k\Delta t$, $k = 0,1,2,\ldots$. For each of $i = 1,2,\ldots,N$, let P_i at t_k be located at $\vec{r}_{i,k} = (x_{i,k}, y_{i,k})$, have velocity $\vec{v}_{i,k} = (v_{i,k,x}, v_{i,k,y})$, and have acceleration $\vec{a}_{i,k} = (a_{i,k,x}, a_{i,k,y})$. Let position, velocity, and acceleration be related by the recursion formulas

$$\vec{v}_{i,\frac{1}{2}} = \vec{v}_{i,0} + \tfrac{1}{2}(\Delta t)\vec{a}_{i,0}, \text{ (starter formula)} \tag{3.1}$$

$$\vec{v}_{i,k+\frac{1}{2}} = \vec{v}_{i,k-\frac{1}{2}} + (\Delta t)\vec{a}_{i,k}, \quad k = 1,2,3,\ldots \tag{3.2}$$

$$\vec{r}_{i,k+1} = \vec{r}_{i,k} + (\Delta t)\vec{v}_{i,k+\frac{1}{2}}, \quad k = 0,1,2,\ldots . \tag{3.3}$$

At t_k, let the force acting on P_i be $\vec{F}_{i,k} = (F_{i,k,x}, F_{i,k,y})$. We relate force and acceleration by the dynamical equation

$$\vec{F}_{i,k} = m_i \vec{a}_{i,k},$$

which, by the assumption of unit mass, simplifies to

$$\vec{F}_{i,k} = \vec{a}_{i,k}. \tag{3.4}$$

As soon as the precise structure of $\vec{F}_{i,k}$ is given, then the motion of each P_i will be determined explicitly and recursively by (3.1)-(3.4) from given initial data. The force $\vec{F}_{i,k}$ is described now as follows. Let $\vec{r}_{ij,k}$ be the vector from P_i to P_j at time t_k, so that $r_{ij,k} = |\vec{r}_{i,k} - \vec{r}_{j,k}|$ is the distance between the two particles. Then the force $\vec{F}_{ij,k}$ on P_i exerted by P_j at time t_k is assumed to be

$$\vec{F}_{ij,k} = \left(-\frac{G}{(r_{ij,k})^p} + \frac{H}{(r_{ij,k})^q} \right) \frac{\vec{r}_{ji,k}}{r_{ij,k}}, \tag{3.5}$$

which is consistent with (2.1). The total force $\vec{F}_{i,k}$ on P_i due to all other particles different from P_i defined by

$$\vec{F}_{i,k} = \sum_{\substack{j=1 \\ j\neq i}}^{N} \left\{ \left\{ -\frac{G}{(r_{ij,k})^p} + \frac{H}{(r_{ij,k})^q} \right\} \frac{\vec{r}_{ji,k}}{r_{ij,k}} \right\}. \tag{3.6}$$

Note finally that the introduction of an additional parameter D is essential to assure that particle interactions are local. We will require that whenever $r_{ij,k} > D$, then (3.5) must be replaced with

$$\vec{F}_{ij,k} = \vec{0} \qquad (r_{ij,k} > D). \tag{3.7}$$

For the convenience of the reader, a typical FORTRAN program of the algorithm is given in Appendix A of Greenspan [7]. Note also that in all examples to be described, the time step used is $\Delta t = 0.01$ and all calculations were done on the DEC-20 system at the University of Texas at Arlington.

4. COMPUTER MODELING OF CIRCULARIZATION

Let us show now how to simulate circularization in the XY-plane. Throughout, we set $p = 3$ and $q = 5$ in (2.1).

First, consider a double-layer, linearly ordered tissue of 100 particles, as shown in Figure 4.1. The ordered particles P_1-P_{50}, which form the lower row, are called row 1 and are located at the points $(-25+i,0)$, $i = 0,1,2,\ldots,49$, respectively. The ordered particles P_{51}-P_{100}, which form the upper row, are called row 2 and are located at $(-24.5+j,0.866)$, $j = 0,1,2,\ldots,49$, respectively. For later consideration, note, in particular, the special relative positions of P_1, P_{50}, P_{51} and P_{100}.

In order to induce the configuration to fold into a circle, note that if we choose $G > H$ on row 1 and $G < H$ on row 2, then row 1 will contract while row 2 expands, and a folding process will ensue. However, a priori, one cannot determine which choices of G and H will yield a circle. But, with some computer experimentation, approximate values can be

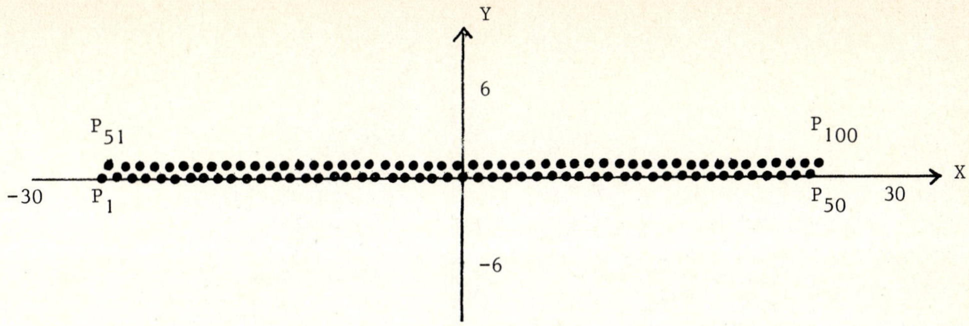

FIGURE 4.1

determined from which circularization can be made to follow easily. To illustrate this, let $G = 1.03$, $H = 0.97$ on row 1 and $G = 0.97$, $H = 1.03$ on row 2. Then, with $D = 1.4$ and all initial velocities set to zero, the resulting motion was calculated from (3.1)-(3.8) for 49000 time steps, the result of which is shown in Figure 4.2 (on a scale which is larger than that of Figure 4.1). It is apparent that the curvature is not great enough to effect the simultaneous bonding of P_1 to P_{50} and of P_{51} to P_{100}, thus forming a double layer. So, at this point, we set $G = 1.05$, $H = .95$ on row 1 and $G = .95$, $H = 1.05$ on row 2. In 7000 further time steps, the indicated bonds were achieved, as is shown in Figure 4.3. At this point, we reset $G = 1.03$, $H = .97$ on row 1, $G = .97$, $H = 1.03$ on row 2, and continued the calculations for 14000 more time steps. The result, as shown in Figure 4.4, when compared to that of Figure 4.3, indicates excessive elastic vibration, which was next damped as follows. The calculations were continued for 7000 time steps, but with the change $D = 1.5$. Then, still with $D = 1.5$, the calculations were continued for 14000 more time steps but with $G = H = 1.00$ on rows 1 and 2 and with all velocities reset to zero at the beginning of the calculation and again after 7000 time steps. The final circular, double-layer configuration is shown in Figure 4.5. The positions and velocities of all particles at this final time are given in the Table.

5. COMPUTER MODELING OF GASTRULATION

In order to show how to model gastrulation, we will proceed, in particular, with the configuration shown in Figure 4.5. Of primary importance will be the selection of G and H along sections of the tissue so as to induce the appropriate convexities and concavities. However, from a biological point of view, it will be necessary, first, to add a liquid interior to the bounding tissue. This will also be of value physically, since it will prevent excessive elastic motions of the boundary. We proceed then as follows.

As shown in Figure 5.1, thirty "liquid" particles, P_{101}-P_{130}, have been added to the interior section at the points (-2,6), (2,6), (-3,5), (3,5), (-4,4), (0,4), (-5,3), (-1,3), (3,3), (-4,2), (2,2), (6,2), (-5,1), (-1,1), (5,1), (-2,0), (4,0), (-5,-1), (1,-1), (5,-1), (-2,-2), (2,-2), (6,-2), (-3,-3), (1,-3), (-4,-4), (2,-4), (-3,-5), (1,-5), (2,-6). The fluid character of these particles is maintained in the following simple fashion. Let P_i be any one of the new particles. Let P_j be any particle, new or old. Then if $r_{ij,k} > 1.5$, the force between the two particles is set equal to zero. If $r_{ij,k} \leq 1.5$, then the force between the two particles is taken to be repulsive only and to have a

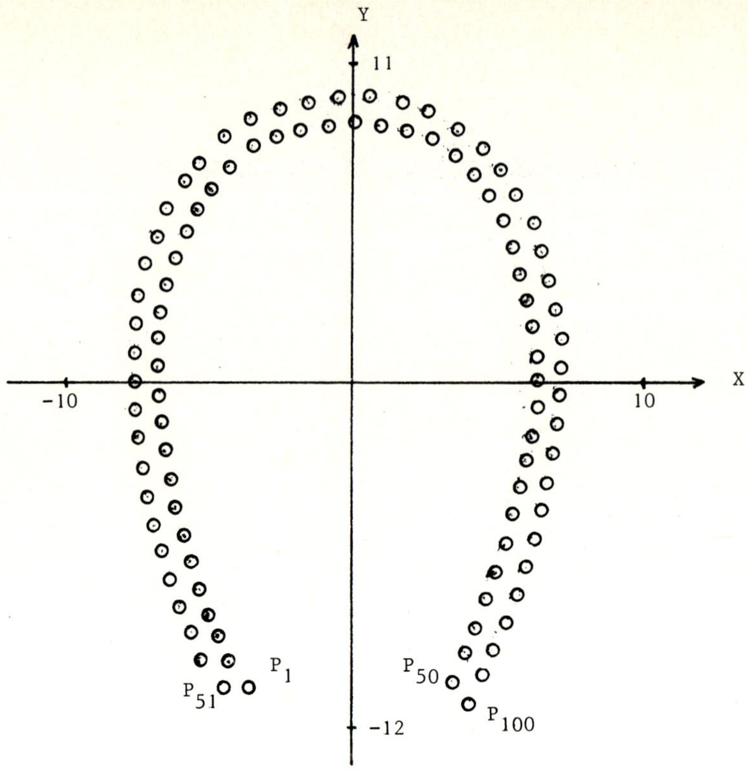

FIGURE 4.2

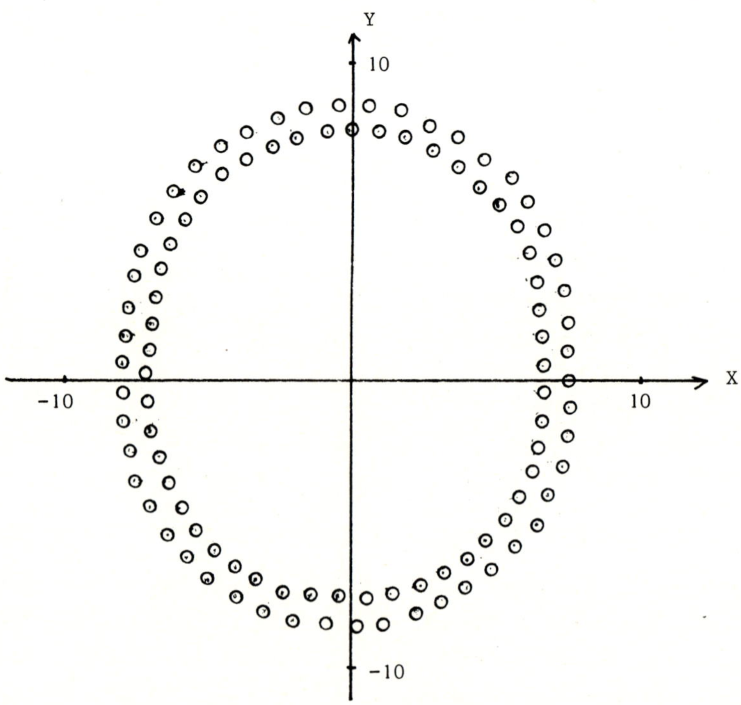

FIGURE 4.3

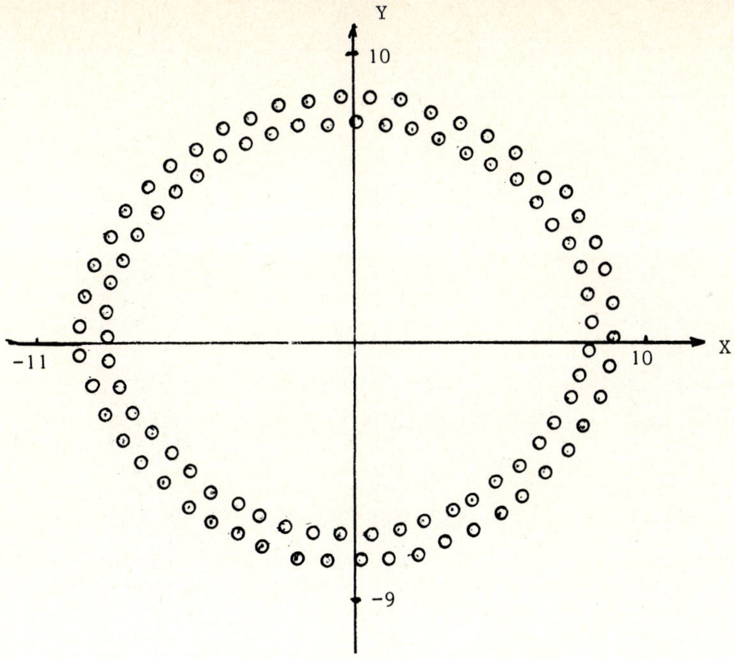

FIGURE 4.4

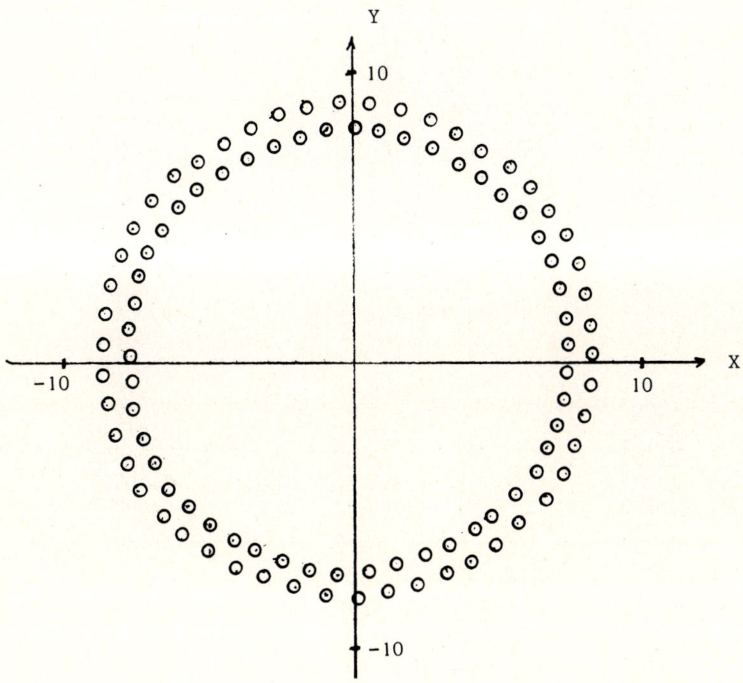

FIGURE 4.5

TABLE

i	x_i	y_i	vx_i	vy_i
1	-0.485	-7.261	-0.00639	0.01691
2	-1.421	-7.120	0.00888	0.01355
3	-2.354	-6.869	-0.00015	-0.00903
4	-3.260	-6.523	0.00773	-0.00019
5	-4.130	-6.093	0.00169	-0.02189
6	-4.964	-5.608	0.01317	-0.02060
7	-5.726	-5.029	0.00226	-0.01735
8	-6.366	-4.312	0.01491	0.00399
9	-6.886	-3.508	0.00321	-0.02527
10	-7.267	-2.645	0.00504	0.01306
11	-7.591	-1.719	0.00890	0.01277
12	-7.759	-0.765	-0.00660	-0.00853
13	-7.808	0.183	0.01563	-0.00806
14	-7.804	1.130	-0.02422	0.01430
15	-7.656	2.079	-0.02341	-0.00514
16	-7.421	3.013	-0.02433	0.02393
17	-7.115	3.906	-0.00694	0.02424
18	-6.639	4.719	0.01757	0.01940
19	-6.008	5.461	0.01664	-0.01230
20	-5.281	6.093	-0.01184	0.02201
21	-4.487	6.674	-0.00325	0.00254
22	-3.645	7.182	0.00670	0.02366
23	-2.781	7.616	0.00085	0.02161
24	-1.889	7.937	-0.00002	0.00939
25	-0.971	8.165	0.00772	-0.02633
26	-0.032	8.198	-0.00563	-0.02455
27	0.896	8.074	-0.01318	-0.01389
28	1.814	7.805	0.00205	0.00507
29	2.690	7.409	0.00565	0.03183
30	3.561	6.927	-0.02214	-0.00205
31	4.393	6.379	0.00997	0.02696
32	5.152	5.793	0.00031	-0.00046
33	5.812	5.104	-0.01838	0.01903
34	6.393	4.346	-0.00273	-0.00042
35	6.804	3.488	0.02598	-0.00847
36	7.068	2.574	0.01765	-0.00850
37	7.253	1.651	0.00543	0.00117
38	7.298	0.686	0.01636	0.01980
39	7.304	-0.277	-0.00367	0.01165
40	7.202	-1.215	0.00009	0.01110
41	6.999	-2.158	0.00007	-0.00287
42	6.624	-3.051	-0.00826	0.00109
43	6.176	-3.889	-0.03131	0.00715
44	5.607	-4.657	0.00110	-0.01273
45	4.862	-5.282	-0.00067	-0.01269
46	4.057	-5.838	-0.01623	-0.02517
47	3.181	-6.282	-0.00269	-0.00714
48	2.297	-6.658	-0.00680	0.00853
49	1.392	-6.987	-0.00956	0.01256
50	0.463	-7.205	0.00377	0.01574

TABLE (Completed)

i	x_i	y_i	vx_i	vy_i
51	-1.048	-8.069	0.01928	0.03899
52	-2.114	-7.845	0.02089	0.01474
53	-3.109	-7.509	0.01531	-0.01077
54	-4.070	-7.092	-0.00460	-0.01426
55	-4.997	-6.585	0.00975	0.00471
56	-5.898	-5.990	0.00117	-0.00440
57	-6.694	-5.256	0.02763	0.00625
58	-7.362	-4.420	0.02490	-0.00440
59	-7.876	-3.460	0.04221	0.00257
60	-8.252	-2.468	-0.02146	0.02805
61	-8.531	-1.395	-0.00634	0.00740
62	-8.666	-0.332	-0.02602	-0.00639
63	-8.692	0.690	-0.00232	0.01162
64	-8.600	1.739	-0.01173	-0.01107
65	-8.381	2.769	-0.03575	-0.02913
66	-8.092	3.778	0.02146	-0.02089
67	-7.631	4.761	0.03111	-0.02232
68	-7.000	5.627	0.00063	0.02459
69	-6.245	6.418	0.02569	-0.00135
70	-5.410	7.076	-0.03597	-0.03513
71	-4.504	7.670	-0.02469	0.00103
72	-3.592	8.187	-0.00389	0.00499
73	-2.626	8.612	0.02247	-0.00487
74	-1.605	8.912	0.00068	0.00373
75	-0.504	9.049	-0.00491	-0.02076
76	0.558	9.012	-0.00946	-0.02197
77	1.572	8.795	-0.02058	0.01208
78	2.576	8.414	0.01498	0.00103
79	3.531	7.934	0.01400	0.01938
80	4.440	7.363	0.02246	-0.00511
81	5.312	6.790	-0.02642	-0.00432
82	6.117	6.062	0.00535	-0.03113
83	6.811	5.224	-0.00007	-0.00530
84	7.379	4.285	0.02278	0.00548
85	7.769	3.307	0.02616	0.00794
86	8.029	2.281	-0.01306	-0.03154
87	8.144	1.229	0.00089	-0.00077
88	8.189	0.201	-0.00307	-0.00941
89	8.121	-0.858	0.00371	0.00675
90	7.936	-1.914	-0.00391	0.00003
91	7.616	-2.924	-0.00118	0.00506
92	7.160	-3.899	-0.01370	-0.00401
93	6.584	-4.787	-0.00976	0.00383
94	5.800	-5.616	-0.01168	0.01462
95	4.942	-6.287	-0.00021	0.00171
96	4.014	-6.814	-0.00139	-0.02873
97	3.082	-7.279	-0.00002	-0.02503
98	2.108	-7.670	-0.03268	-0.00041
99	1.105	-7.959	-0.02033	-0.00089
100	0.051	-8.104	0.00078	0.00833

magnitude of $(500 + r_{ij,k})^{-1}$. Thus, the new particles can never bond, either with themselves or with tissue particles of the boundary. The initial velocities of the new particles are taken to be zero.

Five calculations were then carried out in sequence, as follows, each for 3500 time steps. In the first one, initial convexities and concavities were induced by fixing G and H as follows for the given particles:

$G = 1.01,\ H = 0.99,\quad P_9-P_{11},\ P_{41}-P_{43}$

$G = 1.02,\ H = 0.98,\quad P_{12}-P_{14},\ P_{38}-P_{40}$

$G = 1.03,\ H = 0.97,\quad P_{15}-P_{17},\ P_{35}-P_{37}$

$G = 1.01,\ H = 0.99,\quad P_{18}-P_{20},\ P_{32}-P_{34}$

$G = 0.99,\ H = 1.01,\quad P_{21}-P_{23},\ P_{29}-P_{31}$

$G = 0.98,\ H = 1.02,\quad P_{24}-P_{28}$

$G = 0.99,\ H = 1.01,\quad P_{58}-P_{60},\ P_{91}-P_{93}$

$G = 0.98,\ H = 1.02,\quad P_{61}-P_{64},\ P_{87}-P_{90}$

$G = 0.97,\ H = 1.03,\quad P_{65}-P_{67},\ P_{84}-P_{86}$

$G = 0.99,\ H = 1.01,\quad P_{68}-P_{70},\ P_{81}-P_{83}$

$G = 1.01,\ H = 0.99,\quad P_{71}-P_{73},\ P_{78}-P_{80}$

$G = 1.02,\ H = 0.98,\quad P_{76}-P_{77},$

For each of the next four calculations, the convexities and concavities were accentuated by fixing G and H as follows for the given particles:

$G = 1.02,\ H = 0.98,\quad P_9-P_{11},\ P_{41}-P_{43}$

$G = 1.04,\ H = 0.96,\quad P_{12}-P_{14},\ P_{38}-P_{40}$

$G = 1.06,\ H = 0.94,\quad P_{15}-P_{17},\ P_{35}-P_{37}$

$G = 1.02,\ H = 0.98,\quad P_{18}-P_{20},\ P_{32}-P_{34}$

$G = 0.96,\ H = 1.04,\quad P_{21}-P_{23},\ P_{29}-P_{31}$

$G = 0.94,\ H = 1.06,\quad P_{24}-P_{28}$

$G = 0.98,\ H = 1.02,\quad P_{58}-P_{60},\ P_{91}-P_{93}$

$G = 0.96,\ H = 1.04,\quad P_{61}-P_{64},\ P_{87}-P_{90}$

$G = 0.94,\ H = 1.06,\quad P_{65}-P_{67},\ P_{84}-P_{86}$

$G = 0.98,\ H = 1.02,\quad P_{68}-P_{70},\ P_{81}-P_{83}$

$G = 1.04,\ H = 0.96,\quad P_{71}-P_{73},\ P_{78}-P_{80}$

$G = 1.06,\ H = 0.94,\quad P_{74}-P_{77}.$

Figures 5.2, 5.3 and 5.4 show the developing gastrulation at the ends of the first, the second, and the fifth calculations. The computer program for these calculations is given in Appendix B of Greenspan [7]. The liquid particles showed no significant motions, but simply sloshed about, as can be verified from the figures in Appendix C of Greenspan [7], and so they were excluded from the present figures.

6. REMARKS

From the extensive calculations which supported the development of the methodology of Sections 4 and 5, the following general observations were made. Strictly local interaction could not be maintained with $D > 1.5$. Various combinations of p and q with $p > 3$ and $q > 5$ yielded a degree of elasticity which seemed too high for that usually associated with biological tissues. Examples in which P_1 and P_{50} were bonded, but P_{51} and P_{100} were not, were not amenable to gastrulation because the partially bonded ends would slide excessively in the vertical direction in response to changes of curvature elsewhere. Use of the force formula $(R+r_{ij,k})^{-1}$ for the liquid particles in Section 5 required a decrease in the time step for $R < 250$, in response to large fluid motions, and did not yield the desired effect for $R > 1000$, in which cases, the effective force was too small.

Finally, we recognize that for some basic biological phenomena [1], it would be of interest to have the upper half of the tissue actually gastrulate to the point where it touches the lower half in at least one point. With only 100 particles, this was not possible. The number of particles and the given local interaction distance D limit the amount of curvature one can obtain before the tissue breaks.

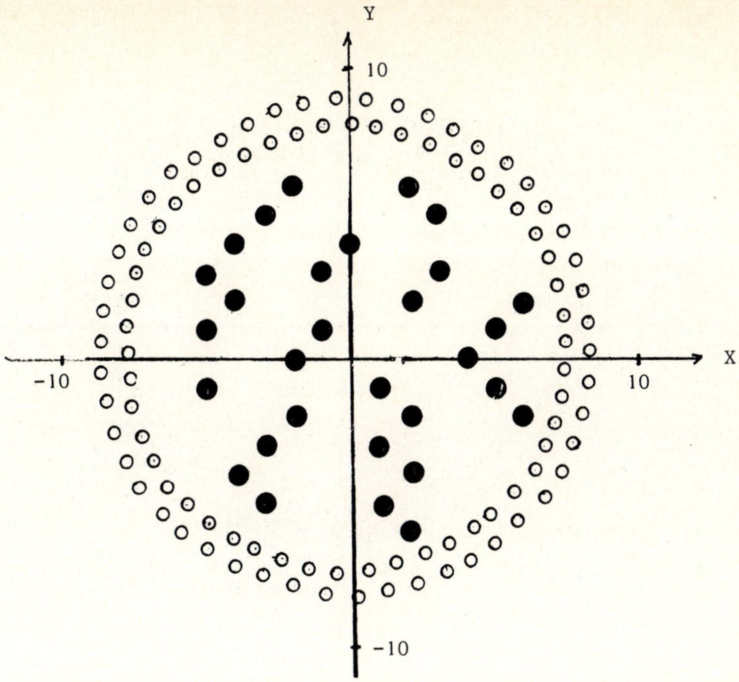

FIGURE 5.1

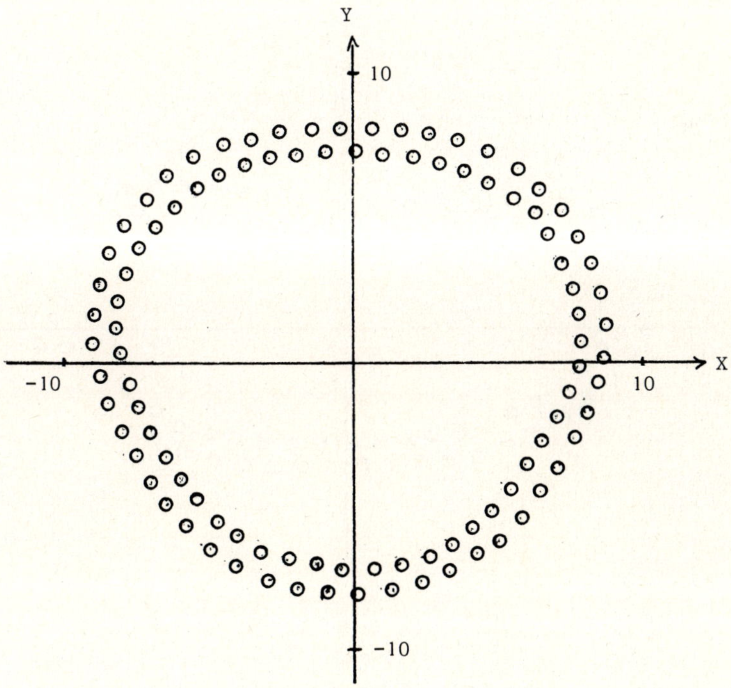

FIGURE 5.2

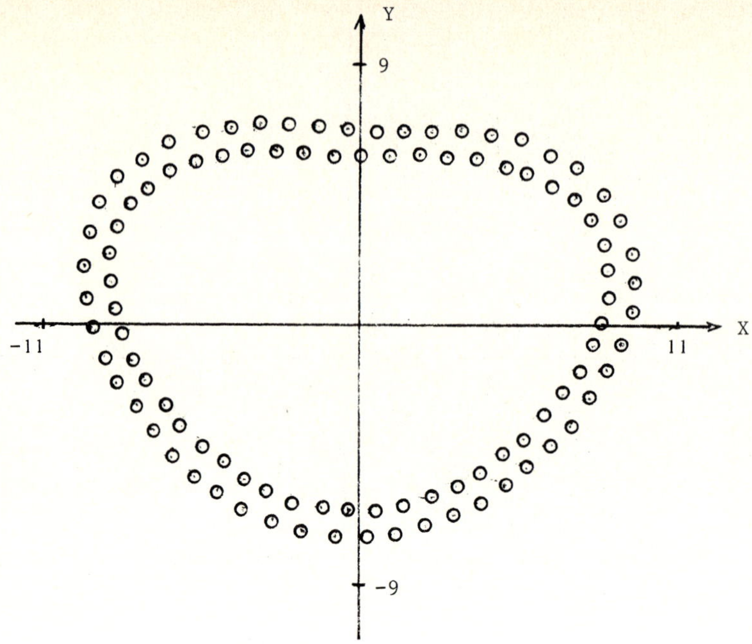

FIGURE 5.3

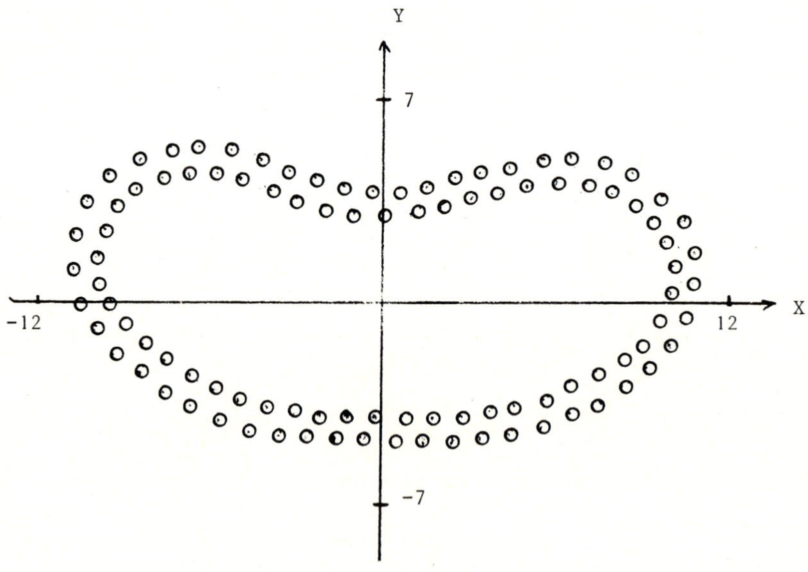

FIGURE 5.4

Therefore, an increase in the number of particles was explored. A 160 particle tissue, completely analogous in structure for that shown in Figure 4.1, was generated by setting $G = 1.03$, $H = 0.97$ on the lower row and $G = 0.97$, $H = 1.03$ on the upper row. Without any of the additional manipulations described in Section 4, the tissue evolved into a double-layered oval in 87000 time steps. An additional 14000 time steps were expended in trying to circularize the oval, but the process appeared to be exceptionally slow. For this reason, thirty liquid particles were added to the interior and gastrulation was attempted immediately. No results were obtained because the storage requirements now exceeded that allowed by the DEC-20 system. Thus, the project had to be abandoned for the present, but should be implementable easily on a larger computer system.

REFERENCES:

[1] Mostow, G. D. (Editor), Mathematical Models for Cell Rearrangement, Yale Univ. Press, New Haven, Conn., 1975.

[2] Greenspan, D., Arithmetic Applied Mathematics, Pergamon Press, Oxford, 1980.

[3] Feynman, R. P., Leighton, R. B., and Sands, M., The Feynman Lectures on Physics, Addison-Wesley, Reading, Mass., 1963.

[4] Hirschfelder, J. O., Curtiss, C. F., and Bird, R. B., Molecular Theory of Gases and Liquids, Wiley, New York, 1954.

[5] Von Neumann, John, "Proposal and analysis of a new treatment of hydrodynamical shock problems", in The Collected Works of John von Neumann, Vol. VI, No. 27, Pergamon, New York, 1963.

[6] Greenspan, D., Discrete Models, Addison-Wesley, Reading, Mass., 1973.

[7] Greenspan, D., "Numerical studies of double-layer circularization and gastrulation", TR 136, Mathematics Dept. University of Texas at Arlington, 1980.

DISCRETE SIMULATION AND RELATED FIELDS
A. Jávor (editor)
North-Holland Publishing Company

MATHEMATICAL MODELLING FOR EMPIRICAL SPATIAL FORECASTING OF COMMODITY FLOWS - A METHODOLOGY AND AN APPLICATION

C. S. Lalwani

Department of Maritime Studies
University of Wales Institute of Science & Technology
Cardiff CF1 3NU United Kingdom

Effective decision making in the transport field depends upon the facility to extrapolate in space as well as time. In this paper an attempt has been made to develop a simple format to present a data set on commodity movement statistics which usually comprises of several hundred thousand individual flows. A class of spatio temporal techniques to model commodity movement system has been presented. The data used for the case study are on General Steels movements in the United Kingdom for calendar years 1974 and 1975.

1. INTRODUCTION

The use of modelling techniques in the area of commodity flows and freight transportation in general is not a recent innovation. But almost all the attempts have been on the use of static spatial methods for the study of interzonal commodity flows. Three sets of model typologies have been used extensively. They are Linear programming, Entropy maximising (gravity modelling) and Network formulations. References (1) - (6) have all used linear programming algorithm to study the inter-regional movement of different commodities. Chisholm and O'Sullivan (7) have recently published an integrated approach to commodity flows over one large national area and a range of commodities in the United Kingdom. They have applied linear programming and gravity modelling to Road Goods Transport Survey data (8) for eleven commodity categories between 78 origin and destination zones. Black (9) has attempted gravity modelling on United States inter-regional commodity flows. A small number of attempts has also been made on the use of network models in commodity flow systems. King et.al.(10) used an 'Out-of-Kilter Algorithm' (11) to determine the optimal transportation patterns of bitumenous coal in the Great Lakes region of North America.

There has been a considerable amount of criticism of the above-mentioned cross-sectional (spatial) modelling methods. Massey (12) has pointed out several problems with linear programming including a problem of feedback, linearity and need for continuous rather than discrete variables requirement.(1) Heggie (3) finds fault with the gravity models - "In general, the gravity and interactance models give a very poor explanation of observed traffic flows. The margins of error are so wide that they cannot consequently be accepted as a valid means of explaining present traffic behaviour or of predicting future traffic patterns." Coopers and Lybrand (14) consider gravity model as inappropriate in their study to predict possible freight movement through the Channel Tunnel. The network solutions in commodity flows are only useful, however, where problems can be framed in network terms and such a formation may not always be possible.

All the three sets of model typologies discussed above have a common limitation and that is their inability to incorporate temporal processes which gives rise to the existing spatial structure and to some extent determines future spatial structure.

None of the spatial methods discussed above seems suitable for General Steels data basically due to their static nature and also strict deterministic formulation in the case of linear programming and network models which limit their forecasting ability. Also, these models may only prove useful for the systems with a large number of origins and destinations, commodities, etc. In relation to the commodity flow systems under consideration here there is a need to look at flows between a smaller number of origins and destinations and, in consequence, these latter techniques may be inappropriate. This raises the need for development of stochastic dynamic models in general suitable for application to the types of problems raised in commodity flow systems under consideration.

Spatial methods such as linear programming, gravity modelling have been rejected for being static, deterministic and needing large O-D matrices. Temporal methods such as time series models (15). (16) could also be rejected because they relate to only one specific point in space. Computer simulation models in this context (17)could also be rejected due to the spatio-temporal nature of the system.

A simplified approach is to consider the commodity movement systems as a space and study a small number of time series for given points which would enable simple inferences to be made about the nature of the space between them. Discussion in this paper is based on this approach.

2. PROBLEM FORMULATION AND DATA

Data on commodity movement should be collected with a view to obtaining spatio-temporal statistics, i.e. disaggregated in both space and time.

The primary source of data for this research for General Steels movements were obtained from the British Steel Corporation as a complete order entry file, on magnetic tapes, for calendar years 1974 and 1975. Each order is entered into this file on the date of its despatch from the manufacturing works, with grid reference co-ordinates for origin and destination. Other useful variables included for each order are product type and weight, details of transport mode and the actual distance in miles between origin and destination.

The major problem in dealing with a data set comprising several hundred thousand individual flows is to reduce the sheer volume of information to a comprehensible order. Figure 1 illustrates the pattern of flows for General Steels on a sample day during 1974. The complexity of flows just for one day itself provides a fairly clear indication of possible difficulties if modelling is based on individual origin-destination flows in the traditional manner.

It is proposed here that this data set be aggregated for $i = 1, 2, \ldots, n$ zones over $t = 1,2,..,T$ time periods. The term 'zone' has been used in a wide sense to define an areal aggregate of a point location.

The problem now should be formulated to use such a data set to identify possible models for use in forecasting and predictive analysis. Calibration of the identified models and the development of appropriate algorithms should then be attempted.

The zones for the initial study could be the 100 kilometre square cells taken from the appropriate Ordnance Survey map. The tonnage arriving in them aggregated by monthly periods could be illustrated in the format suggested in Figure 2.

For example, consider the tonnage distribution of a commodity from a mill to nine zones in the south-west of the United Kingdom. Suppose that the tonnage arriving in zone i in month t is represented by variable Y_{it} which takes on values denoted by y_{it}. An example using this format is given in Figure 3. The tonnage matrix Y_{it} for these nine zones in the first four months is written as

$$Y_{it} = \begin{bmatrix} 15 & 20 & 14 & 13 \\ 16 & 7 & 8 & 11 \\ 13 & 11 & 9 & 14 \\ 15 & 10 & 15 & 20 \\ 10 & 15 & 18 & 12 \\ 12 & 12 & 12 & 15 \\ 12 & 14 & 5 & 11 \\ 18 & 12 & 15 & 10 \\ 10 & 13 & 10 & 12 \end{bmatrix} \qquad (2.1)$$

This could be written for all the twenty-four months, t varying from $1,2,\ldots,24$ for General Steels and i varying from $1,2,\ldots,n$ where n is the total number of zones to be considered in this study.

This format represents the commodity flows from one mill to different zones in the country. Through this approach the dependency of commodity flows in both space and time becomes clearer than if subjected to analysis in either dimension in isolation.

The problem now is to speciy the dynamic equations describing the structure of the model with the view of achieving satisfactory predictive performance for lead times at different spatial locations.

3. MODELLING USING SPACE TIME CORRELATION FUNCTIONS

In recent literature (18) - (22) geographers, control engineers and regional scientists have shown considerable interest in the construction of dynamic spatial models of socio-economic and physical systems.

Several authors have attempted to reformulate the time series techniques discussed by Box-Jenkins (23) and to apply them to space-time problems. Bennet (19) and Martin and Oeppen (18) have both described a family of such methods based on space-time correlation functions and this seems to be very suitable for the problem under consideration.

Let the expected value of Y_{it} be defined as $\hat{y}_{it}$ conditional upon the observed values of Y in zone i, and certain other zones in the previous time period, and upon the explanatory variables. Following Martin and Oeppen (18), let M be a spatial lag operator so that

$$\underline{M}^s y_{it} = \sum_{z \varepsilon Z_s} w_{iz} y_{zt} \qquad \text{for } s>o$$

$$= y_{it} \qquad \text{for } s=o \qquad (3.1)$$

Z_s is the set of zones at spatial lag s from zone i, and (w_{iz}) are weights whose summation over Z_s is equal to unity and for any t and s is equal to n where 'n' is the number of zones. Let y_t be the vector of observations i=1m...,n on Y at time t, then using (3.1)

$$\underline{M}^s \underline{y}_t = W^s \underline{y}_t \qquad \text{for } s>o$$

$$= \underline{I}_o \underline{y}_t \qquad \text{for } s=o \qquad (3.2)$$

where $\underline{I}_o$ is the (n x n) identity matrix and W^s is the (n x n) matrix of scaled weights for the sth spatial leg. Using these definitions some of the important aggregate space-time models could be defined as follows.

The space-time autoregressive (STAR), moving average (STMA) and mixed autoregressive and moving average (STARMA) models are the family of models very similar to time series models (23) but including the spatial dependence lagged in time and could be written (18) as

STAR:

$$\underline{y}_t = \sum_{s=o}^{\ell} \sum_{k=1}^{\rho} \alpha_{sk} \underline{M}^s \underline{y}_{t-k} + \underline{\xi}_t \tag{3.3}$$

STMA:

$$\underline{y}_t = \underline{\xi}_t - \sum_{s=o}^{r} \sum_{k=1}^{j} \beta_{sk} \underline{M}^s \underline{\xi}_{t-k} \tag{3.4}$$

STARMA:

$$\underline{y}_t = \sum_{s=o}^{\ell} \sum_{k=1}^{\rho} \alpha_{sk} \underline{M}^s \underline{y}_{t-k} - \sum_{s=o}^{r} \sum_{k=1}^{j} \beta_{sk} \underline{M}^s \underline{\xi}_{t-k} + \underline{\xi}_t \tag{3.5}$$

where α_{sk}, β_{sk} are the parameters to be estimated, $\underline{\xi}_t$ is the random noise satisfying,

$$E\left[\underline{\xi}_t\right] = o$$

$$E\left[\underline{\xi}_t \, \underline{\xi}_{t-k}^T\right] = \sigma^2 I \quad \text{for } k = o$$

$$= o \quad \text{for } k \neq o$$

$$E\left[\underline{\xi}_t \, \underline{y}_{t-k}^T\right] = o \quad \text{for } k > o \tag{3.6}$$

(T denotes transpose)

In order to choose the best possible (parsimonious) model the identification process requires a considerable amount of computation. The estimated correlation and partial correlation functions have been suggested (19) as the techniques to guess the spatial and temporal orders of the equation. The next step is to estimate unknown parameters of the model. Ordinary least-squares estimator could be used if the model does not have any moving average parameters. For general STARMA model or STMA model, the least-squares approach is not suitable for estimation (19) and further research is required to develop a suitable method.

4. APPLICATION OF SPACE TIME CORRELATION FUNCTIONS

In the context of commodity movement systems, distribution of a commodity from a mill to different zones in the country is shown in Figure 3. In order to develop a space-time model for such a system, the first step is to compute spatial autocorrelation functions and partial autocorrelation functions. The shape of correlograms suggests whether the process is STAR or STMA or STARMA and also possible values for model order.

Let us assume that the process described in Figure 3 is STAR with $\ell=1$ and $\rho=3$ in Eq.(3.3). The model equation could be written as

$$\underline{y}_t = \sum_{s=o}^{1} \sum_{k=1}^{3} \alpha_{sk} (\underline{M}^s \underline{y}_{t-k}) + \underline{\xi}_t \tag{4.1}$$

In order to have an idea of the complexity involved in the formulation of a simple space-time model, it may be appropriate here to expand Eq. (4.1) for the example with t = 1,2,3,4 and i = 1,2,...,9 (Figure 3). Although no conclusion could be drawn with small dimensions in time and space, it should be possible to see the computational demands when the method is used for a full sized problem such as General Steels distribution from one mill to a large number of zones and also the distribution from a large number of mills to a large number of destinations at a disaggregated level. Thus re-writing Eq. (4.1) in expanded form

$$\underline{y}_1 = \alpha_{01}(\underline{M}^o \underline{y}_o) + \alpha_{11}(\underline{M}^1 \underline{y}_o) + \underline{\xi}_1$$

$$\underline{y}_2 = \alpha_{01}(\underline{M}^o \underline{y}_1) + \alpha_{11}(\underline{M}^1 \underline{y}_1) + \alpha_{02}(M^o \underline{y}_o) + \alpha_{12}(\underline{M}^1 \underline{y}_o) + \underline{\xi}_2$$

$$y_3 = \alpha_{01}(\underline{M}^o \underline{y}_2) + \alpha_{11}(\underline{M}^1 \underline{y}_2) + \alpha_{02}(\underline{M}^o \underline{y}_1) + \alpha_{12}(\underline{M}^1 \underline{y}_1) + \alpha_{03}(\underline{M}^o \underline{y}_o) + \alpha_{13}(\underline{M}^1 \underline{y}_o) + \underline{\xi}_3$$

$$y_4 = \alpha_{01}(\underline{M}^o \underline{y}_3) + \alpha_{11}(\underline{M}^1 \underline{y}_3) + \alpha_{02}(\underline{M}^o \underline{y}_2) + \alpha_{12}(\underline{M}^1 \underline{y}_2) + \alpha_{03}(\underline{M}^o \underline{y}_1) + \alpha_{13}(\underline{M}^1 \underline{y}_1) + \underline{\xi}_4 \tag{4.2}$$

where $\underline{y}_1$, $\underline{y}_2$, $\underline{y}_3$ and $\underline{y}_4$ are the vectors of tonnage arrivals in zone i = 1,2,..., 9 in months 1,2,3 and 4 respectively and could be obtained from Figure 3 as

$$\underline{y}_1 = [15,\ 16,\ 13,\ 15,\ 10,\ 12,\ 12,\ 18,\ 10]^T$$

$$\underline{y}_2 = [20,\ 7.\ 11,\ 10,\ 15,\ 12,\ 14,\ 12,\ 13]^T$$

and so on. Vectors $(\underline{M}^o \underline{y}_o)$, $(\underline{M}^1 \underline{y}_o)$ etc. could be obtained using Eq.(3.1) and Figure 3. For example to determine the value of $(\underline{M}^1 \underline{y}_1)$, Eq. (3.1) could be written as

$$(\underline{M}^1\underline{y}_{i1}) = \sum_{z \varepsilon Z_s} w_{iz} y_{z1} \quad (4.3)$$

where $i = 1,2,\ldots, 9$. The weights w_{iz} could be chosen by a number of different criteria. It may also be possible here to incorporate a transport cost or policy structure through the assignments of weights to a particular zone. Martin and Oeppen (18) have used the criterion of equal weights to each zone, thus using $w_{iz}^{(s)} = w_{ij}^{*(s)} / \sum_z w_{iz}^{*(s)}$ where for spatial lag = 1, $w_{iz}^{*(1)} = 1$ if zone z is orthogonally adjoining to zone 1, otherwise $w_{iz}^{*(1)} = 0$. Using Eq. (4.3) and Figure 3 for i=1, z takes only three values because of the location of zone 1 on the coastal line but for i=5, z takes up all the eight possible values as eight zones are orthogonally contiguous to zone 5. Thus, the vector $(\underline{M}^1\underline{y}_{i1})$ could be obtained using a suitable weight criterion and it will have the dimension (9 x 1) for the example under consideration. The random noise vector $\underline{\xi}_1$, $\underline{\xi}_2$, $\underline{\xi}_3$ and $\underline{\xi}_4$ in Eq. (4.2) could be assumed as a sequence of independent normal variables with mean zero and unit variance. In model Eq. (4.2) the only unknowns are the parameters α_{01}, α_{02}, α_{03}, α_{11}, α_{12} and α_{13} which could be estimated using least squares algorithm. Once the parameters have been estimated the model could be used in forecasting and predictive analysis.

5. COMPUTATIONAL DIFFICULTIES

The method discussed above is not too difficult to programme and implement on a computer if the distribution data is small in size and the model order is low in space and time. For large data matrix and higher order mixed space-time processes there are a number of computational difficulties. For example, the shape of computed spatial autocorrelations and partial autocorrelations will not always give unambiguous indication of model order and hence one has to try a number of possible orders with an estimation algorithm and this would be very expensive in computer time. For General Steels movements at aggregation in space to town name and in time to a month, the data distribution matrix for one mill is of dimension (400 x 24). It was felt that to programme (Figure 2 for General Steels data) with any of the space-time models Eqs. (3.3) - (3.6) and a suitable estimation algorithm (19) one needs a very big core space (memory) on a computer. This makes the implementation of the whole procedure on an average size computer very difficult. Therefore, one has to aggregate in space to a county level or bigger grid reference zone and this may not be desirable. Also, for a general mixed STARMA or STMA process, Bennett (18) has noted that the least squares estimators are statistically erroneous. This creates the problem of development of an efficient algorithm for the estimation of spatio-temporal model parameters before the application could be attempted to General Steels movement systems.

6. AN ALTERNATIVE MODELLING METHOD

A different approach for looking at the problem of forecasting commodity flows is a production-attraction gravity model approach developed by Wilson (24) in its static form which has been extended to dynamic situation by Bennett (25). Following Bennett's approach, it is possible to estimate a general interaction matrix T_{tij}, for locations i and j at any time period t which can be estimated by the production-attraction constrained gravity model given by

$$T_{tij} = A_{ti} B_{tj} O_{tj} f(C_{tij}) \quad (6.1)$$

$$\text{where } A_{ti} = 1/\sum_{j=1}^{N} B_{tj} D_{tj} f(C_{tij}) \quad (6.2)$$

$$B_{tj} = 1/\sum_{i=1}^{M} A_{tj} O_{ti} f(C_{tij}) \quad (6.3)$$

C_{tij} is the transport cost of the commodity between i and i, O_{ti} is the total volume of interaction flows leaving zone i at time t and the total of interaction flows into j at time t is given by D_{tj}. Equations (6.2) and (6.3) can be solved (25) interactively for successive estimates of A_{ti} and B_{tj}. The number of ways of assigning individual flows at any time t could be written using multinomial probability function

$$W((T_{tij})) = \frac{\sum_i \sum_j T_{tij}!}{\prod_{ij} T_{tij}!} \quad (6.4)$$

and Wilson (24) proved that a time t if log $W((T_{tij}))$ is maximized subject to the constraints

$$\sum_j T_{tij} = O_{ti} \quad (6.5)$$

$$\sum_i T_{tij} = D_{tj} \quad (6.6)$$

$$\sum_i \sum_j T_{tij} c_{tij} = C_t \quad (6.7)$$

where C_t is the total cost, then the resulting T_{tij} has elements given by Eq. (6.2) with function $f(c_{tij})$ replaced by $e^{-\beta c_{tij}}$, where β is the Langrangian multiplier associated with constraint Eq. (6.7).

This approach has been extended by Bennett (25) to temporal or dynamic situations where lagged relationships are present through the use of an adaptive estimation procedure. The algorithm developed by Bennett (25) is still to be tested against a good data set. The application of dynamic entropy models to determine the optimal distribution network for a commodity on which spatio-temporal data could be collected, should prove very useful. This formulation shares the advantage of techniques such as Linear Programming and Gravity modelling, but in addition, incorporates the temporal lagged relationships which are very important in commodity movement systems.

7. CONCLUSIONS

An attempt has been made in this paper to describe some recently developed spatio-temporal techniques which are useful for forecasting within a commodity distribution system. The methods considered are space-time correlation functions and entropy models of spatial interaction. Use of space-time correlation function model is illustrated by using an example. Also a simple format has been presented to formulate the problem based on the General Steels movements data set, so that the spatio-temporal methods could be used.

8. REFERENCES

(1) Whitelegg, J. The potential and applicability of gravity model techniques to hinterland studies, port location and national transport planning (Tech.Note, MAST, UWIST, Cardiff, UK, 1975)

(2) Goldman, T. Efficient transportation and industrial location, Papers and Proceedings, Regional Science Association, 4 (1958)

(3) Henderson, J.M. A short run model for the coal industry, Rev. Economics and Statistics, 1 (1955)

(4) Henderson, J.M. The Efficiency of the Coal Industry: an application of linear programming, (Havard University Press, 1958)

(5) Cassetti, E. Optimal Location of steel mills serving the Quebec and Southern Ontario Steel Market, Canadian Geographer, 10, 1 (1966)

(6) Koch, A.R., Snodgrass, M.M. Linear programming applied to location of and product flow determination in the tomato processing industry, Papers and Proceedings, Regional Science Association, 5 (1958)

(7) Chisholm, M. & O'Sullivan P. Freight Flows and Spatial Aspects of the British Economy, (Cambridge University Press, U.L. (1973)

(8) Road Goods Transport Survey Data United Kingdom (1964)

(9) Black, W.R. Inter-regional commodity flows: some experiments with the gravity model Journal Regional Science, 12 (1) (1972)

(10) King, L,, Cassetti, E., Odland, J. and Semple, K. Optimal transportation patterns of coal in the Great Lakes Region, Economic Geography, 47 (1971) 401-413

(11) Fulkerson, D.R. An out-of-kilter method for minimal cost flow problems, J. Soc. Industrial Application and Maths, 9. 1. (1961)

(12) Massey, D.B. Problems of location; linear programming, Centre for Environmental Studies, Working Paper 14 (1968)

(13) Heggie, I.G. Are gravity and interactance models a valid technique for planning regional transport facilities? Operational Res. Quarterly, 20(1) (1969) 83 - 110.

(14) Coopers & Lybrand Associates Ltd. The Channel Tunnel: Economic Report, Section 2 Freight Studies, Main Report (1973)

(15) Lalwani, C.S., & Lee, P.R. ARIMA Models of Iron Ore flows - by port of entry and grade of ore In: Voght W.C. and Mickle, M.H. (ed) Modelling and Simulation, Vol.8 Instrument Society of America, Pittsburg, (1977) 107-111

(16) Lalwani, C.S., Gardner, B.M. and Wild, P.G. A simulation model for planning of production of steel coils for export, Proceedings of 14th Seminar MDEA Analogova a Hydridni Vypocetni Technika, Praha (1977)

(17) Lalwani, C.S. and Brown J.M. Model Validation - a view of modelling in social sciences, paper presented at Summer Computer Simulation Conference on 19th July 1977, Chicago, Illinois (1977)

(18) Martin, R.L. and Oeppen, J.E. The identification of original forecasting models using space-time correlation functions. Trans. Inst. Br. Beogr., 66 (1975) 95 - 117

(19) Bennett, R.J. The representation and identification of spatio-temporal systems: an example of population diffusion in North-West England. Trans. Inst. Br. Geogr (1975) 73 - 94

(2) Polis, M.O. & Goodson, R.E. Parameter identification in distributed systems : a synthesising overview, Proc. IEEE (1976) 64(1)

(21) Haggett, P., Cliff, A.D. & Frey, A Locational Analysis in Human Geography (Arnold, UK, 1977)

(22) Bennett, R.G. Spatial Time Series Analysis Forecasting and Control,(Pion,London 1979)

(23) Box, G.E.P. & Jenkins, G.M. Time Series Analysis Forecasting and Control,(Holden Day 1970)

(24) Wilson A.G. Entropy in Urban and Regional Modelling, (Pion, London, 1970).

(25) Bennett, R.J. Adaptive parameter space-time models; an entropy maximising application. Conference on Dynamic Models and Spatial Representation in Geography and Regional Science, (University College, London, 15th May 1976).

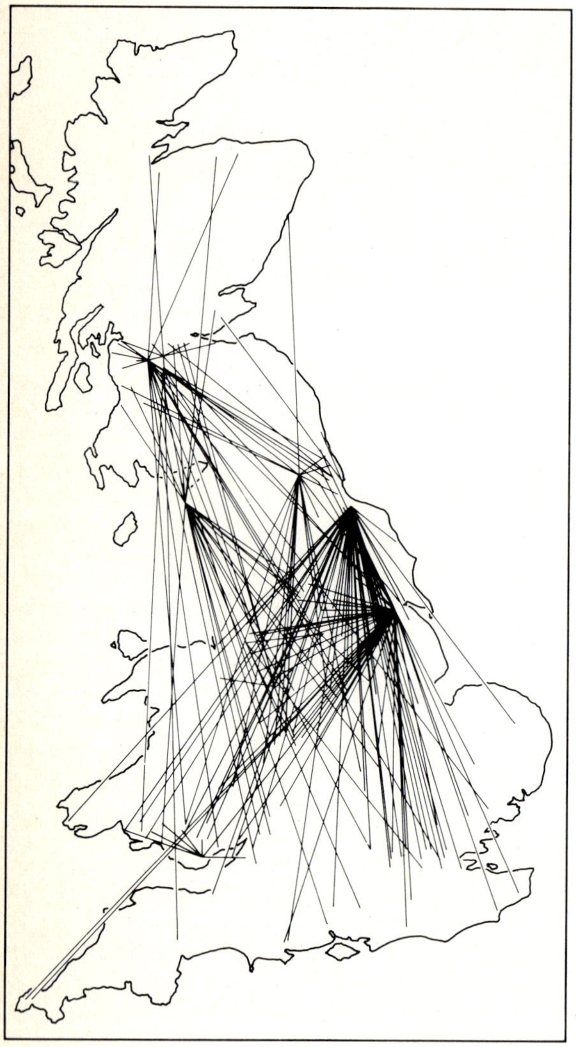

Figure 1. Flows of General Steels on a sample day (Monday, 1st July 1974).

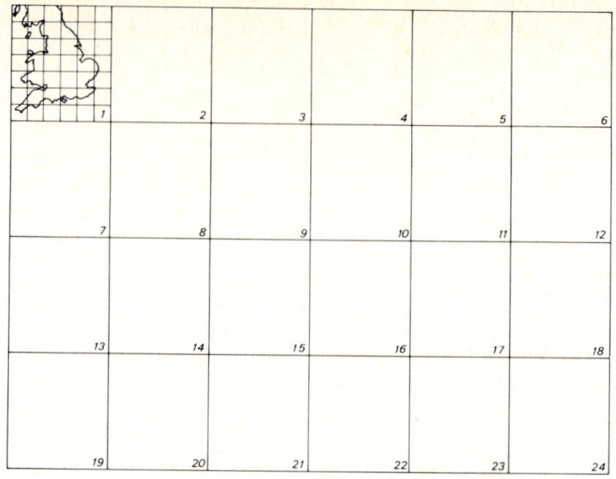

Figure 2. Spatio-temporal display showing the arrival of General Steels for months starting January 1974 until December 1975 (24 months) - a Format.

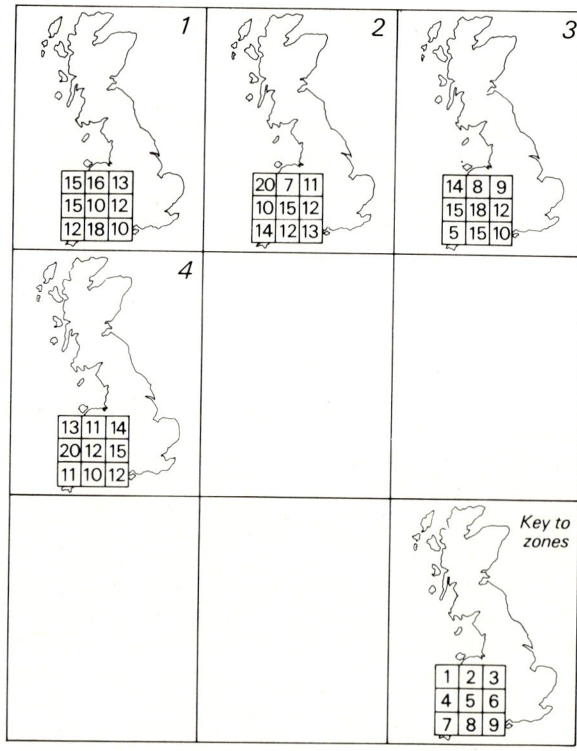

Figure 3. An example for distribution of a commodity from a mill to nine zones in south-west of the country based on Format of Figure 2.

DISCRETE SIMULATION AND RELATED FIELDS
A. Jávor (editor)
North-Holland Publishing Company

DESIGN AND TESTING OF A MINI CONTROL COMPUTER VIA MICROPROGRAMMED SIMULATION

S. G. TZAFESTAS
Control Systems Laboratory
University of Patras
Patras, Greece

A. T. KOSSIDAS
Electronic Eng. Department
Higher Tech. Education College
Maroussi, Attiki, Greece

The systematic utilization of electronic computers in system studies, makes possible the analysis and simulation of systems which are not amenable to explicit analytical techniques. Since a computer is by itself a complex system, the computer designers are using the "simulation" technique as a means for evaluating and modifying its structure and design, before deciding to build and construct the actual computer system. Digital control computers are currently employed in many industrial plants for materializing various arithmetic and logical control functions, and can be designed either for performing a fixed control function, or with programming flexibility in order to be adaptable to some repertory of control function requirements. The aim of this paper is to present the simulation aspects of a mini microprogrammed control computer, designed by using the bottom-up technique, as well as its assembly language (MAL) created for a powerful utilization of the system. This computer can be used for supervisory digital control, or for distributed digital control or for specialized (two-term and three-term) digital process control. Two application examples, worked-out in simulated form, are presented.

1. INTRODUCTION

Simulation is among others, a good tool which helps the computer engineers in the successful design and evaluation of computer systems. In many cases various problems (eg. utilization) related to computer simulation are not yet completely resolved. Recently an alternative technique, called "emulation"was developed which can be used in parallel with simulation. As it is well known, by "computer simulation" we mean the presentation of the function of a computer into another computer, exclusively with software procedures. The simulation language has to be selected so as not to lead to complicated programs. A simulated model is generally composed by logical operations and a number of arithmetic operations, which must be as simple as possible.

The microprogramming approach to the design of digital computing systems has received in recent years great applicability, and gives high flexibility in practical applications. The hardware and software designer can utilize the simulation and emulation techniques for the presentation of the function of a microprogrammed computer into another computer using exclusively software means. So he has the ability to evaluate the computer system under study, by collecting data, elements and parameters arising from the simulation, and modify its structure and functioning in the proper direction.

In this paper the simulation of a control oriented mini computer (CONCOM) will be described and its basic features will be highlighted. The repetitive procedure which characterizes our simulation is: "start searching and executing next instruction". Thus, the simulator translates the instructions of the program by counting the simulation time on the basis of the time needed by the simulated machine. With the exception of the I/O instructions, all instructions are simulated here in some detail.

The present *control computer* (CONCOM) is actually a general purpose one, suitable for both arithmetic and logic control functions, and can be used for the control of multiple loops. It is designed by the microprogramming technique which has replaced the random logic by the programming logic [1-6]. CONCOM was carefully simulated and tested on a CDC-3300 computer. During the design phase many difficulties appeared which have been overcome by modifying the simulation program. Here the finalized model is provided which is presently under hardware construction.

The final results of the simulator are equivalent with those of a real model of the simulated machine. The MAL (Macro Assembly Language) is also simulated on a C.D.C.-3300 computer and has a good portability and adaptability to various applications. The MAL was tested in actual problems through the CONCOM mini control computer and showed an excellent performance.

2. A FEW WORDS ABOUT THE MICROPROGRAMMING APPROACH

The best and safest approach to the study and design of complex systems, like industrial processes, computers etc., is the *simulation* using an electronic computer. Microprogramming is a rather old concept originated by M. Wilkes [3,9,10], but there does not yet exist an accepted concrete definition of the microprogramming concept. The microprogramming was developed and used as a method of designing flexible control units. Since the hardware and software designers are just developing algorithms with different ways of building them, the microprogramming can be considered as a method of designing algorithms, which is more flexible than the hardware and more effective than the software method. The term *"micro"* doesn't mean that microprogramming is the programming of microcomputers. A μ-Computer may be designed as a microprogrammed machine (most μ-Computers are not), but the art of writing programs for a μ-Computer is standard programming, not μ-programming. The basic question is:what is microprogramming? *A type of programming or a kind of logic design* (engineering)? [13]. It is generally accepted that the purpose of microprogramming is entirely different than that of programming. A recent more acceptable term for microprogramming is the term *"firmware"*, which is used to denote something between hardware and software. From the above it is clear that:*"Microprogramming is a systematic technique for the design and implementation of flexible control units for dynamically varying data processing systems"*. This is presently a well accepted definition.

During the design phase of microprogrammed systems we generally use a structure in levels called "level structures". In practice there are two different ways of design; the *"Top-Down"* and *"Bottom-Up"* method. Clearly, any level is formed from a number of intermediate levels. Classical examples are: the study of microprogrammed translators or the study of microprogrammed operating systems. Any didital computer system can be always realized with two, simultaneously acting sequential machines; the *control part* (C.P.) and the *operating part* (O.P.) of the system. These sequential machines are connected as shown in Fig. 1.

In μ-programmed systems the C.P. machine contains a *control memory* (CM) where all microprograms are stored. These microprograms describe the execution of the system instructions. The O.P. machine executes the operations of the system with

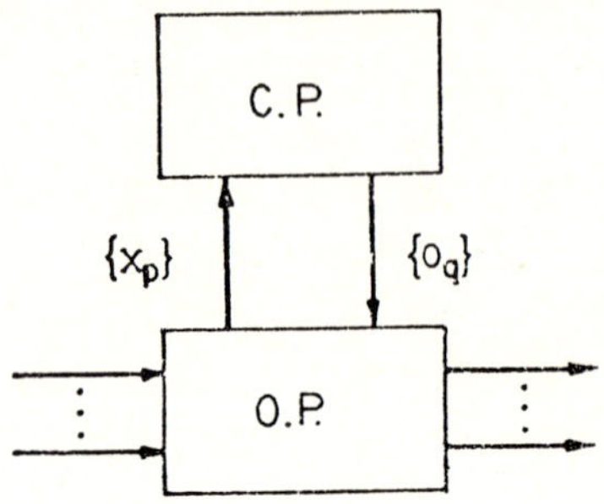

Fig. 1. C.P. and O.P. structure of a digital system.

the aid of μ-instructions formed by one or more elementary operations (micro-operations). The execution and sequencing of the μ-instructions are controlled by the C.P. machine which sends to the O.P. machine a group of signals (O_q:q=1,2,..,t) called commands. These commands take into account a set of signals X_p(p=1,2,...,s), called state variables, which are originated from the machine O.P.

Microprogramming is dinstinguished in two types;*vertical* (ps) and *horizontal* (ts). In the first any μ-operation contains only one elementary operation, whereas in the second more than one elementary operations are executed simultaneously. The horizontal μ-Programming is called, by many authors, "structural micro-programming", and the vertical is called "functional microprogramming".

In a μ-programmed machine the maximum operation speed is achieved by using the minimum possible number of "no-operation" μ-instructions. If no μ-instruction "no-operation" exists the O.P. machine is always in work.

The operation speed is also increased by increasing the complexity of the micro-language used, i.e. by increasing the allowed number of changes per μ-instruction.

3. SIMULATION OF COMPUTER SYSTEMS

Simulation has been proved to be a powerful tool for the design and evaluation of both physical systems or control systems, and computer systems [3,11,14,15]. However many problems arised in the application of simulation for computer systems are still not completelly defined and solved. In the last years a new method, called *"emulation"* was developed and used.

The digital computer is a concrete machine with a predetermined function. A model of this machine can be described functionally on the basis of the changes of the data processed by the machine. The idea to use the microprogramming for the realization of a virtual machine in a real computer is recent and inspired new developments. The utilization of microprogramming for this purpose is what is called "emulation".

The main element of a μ-Programmed system is the control memory which contains the μ-Programs. With the capability to place the microprograms in the control memory, one can emulate a number of virtual machines in a real computer. The capability to create control memories along with the capability of easily modifying their contents made it possible the design of real machines, with high adaptability, by the user side, to a wide range of applications. This is one of the reasons for which the design of "special purpose machines" has lost the interest which had in the past, especially in the application field concerning industrial processes.

One problem not yet fully solved is the automatic creation of powerful microprograms. The translation of high-level language programs into the corresponding microprograms was by itself a goal for the expansion of μ-Programming. The basic concept upon which the development of microprogramming was based is the translation of machine-language programs into the corresponding μ-Programs, oriented towards a better description of elementary operations executed by the logic structure of the computer. Much effort has been made towards the end of converting high-level languages programs in μ-Programs, and not in machine-language programs. This is because in this way computer time and memory are saved.

Below an outline of the basic differences between emulation and simulation of computer systems is given with a view to highlight the relative advantages and disadvantages.

Simulation of a computer system is actually the presentation of the computer in a real computer exclusively by means of software procedures. A particular case is the simulation of a computer during the design phase. The main steps of this are the following:

- Prepare the software is parallel with the hardware, so as to have all parts of the system ready at the same time.
- Evaluate the simulated system.
- Determine the capabilities of the system and make appropriate modifications.

Emulation is defined to be a special type of simulation, in which the software procedures are completed or fully replaced by microprogrammed (firmware) ones. Actually emulation is very close hardware simulation.

There are two types of emulators:
a) Functional Emulator: A functional emulator is composed by a group of software routines combined with operations which are performed by the hardware of the real machine. The emulation of the I/O is done with the help of *"special instructions"* and other *"standard instructions"*.

The outside information enters the real machine through its I/O, and subsequently it is transferred to the simulated machine by using the "special instructions". This method is gradually abandoned due to its low flexibility. An emulator of this type can be modified very hardly because of the close connection between hardware and software, and also because it is strongly dependent on the "host machine" in which it is realized.
b) Procedural Emulator: A procedural emulator does not analyze step by step all operations of the emulated machine, but it is concerned with the correctness of the final result. The procedural emulator is mainly used for I/O simulation. For simplicity, it simulates data transfers,e.g. the reading of a data block from the disk, and puts the required data in the address determined by the program, During this procedure the states of the peripheral units, or the control action on the I/O of the supervisor (during the request process) are not described. The core of a simulated computer system is the package of translation routines which are built using the instruction repertory of the simulated machine. The final result of the simulation is equivalent to that expected from a real model of the machine under simulation.

The repetitive property which characterizes the simulation is *"start searching next instruction"*. The simulator translates the instructions of the program in sequential steps by measuring the simulation time on the basis of the time required by the simulated machine to execute the various instructions. The majority of the simulators don't make an extensive analysis of the I/O instructions. They simply simulate them superficially, compared with the rest instruction repertory of the simulated machine.

Another purpose of a simulated machine, besides that of executing programs, is the collection of statistical data concerning the executed simulated programs. The above features determine the boundaries of the majority of existing simulators, which are characterized as classical simulators. More sophisticated simulators are the "extended simulators" which provide details about the I/O of the simulated system, about the status of the supervisor and about the conditions of the programs under execution. The simulated machine is described by means of the class of variables upon which the simulated program acts. These variables contain all the information needed for the simulation of the supervisor and the I/O. Their values represent the state of the simulated machine which is the result of the execution of an application program.

The general organization of an extended simulator is shown in Fig. 2. Finally it is remarked that a simulated model is mainly composed by logical operations and there are also a few simple arithmetic operations.

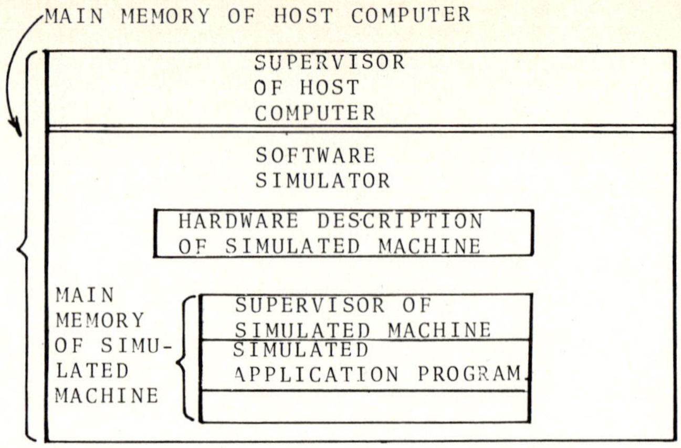

Fig. 2. General organization of an extended computer-simulator.

4. ARCHITECTURE OF THE PRESENT SYSTEM

The simulated computer system is μ-programmed and expandable. It has a general purpose architecture (Fig.3) and programming flexibility and efficiency. (Flexibility is a measure of how readily a system can be used in various situations, either through manipulation of parameters or through modification of components. Efficiency is a measure of the expenditures required to achieve a desired result). It rather uses the firmware technique,

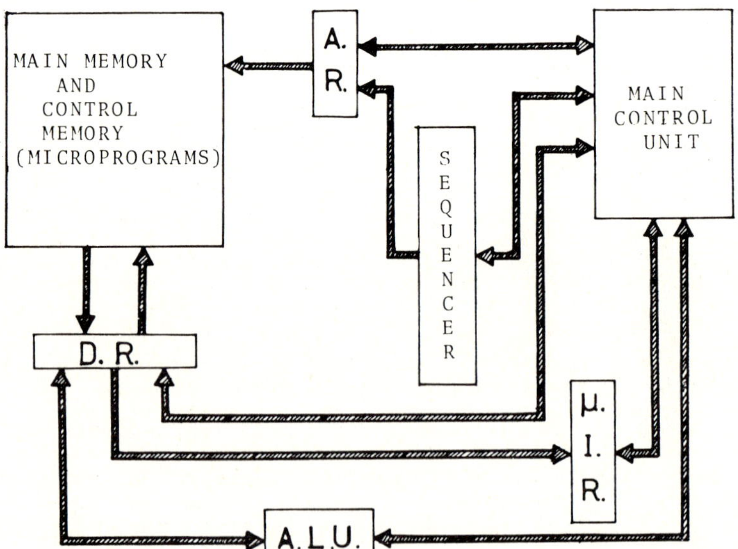

Fig. 3. Organization of CONCOM

with the capability of being modified in case of special purpose applications. The A.L.U. (arithmetic and logic unit) contains the R,B,A, and MQ Registers (R= main Register , A=Accumulator). The format instructions have 16 bits length and are given in Table 1. Table 2 gives a presentation of the I/O and transfer instructions of "CONCOM". Each instruction is μ-programmed through appropriate μ-routines as described in the following.

The mnemonics shown in Tables 1 and 2 are used for MAL assembly language.

Some more mnemonics are also used according to the function of each instruction (e.g. direct-indirect, etc). More details about the use of the instructions are given in the CONCOM Assembly language user's Manual(8). In Table 3 we give the μ-routines, and Table 4 shows the way of connecting the various μ-routines for performing each instruction. Finally an explanation of each μ-instruction is given in Table 5, and an analysis of the mixed μ-instructions is shown in Table 6.

TABLE 1

CONCOM'S INSTRUCTIONS

No.	Instruction			Symbolic	Description of operation
	Code	DR IB	operand		
1.	00001	001	← X →	NOP	No Operation
2.	00010	-01	← D →	JMP	Jump if Positive (R)
3.	00011	-01	← D →	JMN	Jump if Negative (R)
4.	00100	-01	← D →	JMO	Jump if Overf. of R
5.	00101	-01	← D →	JMU	Jump Unconditional
6.	00110	-01	← D →	OR	Or R with (D)
7.	00111	-01	← D →	SUB	Subtract (D) from R
8.	01000	-01	← D →	ADD	Add R with (D)
9.	01001	-01	← D →	EOR	Exclusive OR with (D)
10.	01010	-01	← D →	AND	AND R with (D)
11.	01011	--1	← D →	LDR or B	Load with (D) R or B
12.	01100	--1	← D →	STR or B	Store R or B in (D)
13.	01101	001	← X →	CMR	Complement R
14.	01110	0-*	← C →	ENR or B	Enter in R or B
15.	01111	001	← X →	CLR	Clear R
16.	10000	-01	← D →	MUL	Multiply R with (D)
17.	10001	001	←---→	TR	Transfer
18.	10010	001	← X →	HLT	Halt
19.	10011	001	← X →	SHR	Shift R, MQ Right
20.	10100	0-1	←---→	INR or B	Input in R or B
21.	10101	0-1	←---→	OUR or B	Output from R or B
22.	10110	001	← X →	SHL	Shift R Left
23.	10111	01*	← C →	ICR	Increase Decrease R
24.	11000	001	← X →	ADRB	Add R and B
25.	11001	001	← X →	SURB	Subtract from R, B
26.	11010	-01	← D →	DIV	Divide R with (D)

TABLE 2

I/O AND TRANSFER INSTRUCTIONS

	INSTRUCTION	OPERAND (Constant)	Description
1.	OUR	0	PRINTER
2.	OUR	1	DISPLAY
3.	OUB	0	PRINTER
4.	OUB	1	DISPLAY
5.	INR	0	KEYBOARD
6.	INR	1	Paper tape reader
7.	INR	2	from C.D.C. 3300
8.	INB	0	Keyboard
9.	INB	1	Paper tape reader
10.	INB	2	from C.D.C. 3300
11.	TR	0	(B) → (R)
12.	TR	16	(B) → (MQ)
13.	TR	32	(MQ) → (B)
14.	TR	34	(R) → (B)

TABLE 3

μ-ROUTINES IN CONCOM

No.	Name	No. of instr.	Entry address	μ-instructions which form any μ-routine
1.	Fetch Instruction or Address if Indirect	any instruction	0.	00 23 38 16 49 51/136 14 34 17 50/65
2.	Fetch Data	6,7,8,9,10, 11,16	10.	23 10 51/147 9 1 14 9 6 18 51/149 14 18 50/66
3.	Store Data	12	23.	10 51/160 1 9 6 19 1 6 18 51/339 19 18 51/339
4.	Arithmetic and Logic Operations (ARLO)	6,7,8,9,10, 3,4,5	36.	1 9 6 1 9 6 23 26 27 28 9 6 1 9 6 51/339
5.	Transfer	17	52.	23 45 51/190 46 51/188 1 9 6 51/339 7 51/339 47 51/194 9 51/339 8 23 51/339

Table 3 (Contd.)

No.	Name	No. of instr.	Entry address	μ-instructions which form any μ-routine
6.	Multiply	16	70.	40 44 $\overset{51}{201}$ $\overset{51}{208}$ 1 2 9 6 1 9 6 6 1 9 6 44 $\overset{51}{214}$ $\overset{51}{218}$ 1 2 9 6 8 1 6 35 31 $\overset{51}{232}$ 1 9 27 28 6 1 9 6 22 33 30 $\overset{51}{222}$ 7 1 9 6 23 42 $\overset{51}{244}$ $\overset{51}{339}$ 1 2 9 6 1 2 9 6 $\overset{51}{339}$
7.	Complement	13	126.	23 1 2 9 6 1 9 6 $\overset{51}{339}$
8.	Increase-Decrease (R)	23	135.	48 41 23 29 $\overset{51}{271}$ 2 7 3 $\overset{50}{66}$ 7 3 23 $\overset{50}{66}$
9.	Enter	14	148	23 10 $\overset{51}{299}$ 29 $\overset{51}{290}$ 48 41 2 9 7 3 1 9 6 $\overset{51}{339}$ 48 41 9 7 3 1 9 6 $\overset{51}{339}$ 29 $\overset{51}{306}$ 48 7 2 3 $\overset{51}{339}$ 48 7 41 3 $\overset{51}{339}$
10.	Input	20	184	20 23 10 $\overset{51}{321}$ 9 1 11 9 6 $\overset{51}{339}$ 11 $\overset{51}{339}$
11.	Output	21	196	10 $\overset{51}{333}$ 1 9 6 5 21 1 6 $\overset{51}{339}$ 5 21 $\overset{51}{339}$
12.	Jump	2,3,4,5	209.	32 43 $\overset{51}{339}$
13.	Conditional SHINOCLE + Increase P.C.	1,15,19,22	212	12 $\overset{51}{128}$
14.	Halt	18	214.	37
15.	Divide	26	215.	40 44 $\overset{51}{346}$ $\overset{51}{353}$ 1 2 9 6 1 9 6 1 9 6 44 $\overset{51}{359}$ $\overset{51}{363}$ 1 2 9 6 44 $\overset{51}{368}$ 33 24 $\overset{51}{363}$ 1 9 6 44 $\overset{51}{375}$ 24 $\overset{51}{371}$ 25 $\overset{51}{379}$ 36 $\overset{51}{375}$ 39 26 27 28 9 6 1 9 6 24 33 30 $\overset{51}{393}$ $\overset{51}{397}$ 25 $\overset{51}{379}$ 13 $\overset{51}{388}$ 42 $\overset{51}{400}$ $\overset{51}{339}$ 7 9 1 2 6 9 $\overset{51}{339}$

TABLE 4

COMMUNICATION BETWEEN INSTRUCTIONS AND μ-ROUTINES

No.	Symbolic	Code	Communication bit		No. of μ-routines
			I = 1	I = 2	
1	NOP	00001	211	213	1, 13
2	JMP	00010	208	213	1, 12, 13
3	JMN	00011	208	213	1, 12, 13
4	JMO	00100	208	213	1, 12, 13
5	JMU	00101	208	213	1, 12, 13
6	OR	00110	9	35	1, 2, 4, 13
7	SUB	00111	9	35	1, 2, 4, 13
8	ADD	01000	9	35	1, 2, 4, 13
9	EOR	01001	9	35	1, 2, 4, 13
10	AND	01010	9	35	1, 2, 4, 13
11	LDR or B	01011	9	211	1, 2, 13
12	STR or B	01100	22	213	1, 3, 13
13	CMR	01101	125	213	1, 7, 13
14	ENR or B	01110	147	213	1, 9, 13
15	CLR	01111	211	213	1, 13
16	MUL	10000	9	69	1, 2, 6, 13
17	TR	10001	51	213	1, 5, 13
18	HLT	10010	213	213	1, 14
19	SHR	10011	211	213	1, 13
20	INR or B	10100	183	213	1, 10, 13
21	OUR or B	10101	195	213	1, 11, 13
22	SHL	10110	211	213	1, 13
23	ICR	10111	134	35	1, 8, 4, 13
24	ADRB	11000	35	213	1, 4, 13
25	SURB	11001	35	213	1, 4, 13
26	DIV	11010	9	214	1, 2, 15, 13

TABLE 5
LIST OF μ - INSTRUCTIONS

Type	No.	μ-instructions
E	1.	(A) = (R)
E	2.	Complement A
C	3.	$(B_2) = (A_2)$
C	4.	(R) = (B) if IR bit 10 = 1
C	5.	(O.B.R.) = (B)
C	6.	(B) = (A)
C	7.	(B) = (MQ) καί Clear overflow F.F.
C	8.	(MQ) = (B)
C	9.	(R) = (B)
E	10.	Increase μ.P.C. if I.R. bit 10 = 1 (Register R ή B)
C	11.	(B) = (I.B.R.)
CE	12.	Execute f-μoperation +Increase P.C. (SHINOCLE)
E	13.	Shift MQ left
C	14.	(B) = (Memory content) KJ = 1, KK = 0, RR = 1, FF = 0, RB = 0
C	15.	$(IR_1) = (MQ_1)$
C	16.	(T.P.B.) = (P.B.)
C	17.	$(P.B.) = (B_2)$
C	18.	(P.B.) = (T.P.B.)
C	19.	(Memory content) = (B) KJ = 1, KK = 0, RR = 0
C	20.	(I.B.R.) = (I.B.)
C	21.	(O.B.) = (O.B.R.)
M	22.	Shift R_2, R_1, MQ right
E	23.	Wait
E	24.	Shift R left
E	25.	Increase μPC if R < B
E	26.	Complement A if subtruction INSTR(7), INSTR(25), INSTR(26)
Ē	27.	Execute plus 1 if overf.anticip. in SUB, ADD, e.c.c.
Ē	28.	Execute μ-operation in SUB, ADD_2, ADD, AND, OR, MUL, DIV. e.c.c.
E	29.	Increase μPC if IR bit 9=1
E	30.	Increase μPC if OV of Counter
E	31.	Increase PC if last bit of MQ=1
E	32.	Increase PC if jump logic = 0
E	33.	Increase counter (counts 16 steps)
C	34.	$(IR_1) = (B_1)$
E	35.	R = 0
E	36.	Shift B Right
E	37.	Stop
C	38.	(I.R.) = (Memory content) KK=0 KJ=0 RB=1 RR=1 FF=0
M	39.	Shift MQ left and put 1 in last bit MQ
M	40.	Find sign
E	41.	Clear A

TABLE 5. (Contd.)

Type	No.	μ-instructions
$\dot{E}$	42.	Increase μPC if sign bit=0
C	43.	(P.C.) = $(IR)_1$
$\dot{E}$	44.	Increase μPC if bit 16=0 of R Register
$\dot{E}$	45.	Increase μPC if bit 6=0 of I.R.
$\dot{E}$	46.	Increase μPC if bit 5=0 of I.R.
$\dot{E}$	47.	Increase μPC if bit 2=0 of I.R.
C	48.	(MQ_1) = (IR_1)
$\dot{E}$	49.	Increase PC if I.R. bit 11=1
C	50.	μ Conditional jump
C	51.	μ Unconditional jump

TABLE 6

ANALYSIS OF μ-INSTRUCTIONS

Type		Expansion to simple μ-instructions
CE_{12}	$\bar{E}_{12}$	Is composed from: "No Oper if(INSTR.1) = 1" "R=0 if (INSTR.15) = 1" "shift R,MQ right if (INSTR.19) = 1" "shift R left if (INSTR.22) = 1". Instructions: NOP, CLR, SHR, SHL (SHINOCLE)
	E_{12}	Increase Program Counter
M_{22}	E_{22} C_{22} E_{22}	Shift R_2-R_1 right Shift R_1, MQ right Shift MQ
$\bar{E}_{27}$	$\bar{E}_{27}$	Plus 1 R_2-R_1 if overflow anticipation for the following Instr. ADD,SUB,MUL,IDR,ADRB,SURB depending on INSTR.
$\bar{E}_{20}$	$\bar{E}_{28}$	Execution function μ-operation for the following Instructions depending on the value of INSTR. ADD, SUB, MUL, AND, OR, FOR, ICR, ADRB, SURB
M_{40}	E_{40} C_{40}	Find Sign (BAL) = τό 16o bit τοῦ B καί R
$\dot{E}_{32}$	$\dot{E}_{32}$	Increase μPC if jump logic = 0. This μ-instruction controls the instructions: JMP, JMN, JMO, JMU
M_{39}	E_{39} E_{39}	Shift MQ left Put 1 in MQ

The simulating computer system can use subprograms according to the applications. The subprograms can be, a) Fixed, available in the library of the simulated system b) Temporary, written by the programmer. The following examples show how to connect the main program with subprograms. The system is designed so as, during the execution of a direct jump instruction, to refer to an address greater by one than that indicated by the address part of the instruction (Table 7).

The simulated machine is described with the aid of a number of variables with which the simulated program works. These variables contain all the necessary information for the simulation of the system. During the execution of a program in the simulated machine, the values which the variables take at any instant represent the state of the simulated machine.

The simulated program is written in

TABLE 7

Connection Between Main Program and Subprograms

```
1) Main program (page 1)                 Subprogram (page 1)
           :                             a)       :
      a)   (B)=(i)                       b)       :
    a+1)   Store B to s                           :
           :                             s) Jump to d+1
      d)   Jump to ℓ                              : } data
    d+1)   Output                           Subprogram (page 2)
           :                             1)       :
        -------                                   :
      i)   Jump to d+1 }                 s) Jump indirect to s+1
           :           } data          s+1) Page o, address d+1
2) Main Program (page 1)                          : } data
           :
      a)   (B)=(i)
    a+1)   Store B indirect to k
           :
      d)   Jump indirect to ℓ
           Output
           :
        -------
      i)   Address d                }
      k)   Page 2, address s+1      } data
      ℓ)   Page 2, address 1        }
```

5. SIMULATION OF THE PRESENT COMPUTER SYSTEM

The core of our simulator system is composed by translation routines of the μ-instructions of the machine under simulation. The main purpose of the real computer is just to load the simulated computer system, and, using its I/O, continuously to transfer the instructions and the data of the program under execution, in machine language, to the memory units of the simulated machine.

FORTRAN and is runned in a C.D.C-3300 Computer. It is portable, and is characterized by very good flexibility.

The programs in the simulated machine are written in machine language (Assembly language programs are also submitted through the simulated Assembly). In Fig. 4. we give the flow-chart of the simulated system. In the flow-chart the four phases and the use of each Flip-Flop are shown.

CONCOM has the capability to store more

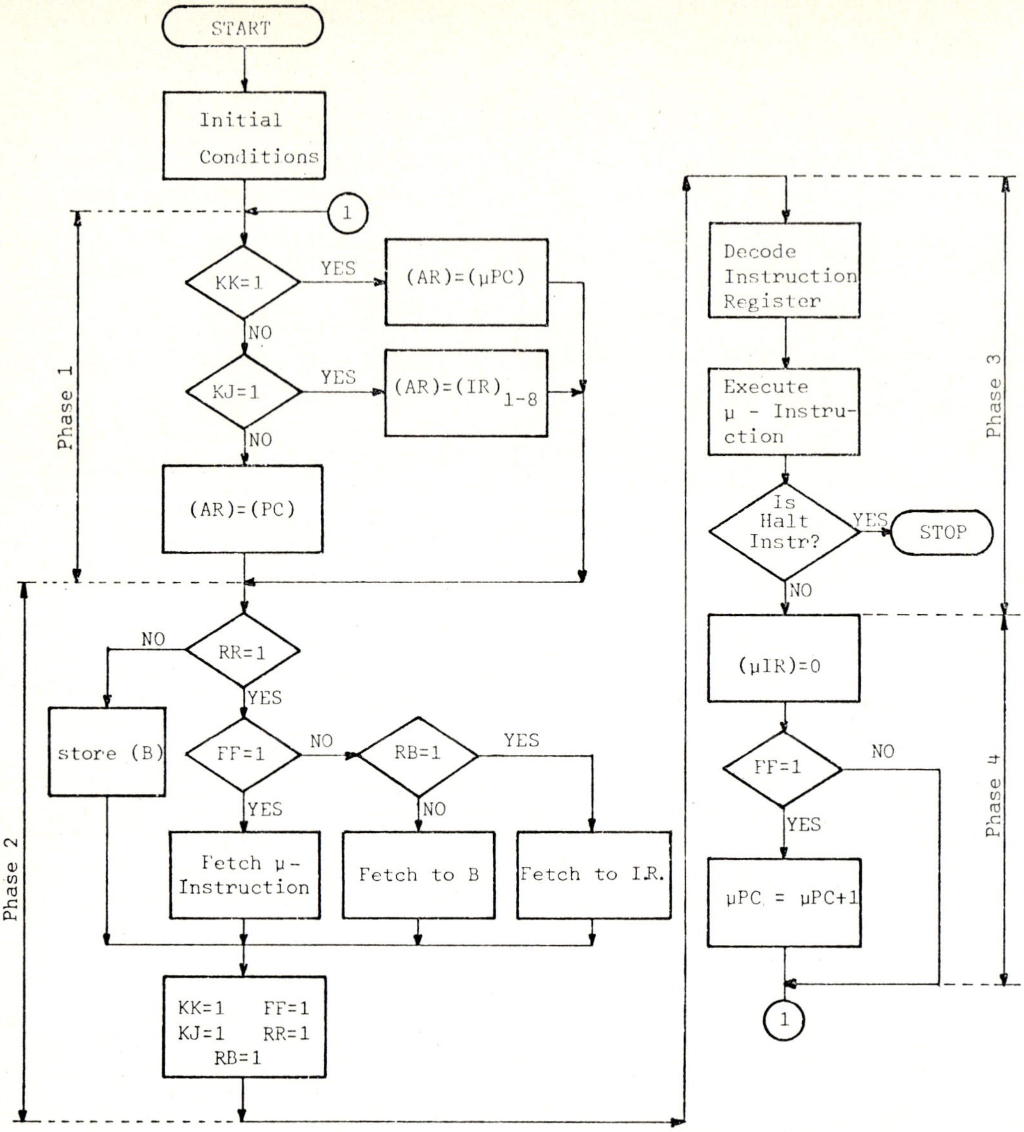

Fig. 4. Flow-chart of CONCOM simulated program

than one program and execute them in batch processing one at a time. The "user's manual" gives details on how to write programs in CONCOM'S machine or assembly language. The simulated program is composed by four phases plus the preparatory phase.
Preparatory phase: The system variables take their initial values. The system is updated by the μ-routines, the linkage table, the μ-instructions table, etc. The program under execution is given to the simulating machine and from that time the control is given to this machine.

Phase one: Put the appropriate address (Flip-Flops KK,KJ) to the address register.
Phase two: Transfer the information between memory and Registers according to the values of FF,RR,RB Flip-Flops.
Phase three: Decode the I.R. and execute the μ-instructions.
Phase four: Increase μPC and fetch the next μ-instruction.

6. CROSS-ASSEMBLY LANGUAGE OF CONCOM

In control applications assembly languages are very efficient. Our Macro-Assembly Language (MAL) is a two pass assembler

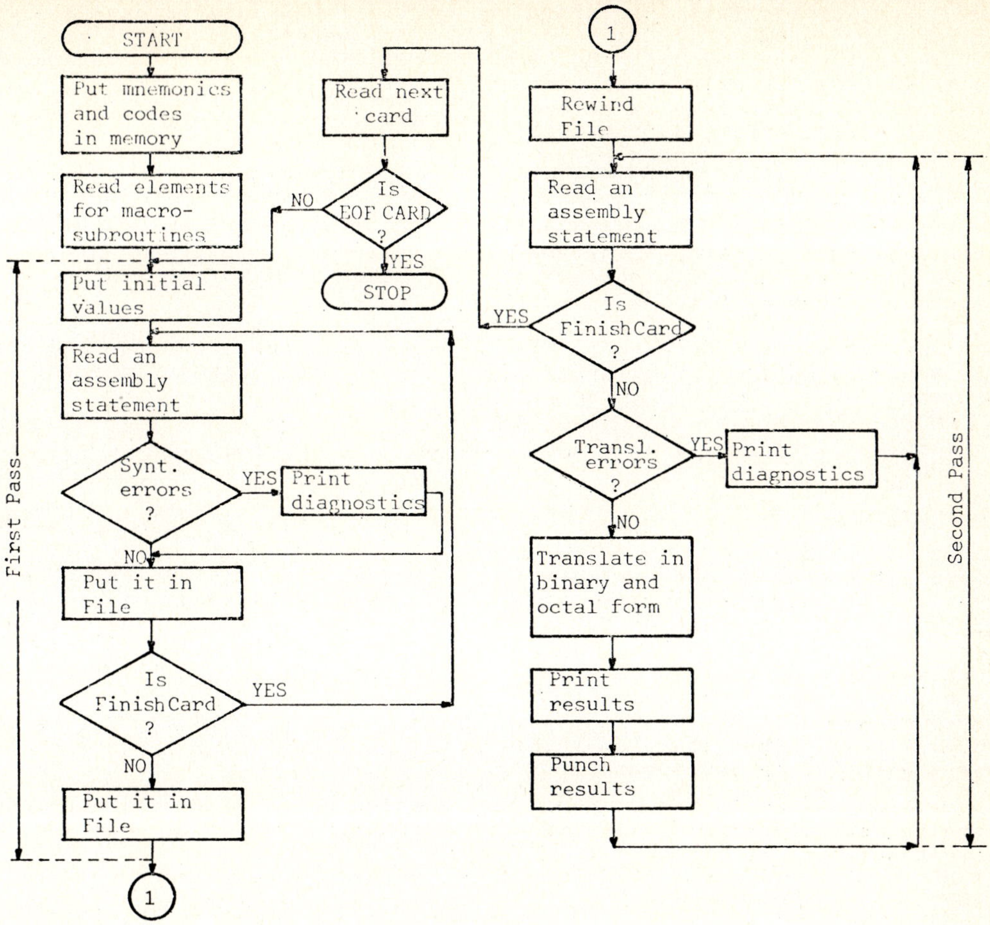

Fig. 5. Flow-chart of CONCOM Assembler.

designed for "CONCOM"so as to simplify its use. The assembler involves the following phases:

a) Preparatory Phase: In this phase the system is initiated by defining the initial values (entry points, etc.) of the simulated program, the mnemonics of the instructions and the macro-subroutines if they exist. We set to zero the program counter (P.C.) and the label counter (L. C.).

b) First pass-Syntactic analysis: The assembly statements starting with the declarative one are read. Diagnostic messages give information about the correctness of the program statements. It follows the creation of a variable array from the declarative statements, and the existing labels of the executable statements are stored in an appropriate table. The "Finish card" determines the end of the first pass.

c) Second Pass: In the second pass the assembly statements are transformed in absolute form. The simulator starts with the declarative statements and then proceeds with the executable ones. As output we obtain the binary form of each instruction. The output can be given in "list form" or can be punched directly and used as input in the CONCOM computer, for the execution of the program. Extra information such as the value of program Counter in binary form, and the corresponding instruction in binary and octal forms are also given. Fig. 5 shows the flow chart of the assembler.

More than one programs can be translated consecutively at the same run of the assembler simulator.

In the following we show how to create

and store macro subroutines according to the application at hand. The data and the address are manipulated through the "Subroutine MACROGEN". The main purpose of this subroutine is to create in software way the instructions "CALL SUBROUTINE" and "RETURN JUMP". The MACROGEN subroutine is updated by a table containing the elements of the macro-subroutine under translation, and replaces the macro-subroutine with a group of simple instructions. Two different ways for connecting the macrosubroutines with the main program are:

1) Macro subroutine with data-part. The Macro is replaced by the following simple instructions

```
STRI    ADD1
LDR     VAR
STRI    ADD2
LDR     ADD5
STRI    ADD3
JMUI    ADD4
```

ADD1: Address to maintain the content of R.
VAR: Data part of Macro subroutine.
ADD2: Address to put the data of Macro-subroutine.
ADD5: Address which specifies the return into the main program from the subprogram.
ADD3: Address to put the return address.
ADD4: Entry point of the subprogram.

2) Macro subroutine without data part. The Macro is replaced by the following simple instructions

```
STRI  ADD1
LDR   ADD4
STRI  ADD2
JMUI  ADD3
```

The meaning of the various addresses is similar to that of the previous case.

The Cross-Assembler gives:

a) A degree of independence from the hardware structure.
b) Increased understandability during the debuging of the program.
c) Increased flexibility and ease in changing and modifying the written program.
d) Error checking. It is capable to detect certain types of errors in the program, such as branches to non-existent micro-instructions, etc.

7. APPLICATION TO DIGITAL SIMULATION OF DYNAMIC SYSTEMS

There exist several digital simulation methods of dynamic and control systems . All these methods convert the continuous time model of the system to be simulated in discrete time. The two standard methods are [16,17]:

(i) The Tustin integration operator method.
(ii) The Z-transform method.

Consider a single-input single-output dynamic system with transfer function

$$G(s)=\frac{b_m s^m+b_{m-1}s^{m-1}+\ldots+b_1 s+b_o}{a_n s^n+a_{n-1}s^{n-1}+\ldots+a_1 s+a_o} \qquad m\leq n \qquad (1)$$

Without loss of generality we take here m=n=4.

Dividing the numerator and denominator by s^4 (the highest power of s) yields

$$G(s)=\frac{b_4+b_3(\frac{1}{s})+b_2(\frac{1}{s})^2+b_1(\frac{1}{s})^3+b_o(\frac{1}{s})^4}{a_4+a_3(\frac{1}{s})+a_2(\frac{1}{s})^2+a_1(\frac{1}{s})^3+a_o(\frac{1}{s})^4} \qquad (2)$$

Tustin Method: The Tustin method is based as the replacement of the Laplace integration operator 1/s and its powers by the approximate digital operator (Tustin operator) $T(z+1)/\{2(z-1)\}$ i.e.

$$\frac{1}{s}\to\frac{T}{2}(\frac{z+1}{z-1}),\quad (\frac{1}{s})^2\to\left[\frac{T}{2}(\frac{z+1}{z-1})\right]^2,\ldots \qquad (3)$$

where z^{-1} is the delay operator by one sampling period T.

Using (3) in (2) one obtains

$$G_A(z)=\frac{B_4z^4+B_3z^3+B_2z^2+B_1z+B_o}{A_4z^4\ A_3z^3+A_2z^2+A_1z+A_o} \qquad (4)$$

where

$$A_4=a_oT^4+2a_1T^3+4a_2T^2+8a_3T+16a_4$$
$$A_3=4a_oT^4+4a_1T^3-16a_3T-64a_4$$
$$A_2=6a_oT^4-8a_2T^2+96a_4$$
$$A_1=4a_oT^4-4a_1T^3+16a_3T-64a_4$$
$$A_o=a_oT^4+2a_1T^3+4a_2T^2-8a_3T+16a_4$$

$$B_4=b_oT^4+2b_1T^3+4b_2T^2+8b_3T+16b_4$$
$$B_3=4b_oT^4+4b_1T^3-16b_3T-64b_4$$
$$B_2=6b_oT^4-8b_2T^2+96b_4$$
$$B_1=4b_oT^4-4b_1T^3+16b_3T-64b_4$$
$$B_o=b_oT^4-2b_1T^3+4b_2T^2-8b_3T+16b_4$$

The corresponding input-output (simulation) model in the time domain is

$$y_k = \frac{1}{A_4}\{-A_3y_{k-1} - A_2y_{k-2} - A_1y_{k-3} - A_oy_{k-4}$$
$$+B_4u_k + B_3u_{k-1} + B_2u_{k-2} + B_1u_{k-3} + B_ou_{k-4}\} \qquad (5)$$

In the case of a closed-loop system, one must simulate each one of its blocks and design the overall closed-loop digital simulation by placing samplers between them. The existing D/A converters are simulated by combining in series a perfect sampler with a perfect zero-order hold.

The actual system which contains the D/A converters and the system G(s) gives the same response as the digital system $G_A(z)$ only at the sampling instants.

Ƶ-Transform Method: This method is based on the general formula which gives $G_A(z)$ via the Ƶ-transformation of G(s), i.e.

$$G_A(z) = (1-z^{-1})\mathcal{Z}\{\mathcal{L}^{-1}[\frac{G(s)}{s}]_{t\to kT}\} \qquad (6)$$

The procedure involves the following steps:

i) Determine the inverse Laplace transform

$$\hat{g}(t) = \mathcal{L}^{-1}\{\frac{G(s)}{s}\} \qquad (7)$$

ii) Compute $\hat{g}(t)$ at the sampling instants t=kT, k=0,1,2,...,i.e.

$$\hat{g}(kT) = \hat{g}(t)]_{t=kT}$$

iii) Determine the Ƶ transform of $\hat{g}(kT)$ and multiply the result by $(1-z^{-1})$.

Using this procedure one can construct a table of continuous transfer functions (in the Laplace domain) with the corresponding pulse transfer fucntions (in the z domain). This table can then directly be used for the digital simulation of any linear dynamic system.

8. TESTING EXAMPLES

Here we give two testing examples of dynamic system simulation by using the present mini-Computer in simulated form. For comparison purposes the same examples were also simulated via a cross-assembler of the INTEL-8080 μ-Computer and its simulation language. The programs of both computer systems are in permanent files and are called with the aid of special control cards. The same systems were also simulated on the Hewlett Packard computer HP9830 in BASIC.

Example 1: Application of Tustin's Method

Consider the closed loop control system

$$\frac{\bar{y}(s)}{\bar{x}(s)} = \frac{G_c(s)G(s)}{1+G_c(s)G(s)}$$

where the system under control is

$$G(s) = 2/(s+2)$$

and the series compensator (controller) is of the PI (proportional+integral) type, namely

$$G_c(s) = K_p(1+\frac{1}{s\tau_i})$$

Applying the Tustin method we obtain

$$\frac{Y(z)}{X(z)} = \frac{2K_p+(Tz+T+2\tau_iz-2\tau_i)T(z+1)}{(\text{Numerator})+2\tau_i(z-1)(2z-2+2Tz+2T)}$$

which gives the following discrete-time simulation model

$$y_{k+2} = \frac{1}{D}\{-Ay_{k+1} - By_k + Ex_{k+2} - Fx_{k+1} + Gx_k\}$$

where

$$A = 4K_pT^2 - 8\tau_i$$

$$B = 2K_pT(T-2\tau_i) - 4\tau_iT$$

$$D = 2K_pT(T+2\tau_i) + 2\tau_i(2+2T)$$

$$E = 2K_pT(T^2+2\tau_i)$$

$$F = 2T$$

$$G = T-2\tau_i$$

The parameter values are chosen as T=1, τ_i=0.5 and K_p=2.

The results obtained with the CONCOM, the INTEL-8080 and the HP-9830 simulators coincide and are shown in Table 8 and Fig. 6 with and without the compensator $G_c(s)$.

The CONCOM program in MAL is given below and involves 36 instructions. The corresponding program written in assembly language of the INTEL-8080 μ Computer involves 157 instructions.

MAL PROGRAM FOR EXAMPLE 1

	ASSEMBLY LANG. LIST		MEMORY ADDRESS	MACHINE LANG. LIST BINARY		OCTAL
	ENTRY POINT 308 PAGE 1		0 1 0 1 1 0 0 1			
	PROGRAM. CONTROLLER					
	ENDM		1 0 0 0 1 0 0 1	0 0 0 0 0 0 0 0	0 0 0 0 0 0 0 0	0
	APOT		0 1 0 0 1 0 0 1	0 0 0 0 0 0 0 0	0 0 0 0 0 0 0 0	0
	ARX1	66	1 1 0 0 1 0 0 1	0 1 0 0 0 0 1 0	0 0 0 0 0 0 0 0	41000
	ARX2	61	0 0 1 0 1 0 0 1	1 0 1 1 1 1 0 0	0 0 0 0 0 0 0 0	-41777
	A	4	1 0 1 0 1 0 0 1	0 0 1 0 0 0 0 0	0 0 0 0 0 0 0 0	20000
	B	2	0 1 1 0 1 0 0 1	0 1 0 0 0 0 0 0	0 0 0 0 0 0 0 0	40000
	CON	1000	1 1 1 0 1 0 0 1	0 0 0 1 0 1 1 1	1 1 0 0 0 0 0 0	13700
	D	12	0 0 0 1 1 0 0 1	0 0 1 1 0 0 0 0	0 0 0 0 0 0 0 0	30000
	COUN	49	1 0 0 1 1 0 0 1	1 0 0 0 1 1 0 0	0 0 0 0 0 0 0 0	-71777
	LDR	ARX1	0 1 0 1 1 0 0 1	0 1 0 0 1 0 0 1	1 1 0 1 1 0 1 0	44732
	OUR		1 1 0 1 1 0 0 1	0 0 0 0 0 0 0 0	1 1 0 1 0 1 0 1	325
	LDR	ARX2	0 0 1 1 1 0 0 1	1 1 0 0 1 0 0 1	1 1 0 1 1 0 1 0	-33045
	STR	APOT	1 0 1 1 1 0 0 1	1 0 0 0 1 0 0 1	1 1 0 0 0 1 1 0	-73071
	OUR		0 1 1 1 1 0 0 1	0 0 0 0 0 0 0 0	1 1 0 1 0 1 0 1	325
EPAN	LDR	COUN	1 1 1 1 1 0 0 1	0 0 0 1 1 0 0 1	1 1 0 1 1 0 1 0	14732
	ICRN	-1	0 0 0 0 0 1 0 1	0 1 1 1 1 1 1 1	1 1 0 1 1 1 0 1	77735
	JMN	TEL	1 0 0 0 0 1 0 1	1 1 0 0 1 1 0 1	1 0 0 1 1 0 0 0	-31147
	STR	COUN	0 1 0 0 0 1 0 1	0 0 0 1 1 0 0 1	1 1 0 0 0 1 1 0	14706
	LDR	B	1 1 0 0 0 1 0 1	1 0 1 0 1 0 0 1	1 1 0 1 1 0 1 0	-53045
	MUL	ARX1	0 0 1 0 0 1 0 1	0 1 0 0 1 0 0 1	1 0 0 0 0 0 0 1	44601
	STR	ENDM	1 0 1 0 0 1 0 1	0 0 0 0 1 0 0 1	1 1 0 0 0 1 1 0	4706
	LDR	A	0 1 1 0 0 1 0 1	0 0 1 0 1 0 0 1	1 1 0 1 1 0 1 0	24732
	MUL	APOT	1 1 1 0 0 1 0 1	1 0 0 0 1 0 0 1	1 0 0 0 0 0 0 1	-73176
	SUB	ENDM	0 0 0 1 0 1 0 1	0 0 0 0 1 0 0 1	1 0 0 1 1 1 0 0	4634
	STR	ENDM	1 0 0 1 0 1 0 1	0 0 0 0 1 0 0 1	1 1 0 0 0 1 1 0	4706
	LDR	CON	0 1 0 1 0 1 0 1	0 1 1 0 1 0 0 1	1 1 0 1 1 0 1 0	64732
	SUB	ENDM	1 1 0 1 0 1 0 1	0 0 0 0 1 0 0 1	1 0 0 1 1 1 0 0	4634
	DIV	D	0 0 1 1 0 1 0 1	1 1 1 0 1 0 0 1	1 0 0 0 1 0 1 1	-13164
	STR	APOT	1 0 1 1 0 1 0 1	1 0 0 0 1 0 0 1	1 1 0 0 0 1 1 0	-73071
	OUR		0 1 1 1 0 1 0 1	0 0 0 0 0 0 0 0	1 1 0 1 0 1 0 1	325
	LDR	ARX2	1 1 1 1 0 1 0 1	1 1 0 0 1 0 0 1	1 1 0 1 1 0 1 0	-33045
	STR	ARX1	0 0 0 0 1 1 0 1	0 1 0 0 1 0 0 1	1 1 0 0 0 1 1 0	44706
	LDR	APOT	1 0 0 0 1 1 0 1	1 0 0 0 1 0 0 1	1 1 0 1 1 0 1 0	-73045
	STR	ARX2	0 1 0 0 1 1 0 1	1 1 0 0 1 0 0 1	1 1 0 0 0 1 1 0	-33071
	JMU	EPAN	1 1 0 0 1 1 0 1	0 1 1 1 1 0 0 1	1 0 0 1 0 1 0 0	74624
TEL	HLT		0 0 1 0 1 1 0 1	0 0 0 0 0 0 0 0	1 0 0 0 1 0 0 1	211

36

TABLE 8

Closed-Loop Step Response with $\tau_i=0.5$, $K_p=2$ and T=1

k	1	2	3	4	5	6	7	8	9	10
y_k	0.67	0.61	0.74	0.69	0.73	0.71	0.72	0.71	0.72	0.71
k	11	12	13	14	15	16	17	18	19	20
y_k	0.71	0.71	0.71	0.71	0.71	0.71	0.71	0.71	0.71	0.71

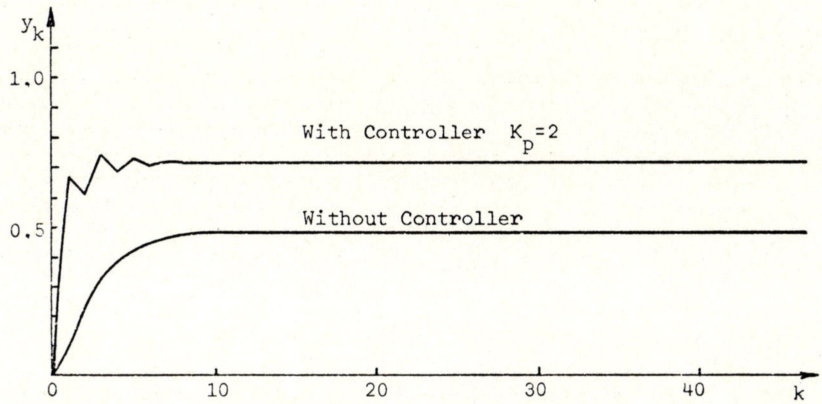

Fig. 6. Response of the closed loop discrete system.

Example 2: Application of Ƶ-Transform Method

The Ƶ-transform method was applied to the simulation of first, second, and third-order systems. The program was written in general form so as in each particular case only the additional parameters have to be read without the need to modify the instructions of the program.

The three systems studied are

1st-order

a) $G(s)=\frac{A}{s}$

b) $G(s)=\frac{A}{s+r}$

2nd-order

$$G(s)=\frac{A}{(s+r)(s+p)}$$

3rd-order

$$G(s)=\frac{A}{s(s+r)(s+p)}$$

The corresponding digital simulation models found by the Ƶ-transform are (where the parameter values were selected for the simulation):

1st-order

a) $y_k=a_1y_{k-1}+b_1u_{k-1};\ a_1=\underline{0.8},\ b_1=AT=\underline{0.18}$

b) $y_k=a_1y_{k-1}+b_1u_{k-1};\ a_1=e^{-rT}=\underline{0.5},$

$$b_1=\frac{A}{r}(1-e^{-rT})=\underline{0.5}$$

2nd-order

$$y_k=a_1y_{k-1}+a_2y_{k-2}+b_1u_{k-1}+b_2u_{k-2}$$

$$a_1=e^{-rT}+e^{-pT}=\underline{0.5},\ a_2=-e^{(r+p)T}=\underline{-0.1}$$

$$b_1=\frac{A}{rp(r-p)}\{(r-p)-re^{-pT}+pe^{-rT}\}=\underline{0.4}$$

$$b_2=\frac{A}{rp(r-p)}\{(r-p)e^{-(r+p)T}+pe^{-pT}-re^{-rT}\}$$

$$=\underline{0.15}$$

3rd-order

$$y_k = a_1 y_{k-1} + a_2 y_{k-2} + a_3 y_{k-3} + b_1 u_{k-1} + b_2 u_{k-2} + b_3 u_{k-3}$$

$$a_1 = 1 + e^{-rT} + e^{-pT} = \underline{0.5}$$

$$a_2 = -\{e^{-rT} + e^{-pT} + e^{-(r+p)T}\} = \underline{-0.1}$$

$$a_3 = e^{-(r+p)T} = \underline{5}$$

$$b_1 = \frac{A}{rp}\{T + \frac{r+p}{rp}(1 + e^{-rT} + e^{-pT}) + \frac{p}{r(r-p)}(2 + e^{-pT}) - \frac{r}{p(r-p)}(2 + e^{-rT})\} = \underline{0.4}$$

$$b_2 = -\frac{A}{rp}\{T(e^{-rT} + e^{-pT}) + \frac{r+p}{rp}(e^{-rT} + e^{-pT} + e^{-(r+p)T}) - \frac{r}{p(r-p)}(1 + 2e^{-rT}) + \frac{p}{r(r-p)}(1 + 2e^{-pT})\} = \underline{0.15}$$

$$b_3 = \frac{A}{rp}\{\frac{rpT + r + p}{rp} e^{-(r+p)T} + \frac{p}{r(r-p)} e^{-pT} - \frac{r}{p(r-p)} e^{-rT}\} - \underline{0.45}$$

The step responses of these systems computed by the CONCOM computer, the INTEL 8080, and the HP-9830 are as follows.

1st-Order Systems

(a)

k	1	2	3	4	5	6	7
y_k	0	0.18	0.32	0.43	0.53	0.60	0.66

k	8	9	10	11	12	13	14
y_k	0.71	0.74	0.77	0.80	0.82	0.83	0.85

k	15	16	17	18	19	20
y_k	0.86	0.86	0.87	0.87	0.88	0.88

(b)

k	0	1	2	3	4	5	6
y_k	0	0.5	0.75	0.87	0.93	0.96	0.98

k	7	8	9	10	11	12	13
y_k	0.99	0.99	0.99	0.99	0.99	0.99	0.99

k	14	15	16	17	18	19	20
y_k	0.99	0.99	0.99	0.99	0.99	0.99	0.99

2nd-Order System

k	1	2	3	4	5	6	7	8
y_k	0	0.4	0.6	0.81	0.89	0.91	0.91	0.91

k	9	10	11	12	13	14	15
y_k	0.91	0.91	0.91	0.91	0.91	0.91	0.91

k	16	17	18	19	20
y_k	0.91	0.91	0.91	0.91	0.91

3rd-Order System

k	1	2	3	4	5	6	7	8
y_k	0	0.4	0.6	0.81	0.64	0.64	0.76	0.73

k	9	10	11	12	13	14	15
y_k	0.71	0.76	0.77	0.77	0.78	0.80	0.81

k	16	17	18	19	20
y_k	0.81	0.83	0.83	0.84	0.84

The pictorial representations of the above step responses obtained by the Plotter are given in Fig. 7.

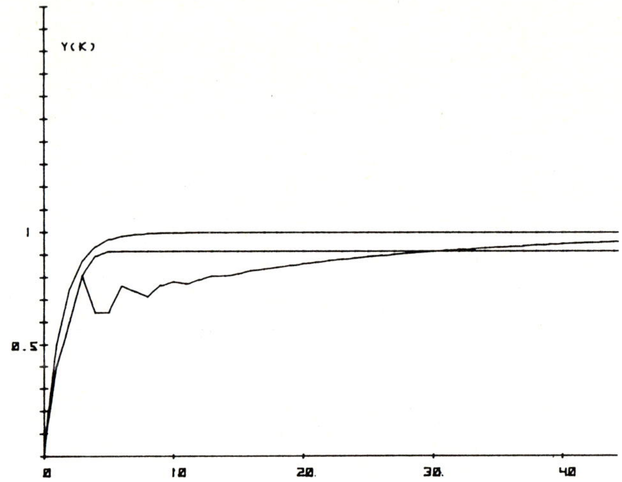

Fig.7. Plotted step responses for the three systems (1st, 2nd and 3rd order).

8. CONCLUSIONS

In general, digital control computers are designed for performing either a fixed control function or for being adaptable to multiple control function requirements. Here we have described the simulation of a micropogrammed mini control computer and its assembly language, which belongs to the latter category [7,8,12]. It was found that the execution time of the simulation programs for the testing examples for both the CONCOM and INTEL 8080 computers are nearly the same, if the same "host" computer is used for the machines simulation. The simulation program in MAL for the dynamic system was written in general form so that any system of up to third-order can be simulated with or without a compensator. This shows among others the usefulness of the CONCOM computer in process control applications. The main goal of the project was to understand microprogramming and design a microprogrammed mini computer, using the simulation approach, which is suitable, among others, for direct digital control. The designed computer is currently under hardware construction. The simulation programs of the machine language, the symbolic language, and the cross-assembler are available from the authors.

REFERENCES

[1] Robert V. Jacobson, "Digital Simulation of Large-Scale Systems", Proc. Spring Joint Computer Conf., 1966, pp. 159-164.

[2] A. Mathis, "La Simulazione dei Processi Industriali per la Progettazione dei Sistemi di Controllo Automatico". Informatica, Vol. II, No.3,1971, pp.69-96.

[3] D.P. Boret, C. Petacchi. "Simulazione di Input-Output per Piccoli Elaboratori", Informatica, Vol. VII, No.2, 1977, pp.185-197.

[4] J. Kontos-A. Kossidas, "Digital Computer CYBERN IV", Tech. Report, N.R.C. Democritos, 1969.

[5] Luigi M. Rispoli, "Operating System Flexibility for Digital Control", Instruments and Control Systems, Jan. 1972, pp.93-95.

[6] S. Tzafestas-P.Cosmatos, "Logical design of a digital control computer", Tech. Report, N.R.C. Democritos, 1972.

[7] A. Kossidas, "CONCOM ASSEMBLY Language User's Manual", Report, Electronic Eng. Dept., Higher Tech. Educational College SELETE, Athens 1979.

[8] S. G. Tzafestas and A.T. Kossidas, "Design and Simulation of a Mini Control Computer, Foundations of Control Eng., Tech. Univ.Poznan, "Ars" Polona Press, 1981.

[9] G.B. Gerace, "Introducione all a Microprogrammazione", Informatica, Vol.V, pp. 197-199, Dicembre, 1974.

[10] C. Batini and A. D'Atri, "Il Progetto di Sistemi Microprogrammati Strutturati a Livelli", Informatica, Vol.V, pp. 377-382, Dicembre 1977.

[11] N. Alexandridis and S. Tzafestas, Microcomputer Aspects for Control Applications", Proc. 20th Midwest Symp. on Circuits and Systems, Texas Tech. Univ., Aug. 1977.

[12] S. Tzafestas and A. Kossidas, "Simulation of a Microprogrammed Mini Control Computer System and its Assembly Language", Preprints IMACS Europ. Simulation Meeting on "Discrete Simulation and Related Fields (A. Javor, Ed.), pp.67-79, Keszthely, Hungary Sept. 1980.

[13] G. J. Myers, "Digital System Design with LSI Bit-Slice Logic", J. Wiley, N. Y. 1980.

[14] B.P. Zeigler, Modelling and Simulation Methodology: State of the Art and Promising Directions, in Simulation of Systems (L. Dekker, G. Savastano, G. Vansteenkiste, Eds), pp. 819-823, North-Holland 1980.

[15] B.P. Zeigler, M.S. Elzas, G. Klir and T. Ören (Eds.) Methodology in Systems Modelling and Simulation, North-Holland, 1979.

[16] S.G.Tzafestas, Advanced Techniques of Digital-Model Design and Real-Time Simulation for Direct Digital Control, Proc. AICA Symp. on "Simulation of Complex Systems", paper D-6, Tokyo, Sept. 1971.

[17] S.G. Tzafestas, Automatic Control Systems, Vol.3, Ch. 4 (Digital Simulation), Univ. of Patras, Greece, 1976.

DISCRETE SIMULATION AND RELATED FIELDS
A. Jávor (editor)
North-Holland Publishing Company

DISCRETE MODELLING OF STRUCTURAL CHANGES IN EDUCATION SYSTEMS

A. Benedek, A. Csákány

Research Institute for Education, Central Research
Institute for Physics; Budapest, Hungary

By demonstrating one of the feasible methods of investigating social progression, the study considers the possibility of computer simulation in the context of educational planning. Analysis of the kind of dynamisms of the educational system that may be expected in the next few decades is carried out by the condition-dependent variation of general schooling and by a method which analyses the state of the system by describing an event. With the aid of discrete simulation the procedure furnishes planners with useful information (as a function of the varied conditions) on the moment of optimum „changeover", rendering it thus possible to draw up alternatives for improvement.

1. INTRODUCTION

For two decades now, one of the universal questions of the day has been how to remodel the various systems of public education and how to increase the period of general schooling. Attempts to settle this problem brought on, during the 60's and the 70's, a whole series of educational reforms in almost every country. It was a common feature of those reforms that they occurred in an earlier – so-called „running-in" – period in the progress of educational systems, at a time when the school-age population had not yet attained full capacity. No structural reforms of public education existed in Hungary at that time; however, the demand for general schooling as well as the social encouragement for it went from strength to strength. It seems, at the same time, to be likely that the structural reform – may actually appear under such conditions when 90-95% of school-age population are already participating in compulsory education. Therefore, the wider application of schooling in Hungary, at present comprising eight grades, by changing of it to a nine-grade or ten-grade system one may give rise to considerable strains.

The feasible point of „,changeover" depends on a multitude of socio-econo conditions and, all things considered, it is the subject of policy decision. In the course of preparing for this decision there will be a need for the results of a great number of researches carried out in numerous disciplines, affording thus the possibility to determine the optimum point. Among the various researches, computer simulation can assert its own particular approach by investigating the dynamic features of the educational system as a function of the system's most characteristic parameters.

Insofar as the modelling of educational processes, taking place on a scale of social proportions, can be realized by suitable means, it will render possible such – relatively inexpensive – computer analyses which may help disclose the inner correlations of these processes as well give information enabling opinions to be formed of the alternatives, plans and prognostics.

Computer modelling of the educational process and structure entails two important methodological advantages:

a/ in the course of developing the model it is the entirety of the educational process that ought to be – and, in fact, must be – very thoroughly deliberated on, certainly much more thoroughly than is allowed by verbal models;

b/ the evaluation of such characteristics which are difficult to define numerically will result in a more profound understanding of them.

It must be accepted as a fact that the development of the present structure and meaning of public education will, at some time in the future and in some way or other, turn into a new system in the course of the changes taking place. This process – which is difficult to grasp from a distance of the present – may be accelerated or impeded by numerous factors. When taking these factors into consideration one may find that some of them limit the possibilities of development. In short, though the parameters of the educational system may not perhaps exert the sole influence they do have a considerable one in determining the possibility of the „changeover" or of other dynamic „activity".

Most educational models provide – a series of discrete values: the calendar year, the school-year, the semester etc. which usually give the measure of the time-scale.

By taking account of the appropriate historical or social interval, the series of discrete values produces a continuous effect. Because the educational structure in our model is undergoing such drastic changes what we needed was the elaboration of the oriented simulation method of an event. The simulation must supply the most important paramteres that were prevalent prior to the occurrence of the „event", as well as those characteristics existing after: that is to say, with the aid of an appropriately selected target-function the simulation programme must produce some sort of an optimum value for that moment when the occurrence of the „event" is desired.

Accordingly, the simulation system described below is an expedient mixture of a continuous (or what may be regarded as continuous) and an event-oriented discrete simulation.

By means of the DYNEDU (Dynamics of Education) model developed jointly by the Research Institute for Education and the Research Institute for Measurement and Computing Techniques of the Central Research Institute for Physics of the Hungarian Academy of Sciences, we have attempted to describe such correlations of primary importance which fundamentally limit the scope of structural development.

2. FEATURES OF DYNEDU

In the course of creating the model the following factors were regarded as of deterministic nature:

a/ Demographic factors, or to be more exact, the formation of the number of those entering school. With respect to this, we have at our disposal numerical prognostics up to the year 2021.

$D(T_i)$ number of six-year old age-group entering school,

where i=1,2, ..., 30 is the period of simulation in years.

b/ Structure of education, the time element spent by the population in regular education, the number and „depth" of education-related „branch-offs" following the period of public elementary school.

c/ The most essential conditions of schooling, the number of classrooms and teachers, as well as their predictable changes, respectively.

The interdependency of these overall factors is illustrated by the following causal loop diagram (Fig.1).

A certain number of children – determined by demographic factors – enters school each year. Since this number entering school fluctuates, education registers an increasing or diminishing amount of strain in the participation rate in proportion to the number of those already receiving instruction. In like manner, those leaving the educational system may also add to the increase or decrease of the inner crowdedness pending the number of that age-group. In fact, by reason of the phenomenon of dropping out the educational system does not release entrants in a constant number. The state of an educational system is substantially determined by conditions pertaining to personnel and the available financial means such as the number of teachers and classrooms. The purposeful development of these may bring about conditions of which the changeover of the structure can be effected. Here, the length of schooling should be augmented so that the pupil (teacher and student) classroom ratios – peculiar to the structure of education – change to the slightest possible degree only.

Our aim was to develop such a model out of the system, comprising three major loops, in which an opportunity would be provided – on both macro- and regional levels – for an analysis of the dynamic qualities of the system, and for the alternative and condition-dependent determination regarding the points of „changeover". /In our view the „changeover" is a state that has a substantial bearing on the number of population attending school and on the length of time of schooling./

The modell was constructed in conformity with these loops in the following steps:

The predicted passing of the population through public elementary school in n steps of schooling is known. Assume it to be A_m, where the period of schooling (school years) m=1,2,...,n is n=8 in the basic state of the system.

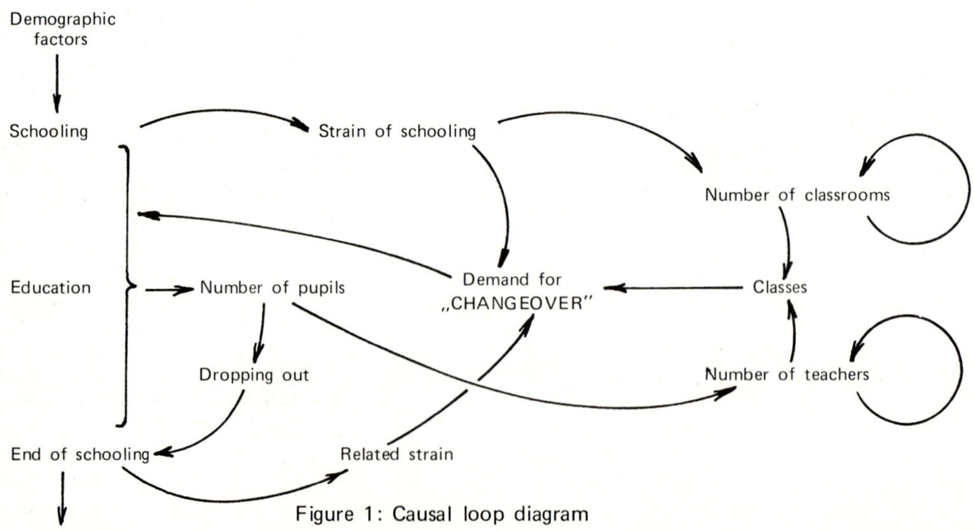

Figure 1: Causal loop diagram

The population undergoing schooling

$$Q\ (T_i) = \sum_{m=1}^{n} A_m\ (T_i)$$

is given. It is conditional on the number of those entering and withdrawing.

The number of those finishing schooling can be determined as

$$A_{out}(T_i) = A_8(T_{i-1}).(1-c_8-d_8)$$

(where c designates the percentage of repetition and failure to satisfy requirements,
and d the percentage of those leaving school)

On Fig. 2. these relations are graphycally pictured.

This will caution us so much the more – particularly in planning – as it is obvious that a disorder in the magnitude of demographic changes could be caused in the school system by an educational measure (c_1=0). Therefore, it is evident that the change of pupils depends, first of all, on the demographic factor as well as on the extent of dropping out.

Both loops, the one describing the changes in the number of teachers and the other representing those in the number of classrooms, may be traceable to the following basic schema (Fig.4):

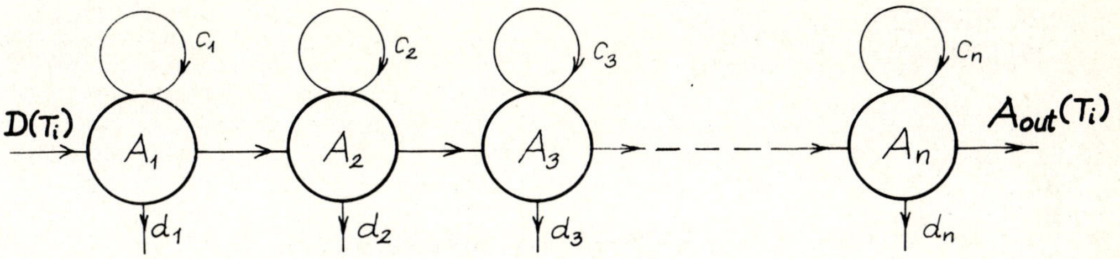

Figure 2: State graph of the school

By means of the above given graph, one can determine the number of pupils in consecutive classes as a function of demographic input, failure rates and drop-out rates.

For some value $2 \leq m \leq n$

$$A_m(T_{i+1}) = A_m(T_i).c_m + A_{m-1}\ (T_i).(1-c_{m-1}-d_{m-1})$$

and for m=1 (a special case because in Hungarian schools the value of c_1 is zero)

$$A_1\ (T_{i+1}) = D\ (T_{i+1})$$

This system appears to be worthy of attention in itself even. If, for example, the participation rate of pupils in individual classes is represented as a function of m,provided that the entry is of a constant value, then in the cases of

$$d_1 = d_2\ \ldots = d_8 = 0{,}01$$

and

$$c_2 = c_3 = \ldots = c_8 = 0{,}03$$

the diagram Fig.3. is obtained:

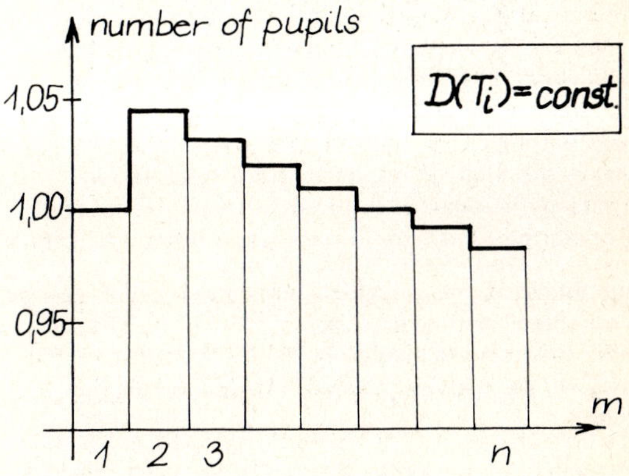

Figure 3: Population fluctuation due to C_1=0

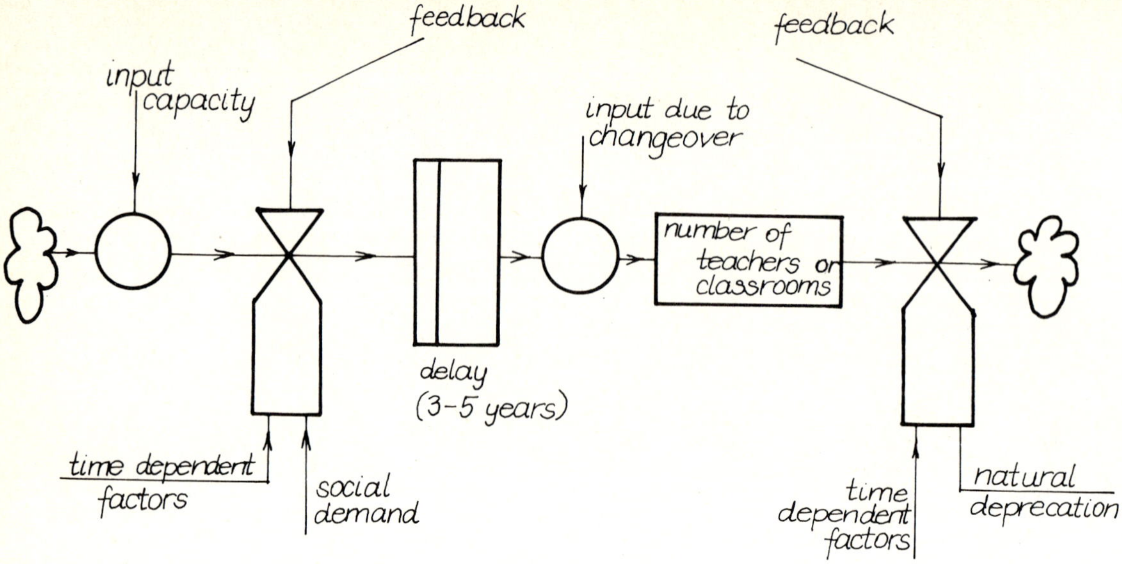

Figure 4: The components of the basic loops of the system

3. SIMULATION WITH DYNEDU

The analysis of the system dynamism of public education may be regarded as a recursive process. The given model construction enables the analyses to be repeated using different parameters under normal conditions. It is, at the same time, an important task that the parameter values be properly chosen as regards both the inner, functional data of the model as well as the external ones describing the conditions that the analysis is subject to. Only in this case can we expect to obtain the kind of results that are suitable for determining the tendencies of such development which is in conformity with the diverse possibilities and means.

The details of the DYNEDU simulation model can be seen on the general block diagram of Fig. 5. The symbols used on the figure are almost identical to the symbols of the widely known DYNAMO simulation concept.

In the course of computer simulation we have selected the activity describing method. The essential character of the procedure is that the event of the „changeover" within the system occurs at a time – and only at that time – when the variables of state and the value of the system-time of simulation comply with certain requirements.

During the simulation the state is put through an analysis which decides whether the increment of the value n – the number of school years – of the activity can be fulfilled.

Several strain-paramteres are defined in the model: for example the so-called entry- or schooling-strain which, by knowing the number of six-year olds entering school and the number of those receiving instruction, can be computed according to the following relationship:

$$S_{in}(T_i) = \frac{Q(T_i) - n\,D(T_i)}{Q(T_i)}$$

Similarly, an output-strain can be given too by the formula

$$S_{out} = \frac{Q(T_i) - n\,A_{n+1}(T_i)}{Q(T_i)}$$

Importart strain parameters strongly influencing the general level of education are the pupil per teacher ratio (S_1) and the number of pupils per classroom ratio (S_2). Further on other complex strain parameters can be defined by adequatly mixing different strain parameters. The complex strain parameter (S_{compl}) was chosen so as to represent the components symmetrically and to give

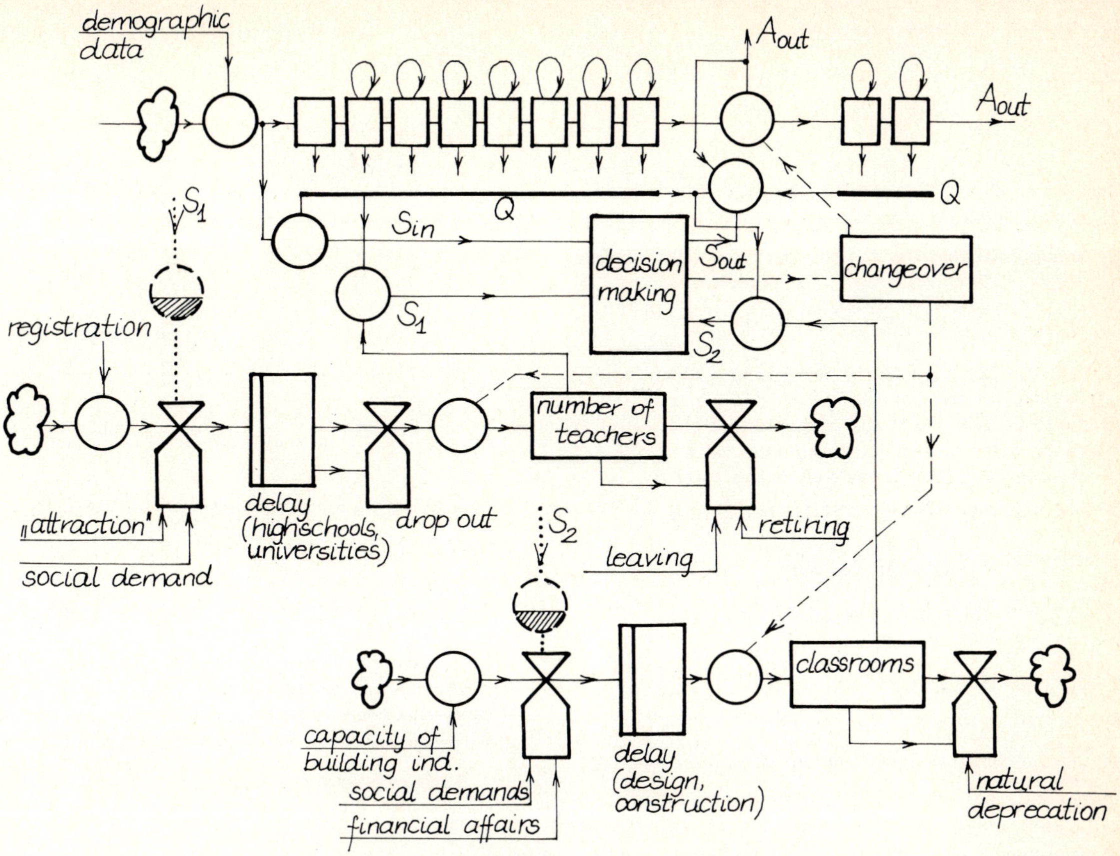

Figure 5: General block diagramm of DYNEDU

some sort of geometric character of the resultant. Thus the following expression was used:

$$S^2_{compl} = \left(\frac{S_1}{S_{10}}\right)^2 + \left(\frac{S_2}{S_{20}}\right)^2$$

where S_{10} and S_{20} are normalising parameters. Due to this choice the contours of constant values of the complex strain parameters are circles. (See Fig.6)

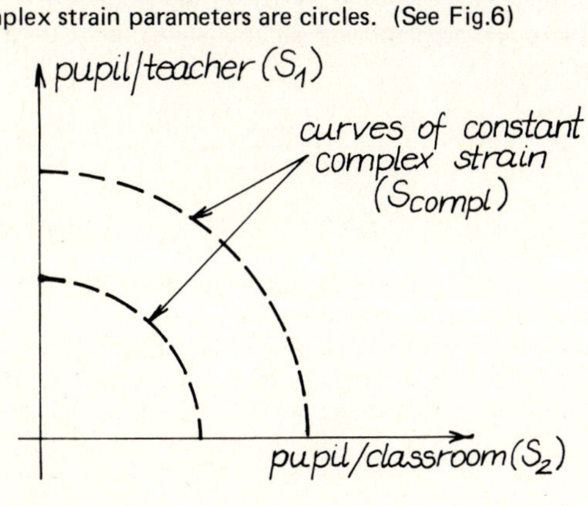

Figure 6: S_{compl} as a function of S_1 and S_2

If the analysis regarding the state of the system realizes the „changeover", the program ensures that the change in the value of the state-variables and the value actualization of the variables of time are done. The input data relating to the analysis of state are obtained in this way (Fig. 7)

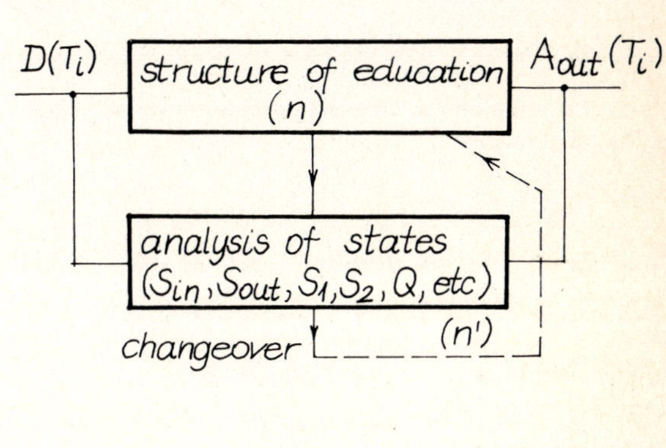

Figure 7

The process of the analysis of state is described by the following difference equation:

$$\Delta f_i = f_i \Big[Q(1), \quad Q(2), \ldots, Q(k); S_{in}(1), S_{in}(2), \ldots, S_{in}(k); S_{out}(1), S_{out}(2), \ldots, S_{out}(k) \ldots\ldots\ldots \Big] \cdot \Delta t$$

where i=1,2,...,k (in our case the computer counts over k=30 cycles).

It is supposed that the characters do not approximate their steady-state condition, i.e. the process does not attain its steady-state condition $0 \leq i \leq k$ in the given domain of time.

Reduce the process into discrete phases and put the characteristics of state of each phase through an extreme value analysis. If the parameters of the analysis of state are of a local minimum value in the given time phase, the n is incremented as follows:

Define the state function of three variables C

$$f{:}C \longrightarrow F(S_{in}, S_{out}, S_{compl})$$

$\varepsilon > 0$ in the chosen interval M. If at the minimum place T_i

$$f(C) \geq f(\overset{*}{C}),$$

and $$(C - \overset{*}{C}) < \varepsilon,$$

then the function has a local minimum value.

(When the parameters of the analysis of state were investigated in the interval M it was assumed that T had an ambience of ε radius, and the values of

$$\dot{S}_{in}(t), \quad \dot{S}_{out}(t) \quad \text{and} \quad \dot{S}_{compl}(t)$$

were determined.

For the sake of simplicity we supposed that a continuosly differentiable function can be used as an approximation instead of the discrete data values.)

If any of the variables has a local extreme value, then the second derivative of the given function is to be examined.

If $\dot{S}_{in}(t)=0$ and $\ddot{S}_{in}(t) > 0$

then the value of the discrete variable of state $\alpha(S_{in})$ is to be taken as 1.

If $\dot{S}_{out}(t) = 0$ and $\ddot{S}_{out}(t) > 0$

then the value of the discrete variable of state $\beta(S_{out})$ is to be taken as 1.

If $\dot{S}_{compl}(t) = 0$ and $\ddot{S}_{compl}(t) > 0$

then the value of the discrete variable of state $\gamma(S_{compl})$ is to be taken as 1.

Failing these conditions the value of α, β, γ is, in each case 0.)

The α, β, γ discrete variables of state determine the value-set function, the truth-table of which is shown on Fig.8.

α	β	γ	Δ
0	0	0	0
0	0	1	0
0	1	0	0
0	1	1	1
1	0	0	0
1	0	1	1
1	1	0	0
1	1	1	1

Figure 8.

The following logic function may be stated from this:

$$\Delta = \gamma \cap (\alpha \cup \beta)$$

The value $\Delta = 1$ increments n, for example for n = 10.

Further, the restructuring of the process to be regarded as of a discrete type is made up of a series of successive analyses and decisions connected decisively with the increment conditions of the value n.

During computer processing the characteristics of state were computed periodically (in discrete time phases).

4. CONCLUSIONS

By means of the foregoing method we have performed and analysis of the Hungarian system of education. In the Fig.9 (which is actually a computer printout) one may follow the effect of „changeover" ensuing in the eighteenth year of simulation time. The change in the values of three different strain-parameters, viz. S_{compl}, S_1, S_2 and are shown in the figure. The „changeover" occurred at the extreme value of S_{compl}. By a modification of the parameters of the model the dynamic qualities of the educational system as well as the possibilities of planning and development can be analysed under different conditions.

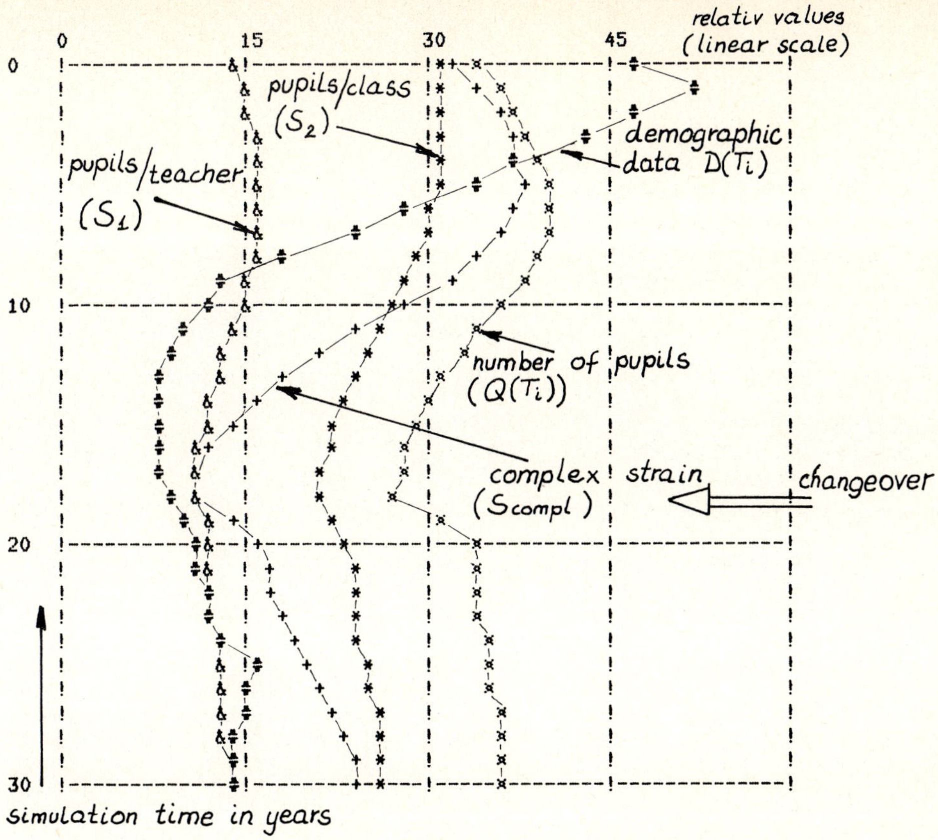

Figure 9: An example: the effect of a changeover in the 18th year of simulation time

Bibliography

1 Cole, S., Towards a modell for long-term education policy, Computers in Education 4 (1980) 147-165.

2 Cook, P.D., Gillet, J., Stainforth, J.A.L., An experimental education planning system. (IBM United Kingdom, Winchester, 1979).

3 Smith, Wm., Computer simulation and logistic analysis in educational planning and administration, in Lecarme, O. and Lewis, R. (eds.), Computers in education (North-Holland, Amsterdam, 1975).

4 Vangton, J.H., Alternate scenario planning, Technological Forecasting and Social Change 10 (1977) 169-180.

5 Pox, Jenkins: Time series analysis: forecasting and control (Holden-Day Ins. 1976.)

6 Athans, Dertouzos, Spann, Mason: Systems, networks, computation: multivariable methods. (McGraw-Hill, 1974.)

7 Forrester, J. W.: Urban dynamics. (M.I.T. Press, 1969.)

8 Gelovani, V.: An interactive modelling system as a tool for analysing complex socio-economic problems. Impact, 31. (1981.) p.: 413-422.

DISCRETE SIMULATION AND RELATED FIELDS
A. Jávor (editor)
North-Holland Publishing Company

IMPROVING THE CONTROL OF AN EXPERIMENTAL EXTRUDER BY A DISCRETE FORMULATION

Yvon JARNY

Laboratoire d'Automatique (ERA - CNRS)
E.N.S.M. 1, rue de la Noë - 44072 NANTES Cedex, France

The on-line implementation of a control law for an experimental distributed parameter system is described. By using a spatially varying parameter model instead of constant parameters it is shown that the results can be improved.
In this way a discrete formulation which preserves the distributed property of the model is used. From this discrete formulation a parameter identification can be derived. The control law for the discrete system is deduced from the minimization of a cost functional defined on a receding horizon. A state observer is required. Experimental results are presented.

1. INTRODUCTION

The control theory for systems governed by partial differential equations has been largely developed during the last fifteen years [1]. But the application to the control of actual processes is still less developed.

For a digital simulation, an approximation of the distributed equations is obviously needed. In many applications the Galerkin approximation [2] is often used to implement the control of linear parabolic systems, but in our sense, it is not convenient when a parameter identification is previously required. Especially when the parameters are spatially varying the finite element method seems to be more suitable. It allows a spatial discretization that leads to discrete state equations which are easy to solve, furthermore the distributed property of the system is preserved : parameters and state are considered as functions of the spatial variable.

This method is used to describe an experimental distributed parameter system by a discrete state equation. Parameters are then identified from the measurements of the temperature process evolution. An optimal control law which requires a state observer is studied for the discrete model. Its implementation is illustrated by experimental results which show the improvement realized by the choice of a spatially varying parameter model.

2. DESCRIPTION OF THE PROCESS

The extruder (Fig. 1) consists of a rotating screw within a cylindrical barrel followed by a die.

It is considered as a unique cylinder along which the temperature profile is controlled by three electrical heating elements. Temperature is measured by three thermocouples.

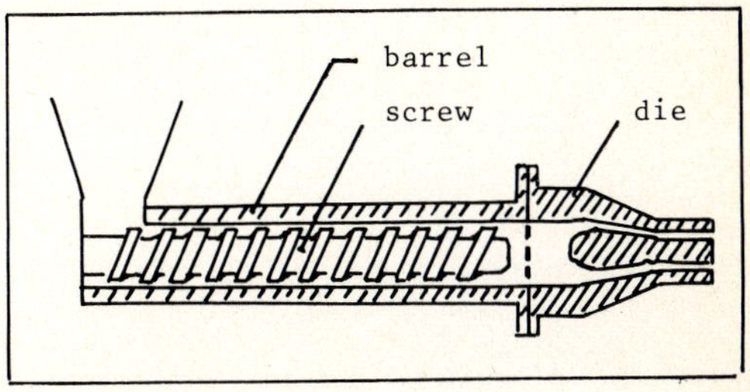

Fig. 1 - The extruder

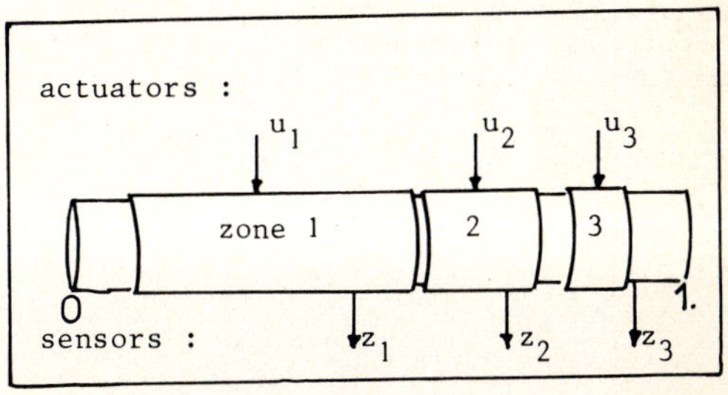

Fig. 2 - Actuator and sensor location.

Notations : L : length, D : diameter, S : cross section of the cylinder, λ : thermal conductivity, C_p : specific heat ; h_1, h_2 : heat transfer coefficients ; ρ : density.

$\theta(x,t)$: cylinder temperature
θ_e : external temperature assumed to be constant
u_i : power dissipated in zone i
L_i : length of zone i

Let $y(x,t) = \theta(x,t) - \theta_e$

$$a = \rho\, C_p\, S \; ; \; b = \lambda S \; ; \; c = \pi\, h_1\, D \; ; \; \delta = h_2\, S$$

$$f(x,t) = \sum_{i=1}^{3} \chi_i(x)\, u_i(t)$$

$\chi_i(x) = 1/L_i, \quad x \in \Omega_i, \ \Omega_i$: interval of zone i
$= 0$ otherwise

The evolution of y can be described by the solution of the following equations :

$$y(x,0) = y_o(x) \tag{1}$$

$$a\frac{\partial y}{\partial t}(x,t) - \frac{\partial}{\partial x}\left(b\frac{\partial y}{\partial x}(x,t)\right) + cy(x,t) = f(x,t) \tag{2}$$

$$x \in]0,L[, \quad t > 0$$

$$b(0)\frac{\partial y}{\partial x}(0,t) - \delta y(0,t) = 0 \tag{3}$$

$$b(L)\frac{\partial y}{\partial x}(L,t) + \delta y(L,t) = 0, \quad t > 0 \tag{4}$$

3. STATE EQUATION OF THE MODEL

The solution y of Eq.(1) - (4) can be considered as the element of $L^2(0,T;V)$ such that :

$$\int_\Omega [a\frac{dy}{dt}v + b\frac{dy}{dx}\frac{dv}{dx} + cyv]dx + \int_\Gamma \delta y.vds = \int_\Omega fvdx \tag{5}$$

$\forall\, v \in V$, with: $\Omega =]0,L[$, $\Gamma = \{0,L\}$
and V is an appropriate Hilbert space [3].

The spatial discretization of Eq.(5) is carried out by a finite element method and the time discretization by an implicit method.

It comes the following discrete state equation :

$$[\alpha]\,\underline{y}^{k+1} = [\beta]\underline{y}^k + [\gamma]\underline{u}^{k+1/2}, \quad k = 1,\dots, M \tag{6}$$

The numerical computation of the tridiagonal matrices $[\alpha]$, $[\beta]$ can be carried out without approximation. The numerical solution of Eq.(6) is obtained by the THOMAS algorithm [5].

The solution $\underline{y}^k$ satisfies the following relations :

$$\underline{y}^k = [y_i^k]_{i=1}^{N+1}, \quad y_i^k = y(x_i,t_k) \quad \forall_i, \forall_k,$$

and $y(x,t_k) = \sum_{i=1}^{N+1} y(x_i,t_k)\, s_i(x)$

where $\{s_i,\ i = 1,\dots, N+1\}$ is an appropriate basis $\mathcal{B}$ of functions defined on Ω [3].
In the same way, the spatially varying parameters a, b and c are decomposed on $\mathcal{B}$, for example :

$$a(x) = \sum_{i=1}^{N+1} a_i\, s_i(x) \text{ and } a_i = a(x_i),\ i=1,\dots,N+1$$

4. THE IDENTIFICATION PROBLEM

From this discrete formulation a parameter identification method is derived.
Let P_{ad} the convex set of admissible parameters, for $\mu = (a, b, c, \delta) \in P_{ad}$, let :

$\underline{y}(\mu)$ be the solution of Eq.(6),

the observation is defined by :

$z_j^k(\mu) = y^k(x_j;\mu)$ at point x_j,

corresponding to the given input $[\underline{u}^k]_{k=1}^M$ of the process, the sensor j gives the output denoted by $[\hat{z}_j^k]_{k=1}^M$
Then, the cost functional J_1 is introduced :

$$J_1(\mu) = \sum_{k=1}^{M+1} ||\underline{z}^k(\mu) - \hat{\underline{z}}^k||^2_{\mathbb{R}^3}, \text{with } \underline{z}^k = [z_j^k]_{j=1}^3 \tag{7}$$

The identification of the parameters μ is set as the optimization of J_1, it consists in finding μ^*, if $\mu^* \in P_{ad}$ exists, such that :

$$J_1(\mu^*) = \inf J_1(\mu),\ \mu \in P_{ad} \tag{8}$$

J_1 is assumed to be derivable on P_{ad} and μ^* to exist. In order to find a numerical approximation of μ^*, a steepest descent method is used, it is iterative and consists in minimizing a function ψ^n in one variable defined at the step n by :

$$\psi^n(\rho) = J_1(\mu^n - \rho\nabla J_1(\mu^n)),\ \rho \in I_{ad} \tag{9}$$

where $\nabla J_1(\mu^n)$ is the gradient of J and I_{ad} is an interval derived from the definition of P_{ad}.
The computation of ∇J_1 is achieved by differentiating the Lagrangian $\mathcal{L}$ defined by :

$$\mathcal{L}(y,P,\mu) = J_1(\mu) + \sum_{k=1}^{M} (\underline{P}^k)^\dagger([\alpha]\underline{y}^{k+1} - [\beta]\underline{y}^k - [\gamma]\underline{u}^{k+1/2}) \tag{10}$$

when $y = y(\mu)$

$$\text{then } \mathcal{L}(y,P,\mu) = J(\mu) \tag{11}$$

by taking $P = [\underline{P}^k]_{k=1}^M$ such that :

$$\frac{\partial\mathcal{L}}{\partial y}(y(\mu),P,\mu)\,\delta y = 0 \quad \forall\,\delta y \tag{12}$$

then it follows that :

$$\nabla J_1(\mu) = \frac{\partial\mathcal{L}}{\partial\mu}(y(\mu),P,\mu) \tag{13}$$

The equation (12) is called the discrete adjoint state equation and its solution :

$P \in [\mathbb{R}^{N+1}]^{M+1}$ verifies :

$$[\alpha]\,\underline{P}^{k-1} = [\beta]\,\underline{P}^k + [\eta](\hat{\underline{z}}^k - \underline{z}^k) \quad k = M+1,\dots,2$$
$$\underline{P}^{M+1} = 0 \tag{14}$$

where $[\eta]$ is an $(N+1,3)$ matrix with :
$\eta_{ij} = 1$ if the location of sensor j is x_i
$= 0$ otherwise.
More details can be found in [3].

($\dagger$) denotes the transposition.

5. THE RECEDING HORIZON CONTROL PROBLEM

Let $\mathcal{U}_{ad}$ be the convex set of admissible controls :

$$\mathcal{U}_{ad} = \{\underline{u} \in \mathbb{R}^3 : 0 \leq u_i \leq u_{imax}, \; i = 1,2,3\}$$

and $\underline{y}_d \in \mathbb{R}^{N+1}$ a desired state.

For $\mu^* \in P_{ad}$ and $\underline{u} \in \mathcal{U}_{ad}$, let :

$[\underline{y}^k(\underline{u})]_{k=0}^{L}$ be the solution of Eq.(6) on the horizon $]0, L\tau[$

then the cost functional J_2 is introduced :

$$J_2(\underline{u}) = \sum_{k=0}^{L} \|\underline{y}^k(\underline{u})-\underline{y}_d\|^2 + \varepsilon\|\underline{u}\|^2, \; \varepsilon > 0 \tag{15}$$

The receding horizon control problem is set as the optimization of J_2, it consists in finding the constant control $\tilde{\underline{u}} \in \mathcal{U}_{ad}$ such that :

$$J_2(\tilde{\underline{u}}) = \inf J_2(\underline{u}), \quad \underline{u} \in \mathcal{U}_{ad} \tag{16}$$

The following properties of $\tilde{\underline{u}}$ can be obtained :

i) $\tilde{\underline{u}}$ exists, is unique and is characterized by :

$$\nabla J_2(\tilde{\underline{u}}).(\tilde{\underline{u}}-\underline{u}) \geq 0 \qquad \forall \, \underline{u} \in \mathcal{U}_{ad} \tag{17}$$

ii) without constraint, the optimal control law can be written :

$$\tilde{\underline{u}} = G[\underline{y}^o-\underline{y}_d] + R\,[y_d] \tag{18}$$

and the matrices G, R depend on the horizon length $L\tau$.

Proof of Eq.(18). From the linearity of Eq.(6), for $k = 0,\ldots L$, $\forall \, \underline{u} \in \mathcal{U}_{ad}$, there exists (E^k,F^k) such that :

$$\underline{y}^k(\underline{u}) = E^k\,\underline{y}^o + F^k\,\underline{u} \tag{19}$$

then it follows that :

$$J_2(\underline{u}) = \sum_{k=0}^{L} \|E^k\underline{y}^o+F^k\underline{u}-\underline{y}_d\|^2 + \varepsilon\|\underline{u}\|^2 \tag{20}$$

denoting the matrices Q_1, Q_2, Q_3 :

$$Q_1 = \sum_{k=0}^{L} (F^k)^{\dagger}F^k + \varepsilon I$$

$$Q_2 = \sum_{k=0}^{L} (F^k)^{\dagger}E^k \tag{21}$$

$$Q_3 = \sum_{k=0}^{L} (F^k)^{\dagger}$$

$$\text{then : } \nabla J_2(\underline{u}) = Q_1\underline{u} + Q_2\underline{y}^o - Q_3\underline{y}_d \tag{22}$$

For $\varepsilon>0$, Q_1^{-1} exists so the optimality condition without constraint : $\nabla J_2(\tilde{\underline{u}})=0$ implies that :

$$\tilde{\underline{u}} = Q_1^{-1}\,[Q_2(\underline{y}_d-\underline{y}^o) + (Q_2+Q_3)\underline{y}_d]$$

The matrices G, R of Eq.(18) are then defined by :

$$G = Q_1^{-1}\,Q_2 \qquad R = Q_1^{-1}\,(Q_2+Q_3) \tag{23}$$

The computation of (G, R) can be performed by the use of a discrete adjoint state equation as in section (4).

Defining a Lagrangian $\mathcal{L}_2$ by :

$$\mathcal{L}_2(y,P,\underline{u})=J_2(\underline{u})+\sum_{k=0}^{L-1} (P^k)^{\dagger}[[\alpha]\underline{y}^{k+1}-[\beta]\underline{y}^k-[\gamma]\underline{u}] \tag{24}$$

when $y = y(\underline{u})$, then $\mathcal{L}_2 = J_2$, choosing $P = [\underline{P}^k]_{k=0}^{L}$ such that :

$$\frac{\partial \mathcal{L}_2}{\partial y}\,\delta y = 0 \quad \forall \, \delta y$$

then P is solution of :

$$[\alpha]\,\underline{P}^{k-1} = [\beta]\,\underline{P}^k - 2\,[\underline{y}^k(\underline{u}) - \underline{y}_d] \qquad k = L, \ldots, 1 \qquad \underline{P}^L = 0 \tag{25}$$

and the gradient $\nabla J_2(\underline{u})$ is obtained by :

$$\nabla J_2(\underline{u}) = \frac{\partial \mathcal{L}_2}{\partial \underline{u}} = -[\gamma]^{\dagger}\sum_{k=0}^{L} \underline{P}^k + \varepsilon\,\underline{u} \tag{26}$$

From Eq.(26), (25), (22) the matrices Q_1, Q_2, Q_3 can be casily computed in the following way, for example taking $\underline{y}_d = \underline{y}^o = 0$, $\underline{u} = \underline{e}_j$ with $\underline{e}_j$ element of the natural basis of $\mathbb{R}^3$ then : $\nabla J_2(\underline{e}_j) = Q_1\,\underline{e}_j$, i.e. the column vector j of the matrix Q_1.

The properties of the control law (18) are discussed in [4].

6. THE STATE OBSERVER EQUATIONS

The control law (18) requires the knowledge of the state $\underline{y}^o$, so a state observer is defined by the following equations : at time t_k, being given :

$\hat{\underline{y}}^{k-1}$ an estimation of the unknown state $\underline{y}^{k-1}$

$\underline{u}^{k-1}$ the control applied to the process during $]t_{k-1},t_k[$

$\hat{\underline{z}}^k$ the outputs measured at t_k then, $\hat{\underline{y}}^k$ estimation of $\underline{y}^k$ is defined by the unique solution of Eq.(27)-(28) :

$$[\alpha]\,\underline{y}_p^k = [\beta]\,\hat{\underline{y}}^{k-1} + [\gamma]\,\underline{u}^{k-1} \tag{27}$$

$$J_3(\hat{\underline{y}}^k) = \inf J_3(\underline{y}), \; \underline{y} \in \mathbb{R}^{N+1} \tag{28}$$

with $J_3(\underline{y})=\|\underline{z}^k-\hat{\underline{z}}^k\|^2+\varepsilon\|\underline{y}-\underline{y}_p^k\|^2$, $\varepsilon > 0$

$\underline{y}^k$ is the unknown state of the system,

$\underline{y}_p^k$ is a prediction of $\underline{y}^k$

$\underline{z}^k$ the observation of $\underline{y}^k$, defined in section (4).

denoting by $\underline{e}^k = \underline{y}^k - \hat{\underline{y}}^k$ the estimation error, it can be shown that if the model is exact then :

$$\text{for } \varepsilon > 0,\ \forall\ \underline{e}^o \in \mathbb{R}^{N+1},\ \lim_{k\to\infty} \|e^k\| = 0$$

7. EXPERIMENTAL RESULTS

The numerical algorithms are implemented on a mini computer. The data of the process (measures and controls) are interfaced by A.D. and D.A. converters, the timing is ensured by external interrupts delivered from a logic device.

7.1 - Process identification

From the initial data :

$L = 0{,}5\text{m},\ \pi D = 22 10^{-2}\text{m},\ \lambda = 45\ \text{W/°C/m},$

$\rho = 7800\ \text{kg/m}^3,\ C_\rho = 500\ \text{J/°C/kg},$

$h_1 = h_2 = 20\ \text{W/°C/m}^2$

the parameter identification leads to a first model with constant values and to a second with spatially varying values which are shown on Fig.3.

7.2 - Process control

The process is controlled according to the following iterative algorithm, at time t_k :

i) $\underline{u}^k$ is applied to the process

ii) $\hat{\underline{z}}^k$ is measured

iii) the state observer gives $\hat{\underline{y}}^k$ and $\underline{y}_p^{k+1}$

iiii) the control law gives $\underline{u}^{k+1}$ from $\underline{y}_d$ and $\underline{y}_p^{k+1}$

iiiii) t_{k+1} is waited.

Fig.(4) is a schematic representation of the process control.

Fig.(5) shows the improvement realized when the control is performed with a spatially varying model.

8. CONCLUSION

The on-line implementation of a digital control of an experimental process has been described. The quality of the control depends on the modelling of the process. Thanks to the discrete formulation used, all the algorithms have been developed without losing the distributed property of the model.

9. REFERENCES

[1] J.L. Lions, Contrôle optimal de systèmes gouvernés par des équations aux dérivées partielles. Dunod, Paris (1968).

[2] Ajinkya, M.B., M. Köhne, H.F. Mäder and W.H. Ray, The experimental implementation of a distributed parameter filter, Automatica, 11, 571 (1975).

[3] Y. Jarny, Identification of spatially varying parameters for a distributed system - Application to a thermal process. Mathematics and computer in simulation. Trans. of IMACS, vol.XXIII, n°2, 1981.

[4] J. Burger, Conduite automatique d'une extrudeuse décrite par un système d'équations aux dérivées partielles. Thèse D.S. Nantes 1980.

[5] D.V. Von Rosenberg, Methods for the numerical solution of partial differential equations. Publishing Division, G.L. Farrar & Associate Inc. Tulsa - U.S.A. (1977).

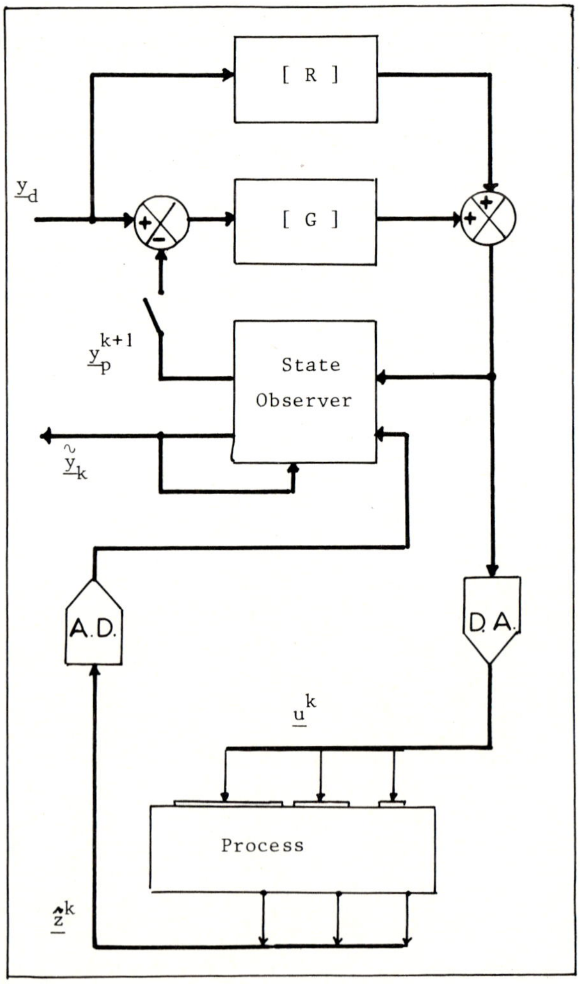

Figure 4 - Diagram of the process control

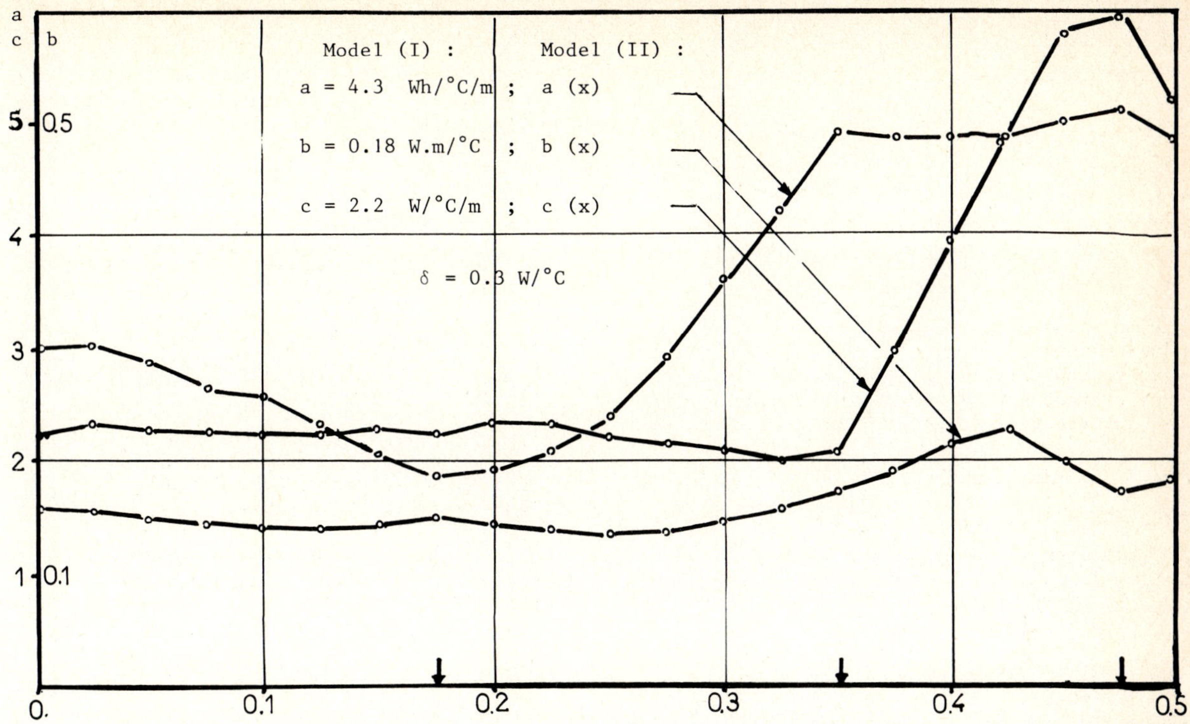

Figure 3 - Parameter values for Model (I) and Model (II)

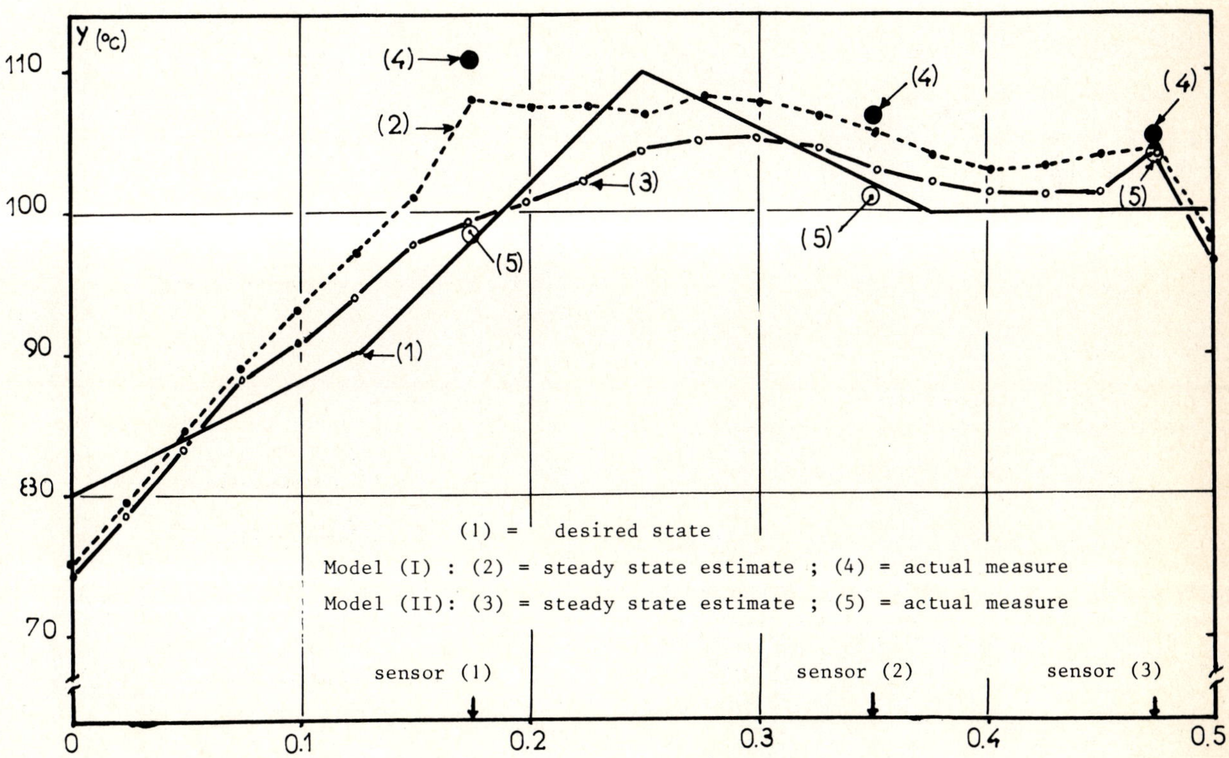

Figure 5 : Steady states reached with Model (I) and Model (II)

DISCRETE SIMULATION AND RELATED FIELDS
A. Jávor (editor)
North-Holland Publishing Company

STRUCTURES OF LINEAR TRANSFORMATIONS AND THEIR SIMULATION ON MULTIPROCESSOR SYSTEMS

O. Lange, W. Ameling, S. Hoener, E. Kempken

Institut für Allgemeine Elektrotechnik und Datenverarbeitungssysteme
Rheinisch-Westfälische Technische Hochschule Aachen
Schinkelstraße 2, 5100 Aachen

Linear transformations which are mappings of the normed spaces E_n and C[0,T] into the space of real or complex number sequences are investigated. It will be shown that these transformations have a common structure. This leads to standard technical implementations of these transformations and their simulation on multiprocessor-systems.

1. INTRODUCTION

Linear transformations play an essential role in the realms of signal processing (ANDREWS /1/) or the realization of linear digital systems (SCHÜSSLER /5/). Linear transformations will be discussed which are mappings of normed linear spaces into the space of real or complex number sequences. The general structure of these transformations depends only on the concrete spaces the transformations are defined on. The exact knowledge of these general structures is of importance when implementing the transformation on multiprocessor systems.

The linear transformations will be regarded as sequences of linear functionals on linear spaces. It will be shown that the structures of these transformations rely on corresponding representation theorems for linear functionals.

2. LINEAR FUNCTIONALS ON NORMED LINEAR SPACES

First of all we have to introduce normed linear spaces. A normed linear space R is a linear space over a scalar field K such that for each $f \in R$ there exists a real number $\|f\|$, called the norm of f, with the properties of positivity, definiteness, homogeneity and triangle inequality.

Examples of normed linear spaces which are of interest in connection with technical applications are the space E^n of all n-tuples of real numbers and the space C[0,T] of all real-valued continous functions defined on the closed interval $0 \leq t \leq T$.

Table I :

class of signals	normed linear space
digital	space E^n of all n-tuples of real numbers
analogue	space C[0,T] of all real-valued continuous functions defined on the closed interval $0 \leq t \leq T$

We are now going to use these two normed linear spaces as mathematical models for the set of digital signals resp. the set of analogue signals (cf. Table I). On the one hand, a digital signal as sequence of n samples can be interpreted as an element of E^n, on the other hand, the behaviour of an analogue signal is continuous due to the fact that we always have to do with limited bandwidths, and therefore, the analogue signal is a model of a real-valued continuous function.

A nice thing about normed linear spaces is that their geometry is much like the familiar Euclidean geometry. Inner product spaces and Hilbertspaces (complete inner product spaces) are even nicer because their geometry is even closer to Euclidean geometry. This "nicer" structure leads to remarkable simplifications.

An inner product space is defined to be an linear space R together with an inner product defined on R. An inner product on R is a mapping that associates to each ordered pair of elements $f,g \in R$ a scalar, denoted by (f,g), with the properties of additivity, homogeneity, symmetry and positive definiteness.

Next we have to introduce the concept of linear functionals on normed linear spaces; it is this a kind of linear transformation that is so important and used so often that it is given a special name: namely, a linear functional.

Let R be a linear space over the scalar field K. A linear transformation F of R into its scalar field K is said to be a linear functional on R.

In the following we want to discuss linear functionals on inner product spaces. A main result is that every linear functional on a Hilbertspace has a particularly simple representation. In other words, it is easy to "get our hands on" all the linear functionals, especially when we think of a simulation of linear functionals on multiprocessor systems.

3. THE REPRESENTATION OF LINEAR FUNCTIONALS

3.1 Linear Functionals on E^n

The normed linear space E^n is a Hilbert space. Our further argumentation is based on:

Theorem 1: Let H be a Hilbert space and let F be a continuous linear functional on H. Then there is one and only one element $g \in H$ such that

$$Ff = (f,g) \quad \text{for all } f \in H.$$

The element g is sometimes called the representation of F. However, F and g are different objects, F a linear functional on H and g an element in H. A proof of theorem 1 is given in COLLATZ /2/.

Theorem 1 adapted to the Hilbert space E^n says that there is a unique $g \in E^n$ such that

$$Ff = (f,g) = \sum_{i=1}^{n} f_i \cdot g_i \quad \text{for all } f \in E^n.$$

Let us now consider a sequence (F_j) of n linear functionals.

$$F_1 f = (f,g_1) = \sum_{i=1}^{n} f_i \cdot g_{1i} = c_1$$

$$F_2 f = (f,g_2) = \sum_{i=1}^{n} f_i \cdot g_{2i} = c_2$$

$$\vdots$$

$$F_j f = (f,g_j) = \sum_{i=1}^{n} f_i \cdot g_{ji} = c_j \tag{1}$$

$$\vdots$$

$$F_n f = (f,g_n) = \sum_{i=1}^{n} f_i \cdot g_{ni} = c_n$$

$c_j \in K, \quad j = 1(1)n.$

The whole of these linear functionals represents a linear transformation of elements $f \varepsilon H$ into the space of number sequences $c = (c_j)$, whose general form will be denoted by

$$G \cdot f = c, \qquad (2)$$

where $G = (g_{ji})$ is a $n \times n$ matrix.

The Discrete Fourier-, the Haar- and the Walsh-Transform are examples of transformations of the kind $G \cdot f = c$.

3.2 Linear Functionals on C[0,T]

C[0,T] is the space of continuous real-valued functions on the interval [0,T]. This is an inner product space where the inner product is

$$(f,g) = \int_0^T f(t) \cdot g(t)dt .$$

The further argumentation is based on

Theorem 2 (Riesz Representation Theorem) Every continuous linear functional F on C[0,T] can be represented by a Stieltjes-integral

$$Ff = \int_0^T f(t) \cdot dg(t) ,$$

where $g(t)$ is of bounded variation and uniquely determined by F.

The proof of this theorem is given in LJUSTERNIK, SOBOLEW /3/.

A function $g(t)$ on [0,T] is of bounded variation (in symbols: $g(t) \varepsilon BV[0,T]$), if for all $t \varepsilon [0,T]$ $g(t)$ can be represented as a difference of two monotone increasing functions.

If additionally $g(t) \varepsilon BV[0,T]$ has a derivative on [0,T] one may write

$$Ff = \int_0^T f(t) \cdot dg(t) = \int_0^T f(t) \cdot g'(t)dt.$$

Let us now consider a sequence (F_j) of continuous linear functionals F_j

$$\begin{aligned} F_1 f &= \int_0^T f(t) \cdot dg_1(t) = c_1 \\ F_2 f &= \int_0^T f(t) \cdot dg_2(t) = c_2 \\ &\;\vdots \\ F_j f &= \int_0^T f(t) \cdot dg_j(t) = c_j \qquad (3) \\ &\;\vdots \\ F_n f &= \int_0^T f(t) \cdot dg_n(t) = c_n \end{aligned}$$

$c_j \varepsilon K, \quad j = 1(1)n .$

The whole of these linear functionals represents a linear transformation on C[0,T] into the space of number sequences $c = (c_j)$, whose general form is given by

$$S \cdot f = c .$$

Symbolically S behaves as a n-dimensional vector, whose components may be expressed by

$$F_j * = \int_0^T * \; dg_j(t), \quad j = 1(1)n.$$

In this context the Fourier transform

$$F_j f = \frac{1}{\pi \cdot j} \int_0^T f(t) \cdot d(\sin j\omega t) = c_j$$

may serve as an example.

4. THE STRUCTURE OF LINEAR TRANSFORMATIONS ON E_n AND C[0,T]

4.1 Linear Transformations on E^n

The structure which is common to all linear transformations $G \cdot f = c$ defined on E^n will be represented by a graph (Fig. 1). A multiprocessor system whose structure is outlined according to the graph structure will be capable in performing all linear transformations $G \cdot f = c$, where the n^2 matrix elements g_{ji} associated with the special transformation G will serve as process-parameters.

Usually the number of multiplications is a measure of expense when performing the linear transformations. The multiplications are represented by the edges of the graph in Fig. 1. Generally n^2 multiplications have to be performed

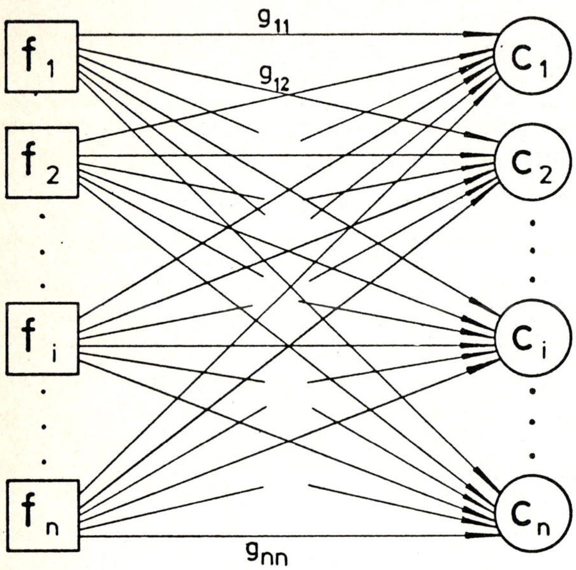

Figure 1: Structure Graph of the Linear Transformation
$G \cdot f = c$

However, a reduction of multiplications is only possible when using specific properties of a concrete transformation G. If G can be written as a Kronecker matrix product a reduction of multiplications is achievable (ANDREWS /1/). Within this paper we are talking about the general structure of linear transformations on E^n such that there will be no further discussion about efficient implementations based on specific properties.

4.2 Linear Transformations on C[0,T]

Similar to the linear transformations on E^n the structure of all linear transformations $S \cdot f = c$ on C[0,T] can be disclosed by a structure graph (Fig. 2). A multiprocessor system, e. g. a digital differential analyzer (DDA), structured according to the graph therefore permits the performance of all linear transformation $S \cdot f = c$ for all possible variants of the parameters g_j, $j = 1(1)n$.

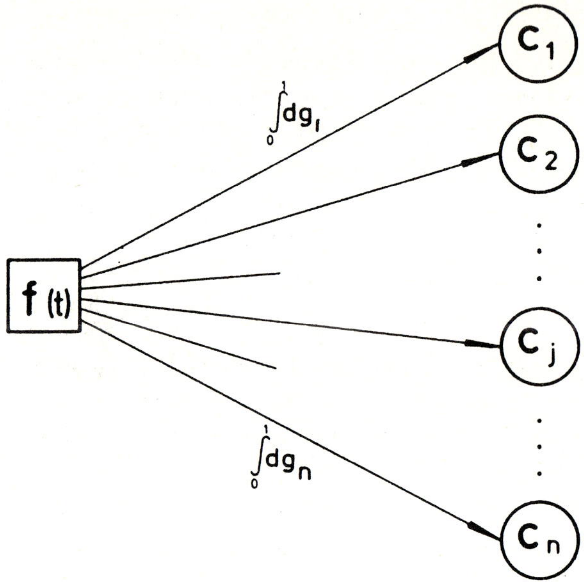

Figure 2: Structure Graph of the Linear Transformation
$S \cdot f = c$

The number of edges in the structure graph again may serve as a measure of expense. In this case n integrations in the sense of Stieltjes have to be performed. Fortunately, a DDA-integrator is capable of integrating in the sense of Stieltjes. Therefore, the linear transformation $S \cdot f = c$ on C[0,T] can be done by n DDA-integrators where the n functions $g_j \in BV[0,T]$ associated with the special transformations S will serve as process-parameters.

5. FINAL REMARKS

We habe presented the general structures of linear transformations on the spaces E^n and C[0,T]. The limitations towards these two spaces are based on the fact that on the one hand the discrete signals can be interpreted as elements of the n-dimensional space E^n, and on the other hand the analogue signals can be interpreted as elements of the space C[0,T] of all continuous real-valued functions on the interval [0,T]. An interpretation of the signals in discrete form as elements of the sequence space l_2 and in analogue form as elements of the Lebesgue space $L_2[0,T]$ leads in fact to similar structures of the multiprocessor system.

With the advent of digital computers especially the investigations of linear transformations on E^n has been stimulated. With regard to the linear transformations on C[0,T] computing devices are asked for which are capable of integrating in the sense of Stieltjes. Here mechanical integrators are highly qualified. But, as soon as real-time problems are involved the computing speed of mechanical integrators does not suffice. In this context digital differential analyzers are suited much better. For the numerical computation by the DDA-integrators one has to approximate the Stieltjes integral by a sum. On the basis of this approximation a digital differential analyzer will suffice the requirements imposed by a real-time simulation.

REFERENCES

/1/ Andrews, H.C.: Computer Techniques in Image Processing, 1st ed., p. 76. New York, London: Academic Press 1970.

/2/ Collatz, L.: Funktionalanalysis und numerische Mathematik, 2nd ed., p. 83. Berlin, Heidelberg, New York: Springer Verlag 1968.

/3/ Ljusternik, L.A., Sobolew, W.I.: Elemente der Funktionalanalysis, 4th ed., p. 125. Berlin: Akademie Verlag 1968.

/4/ Natanson, I.P.: Theorie der Funktionen einer reellen Veränderlichen, 3rd ed., p. 255. Berlin: Akademie Verlag 1969.

/5/ Schüßler, H.W.: Digitale Systeme zur Signalverarbeitung, 1st ed., p. 203. Berlin, Heidelberg, New York: Springer Verlag 1973.

DISCRETE SIMULATION AND RELATED FIELDS
A. Jávor (editor)
North-Holland Publishing Company

SIMULATING THE FLOW OF JOBS OF CYBER-72 INPUT-OUTPUT SUBSYSTEM

Jerzy Kolendowski, Maria Wielgus, Wojciech Zasada

Regional Computer Center
CYFRONET - KRAKÒW
Poland

The paper comprises the following problems:
- the configuration of CYBER computer
- input/output subsystem model
- simulation model of the input/output subsystem
- the comparison of results of the digital simulation and the measurements of the real system
- application of the model and the obtained results to controlling the input/output subsystem.

1. INTRODUCTION

Hundreds of jobs are run daily through the computers used by large computer centers. Their flow is controlled by special systems adjusted to certain work conditions. With certain additional indispensible assumptions, they may yield optimal results. That is why in order to raise the efficiency of a computer in given conditions some changes need to be introduced into the system which controls the execution of programs being run. At the same time it is not possible to experiment on the same computer since that might considerably handicap the performance of the center. Creating a model which is to be a true copy of a certain system allows for a wide range of experiments which would not result in any inconveniences to the center.
Regional Computer Center CYFRONET-Krakow has been using a Control Data computer CYBER-72. In the course of a few years of the computer's exploitation some attention has been given to the mutual load of input-output subsystem and the extent to which the central unit has been utilized. The research aimed at this problem resulted in the construction of an adequate model of the system, compatible with the specific configuration of CYBER-72. The next step was a digital simulation of the empirical model with the help of a language applied for simulating discrete dynamic processes, i.e. SIMSCRIPT I.5. The obtained results were then used in commencing research in the field to seeking an optimal method in controlling a digital system.

2. THE CONFIGURATION OF CYBER

The CONTROL DATA CORPORATION computer of the CYBER series has a very special construction of the central unit and its connection with the external devices. Apart from the central processor proper /CP/ they may have from 10 to 20 peripheral processors /PP/. Every peripheral processor has a memory of 4K twelve bit words. These processors have their own list of commands and an assembler /PP-COMPASS/ and are used for executing all tasks between the central unit and the channels to which the peripheral devices are connected.
CYBER-72 installed at RCC CYFRONET has 10 peripheral processors, out of which three are occupied on permanent basis by the following programs: PP-MONITOR/PPMTR/, a part of the supervisory program it controls, DYNAMIC SYSTEM DISPLAY/DCD/, a system exclusively for the use of computer operators, STACK PROCESSOR/1SP/ controlling disc mass memory.
The remaining seven processors make up the so called POOL PP. They may be assigned to any system or user-program for the time needed to execute a function required by such a program. One program may be assigned to more than one peripheral processor, and this process is controlled by PPMTR. Having executed a required function, the appropriate PP is released and placed again in the POOL PP.
The central operating memory is distributed among the user programs by the control points. The number of programs processed at a time in the operating memory depends in the first place on

the size of those programs and the size of the operating memory. The system under discussion has 10 such control points. The whole disc memory is connected with the rest of the system only through channel 1, which means the computer operation is performed on a so called single access basis.

3. INPUT/OUTPUT SUBSYSTEM MODEL

The configuration presented above imposed the following definition of the empirical model of input/output subsystem /Fig. 1/.

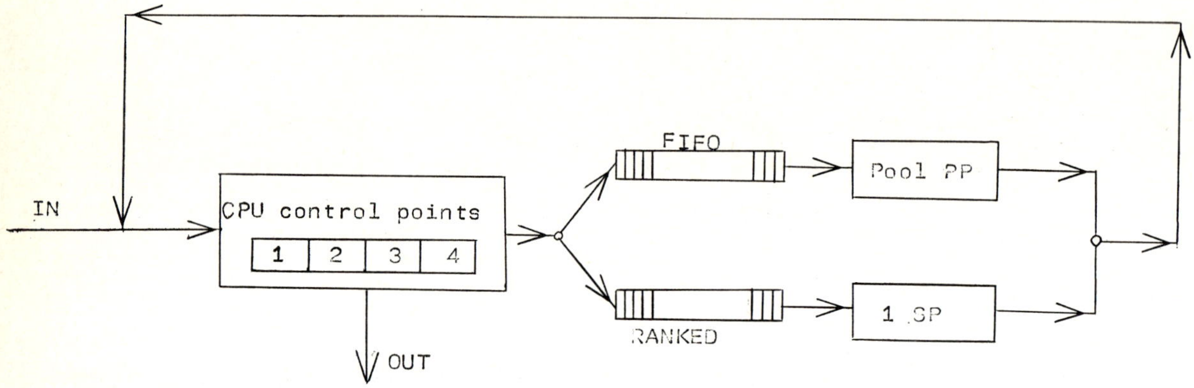

Figure 1 : Input/Output subsystem model

There have been assumed the following simplifying provisions:

- The input queue of the programs waiting for their processing is infinite, which means that right after one program has been finished another one is introduced.
- The peripheral processors which have been assigned to PPMTR and DSD are not considered due to their different function.
- The peripheral processor assigned to STACK PROCESSOR /1 SP/ is separately tested and its work equals that of channel 1 /disc channel/.
- Seven peripheral processors make up POOL PP.
- The multiprogramming level equals 3.62 and it has been computed on the basis of program length measurements and the amount of available operating memory accordingly to the method elaborated by J.P.Clapson [2].
- It has been assumed that the number of control points equals 4. The additional assumption is that a control point occupied by a program becomes available to the next program only after the former has been thoroughly processed, which means when its time limit expires.
- From the above assumption result the following control point statuses:
  FREE /control point free after a program has been processed/
  ACTIVE /the program is being processed in the central processor/
  IDLE - /the program is awaiting the completion of requests sent to POOL PP or 1 SP/
  WAIT - /the program is awaiting the central processor to become available/.
- It has been established that the waiting queue for peripheral processors assignment id of the FIFO /First In, First Out/type, and the queue waiting for 1 SP is of the RANKED type with a priority system.
- The complete time of central processor work for any program is a random choice value generated by random numbers generator with a Poisson distribution.
- The time-quantum a program needs at a control point limits the access of other programs and conditions the dislocation of tasks run through the system.
- Programs are synchronically processed in the central processor and peripheral processors with the help of the system clock.
- When the processing commences /all control points have 0/FREE/status/, the central processor has IDLE status, the channel is IDLE, and POOL PP is made up of seven processors.

4. SIMULATION MODEL OF INPUT/OUTPUT SUBSYSTEM

The assumptions employed by the empirical model have been used to construct a model controlling the performance of input/output subsystem. To commence the processing the programs have to be introduced to all the control points and the time of employing the CPU of a given program has to be specified morever the program must be assigned to the central processor in control point 1.

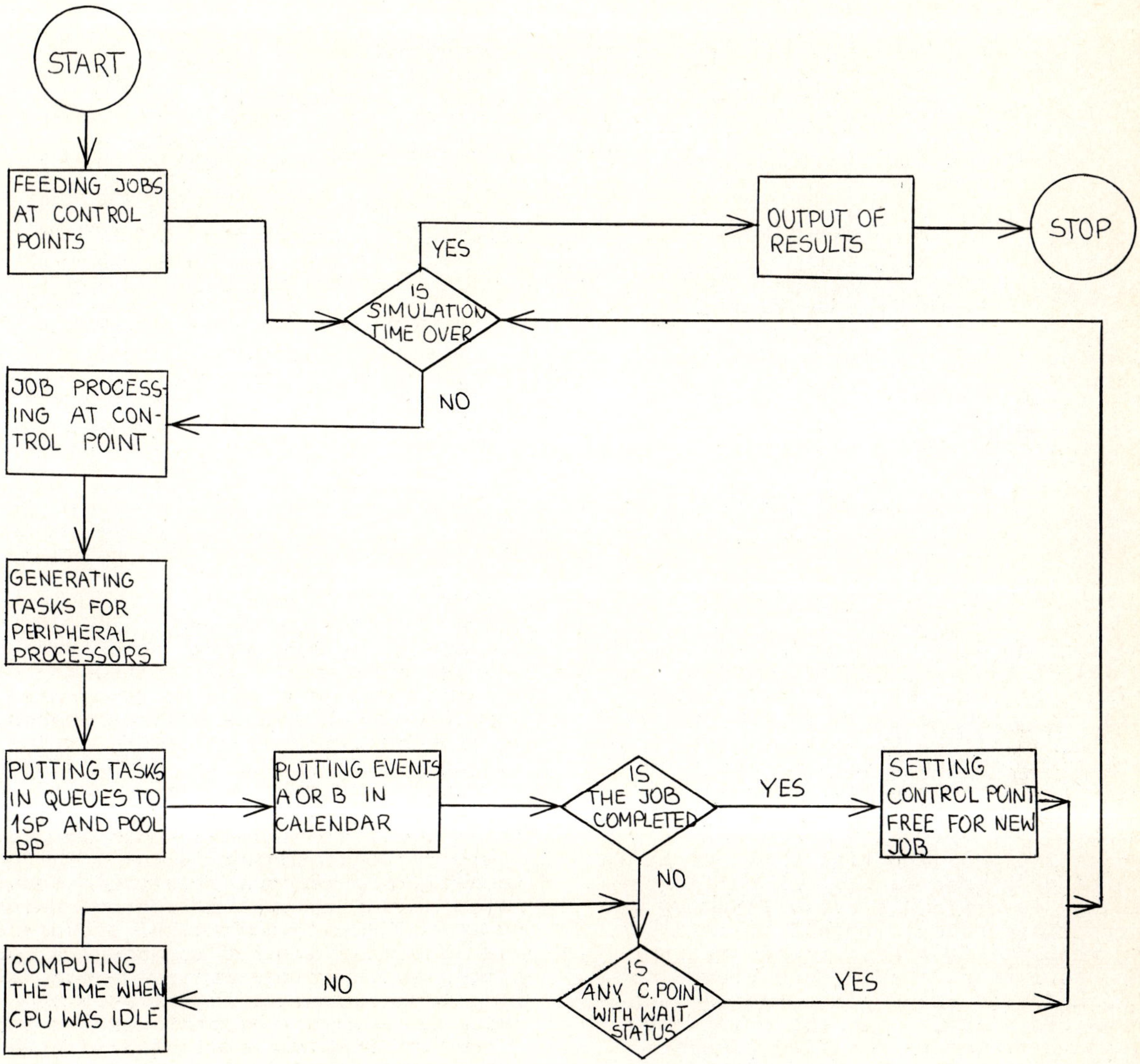

Figure 2 : Simulation of CPU work

After the time unit CPU had lapsed /it is defined by a random number with the value generated accordingly to the specified probability/ that is, when the program which is active at an "i" control point sends a request for the peripheral processors to execute a function. The number of requests sent by a given program and their nature /i.e. whether the request concerns channel 1 /1SP/ or it requires the engagement of POOL PP processors/ has been delimited by appropriate probabilities. Generating requests to peripheral processors causes the "i" control point to take IDLE status, and the central processor is connected with the next control point, providing at the time there is a control point with FREE or WAIT status.

When all the control points have IDLE status, it is assumed that central processor also has IDLE status.

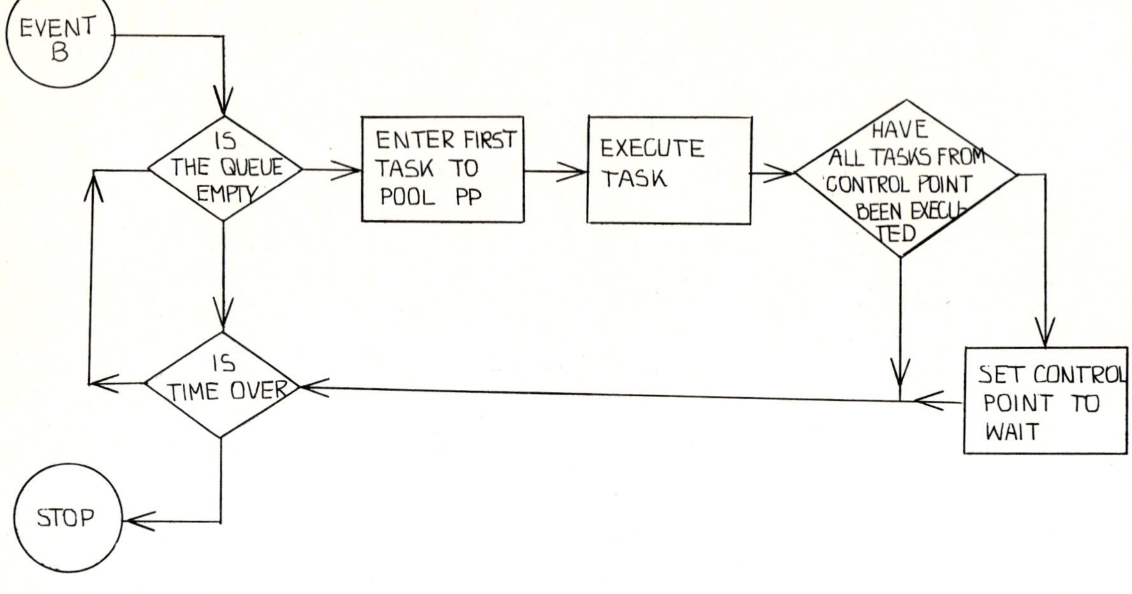

Figure 3 : Simulation of work of peripheral processors

The work of peripheral processors is parallel to the work of the central processor. At the time a request is put into the queue /a queue to 1SP or POOL PP/ the availability of peripheral processors is checked. As has been formulated in the assumptions, requests to POOL PP are put into the FIFO queue and executed one by one on the exit of the proceeding one. The time that the peripheral processor is busy executing particular functions is established by an appropriate random variable.
The requests to transmit information through channel 1 /1SP/ are placed in a Ranked type queue /free access/ and processed according to the priorities assigned to the consecutive requests of the cycle. The priority is a function of the distance between the actual and requested disc cylinder. The number of cylinders for consecutive requests as well as the time of the flow through channel 1 are generated by random numbers generators. When the queues to the peripheral processors have been emptied and the processing of the requests sent to them terminated, the peripheral processors are respectively sent to POOL PP or assume IDLE status in case of 1SP. The termination of processing of all requests sent to POOL PP and 1SP by a program from an "i" control point results in changing the status of that control point from IDLE to WAIT, providing the central processor is connected to another control point, or to ACTIVE if the central processor has IDLE status. At that moment a new time-quantum of the central processor is generated and it is followed by requests sent to the peripheral processors, or if the anticipated program limit has expired - the program is terminated in that "i" control point. That control point then assumed FREE status and in the following cycle it will receive a program from the input queue.

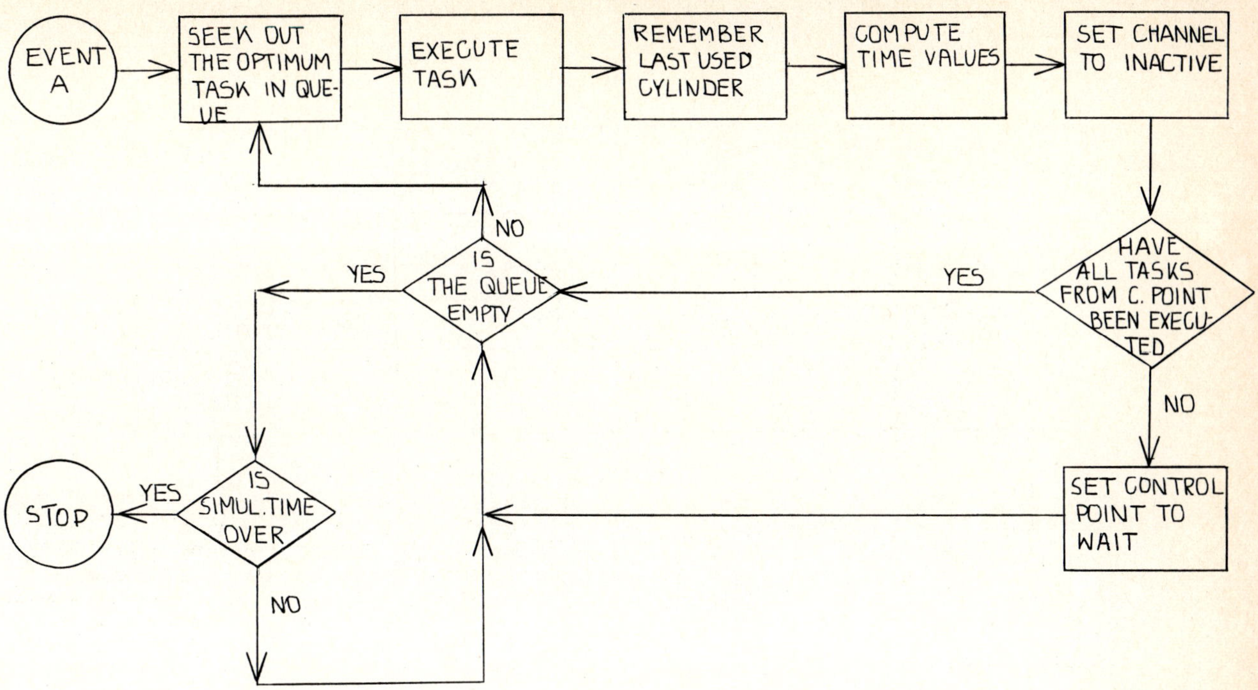

Figure 4 : Simulation of 1SP work

5. DIGITAL SIMULATION OF A MODEL

The language which has been used to describe digital simulation of the above empirical model of input/output subsystem was SIMSCRIPT 1.5 available at RCC CYFRONET-KRAKOW. According to SIMSCRIPT possibilities, the simulator is run in simulation time controlled by timing routine and calendar set. The placing and removing of respective events from the calendar set are triggered by the request to assign the central processor or the peripheral processors. It may also be the termination of the request processing.
The requests, located always in the some part of the set, are processed at the same moment of the simulation time in the order they have been introduced into the set. Processing is terminated when the assumed time of simulation has expired.

To ensure reaching that proper results of the simulation are obtained the time of the simulation should be long enough so that the statistical measurements of the performance of the model are based on a sufficient number of samples. For the purposes of simulation random number generators have been used which are contained within the confines of the library of subprograms of SIMSCRIPT compiler and CERN LIBRARY.

6. MODEL VERIFICATION

The verification of the empirical model of input/output subsystem consisted in the mutual comparison of the results obtained by digital simulation of the model and measurements of the real system done with the help of CIA software monitor [1], [3].
This has been illustrated in the diagram below :

Figure 5 : The table of measurements

	Real system	Simulation model
Time of CPU work for user programs	63,7%	67,6%
Time when CPU was idle	32,6%	32,3%
Time of channel 1 work	61,3%	61,9%
Time when channel 1 was active and CPU idle	24,0%	28,3%

7. APPLICATION OF THE MODEL AND THE OBTAINED RESULTS OF THE CONTROL OF INPUT/OUTPUT SUBSYSTEM

The results obtained from measurements and simulation proved the dependence of the speed of the flow of jobs through the central processor /which also means through the system/ on the efficiency of the input/output subsystem. In periods of maximum load of the system caused by the programs in batch of interactive mode the subsystem of mass memory becomes a "bottle neck" restricting full efficiency of the system. This problem necessitated the research aimed at working out a way of controlling the flow of requests to the mass memories.
It has been attempted to establish how much the increase in the number of requests processed on a parallel basis would influence the speed of processing. Since the existing publications deal quite often with the analysis of a double access to mass memories based on hardware solutions, in our study we investigated software possibilities. Performing additional tests on the system we have established that the organization functions connected with making a request ready for execution take up to 25% of the time of 1SP processor work. The remaining time is shared by

the data transmission and idle time, then the request queue is empty. Simulation investigation of this defined system allows the statement that reorganizing the access to the queue as well as the optimum way of seeking out a request /considering the movement of heads/ makes it possible to reduce the "administration" time to 15% - 18%. The time of overlapping work of 1SP and the central unit is reduced by 20%. The increase of time of activity of the self-same unit amounts to approximately 8%.

REFERENCES

[1]. Bednarz R.: On the interpretation performance measurements. Proceedings ECODU-23, Toulouse, France, May 1977.

[2]. Clapson J.P.: Toward a performance science: A Comparative analysis of computing systems. The computer Journal vol.20 Nr 4 1977.

[3]. Kolendowski J., Zasada W.: Workload characteristics in computer center of Cracow Universities. Proceedings ECODU-25 Liege, Belgium, April 11-13, 1978.

[4]. Simscript Reference Manual - CDC pub. Nr 60358500.

DISCRETE SIMULATION AND RELATED FIELDS
A. Jávor (editor)
North-Holland Publishing Company

APPLICATION OF LOGICAL SIMULATION FOR HAZARD-DETECTING OF MOS-LSI CIRCUITS

P. Keresztes

Central Research Institute for Physics
of the Hungarian Academy of Sciences
Budapest, Hungary

The timing and control unit of a MOS-LSI logic is mainly built up of two-phase, dynamic flip-flop elements, to minimize the chip area. The solutions of different register-transfer control procedures and level-connections have been investigated from the point of view of hazards. The hazardous or hazardless character of the solutions was demonsrated by LOBSTER logical simulation. It is possible to derive important logical design rules from these simulation results.

INTRODUCTION

Special MOS-LSI logical building elements applied for data and control logical units and their LOBSTER-models have been described in our previous paper[1]. The quasistatic storage elements and the three-state bus line are tipically MOS logical building blocks. The most important result of the work mentioned above was the modelling of quasistatic latch and three-state bus line with MOS multiplexers.

Adaptation of MOSGATE, MOSLAVE and MOSTORE elements to the LOBSTER system has made the simulation of MOS-LSI logical circuits possible. Essentially these models are MOS multiplexers with output storage capability.

The most important part of a control--logic is the TIMING circuit consisting of dynamic two-phase MASTER-SLAVE flip-flops.

The application of two phase dynamic MASTER-SLAVE flip-flops has an advantage over the static MASTER-SLAVE flip-flops, because the dynamic storage needs fewer active elements and smaller chip area.

The D-type two-phase dynamic flip-flop and its timing-diagram is shown in Fig. 1. The "next-state" level of the storage will be valid on the output after $\Phi_1 - \Phi_2$ clock signal cycle. The input is sampled by Φ_1, and after the falling edge the input capacity of the first inverter stage stores the sampled level, until the arrival of rising edge of Φ_2 clock signal. (MASTER-cycle). The SLAVE-cycle begins at the rising edge of Φ_2 clock signal, and after the falling edge of Φ_2 the load capacitance stores the state of flip-flop.

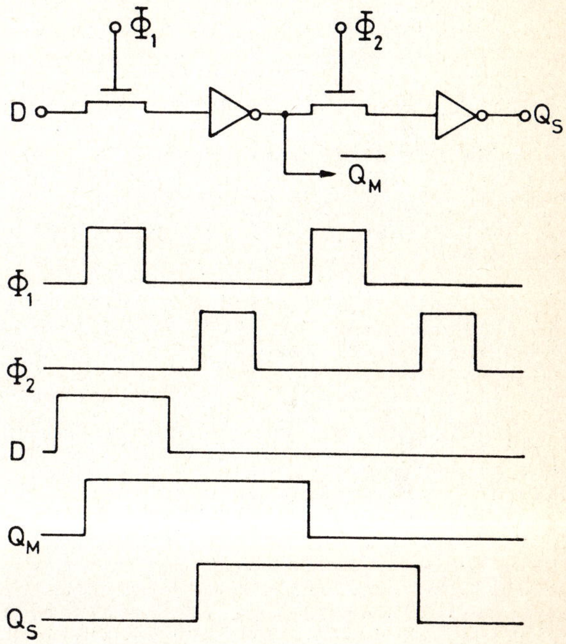

Figure 1 : The D-type, two-phase dynamic M-S flip-flop, and its timing diagram

It is necessary to use non-overlapping clock signals for time-isolation of MASTER and SLAVE cycles.

The control-logic of the data-transfers and the level-connections are built on the basis of the TIMING-circuit consisting of such flip-flops. How is it possible to design these control logics in a hazardless way - this is the subject of our paper. Before showing different control problems, it is necessary to answer the following questions.

- How to distinguish between the hazardous control solutions and the hazardless ones?

- How to classify the control tasks realized by two-phase dynamic timing circuits?

DESCRIPTION OF CONTROL TASKS BY TIMING TABLES

Let us assume, that our investigation begins at the stage of the designing process characterized by the following conditions:

- The TIMING circuitry is given by the designer, i.e. the two-phase, dynamic M-S flip-flops and their feedback logics with the interconnections are described in a certain logical scheme.

- The control tasks of different register-transfers and/or logical level-connections are well known, i.e. the control signal activities depending on timing states and other logical conditions are prescribed for every control signal.

On the basis of such a preparation it is possible to generate ideal timing diagrams for control signals.

An effective method to solve control problems is the construction of timing tables. The first timing table includes the timing states, the "next timing states" with transition conditions, register-transfers and level-connections with their logical conditions. We call this table "register-transfer timing table". At construction of the register-transfer timing table it is necessary to distinguish for a given timing state between the MASTER, the SLAVE, the Φ_1 and the Φ_2 intervals.

The sedond timing table is derived from the register-transfer table. The difference between the two tables is listed as follows:

- The "previous states" stand instead of "next states".

- Instead of register-transfers their control signal level-connections are listed.

The structure of these timing tables will be shown as the illustration of our simulation example.

On the basis of second timing table it is possible to establish logical equations for control signals. It will be shown that to realise the logical functions may be variously. We can construct an ideal solution consisting of delayless logical elements. The logical simulation of this ideal circuit gives us ideal timing diagrams of control signals. These ideal signals will be hazardless, since the logical hazards are the results of the finite propagation delay times of the system. In the real solution we consider finite delay times, and the resulting timing diagrams may show hazard peaks after the simulation process.

A real solution for any control signal is hazardless, if the difference between its timing diagram and the timing diagram of the ideal solution is minimal. Practically it means, that any change of the logical level of the real signal corresponds to a change in the ideal signal. All other changes of the signal level we consider as hazards, that must be eliminated by a different construction of gates generating these signals.

Before giving an example to illustrate the solution of control problems by simulation, we have to classify the control specifications in two-phase dynamic systems.

CONTROL SPECIFICATIONS IN TWO-PHASE, DYNAMIC SYSTEMS

The types of register transfers and level connections are listed as follows:

- Any register-transfer is a T_1 type, if it is executed by Φ_1 clock signal in timing state S_i.

- Any register-transfer is a T_2 type, if it is executed by Φ_2 clock signal in timing state S_i.

- Any level-connection is a C_1 type, if the logical value of the signal is specified in Φ_1 clock interval of timing state S_i.

- Any level-connection is a C_2 type, if the logical value of the signal is specified in Φ_2 clock interval of timing state S_i.

- Any level-connection is a C_0 type, if the logical value of the signal is specified in the MASTER-cycle interval of timing state S_i.

- Any level-connection is a C_3 type, if

the logical value of the signal is specified in the SLAVE-cycle interval of timing state S_i.

It is very easy to understand the following consequences.

- A T_1-type transfer specification in the register-transfer table will be a C_1-type level-connection in the second table.

- A T_2-type transfer specification in the register-transfer table will be a C_2-type level-connection in the second table.

- The specifications of level connections in both tables are the same.

A SIMULATION-EXAMPLE FOR DETECTION OF HAZARDOUS CONTROL-SOLUTIONS

The two timing tables in our example illustrating the application of logical simulation for hazard-detection are shown in Fig. 2. and Fig. 3.

The TIMING unit is an autonom counter circuit including 5 timing states, realized by 5 two-phase dynamic M-S flip-flops. We have written in the register-transfer timing table T_1- and T_2-type clocked transfers, C_o-type and C_3-type level-connections, and a special level-connection described by transfers of logical constants to a dynamic latch.

In the Fig. 4. The logical scheme and input sequences are shown as input-parameters of the LOBSTER simulation program This logical scheme consists of two parts, an ideal and a real logical circuit.

The ideal part consists of delayless gates and MOSTORE elements. The delay times of the gates and MOSTORE elements of the real part are a combination of 4 time-parameters as it is used in LOBSTER system [2]. All time-parameters were 10 ns in our example. The storage time constants of the MOSTORE elements were 1 ms.

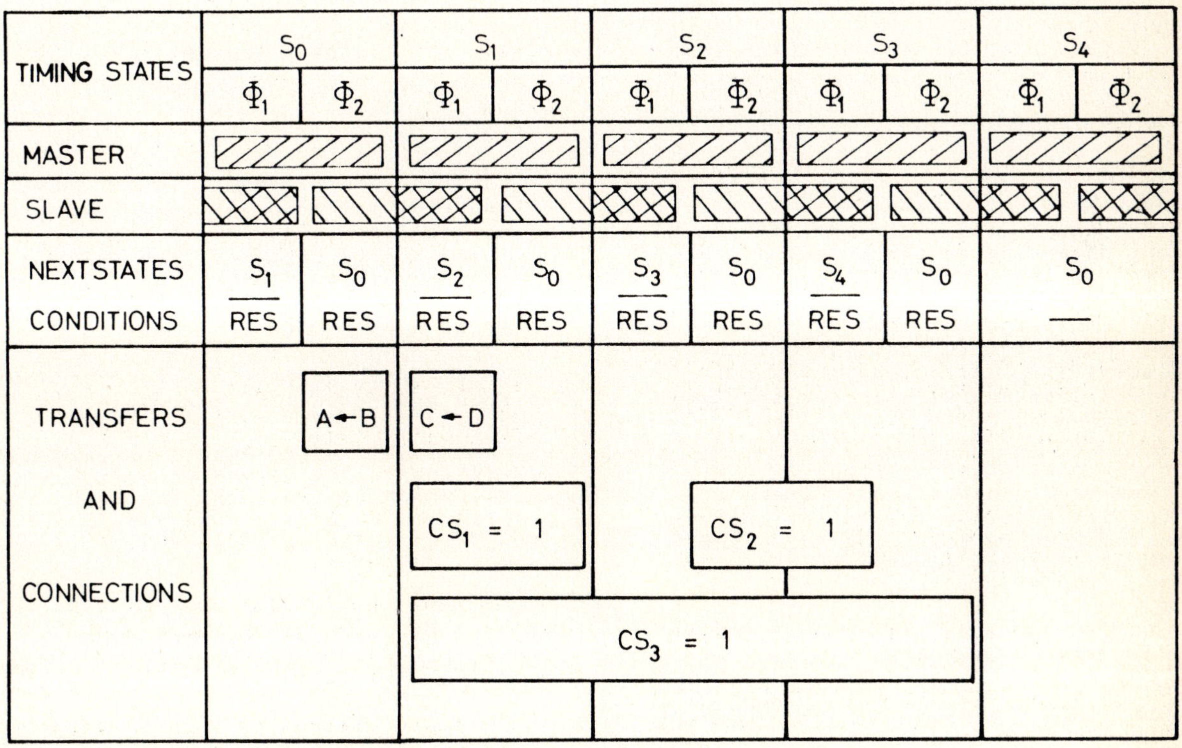

Figure 2 : The register-transfer timing table of our example

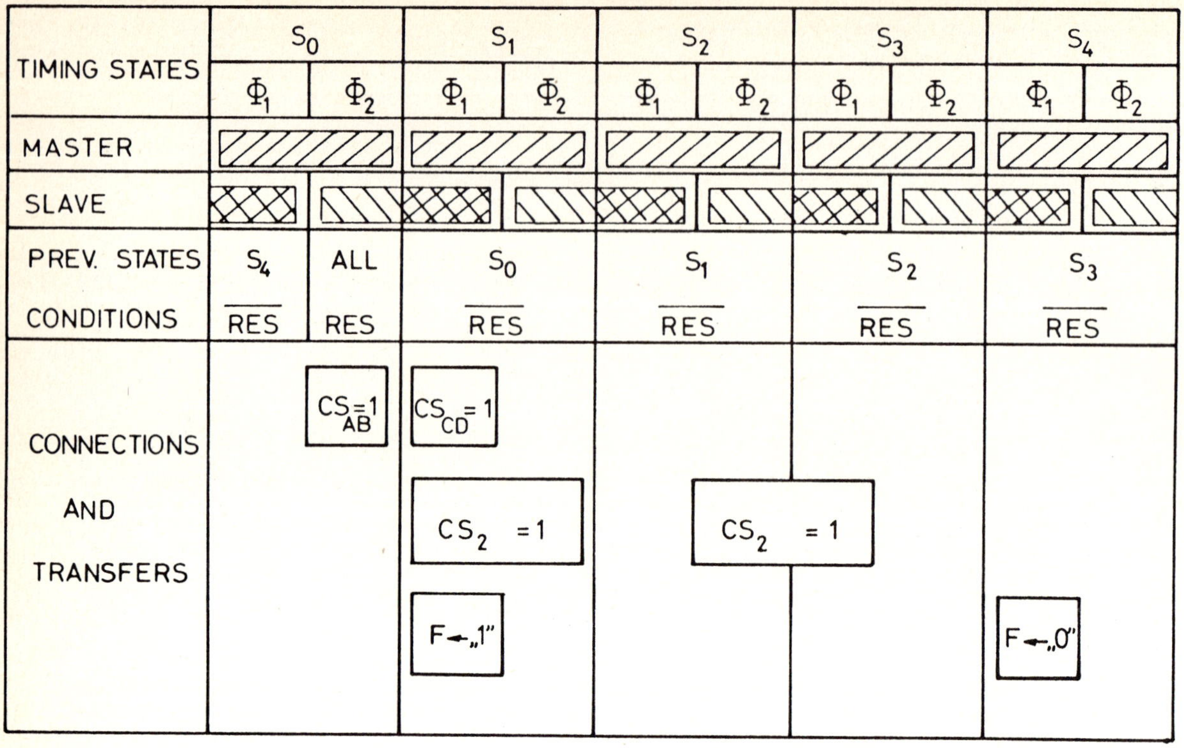

Figure 3 : The second timing table derived from the register-trasfer table

With the exception of C_o and C3 level-connections, each specification may be solved theoretically in two different ways, depending on the choice of the output Q_M and Q_S of the flip-flops for generation of control signal. The results of logical simulation showed, that one of the two solutions is hazardless. The logical designing rules derived from our simulation experiment are listed as follows:

- For a hazardless solution of a C_1-type level-connection in state S_i the designer has to use logical variable D_{Si} representing the transition condition to state S_i from its previous states.

- For a hazardless solution of a C_2-type level-connection in state S_i it is necessary to use logical variable Q_{iM} representing the MASTER-cycle of the state S_i.

- For a hazardless solution of our special level-connection described by two T_1-type transfers of logical constants to a dynamic latch, an OR function is needed as input variable of the dynamic latch. The inputs of this OR gate represent the transition conditions for the states, for which the logical level of the control is prescribed.

Unfortunately, we have no place enough to show the results of the whole simulation in detail. That's why, on Fig. 5. are shown only signals given by the different logical solutions of only CS_{AB} signal which controls the register-transfer (A ← B). The hazardous character of the 1nd solution is obvious.

CONCLUSIONS

In our paper we have applied logical simulation for hazard detection of two-phase MOS-LSI circuits.

In the theoretical part the main steps of the designing process and the classification of control specifications were described. Our simulation example showed, that not all the theoretically possible control solutions for our examples are hazardless. The hazardless solutions for our examples were found as results of the simulation process, and they are presented as logical designing rules of two-phase systems.

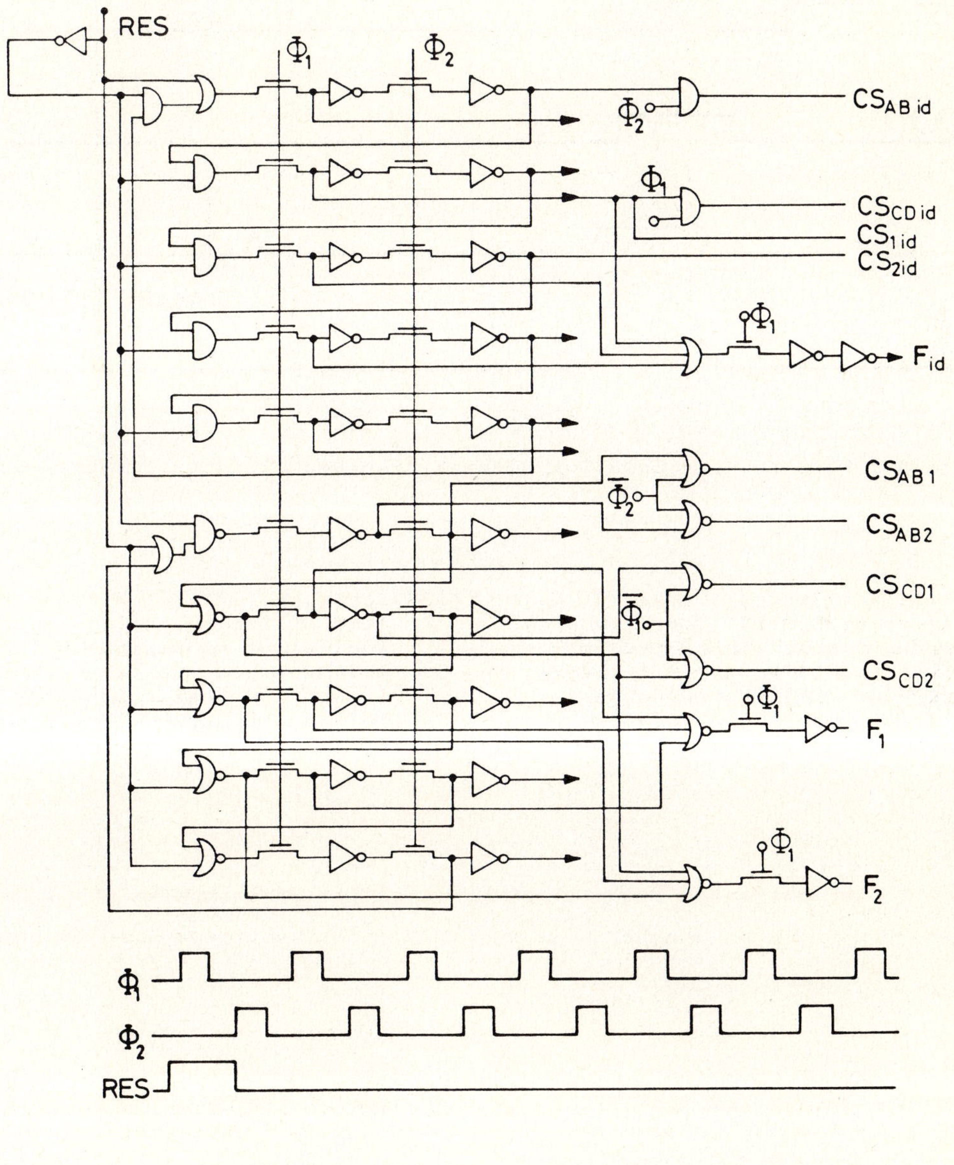

Figure 4 : The logical scheme of our simulation-example and input sequences

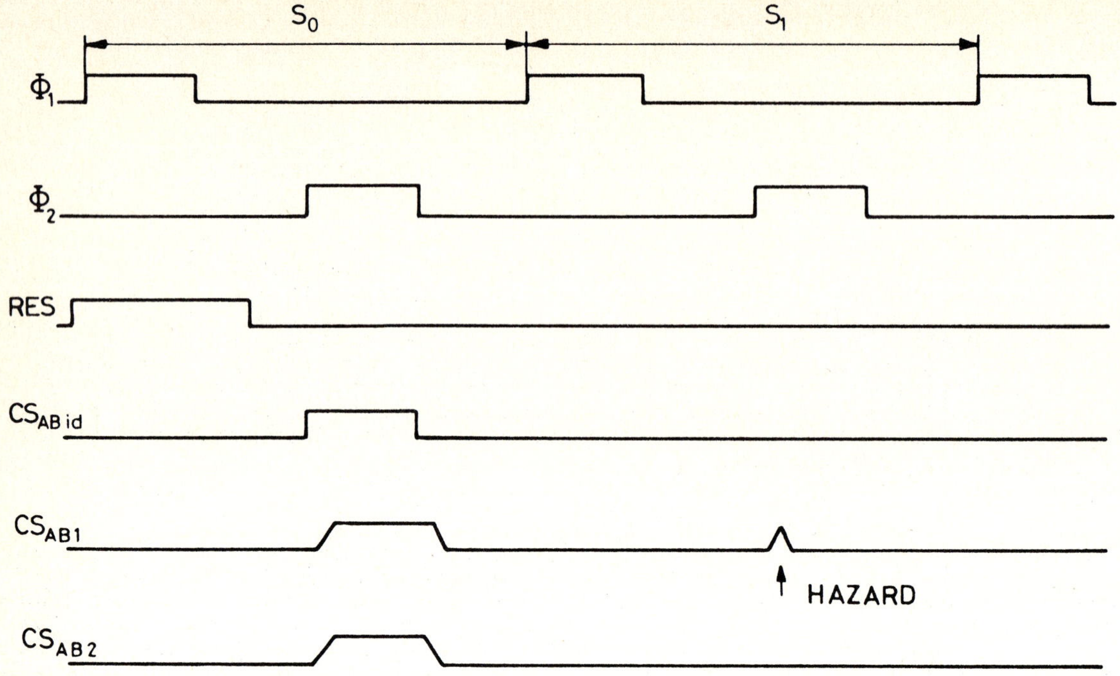

Figure 5 : Results of simulation. Timing diagrams of control signal CS_{AB}

REFERENCES

[1] Jávor, A., Keresztes, P., Benkő, M.: A Solution for MOS-LSI Gate-Level Simulation. Simulation of Systems IMACS Congress 1979 Sorrento, Septemper 24-28. 1979. North Holland Publishing Company, Amsterdam pp. 365-374.

[2] Jávor, A., Benkő, M.: On the Problems of Timing and Hazards in the Simulation of Digital Networks. 1974 European Conference on Circuit Theory and Design 23-26 July, London Conf. Publ. No. 116. pp. 257-262.

DISCRETE SIMULATION AND RELATED FIELDS
A. Jávor (editor)
North-Holland Publishing Company

FUNCTIONAL LEVEL TEST CALCULATION AND FAULT SIMULATION FOR LOGIC NETWORKS

József Sziray

Institute for Coordination of Computer Techniques,
P.O. Box 224, 1368 Budapest, Hungary

An algorithm is presented for calculating tests that detect single or multiple stuck-at faults in logic networks. The networks are assumed to consist of multiple-output combinational and synchronous sequential modules where these modules are treated at the functional level. The test calculation procedure is closely related to fault simulation where the behavior of each possible faulty network is analysed. The paper compares the available fault simulation techniques and designates the most suitable of them which is compatible with the data structures used during test calculation.

1. INTRODUCTION

The rapid advances in the integrated circuit technology have imposed severe demands on designing the test procedures of digital circuits. In order to meet these demands, we need to utilize appropriate test calculation algorithms and circuit modeling which are implemented on computer. In our case, a test calculation algorithm serves for finding input sequences that are capable of detecting faults in the circuits. It is an important feature that the steady growth of the complexity of large scale integration (LSI) chips has made more and more necessary to model the logic elements at a higher level of hierarchy than the gate level. This requirement is mainly due to the fact that the number of equivalent gates for the chips is so large that it renders the gate-level test generation and simulation computationally prohibitive.

It is known that the theoretical basis for the calculation of tests at a low hierarchical level is well-established (1). As opposed to this, in the area of higher level circuit handling, i.e., functional and register-transfer level, the results thus far achieved are much less satisfactory. As a matter of fact, there are a number of open problems of combinatorial nature that have remained to be solved.

This work is intended for reducing the gap mentioned before. It will concern itself with algorithmic test calculation for logic networks that are treated at the functional level. The networks to be considered are composed of multiple-output combinational and synchronous sequential modules. The operation of a module is assumed to be specified by minterm sets, truth-table descriptions or functional algorithms. The type of fault we are interested in is either stuck-at-0 or stuck-at-1 at the primary inputs of the network as well as at the input and output lines of each module. Both single and multiple faults with no constraint on their multiplicity are allowed.

The problem of handling logic networks at a module level for test generation purposes has been considered in (2)-(7). In each of these papers stuck faults are taken into account where, except for (4), single faults are involved. The results obtained in (2) and (3) relate to combinational logic and are primarily of theoretical importance due to the required assumptions and computational means, namely, the knowledge of prime implicant sets (2) and application of Boolean differences (3).

In (5)-(7) sequential modules are dealt with. The extended backtrace method (EBT) in (5) selects a fault propagation path which leads to a primary output and processes this path in a reverse order from the primary output so as to sensitize the path. The EBT method uses truth tables and aims at producing a sequence of input vectors as a test for the fault. However, being essentially a single path sensitizing method, it fails to cope with the problem of reconvergent paths (1). A test calculation concept is presented in (6), (7) which is an extension of the D-algorithm (8), (9) to modular sequential networks. It is remarkable that this approach combines the D-drive, implication and line justification phases with the use of functional algorithms as the means for specifying the behavior of the modules.

In (4) an algorithm has been proposed for calculating tests for module - level combinational logic. The present paper will extend this algorithm to modular sequential logic. The computations employ a 16-valued logic system, and are carried out on the normal and faulty networks simultaneously. This process always starts from a primary output and involves nothing more than successive line-value justification. A detailed description will be given about the use of the multi-valued logic in all the possible situations encountered in the course of computations. Generation of initializing and transfer sequences for faulty networks will also be discussed.

As known, the topic of simulating the network behavior in the presence of faults, i.e., fault simulation, is in a close relationship with test calculation. The paper also deals with this topic. It compares the most important fault simulation techniques from the viewpoint of functional level modeling. Finally, one of these techniques is selected as the most appropriate for supporting the proposed test calculation approach.

2. BASIC CONCEPTS

Let the vector of primary input and output variables for the complete network be $\bar{x} = (x_1, x_2, \ldots, x_n)$ and $\bar{z} = (z_1, z_2, \ldots, z_m)$, respectively. In addition to logic 0 and 1, the indifferent or don't care value d and the unknown value u are applied. Logic inversion is expressed by a prime.

Suppose that a sequence of primary input vectors $X(t) = \bar{x}_1, \bar{x}_2, \ldots, \bar{x}_t$ detects $q \geq 1$ simultaneous stuck faults at a primary output z_j. Now the task of calculating X(t) can be stated in the following way. Find a sequence of input patterns which implies $z_j = \beta$ in the fault-free network and $z_j = \beta'$ in the faulty network, where β is 0 or 1. To reach this goal, we associate the logic values β and β' with z_j and attempt to find a sequence of input patterns wich equally justifies

1) the normal value of z_j for the normal network, and
2) the faulty value of z_j for the faulty network.

In the first case X(t) justifies $z_j = \beta$ through the values of all the necessary network lines in the usual manner. In the second case, however, since the stuck values are self-dependent, they need not be justified by X(t). Thus, in the faulty network X(t) and the stuck values justify $z_j = \beta'$ jointly.

The test sequence can be derived by applying the line justification (consistency operation) concept of the D-algorithm (1),(8). The computations are carried out simultaneously in the normal and faulty network, i.e., in the normal and faulty domain. This is done under the reservation that no stuck values are to be justified in the faulty domain.

Logic values simultaneously representing signal values in both the normal and the faulty networks are called <u>composite values</u>. Line justification performed in terms of composite values is referred to as <u>composite justification</u> (4),(10). This procedure can be done exactly the same way as with single values in the D-algorithm. Clearly, two composite values are consistent iff both their normal components and faulty components are consistent simultaneously. Here two single values are consistent iff they are identical or one of them has the value d. In the following the two components will be separated by a slash with the normal component preceding the faulty one. The four-valued logic system used for the computations in either domain is defined by the basic truth tables shown in Table 1.

Table 1. Truth tables for the four-valued logic system.

a	a'
0	1
1	0
d	d
u	u

	AND 0	AND 1	AND d	AND u	OR 0	OR 1	OR d	OR u
0	0	0	0	0	0	1	d	u
1	0	1	d	u	1	1	1	1
d	0	d	d	d	d	1	d	d
u	0	u	d	u	u	1	d	u

The set of all composite values can be generated by forming the Cartesian product {0,1,d,u} × {0,1,d,u} which yields a set with cardinality 16. This means that the composite justification is performed in a 16-valued logic system. It is interesting to note that the 16-valued logic system proposed in (11) uses a subset of the 16 composite values. It should also be mentioned that the modified versions of the D-algorithm published in (12) and (13) apply a 9-valued logic system for gate-level networks. It can be pointed out that this system is also based upon composite values and forms a subsystem of the 16-valued logic described above.

In the composite justification the computational cost can be greatly reduced by the following considerations (10). The signal values in the normal and faulty networks cannot differ at the lines that do not carry any signals propagating from the sites of the faults. These are called inactive lines for which 0/0 = 0/d = d/0 = 0, 1/1 = 1/d = d/1 = 1, whereas 0/1 and 1/0 represent inconsistency. It should be realized that for our purposes it is sufficient to determine which lines (called potentially active lines) carry signals from the stuck lines to z_j. This holds true, since all the other lines in the network are either inactive or are not involved in the justification process. The set of potentially active lines can be generated by intersecting the set of the lines that are reached from the faulty lines with the set of the lines from which z_j can be reached. The two sets are very easy to obtain by topologically tracing out the signal connections. This is done by starting from the faulty lines and proceeding forward, then starting from z_j and proceeding backward. If a line is encountered in both the forward and backward tracing, then it is potentially active.

Based upon the previous considerations the following concept is proposed for calculating a test of $q \geq 1$ simultaneous faults.

A primary output z_j is taken into account only if it can be reached from at least one faulty line. The calculation process is started by setting z_j to 0/1, while the faulty lines have their stuck values in the faulty domain and the value d in the normal domain. Perform composite justification which is a continuous backtrace procedure with the aim of determining the necessary input values of the individual modules so that these values result in specified output values. The result of one justification pass is a primary input vector of composite values. For sequential networks, one justification pass is done for one particular time unit where two consecutive time units are separated by a network clock-pulse. It should be added that we proceed backward in the time domain whenever more than one justification pass needs to be completed. If the justification process fails, then repeat it for z_j = 1/0. In the case of a consistent solution the test is constituted by the sequence of primary input patterns in the normal domain. If no test has been found with z_j, then select the next appropriate primary output and repeat the computations.

In the following four sections we shall discuss the ways of performing composite justification for a given module.

3. THE USE OF MINTERMS

A module of the network is defined as any package which realizes a single- or multiple-output combinational or synchronous sequential logic where no restrictions are imposed on the module structure. Let the number of primary input variables and primary output variables of a module M_i be s(i) and w(i), respectively. The vector of primary input and output variables of a module M_i is denoted by

$\bar{x}^i = (x_1^i, x_2^i, \ldots, x_{s(i)}^i)$ and

$\bar{z}^i = (z_1^i, z_2^i, \ldots, z_{w(i)}^i)$, respectively.

If M_i is a sequential module with p(i) storage elements, then the vector of its secondary input and output variables is denoted by $\bar{y}^i = (y_1^i, y_2^i, \ldots, y_{p(i)}^i)$ and

$\bar{Y}^i = (Y_1^i, Y_2^i, \ldots, Y_{p(i)}^i)$, respectively.

Furthermore, $z_j^i(\bar{x}^i, \bar{y}^i)$ and $Y_j^i(\bar{x}^i, \bar{y}^i)$ are defined as the logic functions which depend on $\bar{x}^i, \bar{y}^i$ and describe z_j^i and Y_j^i, respectively.

In this section we shall use the so-called truth matrices for the description of a module. The primary truth matrix

$$T_k = \left[t_{ij}^k\right]$$

of a sequential module M_k is a binary matrix having w(k) rows and $2^{s(k) + p(k)}$ columns, where $t_{ij}^k = 1$ iff j-1 is a decimal minterm of the function $z_i^k(\bar{x}^k, \bar{y}^k)$; otherwise $t_{ij}^k = 0$. Analogously, the secondary truth matrix

$$S_k = \left[s_{ij}^k\right]$$

of a sequential module M_k is a binary matrix having p(k) rows and $2^{s(k)+p(k)}$

columns, where $s_{ij}^k = 1$ iff $j-1$ is a decimal minterm of the function $Y_i^k(\bar{x}^k,\bar{y}^k)$; otherwise $s_{ij}^k = 0$.

Note that a combinational module has a primary truth matrix only which can be defined the same way as seen before (4).

As an example consider the sequential module M_k shown in Figure 1. The module is schematically represented by a combinational network with a feedback containing a clocked delay flip-flop. The truth matrices for the module are given in Table 2 where the 0-entries are omitted and the weights of variables x_1^k, x_2^k, y_1^k are decreasing from the left to right in the binary form of a minterm.

Let E_i^k be the minterm set of the function $z_i^k(\bar{x}^k,\bar{y}^k)$, while the complement of E_i^k over the set of all minterms is denoted by $\tilde{E}_i^k$. Analogously, let G_i^k be the minterm set for $Y_i^k(\bar{x}^k,\bar{y}^k)$, while $\tilde{G}_i^k$ is the complement of G_i^k over the set of all minterms.

Now suppose that the module of Figure 1 is a part of a network, and some fault-simulated test sequence has brought M_k to the normal state $y_1^k = 1$, whereas in the presence of some network fault, a faulty state $y_1^k = 0$ has occurred. Further, assume that the composite justification for the complete network has arrived at M_k with

$$z_1^k = 0/0, \quad z_2^k = 0/1, \quad \text{and} \quad z_3^k = d/d.$$

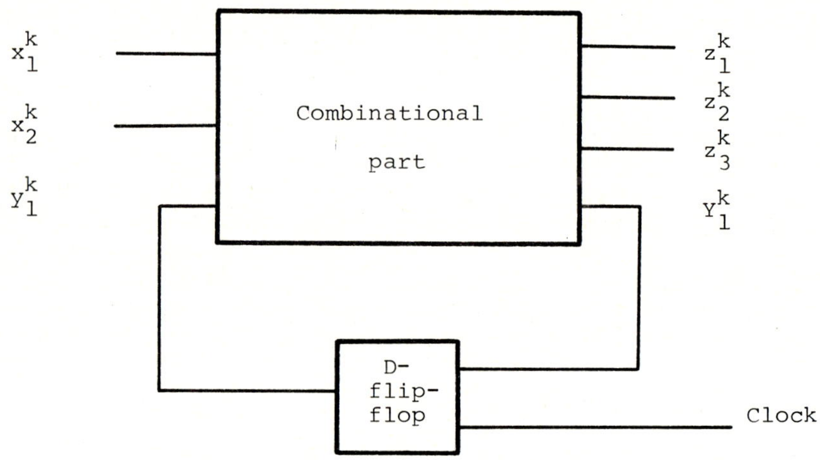

Figure 1. Example for a sequential module.

Table 2. Truth matrices.

T_k:

0	1	2	3	4	5	6	7	
1						1	1	z_1^k
1		1	1		1			z_2^k
		1		1			1	z_3^k

S_k:

0	1	2	3	4	5	6	7	
	1				1			Y_1^k

Now the task of generating the composite values for $\bar{x}^k$ can be solved in the following way.

It can be easily shown (see (4)) that the minterm set that results in $(z_1^k, z_2^k, z_3^k) = (0,0,d)$ for the normal domain is

$$\tilde{E}_1^k \cap \tilde{E}_2^k = \{1,2,3,4,5\} \cap \{1,4,6,7\} = \{1,4\}.$$

Since $y_1^k = 1$, only the minterm 1 meets the requirements.

Likewise, the minterm set that results in $(z_1^k, z_2^k, z_3^k) = (0,1,d)$ for the faulty domain is

$$\tilde{E}_1^k \cap E_2^k = \{1,2,3,4,5\} \cap \{0,2,3,5\} = \{2,3,5\}.$$

Since $y_1^k = 0$, only the minterm 2 can be accepted.

From the results obtained above it follows that the only solution to our problem is

$$x_1^k = 0/0, \quad x_2^k = 0/1.$$

When using minterms the test calculation requires a considerable amount of set operations, namely, intersection and complementation. However, it should be realized that the rows (binary vectors) of the truth matrices represent the minterm sets of the individual functions in the most concise form. Moreover, it can be seen that intersection among the sets is carried out by logically multiplying the corresponding binary vectors in a bit by bit way. Complementation is done by simply inverting each bit of a vector. As for the computer implementation, these operations imply the use of simple machine instructions that are executed very quickly.

4. THE USE OF REDUCED TRUTH TABLES

In essence, the truth matrices represent completely specified truth tables. However, as known from the user's manuals, there are in many cases truth tables available which contain rows with don't care entries for some input variables. Such a row can be obtained by merging two or more minterms, thus a truth table of this kind will have less rows than a completely specified table, and it will be referred to as a reduced truth table. As an illustration, let us take a four-line to one-line data selector (multiplexer) unit with its reduced truth table shown in Table 3. The module considered is a seven-input one-output combinational device.

Table 3. Reduced truth table of a data selector.

Address		Data inputs				Strobe	Output
a_1	a_2	d_0	d_1	d_2	d_3	s	z
d	d	d	d	d	d	1	0
0	0	0	d	d	d	0	0
0	1	d	0	d	d	0	0
1	0	d	d	0	d	0	0
1	1	d	d	d	0	0	0
0	0	1	d	d	d	0	1
0	1	d	1	d	d	0	1
1	0	d	d	1	d	0	1
1	1	d	d	d	1	0	1

The use of reduced truth tables for composite justification may result in a considerable reduction of the computational cost. Suppose, for example, that $z = 0/1$ is to be justified for the given module, where the lines a_2 and d_0 are stuck at 0 and 1, respectively, while all the rest of the input lines are inactive.

If we select the second and sixth rows from Table 3, we obtain

$$(a_1,a_2,d_0,d_1,d_2,d_3,s) = (0/0,0/0,0/1,d/d,d/d,d/d,0/0)$$

which will be consistent with the prespecified input values and yield the desired output values. As can be seen, d_1, d_2, and d_3 need no justification which implies further cost reduction.

In the next example let us take a two-input, two-output sequential module M_i with two storage elements. The reduced truth tables of M_i are shown in Table 4 and 5.

Now suppose that the module M_i is a part of a network, and some fault-simulated test sequence has brought M_i to the normal state $(y_1^i, y_2^i) = (0,1)$, whereas in the presence of some network fault a faulty state $(y_1^i, y_2^i) = (0,0)$ has occurred.

Table 4. Truth tables for the primary output variables.

x^i_1	x^i_2	y^i_1	y^i_2	z^i_1
0	d	d	0	0
1	d	d	1	0
1	1	d	d	0
0	d	d	1	1
1	0	d	0	1

x^i_1	x^i_2	y^i_1	y^i_2	z^i_2
0	0	d	d	0
1	d	0	d	0
1	1	d	0	0
0	1	d	d	1
d	1	1	1	1
1	d	1	1	1
1	0	1	d	1

Table 5. Truth tables for the secondary output variables.

x^i_1	x^i_2	y^i_1	y^i_2	Y^i_1
0	0	1	d	0
d	d	1	1	0
1	d	d	1	0
1	1	d	d	0
0	d	0	d	1
0	1	d	0	1
1	0	d	0	1

x^i_1	x^i_2	y^i_1	y^i_2	Y^i_2
0	1	d	1	0
d	1	0	0	0
1	0	d	1	0
1	d	1	d	0
0	0	d	d	1
d	0	0	0	1
1	0	0	d	1
1	1	0	1	1

Further, assume that the composite justification for the complete network has arrived at M_i with $z^i_1 = 0/1$, and $z^i_2 = 0/0$.

To generate the composite values for $\bar{x}^i$, we use the truth tables of z^i_1 and z^i_2. In the normal domain the vectors (1,d,d,1) and (1,d,0,d) are consistent with each other and with the other prespecified values, thus yielding

$$(x^i_1, x^i_2, y^i_1, y^i_2) = (1,d,0,1).$$

Similarly, in the faulty domain the consistent vectors (1,0,d,0) and (1,d,0,d) yield

$$(x^i_1, x^i_2, y^i_1, y^i_2) = (1,0,0,0).$$

From the results obtained above it follows that the solution to our problem is

$$x^i_1 = 1/1, \quad x^i_2 = d/0.$$

We next turn to the question of handling logic values during the justification process. As shown in Section 2, the composite justification requires in general a 16-valued logic algebra. However, it should be realized that the value u may have to be utilized only at the secondary inputs of a module. In the course of a justification pass the only we have to pay attention to is that we must not assign a logic 0 or 1 to a secondary input having the value u.

If the normal and faulty values of the secondary inputs of a module M_i are computed by means of a three-valued (i,e., 0,1,u) fault simulator, then prior to a justification pass, the composite value of a component $y^i_j (j = 1,2,\ldots,p(i))$ has to be set in the following way.

1) If y^i_j is unknown, then $y^i_j = u/u$.
2) If y^i_j has a known normal value β and
   a) y^i_j is fault-free, then $y^i_j = \beta/\beta$,
   b) a fault has propagated to y^i_j, then $y^i_j = \beta/\beta'$,
   c) a so-called star fault (which means an uncertain fault signal as presented in (14)) has propagated to y^i_j, then $y^i_j = \beta/u$.

5. GENERATION OF INITIALIZING AND TRANSFER SEQUENCES

When working with a given sequential module M_i we may encounter the problem of having to find a sequence of input vectors $X^i(k)$ which is of length k and takes the module from an initial state $\bar{y}^i_1$ to a final state $\bar{y}^i_t$. From our point of view, in a general sense, all the components of $\bar{y}^i_1$ and $\bar{y}^i_t$ are composite values, where both $\bar{y}^i_1$ and $\bar{y}^i_t$ may have faulty components too. If each component of $\bar{y}^i_1$ is unknown, then $X^i(k)$ is called an initializing sequence; otherwise $X^i(k)$ is a transfer sequence,

In order to produce $X^i(k)$, a k-pass composite justification is required for M_i. These passes proceed as follows.

First justify $\bar{Y}^i = \bar{y}^i_t$ by $\bar{x}^i_{t-1}, \bar{y}^i_{t-1}$, then justify $\bar{Y}^i = \bar{y}^i_{t-1}$ by $\bar{x}^i_{t-2}, \bar{y}^i_{t-2}$, etc., until an $\bar{y}^i_{t-k}$ that is consistent with

$\bar{y}_1^i$ has been found. The desired sequence of length k will be

$$X^i(k) = \bar{x}^i_{t-k}, \bar{x}^i_{t-k+1}, \ldots, \bar{x}^i_{t-1}$$

where $\bar{x}^i_{t-k} = \bar{x}^i_1$.

Note that backtracking to previously justified states may be required in this procedure. Whenever a particular $\bar{Y}^i$ cannot be justified, or all of its justifying $\bar{y}^i$-vectors occur among the previously accepted states, we backtrack and attempt to find new state vectors by modifying, as necessary, the results of the previous justification passes.

As an example let us consider the truth tables of Table 5, and assume that

$$\bar{y}^i_t = (0/0,\ 1/0)$$

is to be reached from an arbitrary initial state, i.e., from

$$\bar{y}^i_1 = (u/u,\ u/u).$$

In the normal domain first we select (d,d,1,1) and (0,0,d,d) which result in

$$(x^i_1, x^i_2, y^i_1, y^i_2) = (0,0,1,1).$$

For the second pass

$$(Y^i_1,\ Y^i_2) = (1,1),$$

thus we can select (0,d,0,d) and (0,0,d,d), yielding (0,0,0,d). Finally, for $Y^i_1 = 0$ the vector (1,1,d,d) is taken which is consistent with $(y^i_1, y^i_2) = (u,u)$. Similarly, in the faulty domain (1,d,d,1) and (1,0,d,1) result in (1,0,d,1) for which (0,0,d,d) can be the final choice. In order to have the same length as in the normal domain, this series is to be supplemented by the vector (d,d,d,d). Now if we combine the series of the domains, we obtain the following initializing sequence:

$$X^i(3) = (1/d,1/d),(0/0,0/0),(0/1,0/0).$$

It can be easily seen that the minterm sets of the individual secondary output functions can be used successfully in this algorithm only in that case if each initial state component has a determinate logic value in both computational domains. Under this condition the computations are recommended to be carried out by means of the secondary truth matrices. In the case of unknown initial state components, reduced truth tables or functional algorithms are advisable to use.

6. THE USE OF FUNCTIONAL ALGORITHMS

The logic values of output lines and storage states for a module can also be computed by means of appropriate functional algorithms. The algorithmic manipulation of a module has some remarkable advantages from the viewpoint of computer implementation, such as moderate storage requirement and fast evaluation.

In this section we show through an example how functional algorithms can be applied for composite justification. These algorithms belong to a high level model for an n-bit counter and are taken from (6),(7). The counter performs four functional operations, namely, incrementation by one, decrementation by one, parallel load of bits at the data inputs, and hold operation, i.e., the contents of the register are unchanged. The algorithms that realize these operations are indicated by U, D, P, and H, respectively. The operational mode of the counter is determined by the values of four control signals as specified by Table 6. It should be noted that a logic 1 on the clock input C_p is really a 0-1 or 1-0 transition, i.e., a clocking condition, and a logic 0 is a non-clocking condition.

Table 6. Control codes for functional operations.

C_p	U	G	L	Operation	Algorithm
d	d	d	0	Parallel Load	P
d	d	1	1	Hold	H
1	d	0	1	Hold	H
0	1	0	1	Incrementation	U
0	0	0	1	Decrementation	D

Let $\bar{x}_c = (C_p,U,G,L)$ denote the vector of control bits, while the vector of data input bits is indicated by $\bar{A} = (A_1,A_2,\ldots,A_n)$. Further, $\bar{y} = (y_1,y_2,\ldots,y_n)$ and $\bar{Y} = (Y_1,Y_2,\ldots,Y_n)$ will denote the present state and next state vector of the register elements, respectively. The counter is depicted in Figure 2.

The four basic algorithms are defined in (6),(7) in the following way.

1) P (Parallel Load):

$$Y_i = A_i \quad \text{for } i = 1,2,\ldots,n.$$

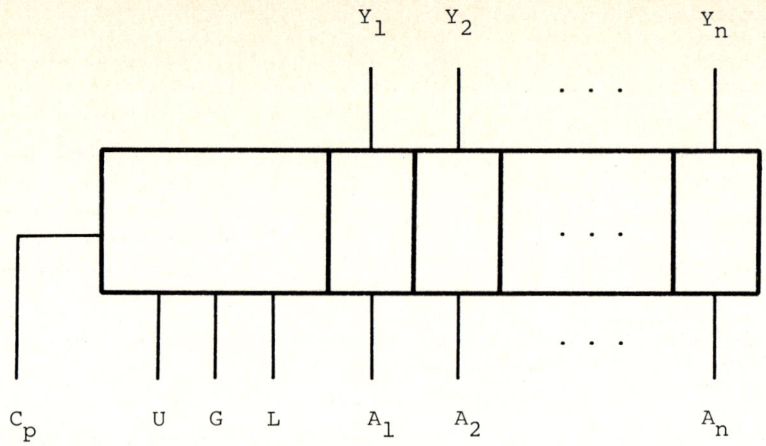

Figure 2. The n-bit binary counter.

2) H (Hold):

$Y_i = y_i$ for $i = 1,2,\ldots,n$.

3) U (Incrementation):

a) all bits to the left of the least significant 0 are unchanged;
b) all bits (if any) to the right of and including the least significant 0 which are also to the left of and including the least significant u become u;
c) the least significant 0 becomes 1 if it is to the right of the least significant u;
d) a rightmost string of 1's (if any) become 0's.

4) D (Decrementation):

It is the same as the U algorithm except for having interchanged 0's and 1's.

Let B_1 be the set of the algorithms that are consistent with a given vector $\overline{x}_c$. For example, if $\overline{x}_c = (0,d,d,1)$, then according to Table 6 we have

$$B_1 = \{U,D,H\}.$$

Moreover, let B_2 be the set of the algorithms that are consistent with the actual components of $\overline{y}$, $\overline{Y}$, and $\overline{A}$ simultaneously.

After this introduction the composite justification will be illustrated with the aid of a 6-bit counter. First assume that the counter possesses the following initial values in the normal domain:

$$\overline{x}_c = (0,d,d,d), \quad \overline{A} = (1,d,0,d,1,1),$$

$$\overline{y} = (0,0,1,0,0,1), \quad \overline{Y} = (d,0,d,d,1,0).$$

Note that an input value of a module is known from a previous justification step performed for another module. In accordance with $\overline{x}_c$ we have

$$B_1 = \{U,D,H,P\}.$$

The only algorithm that complies with the component values of $\overline{A}$, $\overline{y}$, and $\overline{Y}$ is U, hence

$$B_2 = \{U\}.$$

Now the set B of the algorithms that are consistent with all the initial values for the module can be obtained as follows:

$$B = B_1 \cap B_2 = \{U\}.$$

Here the set B implies that $\overline{x}_c = (0,1,0,1)$ and $\overline{A}$ remains unchanged.

As for the faulty domain, let only the vector $\overline{Y}$ differ from its normal domain version by having its last bit faulty, i.e.,

$$\overline{Y} = (d,0,d,d,1,1).$$

The given conditions are met by applying algorithm P only, hence

$$B_2 = \{P\}, \qquad B = \{P\}.$$

From this it follows that

$$\overline{x}_c = (0,d,d,0), \quad \overline{A} = (1,0,0,d,1,1).$$

Combining the results obtained in the two domains we see that a fault signal at the control input L (i.e., L = 1/0) is propagated to the output bit Y_6 by means of the appropriate data input values. It should also be mentioned that $A_2 = 0$ is implied by $Y_2 = 0$ in accordance with the conditions for the parallel load.

7. FAULT SIMULATION TECHNIQUES

Fault simulation is a most important part of computerized test development. In this case the behavior of the fault-free network and the behavior of each possible faulty network are to be simulated for the same input sequence. The simulation for the fault-free network enables us to compare the responses with those obtained for the faulty networks, thus determining whether a fault has been detected at a primary output.

The aim of this solution is twofold. First, it is used to determine the fault coverage of a given test sequence, as part of the test calculation process. Here, fault simulation is done after each test is generated in order to find all the other faults detected by this test. In this way, the need to generate a test for each of these faults is eliminated. Secondly, the results of the simulation procedure provide us with diagnostic information that can be utilized when the testing of the physically existing network is performed.

The relationship between test calculation and fault simulation is demonstrated in Figure 3, where e denotes the number of postulated faults.

The basic difference between a normal logic simulator and a fault simulator is that the latter has to generate and simulate a huge number of faulty network versions. In order for this task to be efficiently solved, special techniques are required.

As known, there are three major and widespread fault simulation techniques: parallel (15), deductive (14) and concurrent (16).

The parallel approach relies on storing the signal values for a logic element in both the good network and the faulty networks in a memory bit field, mostly in one word. Logical operations corresponding to an element function are performed on the memory bit fields, thus simulating the good network in parallel with several faulty ones. This technique is very suitable for basic gates, because it is economical in operational speed and memory consumption. For example, the output bit field of an AND gate can be obtained by performing a bit by bit AND operation among the bit fields assigned to the input lines of the gate.

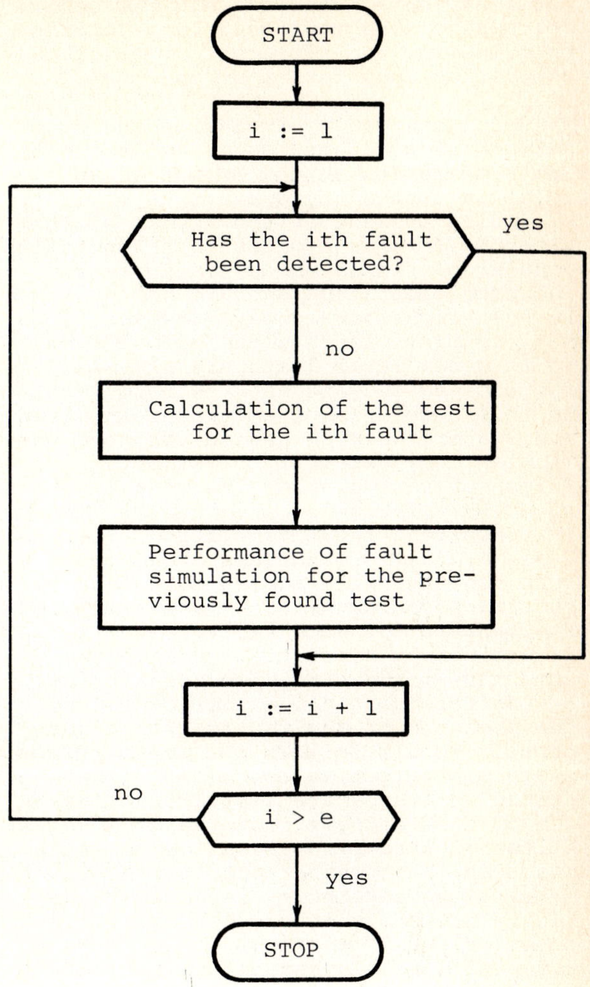

Figure 3. The flowchart of test calculation and fault simulation.

On the other hand, at the functional level when the network elements are far more complex than the gates, for example, shift registers, counters, etc., the above solution becomes much less efficient. Here the elements exhibit different functional behavior with different input conditions. This means that an element can behave differently for the various faults. To accurately simulate this in a parallel environment would necessitate unpacking memory locations to enable the networks to be evaluated separately, and after evaluations repacking is needed. The necessary data transfers and the separate evaluations involve a large overhead, thus loosing the advantage of parallelly simulating many faults at one time.

In deductive fault simulation the good network is simulated only, and the effects of faults on the output of an element is deduced by operations on lists of faults present at the inputs of the element. For basic gates these operations consist of simple union, intersection and complementation and are accomplished in a straightforward way. However, for more complex elements the calculations to form new fault lists are extremely complicated and not easy to formulate. In this case a large amount of involved preparatory work is needed for each particular logic element to establish the rules for manipulating their fault lists.

In concurrent fault simulation, the newest of the techniques, the good network together with any number of singly occurring faulty networks are simulated. The behavior of each faulty network is determined by simulating the good network and at the same time identifying any differences in behavior caused by the presence of any faults. For a particular faulty network the input, present-state and output values of an element are stored in a separate list iff at least one of them differs from the good value. A list of this kind is called <u>super fault list</u> (1). This means that in concurrent simulation only those elements in the faulty network which do not agree, in terms of input, state or output values, with the same element in the fault-free network are explicitly simulated. These elements are evaluated and scheduled in exactly the same way as their fault-free counterpart. Since the method is based on evaluation of the good network plus simultaneously occurring faulty networks, it is ideally suited to functional level simulation. All the techniques developed for logic simulation and element evaluation can be used in a concurrent fault simulator.

Experimental comparisons of the three most common fault simulation techniques at the gate level show that in terms of run time the concurrent technique outperforms the other two (6),(16)-(18). However, this advantage is gained at the cost of serious memory requirements.

As far as the functional level modeling is concerned, the concurrent method is to be favorized. The main reason is that, as we have seen before, this technique is basically independent of the way of modeling, whereas the others are greatly affected and constrained by higher level models.

8. FUNCTIONAL MODELS AND CONCURRENT FAULT SIMULATION

The key operation in concurrent fault simulation is the computation of the output values for the individual logic elements. With knowledge of the input combination and the present-state values of a module, the output combination can be determined by utilizing the suitable operational specifications.

First consider the case of truth matrices. The primary output values are computed by means of the primary truth matrix. It can be easily shown that these values are obtained in the following way.

Let us take a module M_k with the primary truth matrix T_k, and let the weights of bits in the combined input vector $(\bar{x}^k, \bar{y}^k)$ decrease from the left to right. Now, if the decimal value of a combined input vector of M_k is v, then the primary output combination is equivalent to the $(v + 1)$th column in the primary truth matrix, where the ith bit in the particular column represents the logic value of the ith primary output line of the module. The secondary output values can be generated in the same way, by making use of the secondary truth matrix.

The concurrent fault simulation technique is ideally compatible with the data representation chosen for the minterm sets. This is owing to the fact that the normal and faulty module output patterns are readily available in the form of column vectors belonging to the truth matrices.

In the case of reduced truth tables the simple rules for processing truth matrices do not apply. Instead, here we need to carry out a table look-up procedure. To illustrate the evaluation of a module, consider the data selector specified in Table 3. In the following we assume that the module in question is a part of a network, where a super fault list of a module has to be computed for one network fault if at least one input or state bit of the module has become faulty.

Suppose that the input vector of the module in the fault-free version is

$$(a_1, a_2, d_0, d_1, d_2, d_3, s) = (1,0,0,d,1,d,0).$$

The vector is consistent with the 8th row of Table 3, thus the normal output value is

$$z = 1.$$

If, for example, the fifth input bit becomes faulty, the output value can be read out from the fourth row of Table 3:

$$z = 0.$$

Thus, the super fault list comprising the actual input and output values can be written in the following way:

$$(1,0,0,d,0,d,0);(0).$$

Finally, we turn our attention to the use of functional algorithms. For this type of modeling the computations can be carried out in a straightforward manner. The following example illustrates the fault simulation technique for the counter element described in Section 6.

Assume that in the fault-free case the following vectors have been associated with the counter:

$$\bar{x}_c = (1,1,1,1), \quad \bar{y} = (1,0,0,0,1,1)$$

$$\bar{A} = (0,0,0,1,1,1).$$

From $\bar{x}_c$ we know that the counter performs the hold operation, i.e., algorithm H is to be taken. Thus the output vector is

$$\bar{Y} = (1,0,0,0,1,1).$$

Next assume that two control bits have become faulty, namely

$$\bar{x}_c = (0,1,0,1),$$

whereas $\bar{y}$ and $\bar{A}$ are unfaulted. Now we must use algorithm U which yields

$$\bar{Y} = (1,0,0,1,0,0).$$

Hence, the super fault list of the counter will be as follows:

$$\bar{x}_c,\bar{A};\bar{Y} = (0,1,0,1),(0,0,0,1,1,1);$$
$$(1,0,0,1,0,0).$$

9. CONCLUDING REMARKS

A functional level test calculation technique has been described for logic networks consisting of combinational and synchronous sequential modules. The technique involves nothing more than simple line-value justification performed for a given set of initial composite values. This set is constituted by the minimum number of the logic values necessary and sufficient for specifying a fault detection condition. As a consequence of this minimality, the test calculation process yields automatically a path combination for fault propagation. In this way we avoid coping with the problems that are caused by reconvergent paths (1). The other consequences are the following.

In contrast with the D-algorithm and its extensions, the composite justification approach completely leaves out the fault-drive (D-drive) phase along with the successive attempts to justify the different fault propagation possibilities. Hence, it does not require any a priori knowledge of how to propagate one or more fault signals through a module, thus we can avoid the cumbersome task of generating the so-called sets of propagation D-cubes (6),(7).

In the case of multiple faults, attempts are made to propagate different combinations of the individual faults to a particular primary output when using the D-algorithm. If the number of faults is q, in the worst case 2^q-1 attempts are necessary (1). This means that all the computations required for a single fault have to be carried out a maximum of 2^q-1 times. On the other hand, the composite justification algorithm requires only two iterations in worst case, irrespective of the number of simultaneous faults. In this case we do not have to iterate through all the necessary fault propagation combinations. Instead, the justification process automatically results in the subset of those faults that are propagated.

Finally, as we have seen, the composite justification approach is quite flexible in nature in that it can be adapted to a wide variety of functional models. Moreover, it is conjectured that this solution is also compatible with logic models that involve dynamic time processing.

As for fault simulation, it has been demonstrated in the paper that the concurrent technique is the most preferable from the viewpoint of the functional level modeling used in the test calculation.

REFERENCES

(1) Breuer, M.A. and Friedman,A.D., Diagnosis and Reliable Design of Digital Systems (Computer Science Press, Washington, D.C., 1976).

(2) Batni, R.P. and Kime, C.R., A module

level testing approach for combinational networks, IEEE Trans. Computers, Vol. C-25 (June 1976) pp. 594-604.

(3) Savir, J., Testing for single faults in modular combinational networks, Design Automation and Fault-Tolerant Computing, Vol. 3 (April 1979) pp. 69-82.

(4) Sziray, J., A test calculation algorithm for module-level combinational networks, Digital Processes, Vol. 5, No. 1-2 (1979) pp. 17-26.

(5) Marlett, R.A., A comprehensive test generation technique for highly sequential circuits. Proc. 15th Design Automation Conference, Las Vegas (June 1978) pp. 335-339.

(6) Breuer, M.A., New concepts in automated testing of digital circuits, Proc. Symp. Computer-Aided Design, Brussels (Nov. 1978) pp. 69-92.

(7) Breuer, M.A. and Friedman, A.D., Functional level primitives in test generation, IEEE Trans. Computers, Vol. C-29 (March 1980) pp. 223-235.

(8) Roth, J.P., Diagnosis of automata failures: a calculus and a method, IBM Journal of Research and Development, Vol. 10 (July 1966) pp. 278-291.

(9) Roth, J.P., Computer Logic, Testing and Verification (Computer Science Press, Potomac, 1980).

(10) Sziray, J., Test calculation for logic networks by composite justification, Digital Processes, Vol. 5, No. 1-2 (1979) pp. 3-15.

(11) Akers, S.B., A logic system for fault test generation, IEEE Trans. Computers, Vol. C-25 (June 1976) pp. 620-629.

(12) Muth, P., A nine-valued circuit model for test generation, IEEE Trans. Computers, Vol. C-25 (June 1976) pp. 630-636.

(13) Cha, C.W., Donath, W.E. and Özgüner, F., 9-V algorithm for test pattern generation of combinational digital circuits, IEEE Trans. Computers, Vol. C-27 (March 1978) pp. 193-200.

(14) Armstrong, D.B., A deductive method for simulating faults in logic circuits, IEEE Trans. Computers, Vol. C-21 (May 1972) pp. 464-471.

(15) Chang, H.Y., Manning, E.G. and Metze, G., Fault Diagnosis of Digital Systems (John Wiley and Sons, New York, 1970).

(16) Ulrich, E.G. and Baker, T., Concurrent simulation of nearly identical digital networks, Computer, Vol. 7 (April 1974) pp. 39-44.

(17) Chappell, S.G., Chang, H.Y., Elmendorf, C.H. and Schmidt, L.D., Comparison of parallel and deductive simulation techniques, IEEE Trans. Computers, Vol. C-23 (Nov. 1974) pp. 1132-1139.

(18) Crowder, D.E. and Goodall, N.P., An implementation of a concurrent algorithm for functional level digital fault simulation, Proc. Electronic Design Automation Conference, Brighton (Sep. 1981) pp. 198-202.

IV. ROUND TABLE DISCUSSION

DISCRETE SIMULATION AND RELATED FIELDS
A. Jávor (editor)
North-Holland Publishing Company

FUTURE TOOLS OF SIMULATION VERSUS THE FUTURE OF SIMULATION TOOLS

(ROUND TABLE DISCUSSION)

Jávor

According to a proverb "It is difficult to prophecy, especially with regard to the future". Now that is what we want to do, but it is not an easy problem we are trying to solve: to get some ideas which contribute to the future development of simulation tools. What we could do is to change our ideas, our views on the different simulation tools existing today and their future, i.e. the future of the simulation tools, and just think about what the simulation tools in the future will be, whether they will be the same ones or whether some new means will be developed. If we take a look at the present simulation tools, the simulation languages, we see that there is a great-great family of different simulation languages, simulation systems and during our conference it was really very interesting to see the different approaches leading to ideas of what is needed in the future.

The opening address by Prof. Vansteenkiste gave us a set of ideas on how the future simulation tools should be. And then a number of speakers from a variety of countries also added to this subject. Let's just randomly choose; Prof. Schwarze expressed his views as to how a system should be built; then Dr. Kalashnikov; and a very interesting contribution from Prof. Ameling which showed even one step further into the future.

We have also expressed how probably simulation systems should be constructed. I think that these views and these ideas were convergent, which seems to be very encouraging. Now with these ideas at hand and all the ideas we had before let

Round Table Discussion in progress

me ask everybody at this Round Table Session to express their views: either on the ideas expressed here or elsewhere.

So, please, if anybody has something to contribute then you should go ahead.

Zimmerman

I should like to ask the participants the following question. Are you sure the programming languages - simulation languages - will be sufficient in the future, or will there be a need for dedicated simulation languages?

You can distinguish two kinds of machines: one dedicated for a special purpose and a universal simulation machine. I have just visited the meeting in Austria of EAI users: users of the analogue and hybrid computers. There I have seen what I call a survival of the hybrids, because EAI keeps selling large amounts of the 2000 computer at almost one computer per week.

So I am interested, because I am still in the hybrid field, to hear the opinion of the participants. Whether they think the area of discrete simulation will "eat up" the area of analog and hybrid simulation in the future.

Kossidas

Concerning simulation, I think that it is not based only on the language used, but more importantly on the system model. Actually it is not so difficult to write an appropriate program simulating a given model, but the difficult task is to create the model.

The determination of a simple and accurate model of a system, either physical or mathematical is the most crucial part of simulation.

Schwarze

At the beginning we have to clarify what we mean if we take the name simulation. If we look at the contributions here at this meeting we see that several meanings of simulation have been used. The very narrow meaning of simulation is running a model, the computation of a set of data, and nothing more. And the extreme other meaning is: development of a model. Starting with a very little model, model experiments and evaluation in such a form that human decision is possible after this process is realized with the computer.

And so we have also to look carefully at the situation since it may be necessary to integrate such a process in a greater problem solving process.

And if we look at this we have a very wide range and the problem of the language is more than the problem of model description or model modification and the description of some experimentation. It's well known that SIMULA 67 gives help to all this because it is not a simulation language it's only a language with some basic elements we can also use for simulation. But at the beginning we must agree together, here at this discussion, what we mean if we say simulation.

And if I look at the discussion at Berlin, at the end we had to say that simulation is the development and working with models using computers and producing such information which humans can afterwards use for decisions. This is very short and not exact but I think it represents some of the main problems described here.

Ameling

We shouldn't try to define today once more what simulation is.

Our real problem is problem-solving in total, and there are lot of different ways and steps to do this. One way is to go from the physical problem to the mathematical description. This means, that you have only a description of the process and you don't perform the simulation. And then you say this is my mathematical description and I'll try to solve the problems: not for the real world, but the problems for this model. And each possibility to solve the problems of the model by varying parameters is what we call simulation. Simulation has nothing to do with hybrid or digital computers, nothing to do with tools. The tools can be really powerful in hardware and in software. So we should see very clearly what simulation means and I think that most of us will agree with this idea when we talk about simulation.

Strezova

I would like to make some comments on the trends in development of modelling and simulation software tools. When a complex problem has to be solved, e.g. the design of a large scale system with decentralized structure, a case often arising in the real world, then the known methods and techniques are not applicable to handle such kind of systems.

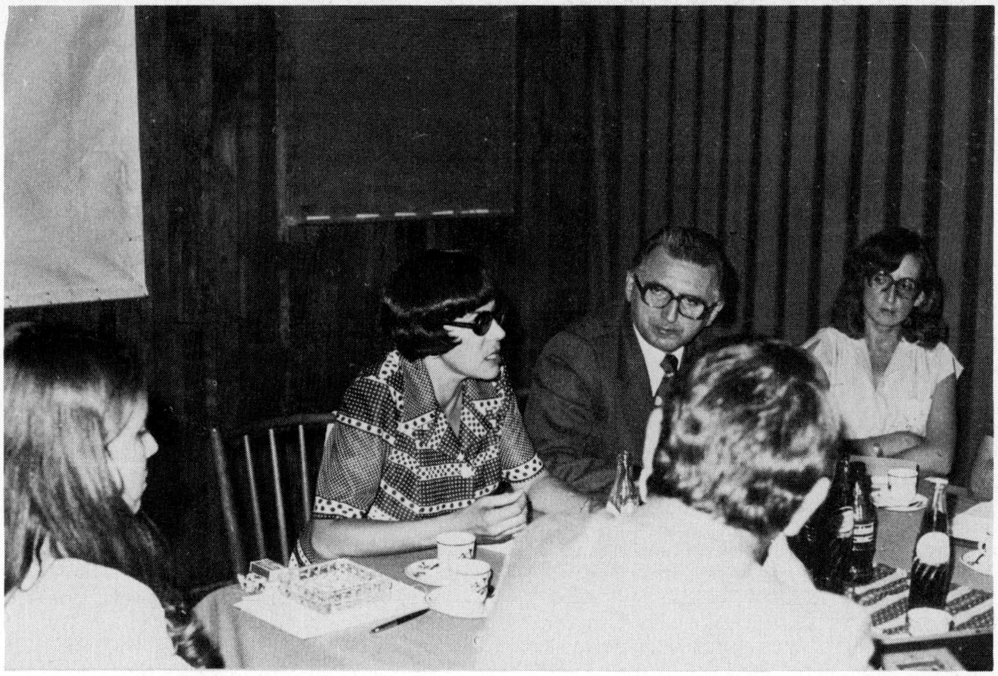

From left to right: Á. Vigh, Dr. Z. Strezova, Prof. G. Schwarze, M. Wielgus

I mean the methods of the modern control theory, the ones of the hierarchical systems theory, even the elegant tools of the mathematical programming. The design of decentralized complex systems requires implicit tools, implicit methods and techniques, instead of explicit ones. Modelling, simulation and alternatives evaluation have to be the main activities in such cases. The problem here is how to perform these activities. On the one hand, general purpose software systems ensuring both system modelling (or simulation) and alternatives comparison are lacking. Obviously, the design of such a universal system is extremely difficult. On the other hand the development of special purpose software systems for particular cases would be an expensive and unfounded process.

There exists to my mind a third way consisting in design of modulars software tools for modelling, simulation and analysis of complex systems. Such a software tool comprises a number of commercialized software products interfaced in a suitable way. Each one of these products performs a given function, e.g., optimization, discrete simulation, sensitivity analysis, etc. Our experience in design of a class of decentralized large scale systems, in particular, management information systems, has argued that applying such a modular software system one is able to generate, analyse and select a set of alternatives in relatively short time.

In a word, an efficient way for development of new tools for treating complex problems, including modelling, simulation and alternatives assessment, consists in using conventional program packages, ordered and interfaced in a manner appropriate for the case under consideration.

Jávor

We now have several different opinions and views that have been expressed on simulation.

I'd like to add my contribution. I'd like to consider the comment by Dr. Zimmerman who asked us - because his main field is hybrid simulation - whether we consider that discrete simulation or digital simulation will "eat up" this. I personally don't think so, and I have the impression, now referring to Prof. Ameling's lecture, that if we are today to speak about the future of simulation tools or future simulation tools, then I think that the real future simulation tools will be a set of processors.

It's quite the same - I think - whether they will be microprocessors or elements of hybrid computers, i.e. let's say operational amplifiers or integrators and so on. If we think that the combined digital and continuous simulation is the future then I think new hardware architecture will be the real future and if we don't look just some months or a few years ahead then such a structure will - to my opinion - be the future and what we have to strive at is to produce - the today possibly not ready - software or at least the outlines of such systems which can handle such new structures.

At first we had analog simulation, analog machines. Then digital machines with their sequential, serial work came and sometimes perhaps some people thought that the other way was outdated. I think we have now come back to it, perhaps on a higher lavel, so that the elements may be micropeocessors and perhaps mixed if the problem is of such mixed nature.

Zimmerman

I agree with this remark about the structures which can be built with the new components that are available now, for example the analog microprocessors, designed for processing analog signals. You know that the Intel 2820 is available now; it is a very mighty component. This component has some disadvantages because its function is only programmable with the erasable PROM part of the chip. But within half a year from the industry in the United States another analog microprocessor will be available, which can have a definable structure. This general structure coupled with the software you suggested to control it, will form a good combination. This new hardware development will force the discrete and the hybrid fields towards each other.

Ameling

I think that it is really difficult to tell what the future will bring. If we are looking back at the last 10 or 15 years (because we are talking about analog computers or hybrid computers) I think nobody would have foretold that it is the best way to go digital. As long as only engineers used equipment for modelling and simulation by means of the analog computer they knew what was going on in each module.

They had a real good understanding about the connections, how the modules work together; they knew the influence of each module on each other. That was a big advantage.

That can be dome digitally as well as it was done earlier in an analog way because that was cheaper, and because the accuracy was high enough at that time. By using a digital computer people want to have a corresponding man-machine interface. That means, e.g. that it would be preferable to have large data bases stored in a totally other form. Anyhow there must be a connection to the digital world. So at least it seems to be easier if all can be done digitally.

If you compare this with the telephone exchange system nobody would say why should we go digital there. If you read the papers and observe the development they are going digital. In 20 years from now there won't be any analog transmission anywhere. That means totally different aspects with corresponding noise problems and other problems.

I think the most important thing will be the "know how" of the user. They must have a better understanding of the model, otherwise there is no progress.

And to the problem you mentioned before; "there should be no special purpose". I feel "general purpose" to be critical anyhow. Only if the user really understands the total system he can sufficiently work with it. In a lot of cases like control systems the engineers really understand what is going on and there is a dedicated system much better to fulfil the task. Even if you'll give them ten times more computer power which is not asked for, than the best system you can think of is of no advantage to them.

I think that will be the further direction of development. Only the market will decide about success. If the market is big enough for dedicated systems, there will be a really great boom in this area, otherwise I think that all engineers, mathematicians, computer science experts will look much more at a combination of the different tools.

I believe tools will be much more specialized than before.

Kalashnikov

I think that the present software is not adequate for the investigation of complex systems and I shall try to explain my opinion.

Let us consider the principal stages of the investigation of some system. First of all, we must construct some mathematical model of the system. And the theory tells us that "It is the most convenient that the model consists of some elements which are as simple as possible". But the software demands that we should not make the model consisting of some simple elements because of the lack of the effectiveness of the corresponding program. So the user needs to keep in his mind some ideas about the effectiveness of the program when creating the mathematical model. And this is the first contradiction. How should we make the model?

How shall we investigate it? The existing simulation tool tells us: "Let this model be the "black box". You need only to investigate "input-output" relations". I think that it is not a scientific approach and you cannot trust the corresponding results. Moreover there exist many important problems which cannot be investigated by "input-output" relations. They are: estimates of small probabilities (e.g. for redundant systems), estimates of stability or sensitivity, estimates of convergence rate, etc.

I believe that one of the ways to solve the above problems is to study the mathematical nature of simulation models. Surely it is evident that no analytical methods can give the decision for complex systems. But analytical methods have another important peculiarity. They can reveal some connections between different properties and parameters of the system. For example, if we consider Markov chains we can show connections between recurrence times and stability estimates or convergence rate estimates. So instead of estimating stability or convergence rate we can estimate recurrence times - it is more convenient and effective.

Using these abilities of analytical methods we can construct some simulation experiments which are very effective and these experiments don't treat the model as a "black box" but some known mathematical object.

Besides investigating a computer model as a mathematical one we can try to make some structural transformations with such models. Then we can permit the user to create any model he likes; then by the above transformations we can make it the most convenient for the simulation program. These transformations are like equivalent transformations of finite automata when you can make a simpler automaton than the initial one, but their behaviour is equivalent.

I would like to point out the difference between continuous and discrete simulation. As a rule, continuous simulation deals with some mathematical scheme (differential equations) and so it is possible to apply the theory of such equations for investigating the model. But discrete simulation deals with descriptive models. And my appeal is: "Let us consider discrete simulation models as mathematical objects. Maybe it will be useful both for computer representation of the model and for computer experiments. Then we can construct software using as much information as possible about the nature of the process being simulated."

Some preliminary results in this direction are in my report presented at this conference.

Vansteenkiste

As to my opinion, future simulators have to fulfil one important goal and that is to realize 1:1 correspondence of the simulated system with the real problem.

I think that the man studying the real system must be in the loop. So that means that the simulator must become transparent for him that he should see he is working on his real problem. So therefore the simulator has as its task to realize a 1:1 correspondence.

Now reality, the real world, is in my opinion hybrid in nature. There are phenomena happening in parallel, there are phenomena happening in series, so that means that the simulator should be able to use that 1:1 correspondence with the real world in that hybrid way.

Further, I think that several disciplines are becoming interested in simulation and I think that they will dictate the line that simulation should follow.

Jávor

If I can join in here, it is really so that if somebody wants to buy a car and it is said that this car has about one hundred different switches and different knobs with which you can do everything, nobody will buy this car. You just want a car in which you can go to, let's say, Lake Balaton if there is sunshine. That is the best. The best would be that you wouldn't have to drive nor even have a gear, but just to tell it. I think really we have to realize that in the old days machine code was the nicest thing because it could do everything and in the future an intelligent tool should be striven for. And I think that users needs have to be met and not the needs of the simulation hobbyists.

Anyway, we should restrict ourselves even if we like nice switches and nice knobs on our software.

Ameling

Excuse me please, I have to disagree with both of you. First: I am really convinced that in the future more and more real time problems will occur. But I think a lot of simulation problems are not of the nature of real time systems.

We had some examples about traffic simulation this morning. Here they work with data from 1974, 1975. What does it mean to do simulation in real time?! You have to work with this data! But things will be completely different. I am sure that if the possibilities for real time simulation will be provided by industry many more real time problems can be attacked and probably solved. Of course, that will be a big advantage.

The next point: The "one button solution" - you know - we technicians always have trouble with non-technical persons. They like these "one button installations" but they have less knowledge of the system and how it works. The system should know it! For example medical people like the "one button system", but the large variety of expectations can not be fulfilled with such a system. Indeed it should be much easier to handle systems. That is right; I

From left to right: Dr. Y. Jarny, Prof. G.C. Vansteenkiste, Dr. A. Jávor, Prof. W. Ameling

think that is what you really mean.

Vansteenkiste

Excuse me but when I say real world simulation or 1:1 correspondence for the user I don't mean that the time scale should be the same. But I mean that he has to see a 1:1 correspondence with his real problem, e.g. a biochemist should understand what the simulator tells him. So that is the 1:1 correspondence, not especially in time. So it would be very difficult to try, for instance, optimal control techniques for very slow processes, if you have to run the process 1000 times.

Jávor

Well, any comments?

Lalwani

I think it is perhaps now time to think about the comments so far. I feel that the debate has been whether the hardware or software should dictate the development of future simulation tools.

I personally would agree with what Dr. Kalashnikov said: that the methods and the models which we are interested in and therefore the systems which we are interested in should actually dictate the development of future simulation tools. As to whether we are interested in general purpose systems or dedicated systems, we should actually look at the problems where we had the difficulties in those systems and what development should be there in the packages which are available and the software which is available.

In considering whether SIMULA is good enough to cope with systems such as the social sciences systems, or whether one should go for the development of some other simulation langauge which is better equipped to deal with illdefined systems, I think the systems in which we are interested, rather than development of the hardware or the available software, should dictate the development of the future tools.

Jávor

Any comments anywhere?

If not, then may I again come back to the ideas we've had up to now. It seems that we have very complex problems to handle from various fields and we need the user friendly interface to different user groups. I don't want to repeat what I have already said in my lecture in the Methodology Session but what I think now is that if the hardware development can take a new trend, or can force a new trend so that some real parallel processing can be done as Prof. Ameling has mentioned, which can be described by or can be an equivalent of some sort of block oriented language then I think if we are going into such a direction that the block oriented language description should be the internal core then if we now make such an internal core for a sequential processor then later all this can be transferred (or parallely we can try to make something similar) to such a new hardware structure.

So what I really want to say is that I think the future tool will be this new hardware architecture but some imminent tasks cannot be solved yet with this. Even so, the development we undertake for the imminent tasks should not be undertaken in a completely different way, nor should there be a quite different way of thinking from what is needed the day after tomorrow. And I think that the real complex simulation software should always be the internal core with user friendly interface languages.

Ameling

I agree with you that at the moment nobody knows what will determine the direction of future development. Is it really only technology or as you mentioned (and I think you are right) is it the better understanding of the physical problems.

But somehow it is too ideal what you think. For example: You can think about the theory of Maxwell. All the problems of electricity are covered by this theory. But the devil is in the detail! And it is really worthwhile to have such a general view and it is also worthwhile to think really much more in this way. It will be possible that such considerations are relevant for the final simulation and modelling.

But up till now it was usually the technique (or the demand) pushing the progress. But I don't know what will push it in the future. If for example there will be an easy-going language to handle real-time and multiprocessor systems, I am sure that will be the way.

If that is not possible in the next years there will be only some special purpose solutions, but they will not be a real break-through in the field of simulation.

Just yesterday we talked about what the future language will be. There are a lot of persons here thinking that it will be PASCAL. And they claim that it is "better" than ALGOL. But in the great society of people using languages, who talks nowadays about ALGOL 68? The mathematicians, the scientists, say that it is so well defined, etc. But a lot of people are not interested and they don't need all the features. And the same can be true for PASCAL.

Only if a large company or governments (or several such bodies) push the language Pascal "PASCAL will then be the language". You know the ideas can be so excellent and brilliant, but if later on there won't be a standardization, then you can forget it!

Probably you have heard, that in the US they are standardizing the ADA-language. For the first time a language is not pushed by the manufacturer (like FORTRAN or PL/1 was by IBM) it is pushed by the customer.

The customer is the biggest customer in the United States: The department of defense. And I am sure that at least the American industry will look very carefully at this language and very soon you will get compilers etc. And I think that if you look at ADA, ADA will cover the total spectrum of data processing.

Lalwani

I think it is a good point that those were the days when FORTRAN was pushed by IBM - a manufacturer - and everybody had to learn it if one was interested to use a machine. Now I think the day has come for the users, and if users want to and unite, then they can dictate the terms on production, I mean to create the demand and then industry would produce and push it.

And I strongly think about PASCAL that there will be, in the very near future, great demand, and people would be inclined to work and do research to develop methodology using PASCAL in simulation.

Ameling

Only one question: Who are "THE USERS"?

At no time there will be one group or a united user group. That is completely impossible. There are totally different fields and directions and priorities; that is the problem you know!

Lalwani

It is a very difficult thing to define the users. They would come from all aspects of life: industry, the universities and the government organizations. And, of course, the universities would play an important role there because they train people to go and work in industry and in government.

Jávor

I think that we have heard a lot of interesting ideas which have shown - at least to me - that there are some ideas which could perhaps provide a foundation for future software and these can be scientifically valid and scientifically good and, on the other hand, there are certain forces - perhaps beyond the control of people who want to design the tools - and this is the user group.

Well I think that the conflict could be resolved by giving the users tools specialized for their purposes. And I agree that there is not such a thing as THE USER but there are plenty of subgroups of users and perhaps every user's need should be fulfilled with its own terminology and own descriptive language and perhaps the internal part is the part that could be standardized, and ADA could be a general descriptive language.

But I personally feel that the block oriented approach will be the best solution, also for today's sequential machines - as Dr. Kalashnikov has expressed in his paper on aggregate systems - as well as for future hardware structures.

Ameling

I think it should be block oriented because (even if the size of a block looks very complex) you can always break it up and you have new relationships between input and output of these blocks, and you can go as deep as you like. I think that is a convenient way of considering for every engineer and also for people with other backgrounds. But I think we should come back to the question of Mr. Zimmerman; "How we feel; what is our opinion, what is going on at the moment with the equipment from EAI"? What is the opinion at our Round Table Discussion here? I think we should try to express our opinions about this.

I can tell you my opinion about this. What EAI did all the time was not only conservative, but they were also developing quite new and flexible tools. That was because the analog computer itself was block oriented and they only had to adapt the possibilities for a really ea easy going interface to the physical outside world. Nowadays in most universities you won't find a computer centre for hybrid computation. Just some weeks ago I was asked: shall we put up a new hybrid computer centre? In my opinion the main reasons for hybrid-computations are fast input-output-transmission and fast calculations in connection with physical units. So it has to be in the loop, it has to be there where the system to be controlled is.

In this sense a centralization of hybrid-computation has only disadvantages. The hybrid-computer really belongs to the outside world and so you'll find in most cases hybrid computers there, where this type of computer is asked for by the problem.

I think that this basic idea can be the main reason for the new equipment of EAI. Because nowadays not only technicians and engineers but also people in other fields use such equipment and these tools, I think that this must influence the price. If the price is going down, there will be a larger community that can use it.

Zimmerman

So your opinion is: No universal machine in that sense?

Ameling

I think the hybrid computer isn't such a universal machine.

This morning we heard that we think too much about dedicated systems. We have to look at the core size. For example, in a very short time memories will be so cheap: that swapping, for instance, won't be worthwhile to discuss. So I feel that the machines are so powerful that there should be one for each field of application.

I would like to say something about simulation-languages. Everybody who really thinks that he needs SIMULA, will learn the language. If a person has other tools which fit quite well to his field he won't do that. That is the same with normal languages.

As long as people can get along with their own language there is no need for another. And that is exactly the case with universities, if the students learn in general a language like PASCAL, they usually will start to solve their problems with this language before they are willing to learn another one.

And so I think the disadvantage of all these new languages is normally that they are not so important that the person will say: "OK there is a big advantage for my problem". That is my opinion.

And so I think that for a long periode of time there will exist a large variety of languages, because the advantages of a new language are measured against the disadvantages of the existing languages. Only if new problem-areas can be attacked easier by the new languages than by the existing ones, the new languages will succeed.

Kossidas

I would like to say that there exist a lot of languages more or less sufficient for most applications. Of course work is still been done by many people to create new languages or expand the existing ones.

In any case it would be interesting to develop an alternative language, or write another compiler, for academic purposes. However this does not always imply that a better result could be obtained. This is actually a game that is played mainly in the research environments.

The main aspect to be considered is the cost of simulation, and most efforts have actually been concentrated towards the end of reducing it. I would be happy to hear what is the opinion of my colleagues here?

Schwarze

I want to return to the future. I agree with the opinion that the block concept is very important, if we incorporate the block concept in the following sense. We have models, we have submodels, components, and so on. We represent these units in our simulation system, and we make the interconnections like the connection in the model and then like the connection in the original system.

This block concept is very important and we shall use this in the future. But we need such a block concept also for the further packages, for instance, optimization and so on. We need such a block concept for possibilities for experimentation as well.

And so we shall have a more extended and wider block concept. This is my opinion. Thank you.

Jávor

I don't know whether there are any more remarks. If not, I think I'll try to summarize that it seems that we can agree on it that such a block concept oriented approach would be or will be the solution and it is on these ideas that user friendly systems should be striven for, and we shouldn't fall in love with a special language but rather fulfil the needs of the users. That is one point.

And beyond that, the promises of hardware development, and the technology should not be left out of sight because otherwise we are definitely going in a wrong direction.

I thank you really very much for your active and I feel extremely useful and extremely interesting contributions to our Round Table Discussion which I personally feel was highly valuable.

And with this I should like to close our Round Table Discussion.